INEQUALITY ACROSS SOCIETIES: FAMILIES, SCHOOLS AND PERSISTING STRATIFICATION

RESEARCH IN SOCIOLOGY OF EDUCATION

(Formerly Research in Sociology of Education and Socialization)

Series Editors: Bruce Fuller and Emily Hannum

Previous Volumes:

RESEARCH IN SOCIOLOGY OF EDUCATION VOLUME 14
(Formerly Research in Sociology of Education and Socialization)

INEQUALITY ACROSS SOCIETIES: FAMILIES, SCHOOLS AND PERSISTING STRATIFICATION

EDITED BY

DAVID BAKER
Pennsylvania State University, USA

BRUCE FULLER
University of California, Berkeley, USA

EMILY HANNUM
University of Pennsylvania, USA

REGINA WERUM
Emory University, USA

Emerald

United Kingdom – North America – Japan
India – Malaysia – China

Emerald Group Publishing Limited
Howard House, Wagon Lane, Bingley BD16 1WA, UK

Reprints and permission service
Contact: booksandseries@emeraldinsight.com

British Library Cataloguing in Publication Data
A catalogue record for this book is available from the British Library

ISBN: 978-0-7623-1061-6
ISSN: 1479-3539 (Series)

CONTENTS

ACKNOWLEDGMENTS

We thank guest editors David Baker and Regina Werum for an enjoyable collaboration in creating this volume. We also value the contributions of Bob Hass, of Hass and Associates, who helped to edit the manuscripts. For their ongoing support and review of manuscripts, we would like to acknowledge our editorial board: Annette Lareau, Temple; Sara Lawrence-Lightfoot, Harvard; Pedro Noguera, New York University; Aaron Pallas, Columbia; Francisco Ramirez, Stanford; Stephen Raudenbush, Michigan; Yossi Shavit, Tel Aviv; and Fran Vavrus, Columbia. Finally, we appreciate the fine work of external reviewers called upon for this volume.

Bruce Fuller
Emily Hannum
Series Editors

INTRODUCTION: INEQUALITY ACROSS SOCIETIES

Bruce Fuller and Emily Hannum

Thank you for faithfully opening yet another book on education and inequality. The role that schooling plays in making a society more fair – or actively reinforcing disparities across groups – is a topic that certainly demands greater attention from scholars and policy makers alike. As capitalism and the neoliberal tenets of everyday life evolve on a global scale, politicians and institutional leaders bank on schooling as the organization that will deliver us from evil, from inequality, from the rough edges of unrelenting materialism.

But indeed, volumes have already been written on the role of education in reproducing inequality, or as the institutional stage on which stratification has been contested throughout the modern era. Nor does the academic record tell a story that typically ends with a happy resolution, or even an intriguing climax. So why did we decide – along with guest editors David Baker and Regina Werum – to craft yet another volume on stratification and the role of schooling?

In a word, possibilities. The stratification literature continues to be largely embedded within the political and economic conditions of particular societies. By looking across nations and cultural settings, new possibilities arise. For example, in this volume, Hyunjoon Park's study examines a half-century of successive generations moving through South Korean schools. He finds that the removal of selective exams reduced the influence of parents status on their son's school attainment. Yet the remarkable expansion of formal schooling has not lessened the overall force of parents' social class in driving their children's educational attainment. The chapter on formal preschools in China, authored by Susan Short and

Inequality Across Societies: Families, Schools and Persisting Stratification
Research in Sociology of Education, Volume 14, 1–5
(Formerly Research in Sociology of Education and Socialization)

ISSN: 1479-3539/doi:10.1016/S1479-3539(03)14001-3

Rongjun Sun, illuminates how this novel institution is serving to reinforce class and gender-based inequality, as it advances the early learning of some children.

Steve Morgan and William Morgan detail how traditional apprenticeship training persists in parts of Nigeria, complementing the skills and modern status awarded by government schools. More successful young merchants appear to draw proficiencies, cultural knowledge, and social networks from these tandem institutions. The social mechanisms of inequality – be they embedded in schools, families, or community organizations – vary dramatically across societies. And this variation in mechanisms holds important consequences both for the magnitude of stratification and for the economic or symbolic markers that signal telling differences among groups.

The effects of "high-stakes testing," preschool expansion, and public support of religious schools are hot topics in the United States and Europe, where income inequality has grown wider even as mass schooling has spread. As we get our heads out of our own context and think cross-nationally, we gain new insights into the peculiarities of stratifying mechanisms and our tacit assumptions about them. By looking across societies and at the forms of difference in each, we discover new dynamics and find more effective policy options available to us.

THEMES, FRESH EVIDENCE, AND THEORETICAL ADVANCES

Beyond reporting on new possibilities, the nine empirical chapters and two commentaries that follow lend order to what scholars are discovering about the mechanisms, motivators, and tacit forms of inequality that characterize stratified societies, and that implicate the school institution at every turn.

We suggest that you put three questions to each author whose work appears in this volume. First, how do these cross-national reports illuminate new mechanisms or locations of where particular groups benefit from differing opportunities? Second, how does the study illuminate facets of the school's inner-workings that broaden or systematically narrow children's life chances? And third, what actions by government can actively reduce the school's stratifying effect?

Empirical knowledge from cross-national perspectives is accumulating on these important topics (Buchmann & Hannum, 2001; Shavit & Blossfeld, 1993). And theory regarding the subtle or vivid character of stratifying mechanisms continues to mature, ranging from the activation of cultural capital between parents and teachers (Lareau, 2002), to curriculum tracking (Lucas & Berends, 2002), to situating children and parents in neighborhoods that possess unequal local institutions and social networks (Brooks-Gunn & Duncan, 2000; Fuller

& Hannum, 2002; Loury, 1977). One persisting issue is whether such causal accounts stemming from the West – that link differing actions in families, schools, or neighborhoods to unequal outcomes for children and young adults – capture the nature of stratification in other societies. Collectively, the chapters in this volume begin to shed light on this question.

Beyond pragmatic questions pertaining to where stratifying mechanisms exist and when government can effectively address them, this volume's contributors advance four specific issues.

Multi-Level Windows into Stratification

Individual differences in one's roles, skills, and social ties are reproduced at various levels – the family, community, region, and society or political economy. The structures of labor and production, and roles cast by age, ethnicity, gender, or religious rules, spread roots into these vertically-conceived levels of social organization. The papers in this volume move beyond conceptualizing status attainment strictly at the level of the individual, instead considering opportunity structures embedded within school institutions, ethnic organization, and the rendered structure of labor. They illuminate how families, community organizations, and the state inadvertently conspire to reproduce educational differences, as well.

Schools and Sectors

Stratification theory remains tied to a structural or correspondence imagery of how inequality is sustained. Indeed, children's life chances and intermediate outcomes (including school achievement) remain strongly tied to the class position of one's parents. But non-structural theorists, especially from neo-institutional circles, emphasize that relatively autonomous sectors may develop – including public schools and universities – where counter norms of difference, equity, and participation may thrive.

While structuralists see a society built like a layer cake, neo-institutionalists suggest that semi-independent sectors of society may coexist, and even contest basic norms and ideologies. For example, Hiroshi Ono's chapter shows how university status and perceived quality can powerfully drive enrollment demand, whether or not prestigious universities impart productive skills. Still, this volume's contributors keep returning to the basic question: How much does schooling matter in moderating class reproduction?

Complementing Structuralist Assumptions

Regardless of whether mass schooling makes societies fairer and more equal, the school institution still keeps on growing. It continues to incorporate more young children into formal preschools, and to credential more young adults within higher education. Across differing societies, the spread and formalization of schooling may act to calcify stratifying mechanisms or to undermine them. But the theoretical advance is to think about how the neo-institutional perspective, determinedly non-structural in its origins, may complement the stratification tradition, a point emphasized by guest editors Werum and Baker.

Governmentality and the State's Inevitable Presence

The volume's authors tacitly assume that western-style modernization provides the backdrop for their stories. Some are critical of whether the ongoing rationalization of young children's lives – as evidenced by preschool expansion in China or the curious persistence of apprenticeship training in Nigeria – acts to deepen or reduce stratification. But what John W. Meyer has called "The Great Rationalization Project" grinds on as nation-states try to look more modern.

This project breeds what Foucault termed a state of governmentality, where citizens come to assume that formal institutions will order and infuse meaning with processes that control and sort persons and groups. It also suggests that only the state can act with legitimacy and authority to make access to schooling and its effects more equal.

But how effective the state really is under neoliberal forms of modernization, and exercising rather mechanical policies, is the final theoretical topic that these new papers address. And when the central state wanes, becoming fragile in its ability to advance fairness, stymied by encounters with the market or cultural tenets, how do stratifying mechanisms evolve? The Morgan and Morgan chapter, for instance, is a story about the Nigerian state's weak legitimacy in delivering modern schools that can rival traditional apprenticeships. Yet families maneuver their children through both systems to advance their interests, at times undoing earlier forms of stratification.

Organization of the Volume

This book includes two sets of papers, along with commentaries intended to enliven the dialogue around cross-cultural varieties of stratification. The first set of papers consists of studies of educational stratification in the U.S. Europe, Israel, and Africa, and guest editors David Baker and Regina Werum place this new work in the context of earlier conceptual frameworks. The second set of papers focuses on East Asia. We provide a commentary on this set of papers, discussing their collective contributions to comparative research on educational stratification.

Together, this empirical work spotlights new locations of stratification mechanisms, and demonstrates how superficially similar systems of educational opportunity are affected by nation-specific labor structures and cultural processes. On the one hand, manifest differences in children's life chances – from eventual disparities in jobs and income to distressing gaps in learning, social opportunities, and status – can be defined along similar indicators across societies. Still, the institutional and cultural mechanisms that drive these inequalities, especially the force of school and state organizations, continue to evolve through culturally specific forms. It is these colorful complexities that this volume illuminates so brightly.

REFERENCES

Brooks-Gunn, J., & Duncan, G. (2000). Do neighborhoods influence child and adolescent development? *American Journal of Sociology*, *99*, 353–395.

Buchmann, C., & Hannum, E. (2001). Education stratification in developing countries: A review of theories and research. *Annual Review of Sociology*, *27*, 77–102.

Fuller, B., & Hannum, E. (2002). Scaffolds for achievement: Institutional foundations of social capital. *Review of Sociology of Education*, *13*, 1–12.

Lareau, A. (2002). *Unequal childhoods: Class, race, and family life*. Berkeley: University of California Press.

Loury, G. (1977). A dynamic theory of racial income differences. In: P. Wallance & A. LaMond (Eds), *Woman, Minorities, and Employment Discrimination* (pp. 153–186). Lexington, MA: Heath.

Lucas, S., & Berends, M. (2002). Sociodemographic diversity, correlated achievement, and de facto tracking. *Sociology of Education*, 75.

Shavit, Y., & Blossfeld, H. (Eds) (1993). *Persistent inequality: Changing educational attainment in thirteen countries*. Boulder, CO: Westview.

GRANDMOTHERS, FORMAL CARE, AND EDUCATIONAL ADVANTAGE IN CHINA

Susan E. Short and Rongjun Sun

ABSTRACT

Among U.S. children, research indicates that early childhood experiences, including the child care environment, affect later educational outcomes. Yet, research on educational stratification in low-income countries rarely features the preschool years. We investigate the organization of child care among preschoolers in China. In-depth interviews reveal that grandmother care and formal care are highly desirable. Formal care, in particular, is perceived to provide educational advantage. Using China Health and Nutrition Survey (CHNS) data, and mixed random effects logit models, we explore the determinants of grandmother care and formal care. Results suggest poverty is associated with gender bias; in low-income households, boys without siblings are especially likely to receive formal care. These results call for greater attention to early childhood in research on educational stratification in China and other low-income settings.

INTRODUCTION

Evidence linking children's experiences during the preschool years to later intellectual development is mounting. In particular, children living in poverty

---

Inequality Across Societies: Families, Schools and Persisting Stratification
Research in Sociology of Education, Volume 14, 7–31
(Formerly Research in Sociology of Education and Socialization)

ISSN: 1479-3539/doi:10.1016/S1479-3539(03)14002-5

during their first years of life do not fare as well later in life on cognitive tests and schooling outcomes (Duncan et al., 1998; Duncan & Brooks-Gunn, 2000). The mechanisms by which poverty affects intellectual development are not entirely clear. One possibility is that poverty is detrimental because of the way it shapes children's home environments – especially cognitive stimulation and parenting style (e.g. Guo & Harris, 2000; Yeung et al., 2002).

The organization of child care (where care takes place and by whom) affects the "environments" in which children grow. Accordingly, to better understand the relationship between children's early experiences and later educational outcomes, we need to attend to the organization of child care. For example, one recent study shows that in their first year of life, children with mothers who work 20 hours or more per week experience small but persistent negative effects on later cognitive outcomes, and these effects are conditioned by the type of child care (Waldfogel et al., 2002).

In limited resource environments, care arrangements may be particularly critical. Low-quality care can reinforce a child's disadvantage, while high-quality care can offset this disadvantage. Further, early education intervention may be beneficial to later cognitive development and academic achievement (Burchinal et al., 1997; Campbell & Ramey, 1994; Entwisle et al., 1997). However, recent research with national sample survey data on the long-term benefits of Head Start suggests caution; not all intervention programs benefit all children in the same way (Aughinbaugh, 2001; Currie & Thomas, 1999). Despite evidence that early childhood experiences are related to later childhood schooling outcomes, until recently, much research in educational stratification in the U.S. has focused on older children and secondary school processes and outcomes (see Entwisle et al., 1997 for discussion). The situation in regard to research on educational stratification in developing countries is similar. A recent review of this literature suggests that researchers have paid little attention to the preschool years in developing country settings, settings where children are even more likely to live in poverty (Buchmann & Hannum, 2001).

Our paper focuses on the early life course, the preschool years, and explores the organization of child care in China, a relatively low-income country. Implicit in our analysis is the assumption that preschoolers' care arrangements are relevant to later child outcomes, and that children with more desirable care arrangements may enjoy an advantage in later school-related outcomes. In the Chinese context, we investigate what constitutes "most desirable" or "best" care for a child, and who has access to "best" care.

In the first stage of our analysis, based on fieldwork, we argue that care in a formal setting, although often not locally available, is highly desirable. Supervision and socialization are thought to be benefits of formal care, but a key component of its desirability is its perceived role in preparing a child well for later school success. Likewise, grandmother care is a highly valued form of care, particularly for the youngest children. Grandmothers are experienced caregivers who usually have more time to supervise children than parents. However, a drawback of grandmother care is the limited ability of the older generation to impart school-readiness skills.

In the second stage of our analysis, with survey data from eight provinces of China, we examine the determinants of formal care and grandmother care for children less than six. Given the well-documented preference for sons in China, we are especially attentive to whether the organization of child care disadvantages daughters. Our results indicate that when family resources are constrained, boys are more likely to receive formal care than girls. The likelihood of grandmother care does not differ for boys and girls. These results suggest that the much discussed disadvantage Chinese girls experience in later schooling outcomes may well begin with decisions made about the organization of child care early in life.

Significantly, the results we present reveal that the organization of child care, including the receipt of formal care, is not entirely determined by access to formal care or urban-rural residence. Our results, based on mixed random effects logit models, confirm strong community effects, particularly in the determination of formal care. However, they also reveal that net of community characteristics, child and household characteristics affect care outcomes.

BACKGROUND

Chinese society places a high value on education (Knight & Shi, 1996; Tsang, 2000). Young children, particularly those in cities, compete for placements at the best schools, and line up for special lessons in piano, art, and other valued skills. Yet, children's experiences vary widely. Research indicates that urban children, children of Han ethnicity, and boys, tend to be most advantaged (Bouma, 1999, with data from early 1990s; Broaded & Liu, 1996, with data from 1992; Connelly & Zheng, 2000 with census data from 1990; Hannum, 1999 with data from 1949 to 1990; Hannum, 2002 with data from 1992; Hannum & Xie, 1994 with data from 1950 to 1985; Zhou et al., 1998 with data from 1949 to 1994).

Disparities in the educational experiences of girls and boys in China have been well documented. Girls suffer lower initial enrollment rates and higher drop-rates, particularly at higher levels of education (Bouma, 1999; Connelly & Zheng, 2000; Hannum & Xie, 1994; Mak, 1996). When they do continue on, they do so at inferior institutions, relative to boys (e.g. Broaded & Liu, 1996). The gender gap has narrowed over time and changed with state policies, but has tended to persist with particularly wide disparities in rural areas (Connelly & Zheng, 2000; Hannum & Xie, 1994). This gap has been attributed to "feudal" ideas related to son preference, as well as structural realities of a labor market and political system that favor men, and a patrilineal, patrilocal kinship system that encourages investments in sons over daughters.

In this paper we extend this examination of gender inequality in education to the preschool years. We do so through analyzing the organization of child care. Previous research suggests that several factors affect the type of care a child receives. These include: the child's characteristics; the availability of care providers; household constraints; and child-rearing preferences (Kuhlthau & Mason, 1996; Leibowitz et al., 1988; Parish et al., 1991; The NICHD Early Child Care Research Network, 1997). These factors should apply across settings. At the same time, cultural and ideological differences, as well as political, institutional, and structural factors, can affect the organization of child care across societies (e.g. Fuller et al., 1995).

In the United States there is popular belief in the primary importance of mothers for children's care. Mothers are thought by many to be the best caregivers (e.g. Mason & Kuhlthau, 1989). Consistent with this attitude, only a few decades ago mothers were the main caregivers of preschool age children. Since that time, an increase in young mothers' participation in the labor force has resulted in an increase in non-maternal child care (Moen, 1992; Spain & Bianchi, 1996). Nonetheless, as of 1991, almost half of the U.S. population agreed that preschool children suffer when mothers work (Rindfuss et al., 1996).

The situation with respect to child care is starkly different in other settings – perhaps nowhere more so than in China. Women's labor force participation rates in China are among the highest in the world (United Nations, 1991). Estimates put the labor force participation of urban women between 25 and 44 years at 90% (Bauer et al., 1992), and higher yet in rural areas. The legacy of Mao's socialist government, which promoted the contribution of women to productive activities, persists today. Women's attachment to the labor force, including mothers of young children, remains strong. Mothers of very young children work, and unlike other settings, tend not to interrupt work for extended periods of time, nor shift to part-time work upon the birth of a child (Entwisle & Chen, 2002). Moreover, unlike the United States, where the rhetoric surrounding women's work is peppered with references to "choice," in China, work is described as a matter of necessity (Short et al., 2002; Tobin et al., 1989). In the Chinese context, most mothers are expected to work. This reality shapes the organization of child care and perceptions of optimal child care arrangements.

CHILD CARE AND THE STATE IN CHINA

The place of early childhood programs in the state agenda is an important backdrop for any understanding of the organization of preschoolers' care. State policies addressing formal child care have been in place since the establishment of the People's Republic of China in 1949. The Ministry of Education propounded its Provisional Regulations for Kindergartens (*youeryuan*) in 1952, which specified the objectives, structure, budget, and educational content of kindergartens.[1] These guidelines have been updated periodically since that time, and the initiation of economic reform in the early 1980s ushered in rapid development of new guidelines regarding formal child care and preschool education.

Numerous documents set norms and standards for the operation of formal child-care institutions. In 1988 the Ministry of Education issued Regulations on Work in Kindergartens, and Regulations on the Management of Kindergartens, which were supplemented by other documents such as a Suggested List of Toys for Kindergartens, and Guidelines for Evaluating the Work of Pre-primary Classes. Together these were judged to constitute a fairly complete set of working documents for the management of early childhood education (Zhang, 2000). The 1995 Law of Education states that preschool education is an important component and the first stage of the education system (Luwan Educational Bureau, 2002). In 1990, there were 170,000 kindergartens and 648,000 preschool classes in China, and about 28% of preschool age children had at least one year of experience in these institutions (Zhang, 2000). By the early 21st century, the state aims to provide access to kindergarten for virtually all young children in large and medium-sized cities, and at least one-year of preschool education to 70% of young children living in rural areas (Zhang, 2000).

Cultural and practical forces drive the emphasis on pre-school education in Chinese society. An example of the value placed on education is found in the traditional saying, "Only the learned rank high, all other trades are low" (*wan ban jie xia pin, wei you du shu gao*). Economic reform over the past 20 years has only served to reinforce such values. Education is thought to lead to desirable employment and social status, and many parents hold the view that college attendance is particularly important to future success; yet, despite the expansion of higher education opportunities in recent years, only 9% of college-age youth gain admission to colleges and universities (Tang, 2001). One consequence is that fierce competition for college admission has extended to high schools, primary schools, and even kindergartens. Many preschoolers are encouraged to "study hard to go to college" and are sent to kindergartens to receive formal education at young ages (Tang, 2001).

In addition to setting in motion policies to promote growth in the availability and quality of early childhood programs, the state has signaled the primary place of women as nurturers of children. In official statements issued by the central government or the government-sponsored Women's Federation, women are reminded that they are responsible for the moral and physical well-being of children (Honig & Hershatter, 1988; Jacka, 1997; Robinson, 1985). For a time, during the collectivization period in the late 1950s, the primary importance of mother or grandmother care was de-emphasized as women were called to work side-by-side with their male comrades, and child care was socialized for some. However, the fundamental idea that child care is women's work was not modified, and women looked after children at the child-care stations. The socialist messages regarding children's care, including the contradictory messages emphasizing and de-emphasizing mothers as essential caregivers, no doubt continue to shape how families think about child care today.

CHILD CARE ARRANGEMENTS IN CHINA: CONTEXTUALIZING "BEST" CARE

To contextualize our analysis we describe, from a child's perspective, the organization of preschoolers' care in China. Using survey data from the China Health and Nutrition Survey (CHNS), we detail where children receive care and who provides care.

The CHNS data is panel data that was first collected in 1989 from 3,800 households in 188 communities in eight provinces and autonomous regions of China. We use the 1993 CHNS, which includes the provinces of Guangxi, Guizhou, Henan, Hubei, Hunan, Jiangsu, Liaoning, and Shandong. The sample is not nationally representative, but the selected provinces vary substantially on economic and demographic measures (State Statistical Bureau, 1994), and they are home to over 400 million people. Furthermore, the CHNS data includes detailed individual, household, and community measures across eight provinces, which is rare.

The CHNS sample is based on a stratified multistage cluster design. Within each of the eight provinces, low-, middle-, and high-income counties were selected. Then within these counties, the county seat and three randomly chosen villages were selected. Also, within each province the provincial capital, a low-income city, and suburban villages located near these cities were included. In the end, the urban sample is comprised of county seats, provincial capitals, and selected low-income cities. The rural sample represents about two-thirds of the total sample and includes villages located outside of cities (suburbs) and villages outside of county towns. Because of the sampling scheme, the urban CHNS sample slightly overrepresents households in smaller urban centers (towns) at the expense of households in larger cities.[2]

The CHNS data is well-suited for this analysis because it includes detailed information for children younger than six on the type of child care received. Unlike other surveys that ask about the *primary* place of care or the *primary* caregiver, the CHNS asks whether children receive any care from a host of potential caregivers within and beyond the household. Thus, the CHNS data allows a more complete picture of children's care experiences.

As with any panel data set, there is loss due to follow-up. Overall, the CHNS has had great success retaining households over the years. Prior to 1993, data was collected in 1989 and 1991 with close to 95% of households followed in each interval. Nonetheless, selectivity processes do operate. Even when households are retained, individuals within them may have moved out. Among those most likely to be lost to follow-up are young couples and their children. Upon marriage, many young couples live with the husband's parents. It is not uncommon for them, however, to move out after a few years. In 1993, new households in the same sampling unit (village or neighborhood) formed by members leaving a CHNS household were followed. Nonetheless, young children were disproportionately lost to follow-up. The average age of the sample of children less than five was somewhat higher in 1993 (3.3) than in 1989 (2.4). Significantly, a component of this aging likely reflects fertility change. The period between 1984 and 1989 roughly corresponds to the most lenient implementation of the one-child policy.

We now turn to the organization of care. Table 1 shows the distribution of children across three categories: those who receive all care inside the household by household members only; those who receive all care inside the household, including some care by non-household members; and those who receive at least some care outside the household. The great majority of children between the ages of 0 and 5 (over three-quarters) receive all care inside the household. Most receive this care from household members. Approximately 11% of children receive all care inside the household, but with some of this care from non-household members. It appears, however, that when families rely on non-household members,

Table 1. Percentage of Children (0–5 Years) Receiving Child Care Inside and Outside the Household ($N = 1{,}005$).

Category	Percent
All care inside the household	
By household members only	66.2
Some by non-members	10.9
Some care outside the household	22.9
Total	100.0

Table 2. Percentage of Children (0–5 Years) Living With and Receiving Child Care by Co-Resident Relatives ($N = 999$).

Caregiver	Co-Residence (%)	Receiving Care (%)
Mother	99.5	81.7
Father	97.0	32.1
Grandmother	36.2	24.8
Grandfather	27.5	8.2
Siblings (≥6 years)	39.0	8.1
Other relative	20.8	5.5
(Uncles or Aunts)	17.1	2.8
Non-relative	0.9	0.2

Note: Sample includes 837 households.

they are much more likely to organize care outside the household. About 23% of children receive care outside the household.

Table 2 provides greater detail on the care of children within the household. It reports the percentage of children living with and receiving care from various adults, highlighting the relationship of the caregivers to the children. The sample includes all children less than six, because we expect that children who receive care from outside the household, or from non-members, are likely to receive care from household members as well. Table 2 indicates that most children, 82%, receive care from a co-resident mother. The others most likely to serve as caregivers within the household are fathers and grandmothers. Approximately one-third of children receive child care from a father, and 25% receive care from a grandmother. These figures are shaped in part by children's experiences of household composition. Over 96% of children in our sample live with a father and mother. Some 36% live with a grandmother.

Table 3 provides more detail on children's care experiences for the subset of children who receive care outside the household. It reports on the location of care. Nearly 65% of all children receiving outside care receive care in a formal

Table 3. Percentage of Children (0–5 Years) Receiving Child Care Outside the Household by Location of Care ($N = 230$).

Location of Care	Percent
Formal setting	64.8
Paternal grandparent house	26.5
Maternal grandparent house	10.4
Other	7.8

Note: Percentages do not sum to 100% because one child can receive care in multiple locations.

Table 4. Time Spent in Outside Care for Children (0–5 Years) Receiving Some Outside Care.

	First Quartile	Median	Third Quartile
Days/Week[a]	6	6	6
Hours/Day[b]	5	8	8

[a] $N = 221$, due to nine missing values.
[b] $N = 201$, due to 29 missing values.

setting. The CHNS asks about a variety of private and public daycare and preschool settings, including those organized by work units, collectives, or local primary schools. We combine all of these settings under the label "formal care." Many children also receive care in the home of their paternal grandparents (about 27%). Given the patrilineal and patrilocal organization of society, care in the home of maternal grandparents is much less common than in the home of paternal grandparents. Still, about 10% of children receive care in the home of their maternal grandparents. Relatively few children (8%) receive care by other relatives or non-relatives, such as neighbors and friends, or by other sources not identified in the survey.

Next we consider the amount of time children spend in the care of people outside the household. The CHNS survey asks: "For how long in a typical day is this child taken care of by people outside the household?"

The distribution of responses is presented in Table 4. When children receive outside care, more than half of children five or younger receive this care for eight or more hours per day. Fewer than 25% of children receive care for less than five hours per day. The vast majority of children receiving care from those outside the household – at least 80% in 1993 – did so for six or seven days per week, with most receiving care for six days per week. This finding is expected. In 1993, six days corresponded to the official workweek, which has since been reduced to five days per week.

Overall, based on the CHNS sample, we draw several conclusions about the organization of child care in China. First, the majority of children receive all of their care in the household by household members. It is relatively uncommon for children to receive care within the household from non-household members. Instead, children who receive care from those outside the household receive care in formal care settings or in the homes of grandparents. Such care tends not to be of the "filling in" variety. Rather, when children receive care outside the home, it is most often for between 40 and 60 hours per week. To better understand these child-care arrangements and their potential implications for children, we turn to a qualitative analysis of the organization of child care from the perspective of families. This analysis is based on two months of fieldwork in Hubei Province in 1995.

CHILD CARE CHOICES

Optimal child care is problematic to measure. A particular location or a particular caregiver does not assure child-care quality. In an analysis of child care for preschoolers of working mothers in the United States, Leibowitz, Waite and Witsberger (1988) reviewed evidence from developmental psychology, and argued that a low ratio of children to adults is optimal when providing care for children less than three. Thus, based on the assumption that paid home care represents one-to-one care, they argued that in-home care is best for infants and toddlers. Because older children benefit from interaction with other children and trained teachers, they argued that children aged three to five received the best care in formal settings such as centers or preschools. They refrained from comparing the benefits of in-home care or formal care to mother care, making arguments instead about the most appropriate alternatives to mother care (e.g. Leibowitz et al., 1988, p. 206).[3]

Although children's developmental needs in China should be similar to those of children in the United States, there are cultural and structural realities that lead parents to value different traits in their children, and contextual differences that affect the set of advantages and disadvantages associated with the care options available in each of the two settings. We draw on a set of in-depth interviews with mothers, fathers, and grandmothers of young children, to examine the care preferences of Chinese families. Similar to the United States, these interviews reveal that, according to parents, children's ages affect the appropriateness of various forms of care. Notably, the families we interviewed in China did not operate on the assumption that mother care is the best care for children, even for children as young as 18 months. Instead, they were more likely to focus on the content of the caregiving and the qualifications of the caregiver.

Our analysis is based largely on a set of in-depth interviews carried out in 1995 in two counties of Hubei Province, one moderately wealthy and the other relatively poor. We interviewed mothers, fathers, and grandmothers separately in a town and village location in each of these two counties for a total of 48 interviews (eight families in each county). All had a child or grandchild seven years of age or younger. Approximately half of the families considered themselves to have split households (*fenjia*) so that the grandmothers lived separately from the children. During the two months in Hubei Province we also visited day-care centers, kindergartens, and pre-primary schools, as well as state-run, collective-run, and privately-run factories and businesses. We discussed child care in all of these venues. We met and formally interviewed local Women's Federation officials and village doctors about preschoolers' care. Though our analysis draws heavily on the family interviews, it is informed by our other discussions and observations during this time.

The subject of the in-depth interviews was caring for children. The interviews were semi-structured and included, for all but one grandmother and one mother, a discussion on the best place to care for children. We asked about the best place to care for an 18-month old baby and a four-year-old child, and about the factors that make one place better than another. Conversations also included discussions about best caregivers. As expected, responses differed by the age of the child. For a baby of 18 months, responses were mixed. Most thought that grandparents, but especially grandmothers, would be best. Significantly, location of grandmother care was not important. Many suggested a grandmother's house was ideal, but others simply replied, "*with* the grandmother." Yet others preferred that grandmothers provide care in the child's house. The general sentiment was that grandmothers should care for the children wherever it is most convenient. As one mother put it:

> If the grandparents and parents have not split households, then (their house) is the best place. If they have split households, then they can put the child in either place.

Those who did not suggest grandmother care as best were likely to say mothers should care for children. About one-quarter of our informants thought the best place would be in the child's own house with care by the mother. Notably, several informants explained that mothers and grandmothers are interchangeable. Many suggested that either the mother or grandmother could provide best care, whoever was most available. Finally, formal care (daycare or kindergarten) was also suggested by almost one-quarter of our informants as best for a child of 18 months, nearly as many as had suggested mother care.

Informants who thought mother care was best tended to emphasize the affection that a mother has for her baby, or the mother's unique ability to know what the baby needs. One mother explained that a mother is best because she can teach a baby to speak. Another thought that mothers were better able to understand babies' needs. Those who thought grandmothers were best usually compared grandmothers to mothers. They offered three reasons for grandmothers' better care: grandmothers have more time; they have more experience and understand children better; and grandmothers are more careful or responsible. In one exchange a village mother explained:

> Grandparents have more experience than younger people . . . because they had children before, they know children better.

Those who thought formal care was best for children of 18 months emphasized the training of the teachers and the learning and social interaction that would be available to a child. Also, many felt that their toddlers could be assured of constant supervision and specialized attention in day care. A town mother explained:

> . . . (daycare is best) because they have teachers whose job is just to take care of children . . . they can do it better.

An exchange with a town grandmother went this way:

> GRMO: A daycare center is best. The children in day care are more active . . . because they have the chance to play with other children.
> INT: What if they stay with their parents or grandparents, would they be active?
> GRMO: No, parents are busy and there is not that much time to play with them. When the children stay with parents or grandparents they just stay alone because the parents or grandparents are busy with housework.

When asked about four-year-olds, the overwhelming majority, all but six informants, told us that formal care was best for children. Many of the reasons were similar to those offered by family members who thought day care was best for children of 18 months. The most important reason had to do with the child's education. Most thought that formal care settings provided the best places to learn. The teachers are trained and the facilities have materials to help children learn. Children in formal care were also thought to benefit through socializing with peers. Some informants mentioned the importance of better supervision.[4] Our informants made it very clear that in-home care has disadvantages. One village grandmother told us:

> Sending them to a daycare center is better than keeping them at home. At daycare or preprimary they have a teacher to watch them all the time. At home they might play with electricity or play in water. Schools are more strict with children.

A second disadvantage of keeping a child at home is that the child may be spoiled. The one-child policy has brought great attention to this issue. Many told us that sending a child to day care is one way to help ensure that a child is not spoiled.

A related reason that families value formal care is that they value community. Many explained that it is important early in life to provide a child with a sense of his or her Chinese identity. One mother explained that some people think that sending a child to formal care early helps the child to develop patriotism and group loyalty. It can also help the child to make friends earlier. Social connections were thought by many to be important to success in later life.

The strength of the positive sentiments our informants expressed about formal care was especially striking given that formal care is not an option for all. Formal care facilities are widely available in cities, but less available in rural areas. Nonetheless, because there was such consensus on the great value of formal care for children and especially for older children, we decided to probe further. We asked our informants why all children did not receive care in formal settings. We were told that what mattered was the availability of such programs, the ability to pay, and child characteristics. Child characteristics were not mentioned often, but one grandmother, when thinking of four-year-old children, explained,

> Some children learn fast and some learn more slowly. Other children can't even count on their fingers. Why should parents waste their money and send that child to school?

Her comment may be especially relevant in light of other work with middle school children that found that children themselves attributed later differences in school enrollment to differences in basic aptitudes, often implying that girls were not as capable as boys (Bouma, 1999).

Overall, our analysis suggests the importance of formal care. Significantly, formal care was not portrayed as the best "replacement" for mother care. Rather, it was *preferred* to mother care by many. Nearly all informants said formal care was best for a four-year-old child. Nearly equal numbers replied that formal care and mother care was best for an 18-month-old child. Grandparent care was preferred by most for infants and toddlers. This strong preference for grandmother care and formal care does not mean that mothers are uninvolved with their children. In fact, other parts of the interviews suggest that mothers are most important in children's day-to-day lives. Instead, Chinese families see advantages in non-parental care. At younger ages, families want to maximize supervision for a child. There is consensus among most family members that grandmothers are often in a better position than mothers to watch over young children because they have lighter work demands.

Our interview informants also made clear the importance of immediate family bonds. Nearly all thought that care by relatives beyond parents and grandparents was not desirable, nor very practical. However, within this inside circle, "best" caregivers were hard to determine. Most especially, women can easily substitute for one another. With these findings, we next look at the determinants of care organization. We emphasize non-parental care. Specifically, we investigate the factors that predict very desirable forms of non-parental care, care by a grandmother, and care in formal settings.

DETERMINANTS OF CARE ORGANIZATION

Using the CHNS data, we explore the determinants of grandmother care and formal care. Our analysis of the in-depth interviews informs the construction of each of the dependent variables. Since respondents indicated that grandmother care was more important than the location of this care, we constructed our dependent variable to be any grandmother care, regardless of where it takes place. We include care by grandmothers that co-reside, care by grandmothers in their own separate residences, and care by grandmothers who live separately and provide care in the child's house.[5]

Formal care, as before, includes all types available to children less than six. Similar to parents in Thailand (Richter et al., 1992), our informants in China used the terms daycare, kindergarten, and pre-primary interchangeably. Because many parents often do not distinguish between the terms, neither do we. Instead we group all such forms of care under the heading formal care. Grandmother care and formal care are not mutually exclusive; children can receive care of multiple types at different times during the day, or on different days, and we model each form of care separately.

Independent variables reflect children's characteristics (age, gender, and number of siblings), the availability of care providers (grandmother's residence, formal care in the community), household constraints (income), and child-rearing ideology (mother's education). We also control for urban or rural residence and the proportion of the community involved in agriculture. Community variables come from a separate community survey administered to local officials in sample communities.

Child Characteristics

Children's characteristics can affect the type of care they receive. In the U.S., older preschoolers are more likely to receive care in formal settings than are younger children (Leibowitz et al., 1988). We expect that age matters to child care arrangements in China as well. It is plausible that boys experience different child care arrangements than girls. Boys are advantaged relative to girls with respect to infant and child mortality, breastfeeding, and educational attainment (Greenhalgh & Li, 1995; Honig & Hershatter, 1988; Ren, 1995). Consistent with boys' advantage in education in later years, we might expect boys to be placed more often in formal care, where it is available. Any such distinction would likely depend in part on the child's number of siblings. As a result, we constructed a set of four dummy variables that distinguish between girls without siblings, boys without siblings, girls with siblings, and boys with siblings. To the extent the one-child policy diminishes distinctions between girls and boys, we might expect only-girls and only-boys to fare similarly.

The Availability of Care Providers

Grandparents, and especially grandmothers, are very involved in child care. The type of care a child receives may depend on the availability of a grandmother (Chen et al., 2000; Short et al., 2001). In these analyses we control for the presence of a grandmother in the household. Because of the patrilineal and patrilocal nature of Chinese society, paternal grandparents are most involved in caring for young children. For this reason we distinguish between paternal and maternal grandparents.

The availability of formal care in the community also affects the set of child-care choices available to parents. The CHNS includes information on whether child-care facilities (including daycare, kindergarten, and pre-primary) are available in the community. Formal care is coded as locally available if any of these three types of facilities is available.

The availability of formal care arrangements differs notably across urban and rural areas and is particularly relevant to this work. In particular, facilities for children less than two or three years are not very common in rural areas. In urban areas, by contrast, day-care facilities can offer extensive services. For example, some cities have centers that take children on Monday morning and allow parents to pick them up the following Saturday (Tobin et al., 1989). In the sample we use for our analysis, 53% of rural children (children who live in rural villages and suburbs outside of cities) live in communities where some formal care option is available. This figure is 78% for children who live in urban areas (in neighborhoods of cities or county towns). Notably, the CHNS question is asked only about availability of formal care in the community where the child lives. Many children may have access to a kindergarten or pre-primary program in a neighboring village or city neighborhood.

Household Constraints

When formal care is available the expense may be prohibitive for the poorest of families. On visits to several kindergartens and pre-primary schools we discussed fees with the school head. In the towns and villages we visited in Hubei Province in 1995, tuition for one year was close to two hundred *yuan*. Given that the corresponding annual household income at that time was several thousand *yuan* in these communities, these fees were substantial, particularly for parents with more than one child. Accordingly, we control for household income in our analysis. Because most of the households in our sample do not derive income from formal steady-wage jobs, household income is largely computed based on income and expenditure reports, including information on economic activities for the year prior to the date of the interview.

Child-Rearing Ideology

We expect that more educated parents will value education more highly and be more likely to seek formal care for their preschoolers notwithstanding other factors. In this analysis we control for mother's education by distinguishing between primary or less, junior high, and senior high or more. In previous analyses we included father's education, but consistently found there to be no effect and dropped it from our final specification. We also expected that differences might exist in child-rearing practices by ethnicity and in early models distinguished between those of Han ethnicity (about 92% of the population) and those of other ethnicity.[6] Models did not indicate a difference and we do not include the variable in our final models.

Previous research has documented large disparities in educational outcomes across rural and urban areas. We expect them in this analysis as well and control for urban-rural residence. We think it an advantage that, in addition to urban-rural residence, we incorporate local level contextual measures, such as formal care availability and the proportion of the community involved in agriculture. Due to data limitations, local community measures are much less frequently included in analyses of stratification in China.

We estimate mixed random effects logit models. An advantage of these models is that they can take into account unmeasured heterogeneity at the community level. The general equation for the logit mixed model is represented:

$$\log\left[\frac{\Pr(P_{ij}=1)}{\Pr(P_{ij}=0)}\right] = aC_j + bX_{ij} + u_j$$

The dependent variable is the log odds that the child receives care from a grandmother (or formal care) relative to receiving no care from this source. C_j is a vector of observed characteristics of community j and X_{ij} is a vector of characteristics associated with child i in community j. The child is the unit of analysis. The u_j in the equation represents unobserved characteristics of communities that may affect the outcome of interest. The assumption is that these effects are additive. The u_j in this model are assumed to be random with a normal distribution and to be independent of other observed covariates. The u_j are also assumed independent of each other with a constant variance.[7]

Because the unit of observation in our analysis is the child, and siblings share parents and a household, there is the additional issue of unobserved characteristics associated with children in the same household that may affect the organization of care. To address this issue, we randomly select one child from each household. We choose this approach rather than taking into account household level effects in our multilevel model, because variation within households on dependent variables is constrained due to the CHNS approach of collecting some of the information about child care at the household level.[8] Our final sample for analysis is 675 children aged 0–5 years. Means and standard deviations for all variables are reported in Table 5.

Table 5. Means and Standard Deviations of Variables Used in Mixed Random Effects Logit Models.

Variable	Mean	S.D.
Individual/household level ($n = 675$)		
Formal care	0.161	0.368
Grandmother care	0.359	0.480
Age		
0–1	0.231	0.422
2–3	0.308	0.462
4–5	0.461	0.499
Sibling composition		
Only boy	0.261	0.439
Only girl	0.194	0.396
Boy with siblings	0.311	0.463
Girl with siblings	0.234	0.424
Paternal grandmother in household	0.379	0.486
Maternal grandmother in household	0.047	0.213
Annual household income logged (*yuan*)	7.901	1.844
Mother's education		
Senior high school	0.178	0.383
Junior high school	0.421	0.494
Primary or less	0.401	0.491
Community level ($n = 157$)		
Urban residence	0.312	0.465
Proportion of community in agriculture	0.435	0.353
Formal care in community	0.592	0.493

Source: 1993 CHNS.

Table 6 includes results from four models. For each dependent variable we present two models, one additive model and a second model that includes interactions between income and child's gender and number of siblings. We tested other interactions as well, but they did not receive support and are dropped from the final models.[9] Model fit was assessed with deviance statistics, which indicated a good fit for all models.[10] To simplify interpretation, below we report results for the preferred models, the additive model for grandmother care (Model 1) and the model with interactions for formal care (Model 4). We turn to Model 1 for grandmother care first. Consistent with the in-depth interviews, grandmother care is more likely for preschoolers when they are young. Household income increases the likelihood of grandmother care. As expected, children living with a paternal grandmother are much more likely than other children to receive care from a

Table 6. Care by a Grandmother and Formal Care, Mixed Random Effects Logit Estimates.

	Care by Grandmother				Formal Care			
	Model 1		Model 2		Model 3		Model 4	
	coef.	s.e.	coef.	s.e.	coef.	s.e.	coef.	s.e.
Constant	−2.805*	0.656	−4.293*	1.540	−1.977*	0.884	0.931	1.046
Individual/household characteristics								
Age								
0–1	0.814*	0.252	0.797*	0.252	−4.344*	0.532	−4.501*	0.532
2–3	0.510*	0.229	0.496*	0.228	−2.297*	0.295	−2.474*	0.300
4–5								
Sibling composition								
Only boy								
Only girl	−0.202	0.271	1.397	1.789	−0.085	0.323	−5.769*	1.952
Boy with siblings	−0.052	0.271	1.033	1.717	−0.608	0.350	−4.141*	1.335
Girl with siblings	−0.250	0.296	2.710	1.729	−0.425	0.349	−7.282*	2.198
Paternal grandmother in household	2.216*	0.212	2.244*	0.214	−0.454	0.387	−0.430	0.285
Maternal grandmother in household	0.774	0.397	0.789*	0.394	0.502	0.543	0.356	0.536
Annual household income logged	0.198*	0.064	0.374*	0.177	0.149	0.076	−0.214	0.109
Mother's education								
Senior high school	−0.348	0.299	−0.369	0.297	0.696*	0.311	0.704*	0.313
Junior high school	−0.260	0.218	−0.251	0.217	−0.092	0.275	−0.179	0.279
Primary or less								
Community characteristics								
Urban residence	−0.073	0.305	−0.095	0.312	1.398*	0.562	1.503*	0.588
Proportion of community in agriculture	−0.782*	0.396	−0.755	0.404	−1.956*	0.794	−2.085*	0.830
Formal care in community	−0.124	0.230	−0.119	0.234	0.169	0.473	0.248	0.496
Interactions								
Only boy × household income								
Only girl × household income			−0.192	0.212			0.689*	0.231
Boy w/sibs × household income			−0.128	0.206			0.440*	0.161
Girl w/sibs × household income			−0.366	0.209			0.844*	0.263

* $p < 0.05$ (two-tailed test); $n = 675$.

grandmother. The likelihood of grandmother care does not appear sensitive to a child's gender and number of siblings.

Turning to Model 4, age is also an important determinant for formal care. Older children are more likely to be in formal care. In addition, children with the most educated mothers – those with a senior high school education or more – are more likely to be in formal care, net of other factors. In contrast to grandmother care, formal care is sensitive to a child's gender and number of siblings, and this effect is observed when these variables are interacted with household income. Our results suggest that parents try to provide equally well for all children, but when income is constrained, boys are advantaged relative to girls. Poorer families are less likely to send girls, whether or not they have siblings, to formal care relative to boys with no siblings. The effect is especially strong for girls with siblings. Also noteworthy, when income is constrained, boys with siblings are less likely to receive formal care than boys without siblings.

Notably, the variable indicating the availability of formal care in the community is not significant ($p < 0.05$) in either the grandmother care or formal care models. Although the ability to measure the availability of formal care in the community is indeed an asset of the CHNS relative to other multi-province data sources, given the small size of the CHNS sampling units, this measure is nonetheless a rough approximation of availability. Other community characteristics are indeed important predictors of grandmother care and formal care. Children who live in urban areas are more likely to receive formal care. In addition, the proportion of the community in agriculture, net of urban location is inversely related to grandmother care and formal care.[11] Finally, we note that the dependent variable captures only receipt of formal care. It does not measure quality. We expect that quality of formal care varies across communities, and on average, is better in urban locations.

The error terms of the mixed effects models provide additional information for model interpretation. The error terms are composed of two components: a random effect at the community level to control for community heterogeneity and a random effect at the individual level to account for residuals. The relative magnitude of these two components is informative. In the grandmother care model (Model 1) the two effects are estimated as 0.113 and 0.931 respectively, which indicates that the community random effect accounts for 11% of the total error ($0.113 + 0.931 = 1.044$). By contrast, in the formal care model the community level random effect is 4.769 and the residual effect is 0.335. These results indicate that the community random effect accounts for 93% of the total error ($4.769 + 0.335 = 5.104$).

As expected, community heterogeneity is critical to variation in patterns of formal care. It appears much less important to variation in care by a grandmother. Notably, child and household effects persist net of community-level factors.

DISCUSSION

Our results suggest that Chinese girls from low-income families may be disadvantaged in their access to formal care. We discover this result through an analysis of the organization of child care. In this analysis we find that care by a grandmother and care in a formal setting such as a daycare, kindergarten, or pre-primary school, is highly valued. Families want to maximize the supervision their children receive and they value the skills of trained care providers who can help children with school readiness skills. It is notable that even where formal care was not available to children until age five, many people told us that formal care is the best care for children, even for children of 18 months. This unmet demand for formal care suggests that the use of outside care, and formal care specifically, will grow quickly in China as daycare becomes more widely available.

The overwhelming enthusiasm of Chinese families for formal care is among the most striking features of our analysis. Chinese families value education highly (Whyte & Gu, 1987), and the families in our study associated formal care during the preschool years with education. This association is not unique to China, but we found it to be particularly strong in our analysis of the in-depth interviews. One reason may be that working parents in China perceive the set of child care options to be limited. Grandmothers are the most logical alternative to formal care for preschool children in many Chinese families. However, today's grandmothers do not have much formal schooling. More than three-quarters of grandmothers in our sample have primary school education at best. Many have no formal education at all. Some parents expressed concern that grandmothers not only have traditional ways, but that they are not well situated to help children learn to write characters and related school readiness skills. Given the rapid changes in educational attainment for women in recent decades in China, the heavy reliance on grandmothers for care, and the high value placed on education, we might expect families to find formal care especially attractive for young children in this setting.

We caution that while our paper describes formal care as "best" care, it does not demonstrate beneficial effects of formal care. We do not assess the link between child care arrangements and later schooling outcomes. Nonetheless, the in-depth interviews we rely on suggest that formal care is desirable because of the advantages it will offer children later in school and life. That our informants perceive this to be true (whether or not later empirical analyses bear it out) is relevant. Our analysis suggests that, notwithstanding community constraint, families are organizing child care so that boys without siblings are most likely to receive the type of care caregivers *think* is most advantageous to children, particularly in regard to later school success.

On the practical side, our results suggest that in analyses of the organization of child care, separating out formal care from all non-kin care can be important. We expected in setting up this analysis that the primary importance of blood lines and family connections in China would make the distinction between kin care and non-kin care particularly relevant. In fact, based on literature in other settings, primarily the U.S., we thought parents would find non-kin care *less* desirable than kin care (Uttal, 1999). To some extent we did confirm this expectation. Parents did not entertain the thought of neighbors caring for children, and most even spoke negatively of relatives other than grandparents caring for their children. These sentiments are reflected in the scarcity of these types of arrangements. However, one type of non-kin care, formal care, is arguably the *most* desirable of all forms of care. Many parents indicated that they want to start their children in formal care as early as possible.

Given the high desirability of formal care, our results suggest that the Chinese government consider carefully the policies that shape the availability and cost of such care. Current government efforts to persuade parents to treat girls and boys equally are laudatory, but may be more effective if coupled with a greater state subsidy for preschool education. Reducing the barriers to formal care for poor families may help to reduce discriminatory practices in the allocation of child care. Taking a broader view, our analysis points to the potential importance of the organization of child care for later child outcomes in under-resourced settings. The dynamics we describe during the preschool years suggest that to better understand educational disparities in developing country contexts, we might do well to pay more attention to preschoolers' care experiences and the processes that shape them.

NOTES

1. Kindergarten refers to programs (daycare/preschool) that generally accept children aged three and older. Pre-primary is preschool education for children in the year prior to their entry into elementary school. These programs might enroll children between the ages of four and six, depending on the program and a child's readiness.

2. Sample weights are not available for the CHNS. Controls for urban residence are included in all models. Descriptive tables need to be interpreted in light of the sample.

3. Such assumptions were necessary because they did not have access to direct measures of child-care quality.

4. Family concerns about supervision were also uncovered by Wang and Burris (1997) in Yunnan Province using a photographic technique called photovoice for data collection.

5. We assume that children receive care in their own homes from grandmothers who live separately when: (1) these children receive care from a non-household member; and (2) the household does not pay for this care. When grandmothers co-reside and report involvement in child care, we assume that all children under six receive some care.

6. The 1993 CHNS does not provide detailed information on ethnicity.

7. We use the Glimmix macro in SAS to estimate these models.

8. We explored, but did not find necessary, the addition of a control for whether the sample child has siblings less than six.

9. We were also concerned about the potential endogeneity of grandmother residence. To explore this issue further we estimated reduced-form models. Our main substantive findings held in all models. There was some change in magnitude of coefficients in the grandmother model, but virtually no change in the model predicting formal care.

10. Deviance is the difference between quasi-likelihood for the full data and quasi-likelihood under the model. Deviance follows a chi-square distribution with $N - p$ degrees of freedom (where N is sample size and p the number of parameters including the intercept). Lack of significance indicates a good fit, and good fit was indicated ($p > 0.05$) for all models.

11. The CHNS uses administrative designations to define urban areas. One consequence is that farming is practiced in some areas designated as urban, such as county towns in relatively rural counties.

ACKNOWLEDGMENTS

We gratefully acknowledge the support provided for this work by the National Institute of Child Health and Human Development (R01-HD37877) and the Brown Population Studies and Training Center. Our work would not have been possible without the use of data from the China Health and Nutrition Survey. Funds for parts of the project design, data collection, and computerization were provided by the Chinese Academy of Preventive Medicine, the Carolina Population Center, and the National Institutes of Health. We are grateful to Zhai Fengying, Xu Siyuan, and Yang Mingliang for their assistance with the fieldwork. We thank Anne Ilacqua and Juhua Yang for reference assistance, Cendhi Arias for editorial assistance, and Dennis Hogan, Aaron Katz, John Modell, and Michael White for helpful discussions related to this paper.

REFERENCES

Aughinbaugh, A. (2001). Does head start yield long-term benefits? *Journal of Human Resources, 36*(4), 641–665.

Bauer, J., Feng, W., Riley, N. E., & Zhao, X. (1992). Gender inequality in urban China: Education and employment. *Modern China, 18*(3), 333–370.

Bouma, J. E. (1999). *Gender and schooling in contemporary China: Does context matter?* Unpublished manuscript.

Broaded, C. M., & Liu, C. (1996). Family background, gender, and educational attainment in urban China. *The China Quarterly*, *145*(March), 53–86.

Buchmann, C., & Hannum, E. (2001). Education and stratification in developing countries: A review of theories and research. *Annual Review of Sociology*, *27*, 77–102.

Burchinal, M. R., Campbell, F. A., Bryant, D. M., Wasik, B. H., & Ramey, C. T. (1997). Early intervention and mediating processes in cognitive performance of children of low-income African American families. *Child Development*, *68*(5), 935–954.

Campbell, F., & Ramey, C. T. (1994). Effects of early intervention on intellectual and academic achievement: A follow-up study of children from low-income families. *Child Development*, *65*(2), 684–698.

Chen, F., Short, S. E., & Entwisle, B. (2000). The impact of grandparental proximity on maternal child care in China. *Population Research and Policy Review*, *19*(6), 571–590.

Connelly, R., & Zheng, Z. (2000). Determinants of primary and middle school enrollment of 10- to 18- year-olds in China. Paper presented at the Annual Meeting of the Population Association of America, Los Angeles, CA.

Currie, J., & Thomas, D. (1999). Does head start help Hispanic children? *Journal of Public Economics*, *74*(2), 235–262.

Duncan, G. J., Yeung, W. J., Brooks-Gunn, J., & Smith, J. R. (1998). How much does childhood poverty affect the life chances of children? *American Sociological Review*, *63*(3), 406–423.

Duncan, G. J., & Brooks-Gunn, J. (2000). Family poverty, welfare reform, and child development. *Child Development*, *71*(1), 188–196.

Entwisle, B., & Chen, F. (2002). Work patterns following a birth in urban and rural China: A longitudinal study. *European Journal of Population*, *18*(2), 99–119.

Entwisle, D. R., Alexander, K. L., & Steffel Olson, L. (1997). *Children, schools, and inequality.* Boulder, CO: Westview Press.

Fuller, B., Singer, J. D., & Keiley, M. (1995). Why do daughters leave school in southern Africa? Family economy and mothers' commitments. *Social Forces*, *74*(2), 657–680.

Greenhalgh, S., & Li, J. (1995). Engendering reproductive policy and practice in peasant China: For a feminist demography of reproduction. *Signs: Journal of Women in Culture and Society*, *20*(Spring), 601–641.

Guo, G., & Mullan Harris, K. (2000). The mechanisms mediating the effects of poverty on children's intellectual development. *Demography*, *37*(4), 431–447.

Hannum, E. (1999). Political change and the urban-rural gap in basic education in China, 1949–1990. *Comparative Education Review*, *43*(2), 193–211.

Hannum, E. (2002). Educational stratification by ethnicity in China: Enrollment and attainment in the early reform years. *Demography*, *39*(1), 95–117.

Hannum, E., & Xie, Y. (1994). Trends in educational gender inequality in China: 1949–1985. *Research in Social Stratification and Mobility*, *13*, 73–78.

Honig, E., & Hershatter, G. (1988). *Personal voices: Chinese women in the 1980s.* Stanford: Stanford University Press.

Jacka, T. (1997). *Women's work in rural China: Change and continuity in an era of reform.* Cambridge: Cambridge University Press.

Knight, J., & Shi, L. (1996). Educational attainment and the rural-urban divide in China. *Oxford Bulletin of Economics and Statistics*, *58*(1), 83–117.

Kuhlthau, K., & Mason, K. O. (1996). Market child care versus care by relatives. *Journal of Family Issues*, *17*(4), 561–578.

Leibowitz, A., Waite, L. J., & Witsberger, C. (1988). Child care for preschoolers: Differences by child's age. *Demography*, *25*(2), 205–220.

Luwan Educational Bureau (2002). *Report on the construction of regional preschool education systems for children aged 0–6*. From the Luwan Educational Bureau Website: http://www.lwedu.sh.cn/shownews.asp?ID=466

Mak, G. C. L. (1996). The people's republic of China. In: G. C. L. Mak (Ed.), *Women, Education, and Development in Asia: Cross-National Perspective* (pp. 3–27). New York, NY: Garland Publishing.

Mason, K. O., & Kuhlthau, K. (1989). Determinants of child care ideals among mothers of preschool-aged children. *Journal of Marriage and the Family*, *51*(August), 593–603.

Moen, P. (1992). *Women's two roles: A contemporary dilemma*. Westport, CT: Auburn House.

The NICHD Early Child Care Research Network (1997). *Journal of Marriage and the Family*, *59*(May), 389–408.

Parish, W. L., Hao, L., & Hogan, D. P. (1991). Family support networks, welfare, and work among young mothers. *Journal of Marriage and the Family*, *53*(February), 203–215.

Ren, S. X. (1995). Sex differences in infant and child mortality in three provinces in China. *Social Science and Medicine*, *40*(9), 1259–1269.

Richter, K., Podhisita, C., Soonthorndhada, K., & Chamratrithirong, A. (1992). *Child care in urban Thailand: Choice and constraint in a changing society*. Bangkok: Institute for Population and Social Research, Mahidol University.

Rindfuss, R. R., Brewster, K. L., & Kavee, A. L. (1996). Women, work, and children in the U.S. *Population and Development Review*, *22*(3), 457–482.

Robinson, J. C. (1985). Of women and washing machines: Employment, housework, and the reproduction of motherhood in socialist China. *The China Quarterly*, *101*(March), 33–57.

Short, S. E., Chen, F., Entwisle, B., & Fengying, Z. (2002). Maternal work and time spent in child care in China: A multimethod approach. *Population and Development Review*, *28*(1), 31–57.

Short, S. E., Zhai, F., Xu, S., & Yang, M. (2001). China's one-child policy and the care of children: An analysis of qualitative and quantitative data. *Social Forces*, *79*(3), 913–943.

Spain, D., & Bianchi, S. M. (1996). *Balancing act: Motherhood, marriage, and employment among American women*. New York, NY: Sage.

State Statistical Bureau (1994). *China statistical yearbook*. China State Statistical Bureau.

Tang, Y. (2001). Do children still have heavy schoolbags? *Beijing Review*, *44*(40), 11–14.

Tobin, J. J., Wu, D. Y. H., & Davidson, D. H. (1989). *Preschool in three cultures: Japan, China, and the United States*. New Haven, CT: Yale University Press.

Tsang, M. C. (2000). School choice in the people's republic of China. In: D. Plank & G. Sykes (Eds), *School Choice and Educational Change: Evidence from Eight Countries* (in press).

United Nations (1991). *The world's women 1970–1990: Trends and statistics*. New York, NY: United Nations.

Uttal, L. (1999). Using kin for child care: Embedment in the socioeconomic networks of extended families. *Journal of Marriage and the Family*, *61*, 845–857.

Waldfogel, J., Han, W., & Brooks-Gunn, J. (2002). The effects of early maternal employment on child cognitive development. *Demography*, *39*(2), 369–392.

Wang, C., & Burris, M. A. (1997). Photovoice: Concept, methodology, and use for participatory needs assessment. *Health Education and Behavior*, *24*(3), 369–387.

Whyte, M. K., & Gu, S. Z. (1987). Popular response to China's fertility transition. *Population and Development Review*, *13*, 471–493.
Yeung, W. J., Linver, M. R., & Brooks-Gunn, J. (2002). How money matters for young children's development: Parental investment and family processes. *Child Development*, *73*(6), 1861–1879.
Zhang, X. (2000). Education for all: The year 2000 assessment final country report of China. From the United Nations Educational, Scientific, and Cultural Organization. Website: http://www2.unesco.org/wef/countryreports/china/contents.html
Zhou, X., Moen, P., & Brandon Tuma, N. (1998). Educational stratification in urban China: 1949–1994. *Sociology of Education*, *71*(July), 199–222.

EDUCATIONAL EXPANSION AND INEQUALITY IN KOREA

Hyunjoon Park

ABSTRACT

During the past few decades, South Korea has experienced a remarkable educational expansion at its secondary and tertiary levels as well as at the primary level, resulting in extraordinary variation between the educational attainment of recent and older cohorts. Using 1990 data from the Social Inequality Study in Korea, the study examines trends in the influence of social background on educational attainment across three male cohorts born between 1921 and 1970. Although in general the impacts of social origin have changed little at the secondary levels of education, there is a significant reduction in the effect of father's occupation on the odds of completing middle school for the youngest cohort. From a multinomial model of transitions to each type of tertiary education, it is found that family background has a stronger effect in the transition from high school to four-year university than to junior college. Interestingly, there has been an increase *across cohorts in the influence of father's education on the likelihood of entering a university, while such a pattern is not observed for the transition to junior college.*

INTRODUCTION

During the past few decades, South Korea has experienced a remarkable expansion in its educational system along with tremendous economic growth, as have many

Inequality Across Societies: Families, Schools and Persisting Stratification
Research in Sociology of Education, Volume 14, 33–58
(Formerly Research in Sociology of Education and Socialization)

ISSN: 1479-3539/doi:10.1016/S1479-3539(03)14003-7

other industrial societies. The extent of Korea's educational expansion, however, is so dramatic that few other countries have achieved a comparable increase in the last 30 years. Even more impressive is the fact that this educational expansion occurred not only at the primary level, but also at the secondary and even the tertiary levels. According to the Organization for Economic Cooperation and Development (OECD, 2001), among 29 OECD member countries, only Norway exceeds Korea in the proportion of people aged 25–34 who have completed at least upper secondary education.

Surprising is the dramatic change between younger and older cohorts in Korea. Although only 28% of people aged 55–64 have completed at least high school, the proportion is 93% in the age group 25–34. In fact, the proportion of 25–34-year-olds who have at least upper secondary qualification in Korea is similar to that in Japan or the Czech Republic. However, the difference in educational attainment between the age groups of 25–34 and 55–64 is far less dramatic in these two countries than it is in Korea.

The statistics also show that although only 8% of people aged 55–64 in Korea completed a tertiary-type A education (which corresponds to a university education), the proportion has almost tripled to 23% for the age group 25–34. As a result of this growth, Korea now has the same percentage of people aged 25–34 with university degrees as does Japan, Canada, or the Netherlands. Of the 29 OECD countries, there are only two (Norway and the U.S.) that rank higher in this respect. Considering the rapid expansion of Korea's educational system, it is important to ask whether inequality in educational attainment between people with different social backgrounds has declined over the period.

THE KOREAN CASE IN COMPARATIVE PERSPECTIVE

In a comparative educational stratification project, trends in educational opportunities were examined across a variety of societies, including two other countries in East Asia: Japan and Taiwan (Shavit & Blossfeld, 1993). Specifically, the effects of socioeconomic origin – mostly represented by parents' education and occupation – on the odds of making educational transitions have changed little over time, despite significant educational expansion during the same period in most of the countries included in the project. The only exceptions were the Netherlands and Sweden, where the influences of family background on the low and intermediate transitions indeed declined.[1] Thus, the main conclusion drawn from these studies was that educational expansion does not necessarily reduce the association between social origins and educational attainment.

Some studies of educational inequality in the countries not examined in Shavit and Blossfeld's project, such as Ireland (Raftery & Hout, 1993) and the Philippines (Smith & Cheung, 1986), have presented empirical evidence supporting the conclusion of persistent inequality. However, this may not hold true in every context. For instance, in human capital theory, Birdsall, Ross and Sabot (1997) emphasize a feedback effect: increases in labor forces with high productivity contribute to lower income inequality as well as economic growth by weakening the scarcity of more educated workers in the labor market.[2] This low level of income inequality, in turn, results in increased demand for education across all social groups.

Furthermore, since Shavit and Blossfeld's (1993) comparative project on educational inequality, we have seen several studies that in fact found some significant decline over time in the effects of social origin. This was especially true at the lower levels of educational transition in Italy (Shavit & Westerbeek, 1998), Germany and Britain (Jonsson, Mills & Müller, 1996), though at the higher levels of education, class differentials in educational attainment have not changed significantly. Note that studies on the Netherlands and Sweden reported in Shavit and Blossfeld (1993) had already shown such a pattern, as we discussed earlier. These new findings indicate that we cannot generalize the notion of persistent inequality into a society without a detailed investigation of where inequality persists and where progress has been made.

The Korean educational system displays some distinctive features, especially compared to the European or American systems. For instance, at all educational levels Korea shows a high degree of standardization, with the same standards adopted nationwide in the educational system (Allmendinger, 1989; Shavit & Müller, 1998). Under the direct control of the government, teachers' training, school budgets, and even the number of college students are constrained by government guidelines. This standardization is exemplified by nationwide entrance examinations for high schools and colleges and a common curriculum designed to prepare students for the examinations. This is clearly distinct from the lower degree of standardization in the American educational system.

An important feature of the Korean educational system, which is particularly relevant for research on the effects of educational expansion on inequality, is the dramatic expansion of the educational system during recent decades. The fact that the Korean case displays extraordinary variation in educational attainment between old and young cohorts provides an excellent case by which we can assess the genuine effects of educational expansion on inequality.

Moreover, as will be explained in detail later, the Korean government has intentionally pursued policies, especially for higher education, that emphasize competition and quantitative increases in the education of its population rather than equality of educational opportunities (Cheng, 1992). Instead of reducing educational barriers among social classes – for instance, by lowering the tuition or providing subsidies to lower classes – the Korean government's policy for higher education has exclusively concentrated on manipulating the number of students admitted, in response to social demands for higher education. This makes the Korean case a prototype of the "expansion" model, in contrast to the Swedish case, which has paid more attention to the reduction of social differentials in educational opportunity (Hout & Dohan, 1996).

More emphasis on expansion rather than on policy directly geared to reducing social differentials in educational opportunity can also be found in other countries such as the U.S. or Ireland (Hout & Dohan, 1996). However, the more dramatic expansion of educational systems and the more apparent lack of governmental support for higher education make Korea an extreme case of the expansion model of educational opportunity.

These distinctive characteristics of the Korean educational system provide an opportunity to see if previous findings on educational inequality hold in the Korean context. One might be tempted to conclude in advance that persistent inequality would be found in Korea as well since previous research on Japan (Treiman & Yamaguchi, 1993) and Taiwan (Tsai & Chiu, 1993) has found no change over time in the extent of educational equality. It is widely recognized that these three East Asian countries have a similar cultural tradition based upon Confucianism and a process of economic development characterized by export-led industrialization with rapid economic growth.

In addition, their educational systems share many similarities. For instance, their school structure follows the basic 6-3-3-4 pattern: six years in elementary school, three years in middle school, three years in high school, and four years in a university (or alternatively two years in a junior college). All three educational systems are strongly centralized and tightly controlled by the state. Under such strong centralization, national entrance examinations play a major role in selecting students (Ishida, 1998; Tsai, 1998). Moreover, some studies suggest that under the Confucian tradition, which highly values education, education may play an important role for socioeconomic achievement in these three East Asian societies (Smits Ultee & Lammers, 1998).

However, it is also apparent that in some aspects, Korea has adopted educational policies that contrast sharply with those of Japan or Taiwan. The three countries particularly differ in their policies on vocational education, especially at the high school level (Cheng, 1992). In Korea, the proportion of those who attended vocational high school among total high school students was about 45% and it remained stable during the 1980s. Although this seems to indicate that vocational education is playing a substantial role in the country's educational system, vocational programs indeed tend to emphasize general skills rather than improving students' specific skills for corresponding occupations.

Necessary skills are often acquired at the workplace through on-the-job training after graduation rather than within the educational system. In Korea, unlike Japan and Taiwan, the relationship between vocational high schools and employers is very weak.[3] Apparently due to the low level of vocational specificity, vocational education in Korea does not have a significant impact on the chances for graduates to obtain skilled jobs (Sandefur & Park, 2002). Furthermore, since the early 1980s, the curriculum in vocational high schools has become more academic rather than increasing in vocational specificity (Chang, 2001). In this system, vocational education is considered less prestigious, and the more successful students tend to avoid vocational education if possible (Shavit & Müller, 1998).

In contrast, Taiwan's favorable policies toward vocational education, initiated by the government's effort to minimize the mismatch between demand and supply of labor, resulted in a ratio of academic and vocational high school students that already approached 3:7 in 1980 (Cheng, 1992, p. 61). Taiwan's policies for vocational education resulted in preparing students better for skilled occupations and thus reducing the wage gaps between college graduates and vocational high school graduates (Cheng, 1992).

Given that most students who follow a vocational track are far less likely to attend tertiary levels of education, in Korea the preference for academic over vocational tracks led to a much stronger demand for higher education. Indeed, expansion of higher education was more dramatic in Korea, especially since the mid-1970s, than in Taiwan or Japan, where the governments have tried to temper expansion of higher education (Brinton, 2001; Kim, 1993).[4]

Another difference relevant to educational inequality is the extent of governmental support for higher education. Compared to Korea where most of the cost for higher education is covered by individuals or families with a very few governmental subsidies, Taiwan has shown considerably higher levels of public subsidies for tertiary education. Furthermore, among the total students enrolled in higher education, the relative share of students enrolled in private institutions, which usually require higher tuition and fees than public schools do, is much lower in Taiwan than in Korea. Thus, the policies for higher education in Taiwan may be characterized as more equity-oriented (Cheng, 1992).

These characteristics of Korean society lead us to expect substantial inequality of educational opportunity, especially for higher education. However, there is also some evidence suggesting less educational inequality in Korea in the comparative perspective. Park (2002) demonstrates that the effect of social origin on destination among Korean men is significantly lower than in some European countries. Given the mediating role of education between origin and destination, this finding may suggest that in Korea, educational expansion has increased the importance of educational attainment for socioeconomic achievement, while influences of social background on education have become substantially weaker.

In addition, in many comparative studies of income distribution, Korea showed greater equality in its income distribution during the 1970s than did most developing countries, and similar levels of inequality compared to fully industrialized societies such as Japan and the United States (Chenery et al., 1974). Furthermore, it is generally accepted that Korea's relatively low level of income inequality remained virtually unchanged from the 1960s through the late 1980s (Park, 2002; World Bank, 1993).[5] This, along with the remarkably fast expansion of education, might enhance the opportunity of students from disadvantaged social origins to continue their education.

This paper intends to detect the extent to which the dependence of educational outcomes on social background has changed in Korea during a period of remarkable educational expansion. Specifically, the study examines trends in the influence of social origins on educational attainment across three birth cohorts born between 1921 and 1970. Applying methods similar to those used by other studies to investigate this issue, this research adds a comparative insight to the discussion of educational expansion and inequality.

In the next section, I describe the basic structure of the Korean education system and governmental education policies regarding educational expansion. Then I introduce the data and method used in this study. After presenting the results of an empirical analysis of changes in the association between social origins and educational attainment across cohorts, I conclude with a brief discussion of the findings.

EDUCATIONAL POLICIES IN KOREA

In comparison to systems in other countries, the structure of the educational system in Korea is relatively simple. It basically consists of six years of compulsory elementary school, three years of middle school, and three years of academic or vocational high school. After graduating from high school, students may proceed to two years of junior college or four years of university.

Since middle school entrance exams were abolished in 1969, elementary graduates have been assigned to middle schools within their districts by lotteries. There is no tracking at the middle school level. Admission into high school is determined primarily by performance on entrance examinations and achievement records in middle school. There are, however, some differences between the admission processes of academic high schools and vocational high schools. Whereas applicants for vocational schools have the opportunity to choose their school, students who apply for academic high schools are assigned to schools within their districts by lotteries, once they pass the entrance examinations (MOE, 2002). Vocational high school is basically intended to provide students with vocational skills or training to prepare them for the labor market. Thus, most students graduating from vocational high school leave school to enter the labor market, although the proportion continuing to the tertiary level of education has recently increased. Because of the importance of college graduation for life chances in Korea, competition and pressure to earn high scores on the national entrance examinations required to apply for university or junior college is extremely intense.

Policies for the Lower Levels of Education

One highly praised educational policy that has been successfully implemented by the Korean government is its effort to concentrate public expenditures on the basic or primary level of education rather than higher education (Birdsall et al., 1997). As a successful example of the World Bank model, which requires developing countries to allocate school budgets largely to primary schooling (see Brint, 1998, pp. 83–85),[6] the Korean government has given priority to expanding the quantity and improving the quality of primary education, leaving the demand for higher education to the private sector. With this heavy investment in primary education, elementary enrollment rates had already passed 90% by the early 1960s.

The significant rise in elementary enrollment rates during the 1950s increased the demand for middle schools. Given the limited opportunities for a middle school education, this increasing demand caused social problems. Even in elementary school, the curriculum concentrated on preparing students for entrance examinations (in this case for middle school). As a result of this overemphasis on testing, students suffered from intense pressure and competition (Kim, Park & Han, 1997). In an effort to ameliorate these problems and extend educational opportunities, the government abolished middle school entrance examinations in 1969. Since then elementary graduates have been assigned to middle schools on the basis of a lottery within their school districts. The abolition of entrance examinations facilitated rapid growth in middle school education: enrollment rates increased from 41% in 1966 to 95% in 1980.

Just as the rapid growth in elementary education created a greater demand for middle schools, so rising middle school enrollment rates, spurred by the abolition of entrance examinations, created a greater demand for a high school education. As competition increased for entrance to high schools, the middle school curriculum soon became reduced to preparing students for high school entrance examinations. Entrance examinations administered by individual high schools sorted students into different high schools, ranked hierarchically. High-ranking schools selected students with high academic quality, which increased between-school differences in the average academic ability of students.

To reform this system, a new policy, called the "equalization policy" (*P'yŏ ongjunhwa Chŏngch'aek*), was implemented on a gradual basis beginning in 1974. The new system abolished school-specific entrance examinations and replaced them with nationwide entrance examinations.[7] Once they passed the examinations, students were assigned to high schools within their residential districts by a lottery. Although there are still some places where this new system has not been adopted, the policy has been successful in achieving equalization among high schools, thus relieving intense competition for entrance to a few top schools. The government also tried to extend educational opportunities by raising the quota of entrants. This led to a significant increase in high school enrollment rates from only 28% in 1970 to 41% in 1975, just one year after the implementation of the new policy. By 1980, high school enrollment rates had increased to 95%.

Educational Policies for Higher Education

In contrast to the various efforts of the Korean government to extend educational opportunities at the primary and secondary levels of education, its policy of "letting the market decide" – that is, letting people pay for the schooling they want for higher education – has increased the burden on the private sector for higher education. As is clearly shown in Fig. 1, the extent of total expenditures on the tertiary level of education in Korea is comparatively high. Only expenditures in Canada and the United States exceed those in Korea as a percentage of GDP, while expenditures in Australia are similar to Korea.

What is distinct in Korea, however, is that the private sector pays for a much higher proportion of expenses for tertiary educational institutions than does the private sector in any other country, or approximately 1.48% of its GDP, compared to only 0.3% from its public funds. In Korea, therefore, the relative share of private funds for tertiary education is 83%, which is the highest among the 19 OECD countries providing private expenditure data. Indeed, except for Korea, the private sector in only two other countries – Japan (54%) and the U.S. (52%) – pays more than half of all expenditures for tertiary education. In other countries, tertiary education is paid for primarily through public funds.

The situation is also much the same regarding private payments for all levels of educational institutions. In Korea, the proportion of funds that the private sector contributes to all levels of education is 2.51% of GDP, whereas from public sources it is 3.65%. In fact, among the OECD countries reporting private expenditure data,

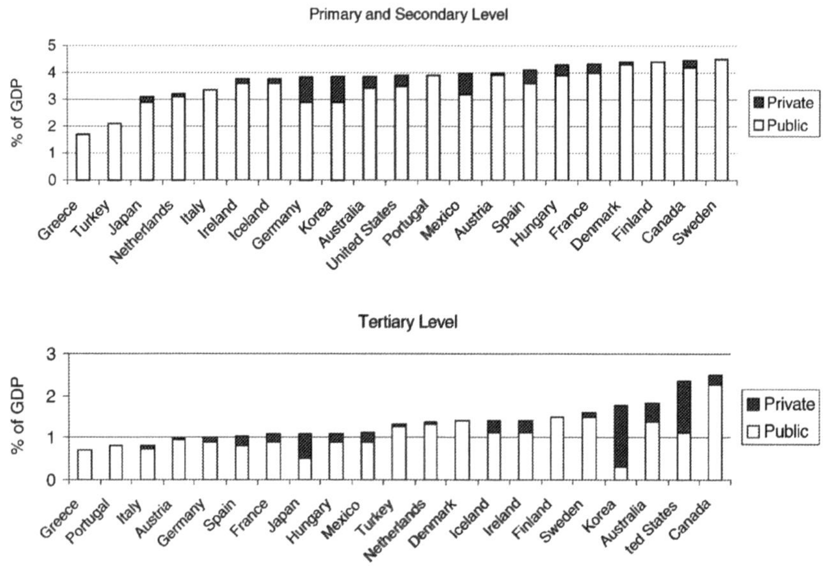

Fig. 1. Educational Expenditure as a Percentage of GDP, by Source of Funds (1994). *Source:* Education at a glance OECD indicators (1997: Chart B1.1).

Korea is the only country where private payments exceed 2% of GDP. Moreover, it should be noted that in Korea most private expenditures come from households, whereas in Germany business enterprises provide a large amount of this funding.

It is not only the very low level of public versus private expenditures for education that distinguishes the Korean case from others, but also the structure of its public expenditures. For instance, in many North European countries, between 25 to 45% of public expenditures at the tertiary level are provided in the form of financial aid to students (through scholarships, grants, and loans), whereas in Korea only 3% of public spending goes toward scholarships and grants, and practically no monies are allocated for student loans (OECD, 1997, p. 76).

The Korean government's educational policies, especially for higher education, can be characterized as an "expansion strategy," and as Hout and Dohan (1996) point out, is similar to that of the United States. Educational policy in Korea has been strongly oriented towards increasing the quantity of education available, rather than improving equality of opportunity across social groups. Over the past few decades, no explicit effort has been made to reduce inequities in educational opportunity. A major focus of the government's policy for college education was to manipulate the number of students admitted, rather than attempting to directly reduce high tuition and fees or increase government subsidies.

For instance, in 1973 the government responded to increasing social demand for higher education associated with rapidly rising high school attendance and industrial development by switching its policy from constraining to extending student quotas, especially in the area of engineering (Kim, 1993). During the 1980s, entrance quotas to universities further increased, leading to a dramatic expansion of higher education.

In this regard, what has shaped the dramatic expansion of higher education in Korea has been the strong demand for education by individuals and a willingness of parents to pay for their children's educational success, in the context of the lack of a substantial governmental effort to reduce barriers to higher education.

Given that cost is an essential element of educational decisions, the high proportion of private expenditures on education might discourage students from disadvantaged families from continuing their studies and thus preserve social inequality in educational attainment, particularly at the tertiary level (Chang, 2000). While it is generally accepted that inequality in the distribution of income is not as great in Korea as in other industrialized countries, the large financial burden placed on individuals who must pay the majority of higher education costs by themselves may help to maintain the effects of family economic background on educational attainment.[8]

Finally, it is necessary to describe how these changes in the educational system and policies apply to the three cohorts in this study, in order to help understand a context for changes in the effects of family background across the cohorts. The oldest cohort was born between 1921 and 1942; most members of this cohort completed their education before the systematic educational system had been established in Korea. The next cohort includes people born between 1943 and 1954 who attended school during the formation of the modern educational system and policies. They had graduated from elementary school prior to 1969 and had to pass entrance examinations to attend middle school. They entered high school taking school-specific entrance examinations before the "equalization policy" was implemented in 1974.

The youngest cohort, aged 20–35 in 1990, was in school during the period of rapid educational and economic expansion observed since the late 1960s, and their experiences were in sharp contrast to those of previous cohorts. Most of the individuals in the youngest cohort entered middle school after middle school examinations were abolished in 1969, and continued on to high school by taking the national common examination. (Older cohorts had to take individual high school entrance exams.) In addition, most members of the cohort who attended higher education had taken college entrance examinations after 1973. Remember that as mentioned earlier, since 1973 the government started substantially extending university student quotas responding to increasing demand for higher education.

This is one of the most important differences between the educational experiences of the youngest and the two older cohorts. Thus, in this analysis, I pay particular attention to differences among the cohorts regarding the impacts of family background on the likelihood of entering the tertiary level of education. A major aim is to examine the extent to which the expansion in tertiary education since 1973 has increased the chances of entering college for students from poor families.

DATA AND METHODS

The data for this research come from the Social Inequality Study (SIS) conducted in 1990 in Korea. Designed especially to study the extent and perception of inequality across various dimensions, the survey includes information about the education and occupation of respondents and their fathers, which are the basic variables used in this research. The survey sampled only males and females who were economically active at the time of the survey, using a multistage sampling method.[9] Information was collected through individual interviews. The total sample size is 1,976 and the ratio of male to female is about 4:1. Because of the small female sample size, this research focuses only on males aged 20–69 in 1990.[10]

The main aim of this empirical analysis is to investigate changes in the effects of social background such as the father's education and occupation on the respondent's educational attainment. As Mare elaborated in his influential papers (1980, 1981), the traditional linear regression model of family background effects on highest completed years of education does not distinguish between the effect of social background and the impact of the expansion of the educational system. Instead, logit models of educational transitions enable an analytical distinction between schooling distribution and schooling allocation.

The former reflects marginal differences, while the latter indicates the association between background and school decisions, controlling for marginal differences. This is done by examining school continuation probabilities that denote the chances to continue to the next level of schooling, given the previous level completed. Stated differently, logit parameters for each transition in the educational system are appropriate for detecting genuine impacts of social origins on school continuation and their temporal changes, because these estimates are not contaminated by variation in the schooling distribution across cohorts.

This study applies logit models for each transition in the educational system to three different birth cohorts in order to explore the trend in the association between social background and educational attainment. In the analysis, three transitions are differentiated and examined:[11] (1) completing middle school; (2) completing high school given middle-school completion; and (3) attending a junior college or university given high school completion. Since the data do not provide information on specific high school tracks that respondents attended, it was impossible to estimate separate models for the transition from middle school to either an academic or a vocational track in high school. Therefore, what is estimated is one binary logit model of whether respondents completed high school or not.

However, because we are able to distinguish between junior college and university attendance, two separate pathways from high school completion to attendance at a junior college, and from high school completion to attending a university are simultaneously analyzed using a multinomial logit model (Breen & Jonsson, 2000). This multinomial model of educational transitions will show clearly how each of the social background variables might have a different impact, depending on the type of institution a student chooses (junior college or university). Regarding the likelihood of making transitions, it is expected that social origin differences will be greater for the more difficult pathways, because greater family support such as socioeconomic resources or cultural capital is necessary to make the relatively difficult transition (Breen & Jonsson, 2000). Thus, social origins will have stronger effects on the transition to university than to junior college because the former, which is more academic and prestigious, is more difficult to accomplish than the latter.

The analysis includes father's education, occupation, and community of origin (metropolitan area/non-metropolitan area) as independent variables. These variables represent the impacts of social background. Father's education is measured by the number of years of completed schooling. Father's occupation, which refers to the occupation when the respondent was an adolescent, is measured by the International Socio-Economic Index of occupational status (ISEI) provided by Ganzeboom, De Graaf and Treiman (1992).[12]

Finally, the community of origin which indicates the place in which the respondent grew up, is obtained by distinguishing five metropolitan areas including Seoul, the capital of Korea, from other areas. A dummy variable is coded 1 if the respondent grew up in one of the metropolitan areas, 0 otherwise. The degree of the effect of this variable describes how residing in one of the five metropolitan areas may provide advantages for schooling continuation, controlling for other independent variables. Considering the extreme concentration of educational and cultural institutions in metropolitan areas, this effect is expected to be substantial.

EDUCATIONAL TRANSITION RATES

Before systematically examining changes in the effects of social origin on educational attainment, it is relevant to look at the extent of educational expansion

Table 1. Descriptive Statistics.

Variable	1921–1942	1943–1954	1955–1970	Total
A				
Educational attainment (%)				
Elementary	43.70	18.63	4.26	22.05
Middle	21.46	23.95	12.96	19.47
High	25.39	39.35	50.68	38.56
Junior college	1.18	3.61	11.99	5.61
University	8.27	14.45	20.12	14.31
B				
Father's years of education[a]	2.62 (3.90)	4.8 (4.50)	7.09 (4.56)	4.85 (4.85)
Father's occupation (SEI)[a]	30.86 (11.79)	34.24 (13.81)	37.64 (14.41)	34.27 (13.81)
Type of community: Metropolitan (%)	19.10	32.5	42.55	31.46
Cases	508	526	517	1551

[a] Means and standard errors (in parentheses) are reported for these continuous variables.

over time from descriptive statistics of the data. Panel A in Table 1, which reports the distribution of the highest level of educational attainment across the three cohorts, reveals how sharp the change in educational attainment was over the last few decades. A comparison of the oldest with the youngest cohort clearly shows the improvement in educational chances for the younger generation. Compared to 44% of the oldest cohort, only 4% of the youngest cohort stopped their educational careers at the level of primary education. On the other hand, the proportion of people who completed the tertiary level of education (junior college or university) dramatically increased from 9 to 32%.

Panel B in Table 1 presents descriptive statistics for variables used in the analysis. Educational expansion in Korea is confirmed by a significant increase over time in the mean years of education completed by fathers.[13] In addition, the table shows an increase for the younger cohorts in the percentage of people who grew up in metropolitan areas. More than 40% of the youngest cohort grew up in metropolitan areas, while only 19% of the oldest did.

Table 2 presents transition rates to the next levels of education given completion of the previous levels and provides another insight into the trend of educational attainment over time. There is a clear pattern of increasing educational attainment across cohorts at the middle and high school levels. Of the youngest cohort, 96% completed middle school, whereas only half of the oldest cohort graduated from middle school. The youngest cohort is advantaged again at the level of high school completion. The probability of completing a high school education,

Table 2. Educational Transition Rates by Cohort.

Birth Cohort	Complete Middle School	Complete High School	Attend Tertiary		
			Junior Col.	University	Tertiary[a]
Total	78.0%	75.0%	11.1%	27.8%	38.9%
1921–1942	56.3	61.9	6.2	29.9	36.1
1943–1954	81.4	70.6	6.6	28.2	34.8
1955–1970	95.7	86.5	16.4	26.6	43.0

[a] Combination of junior college and university.

given the completion of middle school, has monotonically risen from 62 to 87% across cohorts.

The picture is very different at the transition to tertiary education. While there is slight variation in favor of the youngest cohort in the rates of entering the tertiary level, which combines both junior college and university, the proportion entering four-year universities, given completion of high school, does not differ substantially across cohorts. In fact, the proportion even seems to be lowest for the youngest cohort. On the other hand, with respect to the proportion attending junior colleges, there is a significant increase from 6% for the two oldest cohorts to 16% for the youngest cohort. This reflects rapid growth in two-year junior colleges during the last few decades, which contributed to a massive expansion of higher education overall.[14]

RESULTS

Binary Logit Models of Completing Middle/High School

I now turn to a multivariate analysis of the data in order to determine the extent of change of educational inequality over time. A logistic regression is used to assess the effects of social background on the likelihood of making a transition to the next level in educational system. For the two transitions of middle school completion and completing high school given completion of middle school, binary logit models are estimated. I apply a multinomial logit model to the transition from high school to tertiary education, in order to separate two different pathways to four-year universities and junior colleges.

Table 3 presents the parameter estimates of logit models of two sequential transitions: completing middle school and completing high school conditional on middle school completion. To better show cross-cohort differences in the odds of making transitions, each of our three cohorts (1921–1942, 1943–1954, and

Table 3. Conditional Binary Logit Models of Educational Transitions.

	Middle School	High School
Father's years of education (FEDU)	0.245** (0.040)	0.067* (0.036)
Father's occupational status (FSEI)	0.073** (0.015)	0.032** (0.012)
Community of origin (COM: metropolitan = 1)	1.020** (0.327)	1.232** (0.335)
Cohort (Reference: 1921–35)		
1936–1942	0.842** (0.216)	0.221 (0.276)
1943–1949	2.372** (0.629)	0.851 (0.561)
1950–1954	2.602** (0.638)	0.860 (0.568)
1955–1960	4.065** (0.850)	1.398** (0.632)
1961–1970	5.338** (0.999)	1.103* (0.641)
FEDU × Cohort 1943–1954	−0.063 (0.055)	0.088* (0.047)
FEDU × Cohort 1955–1970	−0.050 (0.074)	0.034 (0.049)
FSEI × Cohort 1943–1954	−0.033 (0.021)	−0.021 (0.016)
FSEI × Cohort 1955–1970	−0.055** (0.028)	−0.002 (0.018)
COM × Cohort 1943–1954	−0.644 (0.445)	−0.645 (0.421)
COM × Cohort 1955–1970	−0.797 (0.607)	−0.761* (0.454)
Constant	−2.961** (0.436)	−1.270** (0.447)
Number of cases	1551	1209

*$p < 0.1$.
**$p < 0.05$.

1955–1970) is further divided into two groups, yielding a total of six groups (1921–1935, 1936–1942, 1943–1949, 1950–1954, 1955–1960, and 1961–1970). With the oldest group (1921–1935) as a reference, the five dummy variables indicate an overall trend in the odds of making transitions over time.

Looking at temporal changes in the effects of social background on each transition, the most relevant variables for the current study are interaction terms between each of the socioeconomic variables and cohorts. Given the number of samples, here the effects of social origin are allowed to vary across the three original cohorts – 1921–1942, 1943–1954, and 1955–1970 – instead of six age groups, in order to obtain more stable estimates.[15] These interaction terms indicate the extent of changes across cohorts in the impacts of social origin on the odds of completing middle school or high school conditional on middle school completion.

The three socioeconomic variables – father's education, father's occupation, and respondent's community of origin – significantly affect the chances of completing middle school, implying that with more socioeconomic resources there is a higher probability of making the transition. Subsequently, rising coefficients of five dummy variables for birth cohorts show a significant increase in the odds of middle-school completion across cohorts. This simply confirms the finding illustrated in Table 2: the probabilities of completing middle school have significantly increased across three cohorts.

Not only is there an increase in the likelihood of completing middle school across cohorts, but there is also some evidence of a decline in the effect of father's occupation for the youngest cohort (1955–1970), as indicated by a significantly negative coefficient of the interaction between father's occupation and the cohort of 1955–1970. Although it is not large enough to be statistically significant, the interaction between father's occupation and the second cohort of (1943–1954) also shows a negative sign, indicating a decline in the impact of father's occupational status.

As introduced earlier, middle school entrance examinations were abolished in 1969 and thus most of the youngest cohort (1955–1970) moved on to middle school without having to take entrance examinations, compared to the older cohorts who had to take them. We have already seen that the abolition of entrance examinations led to a significant increase in middle school enrollment rates. Given that dropout in middle school has been very rare in Korea, this increased participation for the youngest cohort might have reduced social origin differences in the odds of completing middle school as well. This partially explains the decline in the effects of father's occupation, especially for the youngest cohort. However, none of the other interactions between father's education or respondent's community of origin and the cohorts is statistically significant, though the coefficients are large.

Having found a decline in the influence of father's education at this same transition of completing middle school in Italy, Shavit and Westerbeek (1998) attributed the decline to a saturation effect suggested by Raftery and Hout (1993). According to their hypothesis, a decrease in social origin differences in the odds of educational attainment is feasible only if educational demand by the privileged groups reaches saturation. As was the case in Italy, the proportion of those who complete middle school has rapidly increased over time in Korea, reaching 96% for the recent cohort, as seen in Table 2. Thus, the proportion of students from higher social strata completing middle school probably reached saturation, and this might be associated with the decline in the effect of father's occupation that we have observed.

Turning to the transition to high school completion conditional on completing middle school, students with fathers who were more educated and/or had higher occupational status are more likely to graduate from high school, as are those who grew up in metropolitan areas. The increase across cohorts in the proportion making the transition is substantial at the level of high school as well as at the middle school level. The odds of completing high school are four or three times as great, respectively, for the two youngest groups born between 1955–1960 and 1961–1970, as for the oldest group born 1921–1935 ($e^{1.398} = 4.05, e^{1.103} = 3.01$).

In general, most interactions between the cohorts and socioeconomic variables are not significant at this educational career level, indicating that the effects of social background have changed little over time. On the one hand, the interaction between father's education and the second cohort (1943–1954) is marginally significant ($p < 0.10$), indicating some increase in the importance of father's education on the odds of completing high school for this cohort as compared to the oldest cohort. On the other hand, the advantage for educational attainment of growing up in a metropolitan area seems to have declined for the youngest cohort, although the effect is only marginally significant ($p < 0.10$).

To summarize, the results of logit models for educational transitions reveal that despite a significant increase in the proportion of students completing middle school and high school across cohorts, which is a reflection of rapid educational expansion, this expansion did not substantially reduce the association between social origins and educational attainment. Although, in general, evident changes in the effects of social origin were not detected from the analysis, it should be noted that the effect of father's occupation on the odds of middle school completion has significantly declined for the most recent cohort. In addition, there is somewhat weak evidence of a declining gap in the likelihood of high school graduation between those from metropolitan and other areas.

A Multinomial Model of Transitions to Tertiary Education

In Table 4, parameter estimates from a multinomial model of transitions to each kind of tertiary education are reported. However, before examining the results, two additional sets of parameters need to be considered. The column labeled "all" presents the parameter estimates of the binary logit model comparing the likelihood of attending any types of tertiary education to that of leaving school without further education, while the column labeled "university only" refers to the estimates of the binary logit model, focusing only on universities by treating attendants at junior college as those who could not make the transition and thus stopped their educational careers at the level of high school.[16]

Regarding trends in the effects of social origin, the most interesting finding is a significant increase in the impact of father's education across cohorts for both columns of "all" and "university all." Father's education did not affect the likelihood of making the transition for the oldest cohort, as the negligible coefficient of FEDU indicates. However, two interactions between the two younger cohorts and father's education are statistically significant, showing the substantial increase over time in the importance of father's education on the conditional odds of attending

Table 4. Multinomial Models of Transitions to Tertiary Education.

			Multinomial Model	
	All[a]	University Only[b]	Junior Col./No[c]	University/No
Father's years of education (FEDU)	−0.047 (0.044)	−0.065 (0.046)	0.017 (0.082)	−0.061 (0.047)
Father's occupational status (FSEI)	0.055** (0.013)	0.054** (0.014)	0.037 (0.024)	0.059** (0.014)
Community of origin (COM: metropolitan = 1)	0.800** (0.349)	0.912** (0.363)	0.196 (0.679)	0.934** (0.372)
Cohort (Reference: 1921–1935)				
1936–1942	−0.060 (0.362)	−0.041 (0.377)	−0.087 (0.677)	−0.055 (0.386)
1943–1949	−0.014 (0.708)	0.166 (0.741)	−0.482 (1.292)	0.102 (0.763)
1950–1954	0.076 (0.714)	0.111 (0.753)	−0.030 (1.290)	0.104 (0.772)
1955–1960	0.346 (0.674)	−0.428 (0.733)	1.344 (1.144)	−0.411 (0.757)
1961–1970	0.292 (0.680)	−0.538 (0.739)	1.370 (1.149)	−0.517 (0.765)
FEDU × Cohort 1943–1954	0.119** (0.056)	0.115** (0.058)	0.090 (0.105)	0.126** (0.059)
FEDU × Cohort 1955–1970	0.138** (0.052)	0.170** (0.055)	0.038 (0.090)	0.181** (0.057)
FSEI × Cohort 1943–1954	−0.021 (0.016)	−0.022 (0.017)	−0.010 (0.030)	−0.023 (0.017)
FSEI × Cohort 1955–1970	−0.024 (0.016)	−0.022 (0.016)	−0.018 (0.026)	−0.021 (0.017)
COM × Cohort 1943–1954	−0.235 (0.436)	−0.216 (0.455)	−0.181 (0.839)	−0.242 (0.465)
COM × Cohort 1955–1970	−0.426 (0.410)	−0.472 (0.437)	0.026 (0.736)	−0.441 (0.450)
Constant	−2.705** (0.583)	−2.988** (0.615)	−3.782** (1.057)	−3.069** (0.630)

[a] A binary logit model of attending any types of tertiary education compared to no tertiary education given high school completion.
[b] A binary logit model of attending four-year university compared to a combined category (no tertiary education and two-year junior college).
[c] No = No tertiary education.
** $p < 0.05$.

higher education.[17] Other interactions between cohorts and father's occupation or community of origin are not significant.

Turning to the results of a multinomial model that allows separate comparisons between junior college and no post-secondary education and between university and no post-secondary education, none of the variables related to the former comparison have significant effects. However, the coefficients of two dummy variables representing the age groups of 1955–1960 and 1961–1970 are large. This suggests a somewhat higher chance of junior college education for the recent cohorts.

However, father's occupation affects the odds of entering a university as compared to no tertiary education. Also, growing up in metropolitan areas provides a substantial advantage for pursuing a university education. These findings confirm the expectation discussed earlier that social origin differences affect the transition to junior college less than to the university. This is because the pathway to the university as opposed to junior college is more demanding academically – it requires much higher test scores and GPA in high school. Consequently, differences in socioeconomic resources play a greater role in determining success at this educational career level (Breen & Jonsson, 2000).

Examining interactions between social origins and cohorts reveals that the increase in the importance of father's education is mainly related to the transition to the university, but not to junior college. Except for a significant increase over time in the effect of father's education on attendance at university, there is no evidence of a significant change in the effect of the father's occupation or community of origin on either transition. This implies that the expansion of higher education, which occurred particularly since 1973 as the Korean government extended student quotas, did not lead to a significant reduction in social origin differences in the probability of continuing to tertiary education.

SUMMARY AND DISCUSSION

The results clearly show that there has been a considerable increase in educational attainment in Korea over the last few decades, and the extent of change is remarkable. The mean years of schooling achieved by younger people has dramatically increased, and the distribution of educational attainment by cohorts shows rapid growth in the proportion of those completing secondary and tertiary education. This expansion has occurred in a context in which academic education is emphasized over vocational education, and the nationwide entrance examinations and similar curricula across schools have yielded a high degree of standardization.

This study also examined the striking growth in Korea's educational system that has resulted from changes in the country's educational policy. The Korean government has invested heavily in primary education, and expanded opportunities for secondary education. Within higher education, it has emphasized efficiency and an increase in the quantity of education, rather than direct intervention to reduce inequality of educational opportunity. A significant result of this policy has been the high proportion of private expenditures on higher education and scarce public support for it.

The main issue addressed in this study was whether there was a decrease in the impact of social background on educational opportunity during the same time as the Korean educational system was expanding. Given the country's remarkable educational growth and low level of income inequality, it was expected that social origin would have a declining effect on educational attainment.

The analysis of the multinomial model of educational transitions revealed that the impacts of social origin are more crucial for entry into the university than entry into junior college. The results also showed a significant rise across cohorts in the effect of the father's education on opportunities for university education, while such a pattern was not observed for the transition to junior college. The finding that the father's education became more important for university entrance for the younger cohorts seems to be unique to Korea. As far as I am aware, such a pattern has not been reported in any other countries (cf. Erikson & Jonsson, 1996; Shavit & Blossfeld, 1993).

However, it should be kept in mind that an alternative explanation attributes this pattern of the rising effect to differential selection. As the proportion of students completing high school increases across all social groups, risk sets eligible for university education also increase. This leads to greater heterogeneity among students on unmeasured determinants of educational success, which, in turn, may result in increasing effects of measured origin variables (see Shavit & Blossfeld, 1993). Although this may not be the case in this study,[18] further analyses with data not presently available would be required to rigorously test this possibility.[19]

Unlike the rising effect of father's education, no substantial changes were seen in the influence of father's occupation or community of origin on the transition to either junior college or university. In general, this confirms the conclusion of previous studies that educational inequality has persisted despite educational expansion in many countries during the 20th century (Shavit & Blossfeld, 1993).

The persistent dependence of educational attainment on social origin for entrance to a university or junior college may be due, in part, to the relatively high private burden for education. With the lack of governmental subsidies or support for higher education, a large proportion of educational expenditure attributable to household payment may discourage students from disadvantaged backgrounds to proceed to the next stage of the schooling process. However, the substantial impact of father's education on university education for the youngest cohorts seems to suggest that in the Korean educational system, not only economic resources but also cultural capital may be producing inequalities in educational attainment. In the literature of educational stratification, parental education is often understood as a crude measure of cultural origin (Hout & Dohan, 1996). An interesting future project would be to create the more refined measures of cultural capital to better test the hypothesis of the increasing importance of family cultural resources on educational attainment.

This persistent inequality, especially at the level of tertiary education, however, should not lead us to neglect the progress at the middle school and high school levels. Although in general the effects of social background on making transitions remained constant at these levels of education, there was strong evidence of significantly larger proportions of the recent cohorts completing high school and/or middle school as compared to the older cohorts. This reflects the rapid educational expansion in Korea during the last few decades, which led to a dramatic increase in educational attainment across cohorts.

We have seen various efforts by the Korean government to extend educational opportunities at the primary and secondary levels. In addition, there is a noticeable decline in the importance of father's occupation on middle school completion for the youngest cohort. This can be attributed in part to the dramatic increase in middle school education for the youngest cohort after entrance examinations were abolished. The advantage of growing up in a metropolitan area for high school completion also seems to have diminished for the youngest cohort, although it was found to be marginally significant in this study.

Before concluding, it is necessary to point out two major limitations of the study, which suggest possible directions for further research. Since the data does not provide information on the specific types of high schools that respondents attended, this made it impossible to examine the two different pathways to higher education – from academic or vocational high schools. The only feasible approach in the current study was to treat all high school graduates as candidates for post-secondary education. However, it is common knowledge that students graduating from vocational high schools are far less likely to continue their education than are graduates of academic high schools. This points out the need in future research to examine how the educational choice at the high school level affects the transition to higher education and how social origins influence this process (Breen & Jonsson, 2000).[20]

Finally, the small number of female samples in the data precluded an investigation of trends in gender differences in educational attainment, which is another major dimension in educational stratification. In particular, given the impressive increase in female participation in higher education,[21] a consideration of gender effects would provide a fuller understanding of trends in educational inequality in Korea.

NOTES

1. Another important finding highlighted by the comparative analysis is that social background has stronger impacts at the beginning of an educational career than at the later transitions. Blossfeld and Shavit (1993) introduced two explanations for the declining effects of socioeconomic origin across educational transitions. The first perspective emphasizes the differential selection process between social strata (Mare, 1981). An alternative to this explanation of the pattern suggests that, as students become older, they are less dependent on parental resources, which leads to declining effects of social origin on later transitions.

2. They illustrated that the wage premium earned by educated workers in Korea declined as numbers of highly educated workers in the labor force sharply increased, consistent with the traditional economic prediction that returns to a factor decrease as its relative supply increases. According to the researchers, in 1976 Korean workers with a high school education earned 47% more than primary school graduates, while that premium declined to 30% by 1986. The premium related to tertiary schooling also declined from 97 to 66% during the same period (Birdsall et al., 1997, p. 105).

3. It is widely known that the institutional linkage between high schools and employers is considerably stronger in Japan (Rosenbaum & Kariya, 1989), whereas in Korea there are few institutional ties between schools and employers. Japanese high schools and employers actively cooperate with each other: the former prepare students for the specific skills needed by employers and the latter recruit students recommended by high schools.

4. Enrollment rates in higher education were substantially higher in Taiwan than in Korea until 1981, when Korea's rates surpassed those of Taiwan. Between 1980 and 1985, enrollment rates in Korea more than doubled from 16 to 35.6%, while the corresponding change in Taiwan was from 17.9 to 23.2% (Kim, 1993).

5. The trend in the Gini index, a rough indicator of income inequality, is not linear in Korea. According to a report, the coefficient that had declined slightly from 0.34 in 1965 to 0.33 in 1970 increased substantially between 1970 and 1975 (0.39). After that, the Gini index remained constant, showing 0.389 in 1980 (Koo, 1985). Another study also reports that there has been no linear trend in the Gini coefficient; it was 0.34 in 1965, 0.39 in 1976, and 0.36 in 1982 (see Tables 1–5 in Leipziger, Dollar, Shorrocks & Song, 1992). Here it should be remembered that over this period, the Gini index in Korea remained primarily in the 0.3–0.4 range, which indicates a relatively low level of income inequality by international standards (Barrett & Chin, 1987).

6. In addition to targeting monies for primary schooling, another element that the World Bank considers essential for educational expansion is emphasizing general education over vocational education. The World Bank has taken a strong stand against vocational education as an inefficient and ineffective means for economic development. In this regard, the educational policy thc Korean government has followed is close to the model of the World Bank.

7. Furthermore, since 1998, entrance examinations for high school were abolished in four large cities including Seoul, the capital of Korea. In those cities students are now selected on the basis of middle school activities records, while in other places entrance examination scores are still considered as a major criterion for selection (Ministry of Education and Human Resources Development, http://www.moe.go.kr).

8. It should also be noted that wealth in Korea is considerably more unequal than income, as is common in other countries. In particular, most of the wealth is accumulated through landownership and real estate (Leipziger et al., 1992). Thus, although income is relatively equally distributed within the population, the more unequal distribution of wealth combined with an inefficient tax system may yield substantial differences between social groups in the amount of money they can contribute toward higher education.

9. This way of sampling only the economically active population at the time of the survey requires us to be careful for any potential biases it might cause on the interpretation of current results. However, the fact that the proportion of men aged 25–64 who participate in the labor force is about 90% regardless of educational levels and even the percentage among men aged 55–64 reaches around 75% without significant differences by educational levels (OECD, 2000, p. 269), implies that this problem should not cause serious bias. If we included women in the analysis as well, of course, we had suffered from more serious selection problem, given that only half of Korean women participate in the labor force. See Whang (1992) for detailed information on the sampling process of the survey.

10. The total sample between ages 20–69 is 1,551. Among them, one case lacks information on the type of community origin. For 79 cases where information was missing on either the father's education or occupation, I imputed average scores. The results did not differ in any significant ways, regardless of whether those missing cases were excluded from the analysis or were included with the imputed average scores.

11. The effects of socioeconomic origin on the completion of elementary school are not separately estimated. Most of the oldest cohort as well as the youngest cohort completed elementary school, so the number of the cases that failed to make the transition is too small to be analyzed.

12. Originally the index was constructed by utilizing comparably coded data on education, occupation, and income for 73,901 full-time employed men from 16 countries. Ganzeboom, De Graaf and Treiman found that the index compares favorably with other competing measures of occupational status such as Treiman's international prestige scores or EGP occupational class categories. For more details, refer to Ganzeboom, De Graaf and Treiman (1992).

13. However, the mean years of father's schooling is only seven, even for the youngest cohort. This reflects the fact that the fathers were mainly farmers who did not need formal schooling. In the data, the proportion of occupations related to farming – including fishing and forestry work – in the father's generation is 68%.

14. Between 1965 and 1990, the number of junior colleges increased from 48 to 117 and the number of students enrolled in junior colleges increased 10 fold from 33,483 in 1970 to 323,825 in 1990 (KEDI, 2000).

15. See Shavit and Westerbeek (1998) for a similar analytical strategy.

16. Breen and Jonsson (2000) showed that these are two alternative strategies that Mare's sequential model can utilize to analyze transitions to tertiary education. (The model does not allow separate analyses of different educational choices at a particular point in educational transitions.) They compared the results of the Mare model with that of the multinomial model and demonstrated the advantages of the latter.

17. Using the same data pooled with another data source, Chang (2000) presented contrasting findings of no temporal change in the effects of father's class, education, and community of origin on any educational transition. But his way of modeling temporal changes in social origin effects assumes linear trends across all age intervals. Thus, it is not appropriate for detecting changes simultaneously affecting people in certain broad age ranges, which consist of a certain cohort.

18. As seen in Table 2, in Korea the proportions of students who complete high school have increased significantly over time. Thus, the increasing effect of father's education on the conditional odds of attending university might be attributable to the growing risk sets for university education, as predicted by the differential selection hypothesis. However, there is no such increase in the effects of father's education on the transitions of completing high school or attending junior college. Because the proportion of students who complete these transitions also increased substantially over time, the same pattern of rising effects of social origins should be expected for these transitions as well. In addition, except for the effect of father's education, there is no change in the effects of other social origin variables such as father's occupation or the type of community on the conditional odds of attending university or junior college.

19. As Mare (1993) showed, utilization of information on siblings, which are not available in our data, might be a possible way to control for unmeasured characteristics and thus reach a more reasonable conclusion on this issue.

20. This data limitation also makes it unfeasible to test another alternative explanation of the increasing effect of father's education on college attendance. The finding that father's education became more important for college attendance among the younger cohorts might reflect increased tracking at the middle school-high school transition. Given that vocational high school graduates, who are more likely to come from disadvantaged origins, are far less likely to attend college, expansion of secondary vocational education relative to academic education may partially explain the increasing effect of father's education on college attendance. Since the data do not provide information on tracking at the high school level, I cannot test this hypothesis empirically. However, official statistics show that the proportion of vocational high school students in Korea has decreased rather than increased over the period from 45% in 1980 to 35% in 1990. During the same period, we observed an increased effect of the father's education on college attendance.

21. For example, since 1985 advancement rates from academic high school have been higher among women than among men, and the proportion of female students among total entrants to universities increased from 27% in 1970 to 39% in 1990. The corresponding percentage among entrants to junior colleges increased from 36% in 1970 to 46% in 1990 (KEDI, 2000).

ACKNOWLEDGMENTS

An early version of this paper was presented at the annual meeting of Research Committee 28, International Sociological Association, Mannheim Germany, April 2001. I thank Adam Gamoran, Robert Hauser, Gary Sandefur, the editors, and two anonymous reviewers for their valuable comments and suggestions on early drafts. I am also grateful to Janet Clear in the Center for Demography and Ecology of University of Wisconsin-Madison for her editorial suggestions.

REFERENCES

Allmendinger, J. (1989). Educational system and labor market outcomes. *European Sociological Review*, *5*, 231–250.

Barrett, R. E., & Chin, S. (1987). Export-oriented industrializing states in the capitalist world system: Similarities and differences. In: F. C. Deyo (Ed.), *The Political Economy of the New Asian Industrialism* (pp. 23–43). Ithaca, NY: Cornell University Press.

Birdsall, N., Ross, D., & Sabot, R. H (1997). Education, growth, and inequality. In: N. Birdsall & F. Jaspersen (Eds), *Pathways To Growth* (pp. 93–127). Washington, DC: Inter-American Development Bank.

Blossfeld, H.-P., & Shavit, Y. (1993). Persisting barriers: Changes in educational opportunities in thirteen countries. In: Y. Shavit & H.-P. Blossfeld (Eds), *Persistent Inequality: Changing Educational Attainment in Thirteen Countries* (pp. 1–24). Boulder, CO: Westview Press.

Breen, R., & Jonsson, J. O. (2000). Analyzing educational careers: A multinomial transition model. *American Sociological Review*, *65*, 754–772.

Brint, S. (1998). *Schools and societies*. Thousand Oaks, CA: Pine Forge Press.

Brinton, M. C. (2001). Married women's labor in east Asian economies. In: M. C. Brinton (Ed.), *Women's Working Lives in East Asia* (pp. 1–37). Stanford, CA: Stanford University Press.

Chang, S. S. (2000). Inequality of educational opportunity: Effects of family background on educational attainment. *Korean Journal of Sociology*, *34*, 671–708 (in Korean).

Chang, S. S. (2001). *Social mobility in Korea*. Seoul: Seoul National University Press (in Korean).

Chenery, H., Ahluwalia, M. S., Bell, C. L. G., Duloy, H. H., & Jolly, R. (Eds) (1974). *Redistribution with growth*. London: Oxford University Press.

Cheng, T.-J. (1992). Dilemmas and choices in educational policies: The case of South Korea and Taiwan. *Studies in Comparative International Development*, *27*(4) (Winter), 54–79.

Erikson, R., & Jonsson, J. O. (Eds) (1996). *Can education be equalized? The Swedish case in comparative perspective*. Boulder, CO: Westview Press.

Ganzeboom, H. B. G., de Graaf, P., & Treiman, D. J. (1992). An international scale of occupational status. *Social Science Research*, *21*, 1–56.

Hout, M., & Dohan, D. P. (1996). Two paths to educational opportunity: Class and educational selection in Sweden and the United Sates. In: R. Erikson & J. O. Jonsson (Eds), *Can Education Be Equalized? The Swedish Case in Comparative Perspective* (pp. 207–231). Boulder, CO: Westview Press.

Ishida, H. (1998). Educational credentials and labor-market outcomes in Japan. In: Y. Shavit & W. Müller (Eds), *From School to Work* (pp. 287–335). Oxford: Oxford University Press.

Jonsson, J. O., Mills, C., & Müller, W. (1996). A half century of increasing educational openness? Social class, gender, and educational attainment in Sweden, Germany, and Britain. In: R. Erikson & J. O. Jonsson (Eds), *Can Education Be Equalized? The Swedish Case in Comparative Perspective* (pp. 207–231). Boulder, CO: Westview Press.

Kim, Y. H. (1993). *Educational inequality in Korea*. Seoul: Educational Science Press (in Korean).

Kim, Y. H., Park, Y. H., & Han, S. H. (1997). *Korean education and national development*. Research Report 97–99. Seoul: Korean Educational Development Institute (in Korean).

Koo, H. (1985). The transformation of the Korean class structure: The impact of dependent development. *Research in Social Stratification and Mobility*, *4*, 129–148.

Korean Educational Development Institute (KEDI) (2000). *Handbook of Educational Statistics*. Seoul: KEDI.

Leipziger, D. M., Dollar, D., Shorrocks, A. F., & Song, S. Y. (1992). *The distribution of income and wealth in Korea*. Washington, DC: World Bank.

Mare, R. D. (1980). Social background and school continuation decisions. *Journal of the American Statistical Association*, *75*, 295–305.

Mare, R. D. (1981). Change and stability in educational stratification. *American Sociological Review*, *46*, 72–87.

Mare, R. D. (1993). Educational stratification on observed and unobserved components of family background. In: Y. Shavit & H.-P. Blossfeld (Eds), *Persistent Inequality: Changing Educational Attainment in Thirteen Countries* (pp. 229–249). Boulder, CO: Westview Press.

Ministry of Education and Human Resources Development in Korea (MOE) (2002). Available: http://www.moe.go.kr

OECD (1997). *Education at a glance: OECD indicators*. Paris.

OECD (2000, 2001). *Education at a glance: OECD indicators*. Paris.

Park, H. (2002) (in press). Intergenerational social mobility among Korean men. *Research in Social Stratification and Mobility*.

Raftery, A. E., & Hout, M. (1993). Maximally maintained inequality: Expansion, reform, and opportunity in Irish education, 1921–1975. *Sociology of Education*, *66*, 22–39.

Rosenbaum, J. E., & Takehiko, K. (1989). From school to work: Market and institutional mechanisms in Japan. *Sociology of Education*, *64*, 78–95.

Sandefur, G. D., & Park, H. (2002, August). Gender and cohort differences in first occupational attainment and early labor force participation in Korea. Presented at the annual meeting of American Sociological Association, Chicago.

Shavit, Y., & Blossfeld, H.-P. (Eds) (1993). *Persistent inequality: Changing educational attainment in thirteen countries*. Boulder, CO: Westview Press.

Shavit, Y., & Müller, W. (Ed.) (1998). *From school to work*. Oxford: Oxford University Press.

Shavit, Y., & Westerbeek, K. (1998). Educational stratification in Italy: Reforms, expansion, and equality of opportunity. *European Sociological Review*, *14*, 33–47.

Smith, H. L., & Cheung, P. P. L. (1986). Trends in the effects of family background on educational attainment in the Philippines. *American Journal of Sociology*, *91*, 1387–1408.

Smits, J., Ultee, W., & Lammers, J. (1998). Educational homogamy in 65 countries: An explanation of differences in openness using country-level explanatory variables. *American Sociological Review*, *63*, 264–285.

Treiman, D. J., & Yamaguchi, K. (1993). Trends in educational attainment in Japan. In: Y. Shavit & H.-P. Blossfeld (Eds), *Persistent Inequality: Changing Educational Attainment in Thirteen Countries* (pp. 229–249). Boulder, CO: Westview Press.

Tsai, S.-L. (1998). The transition from school to work in Taiwan. In: Y. Shavit & W. Müller (Eds), *From School to Work* (pp. 443–470). Oxford: Oxford University Press.

Tsai, S.-L., & Chiu, H.-Y. (1993). Changes in educational stratification in Taiwan. In: Y. Shavit & H. -P. Blossfeld (Eds), *Persistent Inequality: Changing Educational Attainment in Thirteen Countries* (pp. 193–227). Boulder, CO: Westview Press.

Whang, I.-C. (Ed.) (1992). *Inequality and equity in Korean society*. Seoul: Nanam Publishing House (in Korean).

World Bank (1993). *The East Asian miracle: Economic growth and public policy*. New York: Oxford University Press.

EDUCATIONAL OPPORTUNITIES FOR BOYS AND GIRLS IN THAILAND

Sara R. Curran, Chang Y. Chung, Wendy Cadge
and Anchalee Varangrat

ABSTRACT

Within individual countries, the paths towards increasing educational attainment are not always linear and individuals are not equally affected. Differences between boys' and girls' educational attainments are a common expression of this inequality as boys are more often favored for continued schooling. We examine the importance of birth cohort, sibship size, migration, and school accessibility for explaining both the gender gap and its narrowing in secondary schooling in one district in Northeast Thailand between 1984–1994. Birth cohort is a significant explanation for the narrowing of the gender gap. Migration, sibship size, and remote village location are important explanations for limited secondary education opportunities, especially for girls.

INTRODUCTION

As developing societies are integrated into the global economy, the perceived value of education tends to increase in national governments, communities, families, and among individuals. Individuals' levels of educational attainment tend to rise as a result of changes in state policies, community contexts, and family dynamics

Inequality Across Societies: Families, Schools and Persisting Stratification
Research in Sociology of Education, Volume 14, 59–102
(Formerly Research in Sociology of Education and Socialization)

ISSN: 1479-3539/doi:10.1016/S1479-3539(03)14004-9

(Buchmann & Hannum, 2001). Within individual countries, the paths towards increasing educational attainment are not always linear and not all members of the population are equally affected (Shavit & Blossfeld, 1993). Differences between boys' and girls' educational attainments are one of the most common expressions of this inequality as boys are more often favored for continued schooling than are girls (Appleton & Collier, 1995; Fuller & Liang, 1999; King, 1991; King & Hill, 1993; Kurz & Prather, 1995; Richter & Pong, 1995; Stash & Hannum, 2001; Subbarao & Raney, 1995; Tsai et al., 1994; United Nations Development Program, 1994).

Differences in boys' and girls' educational attainment are understood to have important influences upon the extent and pace of social and behavioral change associated with development (Appleton & Collier, 1995; Axinn & Barber, 2001; Axinn & Yobiku, 2001; Behrman et al., 1997; Blossfeld & Huinink, 1991; Hadden & London, 1996; King & Hill, 1993; Malhotra & Mather, 1997; Subbarao & Raney, 1995; Summers, 1994; Tzannatos, 1999). And, targeting women's literacy through informal education programs and girls' expanded educational opportunities has been a central goal of governmental, multilateral, and non-governmental organizational efforts to promote efficient economic development (Knodel & Jones, 1996; Summers, 1994; Tzannatos, 1999).

Explaining why the gender gap persists or why it narrows are questions in educational attainment research that are less well understood (Buchmann, 1996; Fuller & Liang, 1999). Answers vary from family of origin characteristics (e.g. the number and sex composition of siblings) (see Conley, 2000, for a review), cultural institutions (like patriarchy or the structure and character of schools or some combination of both) (Fuller & Liang, 1999; Stromquist, 1998, 1990), or economic institutions (either those within families determining resource pooling and allocation or those outside the family that structure extra-familial labor market opportunities) (Buchmann & Hannum, 2001; Fuller & Liang, 1999; King, 1991; King & Hill, 1993).

We join the growing literature on this topic, with a prospective study of boys' and girls' transitions to secondary school over a 10-year period (1984–1994) of both rapid economic development (especially during the first two-thirds of the decade) and rapid expansion of secondary schools in rural northeastern Thailand. We take up the challenge proffered by Buchmann and Hannum (2001) that research on educational attainment must include analysis of the dynamics of social change with simultaneous attention to the multiple levels at which social change occurs, including the individual, family, and community.

We focus on five factors related to the social change occurring in Thailand from 1984 to 1994 that might diminish the relative schooling advantages of boys over girls. The first factor is birth cohort. We are especially interested in the opportunities afforded to children born after 1976 when the Thai government initiated a significant expansion of primary education. The second is declining fertility as measured by the number of siblings at the beginning of the period (1984) and any additional siblings born after 1984. The third factor is the role of migration, specifically rural-urban migration, in stimulating demand for education through expansion of non-agricultural labor market opportunities and increasing its affordability through remittances. The fourth factor is accessibility of schools, through school building in villages or nearby villages. And a fifth factor is the remoteness of the village location relative to the district town. The district town, Nang Rong, is the center of commerce and trade and is situated at the intersection of highways connecting villagers to migrant destinations.

Our study builds on other work that examines cohort and number of siblings as factors determining educational attainment (for reviews see Conley, 2000 and Shavit & Blossfeld, 1993). We add to these studies in two ways. First, we examine the role of migration, a rarely studied topic in educational attainment research in developing countries (for an exception see Kandel & Kao, 2000, who examine educational aspirations and migration among Mexican youth). Second, we examine the impact of school building and remoteness of village location. To our knowledge, this is the first prospective study of accessibility and educational attainment in the Thai context, and it captures the period when Thai educational policy shifted significantly towards addressing the need for expanded secondary education. Beyond the importance of this study for understanding the Thai context, to our knowledge, this is the first time a systematic analysis of prospective data has been used to analyze the combined influence of individual, family, and community factors, especially migration, upon gendered differences in educational outcomes.[1]

BACKGROUND

Previous International Stratification Research about Gender, Migration, Family Dynamics, and School Accessibility

Previous research on gender stratification in educational attainment shows persistent male advantages in some countries, shrinking sex differentials in others, and growing female advantages in still other countries. The empirical evidence for these patterns yields complex interpretations and explanations that point to the simultaneous importance of family dynamics, labor markets, rates of economic growth or contraction, and social context. Adding to this complexity is some evidence that transition rates from one level of schooling to another do not change at the same pace for boys and girls, nor are the factors predicting the probability of transitions the same at each level for boys and girls (Ashby, 1985; Greenhalgh, 1985; Knodel, 1997; Shavit & Blossfeld, 1993). In this section, we briefly review explanations for gender differentials that include family dynamics, economic change, and school accessibility. We also discuss the ways in which migration might be an important factor for explaining educational attainment and gender differences in attainment as migration offers both increased income and competing alternatives to education.

Much research focuses upon family dynamics to explain gender differentials in educational attainment. These studies emphasize family size, the number of siblings and sex composition, parental attitudes, parental educational attainment, and family economy (current opportunity costs and future returns to the family economy and familial social support systems). Blake's (1989) hypothesized resource dilution effect has been supported with evidence from a number of settings (e.g. Knodel & Wongsith, 1991) in Thailand; Lloyd and Gage-Brandon (1994) in Ghana; Pong (1997) in Malaysia; Anh et al. (1998) in Vietnam; Kaneda (1998) and Ono (forthcoming) in Japan; Powell and Steelman (1993) in the U.S. But the negative effect of number of siblings upon education attainment is not uniform across children within families (Fuller & Liang, 1999). When examined, size tends to have a more pronounced effect upon girls than boys (Lloyd & Gage-Brandon, 1994).

Contrary to the resource dilution hypothesis, others have argued that, in particular settings, large, extended families can provide greater opportunities for educational opportunities. In part, these findings depend on which unit of analysis is considered (household or family) and the porous nature of household boundaries, especially with regard to resource pooling, risk minimization, the spreading of reproductive investment burdens (like family care giving and children's schooling). Thus, researchers have found that extended families can also improve educational opportunities in Botswana (Chernichovsky, 1985), in Thailand (Richter & Pong, 1995), and among some groups in Israel (Shavit & Pierce, 1991) and South Africa (Fuller & Liang, 1999; Kaufman et al., 1998).

Significant research effort has also been devoted to understanding sibling dynamics within families and their effect upon educational attainment. And, again, gender is an important factor. These studies have yielded mixed results (see Conley, 2000 for a review of the literature in the U.S.). In Asia, there is some evidence that although brothers are generally advantaged for schooling, sisters gain access to some schooling insofar as it assists either their marriage prospects or their labor market opportunities and subsequent contributions to the natal family's economy, their brothers' educational attainment (Ashby, 1985, in Nepal; Greenhalgh, 1985, in Taiwan; Lillard & Willis, 1994, in Malaysia) or younger siblings' education prospects (Parish & Willis, 1993, in Taiwan).

Parental attitudes, as well as parental education, is another element of family dynamics that has provided some leverage in explaining sex differentials in education and, in some cases, changing parental attitudes have narrowed gender gaps. Perceptions of limited labor market opportunities constrain girls' educational opportunities in Kenya (Buchmann, 2000) and in the Gambia (Bakarr, 2000). On the other hand, in Asia the constraining factor is parental attitudes about how the education of children may or may not disrupt the family economy.

In Thailand, Knodel (1997) finds that, especially among rural families, sons were preferred recipients of education investments during the early period of economic growth. Daughters, on the other hand, especially youngest daughters, were not preferred recipients for fear they might not be available to care for their parents when they got older (the traditional expectation). However, towards the middle of the economic expansion (early 1990s), parent's gender preferences had diminished considerably, mirroring statistical observations that the gender gap had shrunk. Nevertheless, family economic concerns, especially among rural parents, predominated in discussions about the tradeoffs of children's education versus work and migration. Daughter's remittances, the reliability of their sending behavior, and their greater level of remittance back to their natal home were important alternative considerations for parents.

The preceding discussion highlights how current and future family economic considerations on the part of parents appear to be an important element in the calculus of education resource allocation. These considerations are inevitably influenced by the social and economic context within which the family economy is situated. Rapid expansion of labor market opportunities in countries where educational attainment is low, especially in some developing country contexts, are likely to be disassociated with education or technical skills. In these cases, low-wage, low-skill jobs may provide competing alternatives to education. To the extent that these job opportunities may be sex-segregated, such labor market expansion may also explain sex differentials in education outcomes (King & Hill, 1993; Kingdon, 1998). The dramatic increase in outsourcing of textile and electronics manufacturing throughout Southeast Asia is one such example – where the production technology did not demand a highly skilled labor force. In fact, Richter and Pong (1995) found a drop in school enrollments during the early periods of Thailand's move towards export lead manufacturing (from 1985–1990).

For rural residents, particularly from impoverished agricultural regions, migration to low-wage factory jobs provides an important competing alternative, especially when there are high opportunity costs associated with schooling. This has certainly been the case for Mexican migrants (Massey, 1990), where educational attainment is associated with lower odds of migration. In the Mexican case, Kandel and Kao (2000) found that children with family migrant experience in the U.S. are less likely to aspire to a university education in Mexico, although they do aspire to work in the U.S. and perhaps pursue an education in the U.S. Although a study of aspirations, Kandel and Kao's (2000) study does suggest that there may be multiple stages of behavior that initially select against education in favor of migration, but not over the long run, at least in the Mexican case.

Migration may relieve family economy budgets in very poor settings, freeing up resources that might be invested in the remaining younger family members' education. This would yield a resource concentration effect, rather than resource dilution. This would be especially true if the migrant limits the ties between her/himself and the family in the community of origin, i.e. disassociating her/himself from the family economy in the place of origin.

One way in which ties between migrants and their families in places of origin are maintained is through remittances. The literature on how remittances from migrants are used in places of origin points in two directions. One line of argument is that remittances are used to smooth income, provide insurance, or, even more basically, to ensure survival (Itzigsohn, 1995; Stark, 1991). Another line of argument is that remittances are used for investments (Durand et al., 1996), yielding growing social and economic inequality in places of origin (Reichert, 1982; Stark et al., 1988; Taylor, 1992). Whether and to what extent migrant remittance income is used to invest in education is not known. To our knowledge, until now these relationships have not been explored systematically in the research on education and stratification.

Beyond family dynamics, state policies and community contexts can influence educational opportunities. Initial state education policies to expand educational attainment are usually to build schools and train teachers. These policies are then followed with accreditation, more training, and attention to curricular content – or the improvement of school quality. Accessibility of schooling has been a considerable barrier to children's educational opportunities, especially girls' (Kaufman et al., 1998; King & Lillard, 1987). But, accessibility is not the only factor.

Some argue that school quality is more important than school accessibility for girls (Mensch & Lloyd, 1998; Tindigarukayo, 1996), particularly in the perception of school safety (Knodel, 1997; Mensch & Lloyd, 1998). Schools located close to local communities and families can be monitored by families, and school officials and administrators held accountable by community members for children's safety and school quality. In addition, it is rare that data is available that links school quality, accessibility, and educational achievement, especially in developing countries. It is also rare to show the impact of school building upon educational attainment. In our study, we were not able to examine school quality directly, but we do measure whether or not the establishment of a secondary school during the ten-year period had any impact upon educational attainment.

THE CASE OF THAILAND, 1984–1994

Thailand is on the Indo-Chinese peninsula of Southeast Asia, neighboring Malaysia, Burma, Cambodia, and Laos. Its geographic location, cultural underpinnings, and history have been offered as explanations for a variety of social and economic differences which set it apart from its neighbors, especially concerning the relative status of women and the rapid rate of economic development. Map 1 situates Thailand within Southeast Asia, delineates the regional distinctions in the country, and the location of the study site.

Thailand between 1984–1994 provides an ideal place and time to examine the narrowing of the gender gap in education. This is the time period when Thailand experienced the fastest economic growth rate in the region, with an average increase in Gross Domestic Product of 10% annually (Slagter & Kerbo, 2000; Warr, 1993). Despite this growth, development was not uniform and Thailand remains a predominantly rural country with more than 65% of the populace living in the countryside in 2000. More than 30% of the rural population lives in absolute poverty, and income inequality appears to be growing (Phongpaichit & Baker, 1996; United Nations Development Program, 1994; Warr, 1993). Poor conditions are particularly evident in Northeast Thailand, where people were disadvantaged economically and educationally relative to the rest of the country, even into the late 1980s (Fry & Kempner, 1996).

Nevertheless, educational attainments in all of Thailand have increased dramatically. Data from the Thai National Statistical Office (the Thai Socio Economic Survey) displayed in Fig. 1 shows that those with some lower secondary schooling, some upper secondary schooling, and completed secondary education increased dramatically between 1975 and 1992. This increase in education, however, was not distributed evenly among the population. The gender gap in education changed between 1975 and 1992, narrowing during the 1980s for the country as a whole. Access to lower secondary school shows little difference for boys and girls at the national level, but in the Northeast the gap expanded and narrowed precisely during the time period covered by the survey we will be analyzing (the top graph in Fig. 1). Access to upper secondary school shows a longer period for which a gender gap exists at both the national and regional levels (the middle graph in Fig. 1). Secondary school completion rates are significantly different for men and women at both the national and regional level throughout the 1980s, but narrow in the early 1990s (the bottom graph in Fig. 1).

To understand changes in the gender gap in schooling in Thailand, it is important to briefly consider the history of education in Thailand through 1994. Prior to the establishment of a uniform national education system at the beginning of the 20th century, literacy was gained through study in Buddhist temples, and this

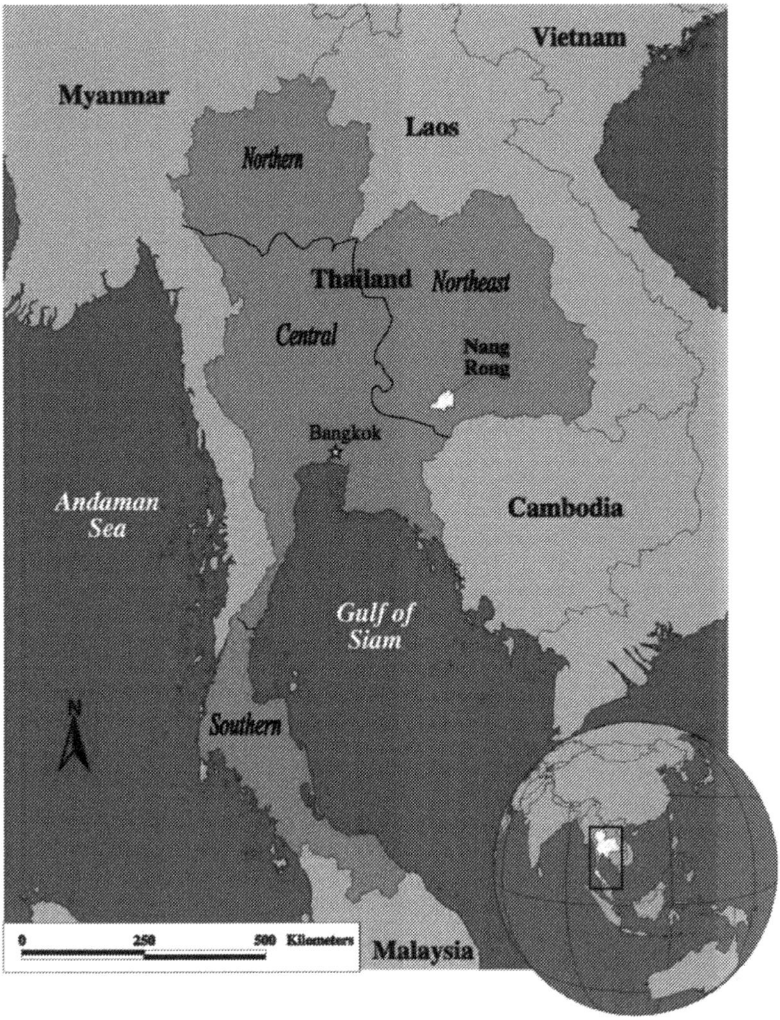

Map 1. Index Map of Thailand, Northeast Region, and Nang Rong, the Study Site. *Note:* Base Map Prepared by the CEP-CPC Project, Carolina Population Center, University of North Carolina, Chapel Hill, North Carolina.

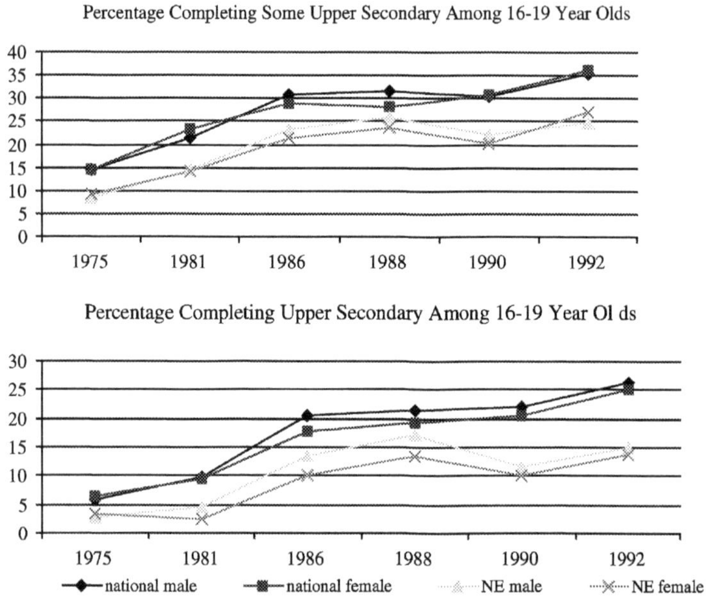

Fig. 1. Secondary School Completion Rates for Thailand and Northeast Region, 1975–1992. *Note:* National Statistics Office. Socio-Economic Survey, 1975–1992. Bangkok: Ministry of Interior, National Statistics Office.

opportunity was only available to males as part of preparation for entry into monkhood (Keyes, 1991). Since the 1930s, primary schooling was mandated for both boys and girls as a way to unite a disparate country and supersede local political power structures and local patronage systems (Keyes, 1991). Between 1960 and 1978, four grades of primary education were mandatory, and in 1978 mandatory schooling was extended through six years. The mandatory policy of primary schooling was preceded by two years of significant primary school construction and training of teachers. Thus, from 1976 heightened awareness of education and its value, at least through primary school, permeated villagers' consciousness (Keyes, 1991). Cohorts of children born since 1976 are likely to have grown up in an atmosphere with a heightened sense of the importance of education compared to older cohorts.

Secondary education is currently divided into two levels, lower level and upper level, each for three years. Following significant school construction and training of teachers during the mid-1990s, in 1997 mandatory schooling levels were again changed and extended through nine years of schooling. These more recent changes to mandatory levels of schooling have not affected the children and time period of interest in this study, but the significant school construction has certainly influenced opportunities for the younger cohorts of students.

Education has been an important part of the most recent national development plans in Thailand, and changes were evident by the early 1990s in terms of national finances, the number of schools, and the number of teachers. Between 1985 and 1995 the percent of Gross Domestic Product (GDP) spent on educational expenditures was fairly consistent, averaging 3.2%. The educational budget increased relative to the national income in the latter part of that period during the 7th National Plan between 1993–1995. Between 1984 and 1994, the total number of schools increased from 1,988 to 7,243. The percentage of schools offering secondary education increased dramatically from 6 to 20%, especially between 1990 and 1994 for the entire country (Ministry of Education, 1984–1994), though the increases in Nang Rong lagged slightly behind the rest of the country (from 3 to 18% over this time period). Nevertheless, the changes were relatively dramatic in Nang Rong: in 1984 there were three schools in the district offering some secondary education, but by 1994 there were 14 schools. The total number of teachers in Thailand also increased between 1987–1994, although the number in Nang Rong remained relatively constant during the period (Ministry of Education, 1984–1994).

In Nang Rong, as in other areas of Northeast Thailand since the 1980s, Thailand's export manufacturing-oriented economic policies have become more important for men's, women's and families' hopes for improved standards of living and even upward mobility (Phongpaichit & Baker, 1996). Migration became an increasingly important social phenomenon in the region during the decade of the 1980s. Much of the migration from the Northeastern part of the country provided the factory and construction labor that contributed to Bangkok's population and economic growth (Chamratrithirong et al., 1995). A majority of the labor provided to the export-manufacturing sector was met by women (Bello et al., 1998; Mills, 1999; Phongpaichit & Baker, 1996), construction sites were equally likely to have male and female laborers, and the rapidly growing service sector provided many jobs for women (Phongpaichit & Baker, 1996). Hence, as opposed to many other contexts, men and women were equally likely to migrate out of the Northeastern region of the country by the early 1990s (Chamratrithirong et al., 1995).

However, as the demands of the global economy shifted, so did Thailand's position as a supplier of labor and producer of manufactured goods relative to its neighbors, Vietnam, Burma, Cambodia, and Laos (Bello et al., 1998; Phongpaichit & Baker, 1996). By the late 1980s, there was a growing demand for higher skilled labor, increasing the returns to secondary education investments, a previously under-invested sector in the Thai economy (Sussangkarn, 1993). In the early 1990s, returns to secondary education in the urban labor market were twice those of primary education (Sussangkarn, 1993). However, in rural areas, knowledge among villagers about these returns to secondary education lagged behind those of urban dwellers (Curran, 1996). The initial solution to this was to take advantage of existing sex differentials in educational attainment, drawing men into the higher-wage sectors while women remained in the low-wage sector (Phongpaichit & Baker, 1996; Richter & Pong, 1995; Warr, 1993). In the next section, we briefly discuss family relations and some qualitative evidence from fieldwork conducted throughout the 1990s.

SCHOOLING, MIGRATION, AND FAMILY DYNAMICS IN NANG RONG

The Thai government's and private sector's economic focus on export manufacturing and associated increase in service sector and construction jobs from 1980 onward, created a large demand for labor, which was met primarily by rural migrants. During the middle to late 1980s, large flows of young people migrated from the Northeast to the Bangkok metropolitan area. A 1992 national study of migration showed that the majority of migrants to the Bangkok region were from the Northeast, were primarily young people between the ages of 12 and 18, and were equally likely to be young women or men (Chamratrithirong et al., 1995).

Further, many of these young people, especially women, sent money home to their families to repay debts, purchase farming supplies and consumer durables, and pay for siblings' education. Young people and families repeatedly indicated that young women were preferred migrants since they were more likely to send wages home, due to their traditional obligation to their families and the lower likelihood that they would spend their wages "unwisely" on entertainment and fun with friends (Curran & Saguy, 2001; Mills, 1999).

The needs of the Thai government, the private sector, and the forces of market globalization coincided with the structure of family relations and family economy in Northeastern Thailand. Qualitative evidence of these relations provides justification for a quantitative analysis to explain how the gender gap in educational attainment may have narrowed. Most of the interview material comes from ethnographic work conducted in 1991 by the first author. This is supplemented by observations from five rounds of briefer ethnographic work conducted since then.[2]

Like many other places in Southeast Asia, Thai family relations are generally described as being governed by bilateral inheritance, little or no son preference, and matrilineal residence preferences (with preference for the youngest daughter and her husband to live with her parents, providing care giving and inheriting most of the property). This is partly due to the family's economic dependence on growing rice, combined with the value of women's labor (planting, weeding, and harvesting) and their knowledge of land use and history (Yoddumnern–Attig et al., 1992).

Family relations in Northeastern Thailand epitomize this generalization. By the mid-1980s, the once-frontier region faced a closing of the frontier, resulting in limited land for growing families, combined with the highest family sizes in the country, and growing poverty. At the time, this region and its population sorely needed economic alternatives, especially for its youth. By the time the first author arrived to conduct fieldwork in 1992, parents were observing:

> All of our children are going and coming back. They are working at temporary jobs. During droughts or after harvesting seasons, they go elsewhere to work. They return during farming season.

And, in another interview with a father:

> (Our children go) to find work. In the village there is no work to do after the farming seasons. As for me, I do not have my own land, I rent all of the land I work on . . . (It is difficult to say whether they should go to the city.) If they stay with us, they would not have anything to do. If they go to the big city, even if they do not have an education, at least they have work to do.

Villagers in Nang Rong are well aware of the gender differential in the labor market and its relationship to education. In 1992 an explanation offered by one 19-year-old woman was an oft-heard refrain:

> If girls and boys finish the fourth or sixth grade, usually girls will find work more easily because they can sew and usually industrial factories have sewing. A boy who finishes at this level will have trouble finding work.

Another 24-year-old woman in a different in-depth interview in 1994, said:

> Most industrial factories want women. They only want men who have a high education, like artisans or professionals. They can then find work. Even if they finish ninth grade, men have a hard time finding work."

When considering the tradeoffs between work and education, Richter (1989) finds that parents tended to favor girls for migration and work earlier than boys, and that boys were favored for education.

One of the reasons parents preferred to have their daughters migrate was their higher remittance rate compared with sons. One parent observed in 1992:

> If girls make 5,000 baht[3] they will send 5,000 baht. The boys would not send us any money! . . . He would not send any money to his mother. They do not even make enough for themselves. You cannot depend on sons.

And in a 1992 focus group interview, one woman explained (with enthusiastic head-nodding among participants):

> I think girls (send more money) because boys use money for cigarettes, whiskey, having fun and partying. Boys use a lot of money. If there is any money left over, they go out again. Girls have chances to have fun, but fewer than boys. They must be more responsible than boys . . . Daughters think more about their future at home because they must wait for money from us.

Migrant women echoed these sentiments during interviews throughout the Bangkok metropolitan area. For example, one migrant woman explained during an interview in 2000:

> We send money home very often. When the end of the month comes, we save and send it all home. We do not have any personal responsibilities. We get money and send it home. We have to take care of the family. We all have to help. The younger ones are still little, and we do not want them to have it tough. We would like them to study. I would like to improve the financial status at home.

In addition, parents in Nang Rong tend to view education as a double-edged sword, as both a risky investment in non-agricultural futures and a challenge to traditional familial hierarchies associated with filial obligation and respect. In a focus group interview among fathers, 40–55 years old, one father explained:

> Parents worry about their children. They send their children to school, but their children cannot find any jobs. They return to the countryside and have nothing to do, which makes their parents worry and become frustrated.

The lack of information about the returns to education pervaded attitudes among parents. In addition, educated children seemed more capable of challenging traditional hierarchies. As one young woman explained in 1992:

> My parents are conservative. They would not send their children (to school). Back then, even for sixth grade, they would not send us. They said I could only go to fourth grade. We had already made my school uniform and they said there would not be anyone to work the fields. They said, "You study and then are naughty; you may have a husband too soon. Why should you study?" So, I did not go.

Parents sometimes went to great lengths to prevent their daughters from studying, as one 19-year-old migrant explained:

> My parents wanted me to quit to help work the fields and stay at home. They did not want me to study. They had to send me to stay with relatives in Bangkok and work there, because if I stayed in the village, the teachers at the school would come after me to make me finish grade six. So my parents sent me to Bangkok. I really wanted to study, but my parents would not let me, so I did what they wanted.

And in a 1992 focus group interview with women, 40–55 years old, the first author asked:

> Your child who finishes grade six and your child who finishes high school, are they different from each other? Do they have different jobs? One woman replied: "They are different. Those

who study are unable to farm. They have enjoyed a comfortable life for a long time. However, those who finish grade six, they can farm. They work harder. Those who study at a higher level do not work hard in the fields." Another woman added: "They do not like to farm, they like to do other things. They like light work. They do not like strenuous jobs.

As the preceding data illustrates, tradeoffs between schooling and migration are commonplace. Limited knowledge of the labor market returns to education and evidence of widespread opportunities in the urban labor market, independent of educational training, seemed to drive choices. These biases work against both boys' and girls' educational opportunities, but especially girls' educational advancement. Nevertheless, parents often observed that daughters are better students than sons. Knodel (1997) has also noted this – daughters are perceived as more diligent and harder working at their studies.[4] Thus, although they may have slightly lower rates of access to secondary education or making the transition from primary to lower secondary, once they do they may be more likely to continue to upper secondary than boys.

Based on Knodel's (1997) research and our fieldwork, parental attitudes concerning school safety and their lack of knowledge about the returns to education are critical factors limiting secondary schooling opportunities. Proximity of schools was seen as extremely important for limiting exposure to bad influences, the adoption of delinquent behavior, or other worrisome behavior (Knodel, 1997, p. 77). According to Knodel's respondents, if villagers, parents, and neighbors could keep a watchful eye on children, this would ease concerns about the risks associated with secondary schooling. Boys were perceived as being more prone to misbehavior and less diligent as students. But, as the young woman quoted earlier noted, parents were overwhelmingly concerned with girls becoming sexually active, eloping with partners, and terminating their schooling as a result. These concerns are also found in Knodel's study (1997, p. 78).

Furthermore, the consequences of such behaviors for girls were understood to be profoundly shameful for the girl and her family and more burdensome for the family than if a boy had become sexually active or eloped. Similarly, threats to physical safety were perceived to be greater for girls than boys, and greater if the school was located outside of the locality (Knodel, 1997, p. 79). Finally, schools in nearby localities reduced travel time and decreased the opportunity costs of schooling, providing students were still able to contribute housework and fieldwork hours to the family economy.

Proximity to the district town increases villagers' exposure to a wide range of evidence relating education to social mobility, and increases access to markets that enhance villagers' incomes. Villagers living in villages less remote from the major district towns are more likely to know about the returns to secondary education and to see successful examples of young people with secondary schooling. The presence of a vibrant middle class in Nang Rong's district town, also known as Nang Rong, includes civil servants from all levels of government (district, provincial, and central), finance officers (mostly bank tellers and bankers), employees of non-governmental organizations, and hospital staff (doctors, nurses, laboratory technicians and administrators).[5] Their presence and contributions to the community, and interactions with villagers may provide concrete examples of how education translates into upward mobility.

The preceding review of the literature identifies five factors that might explain secondary schooling opportunities, the difference between boys' and girls' educational attainment, and why the differential has persisted in some cases and narrowed in others. Following a discussion of the survey data and methodology used in our quantitative analysis (in the next section), we identify the factors suggested by the literature review and the qualitative evidence, and include them in a model to explain educational attainment and the dynamics of the gender differential in educational attainment. These factors include birth cohort, family size, migration, and school proximity and village accessibility to the district town.

Specifically, we hypothesize that if a person is born after 1976 (coming of school age after dramatic primary school expansion throughout Thailand), they are more likely to have an opportunity to continue on to secondary school, and girls are equally likely and possibly more likely to have an opportunity for continued schooling (given perceptions about their studious diligence). We also hypothesize that fewer siblings increase youth opportunities for schooling, but that this is more important for girls than boys. Further, we hypothesize that if additional siblings are born during the time period of observation – at the point when decisions about transitions to secondary school are made – then youth are less likely to continue on to secondary school, with this effect being more pronounced for girls than for boys.

With regard to migration, we offer three hypotheses. One hypothesis predicts that having a remitting migrant in the household might work against continued education, if migration is perceived to be a competing alternative, and an investment with greater returns, lower opportunity costs, and less risk to the family economy. We expect the competing alternatives hypothesis to be more important for limiting girls' secondary school opportunities, especially if the remitting migrant is female. Another hypothesis suggests that remittances are used to enhance educational opportunities; thus, families with remitting migrants are more likely to invest in the education of their remaining youthful members. We consider this hypothesis to be gender neutral, expecting remittance investments to improve younger siblings' schooling regardless of sex.

Finally, a third hypothesis predicts that migration of other household members, particularly if they are non-remitting (indicating a disassociation from the family economy) lightens the social and economic support burden of households, freeing up resources for remaining members. Given the Thai context and the earlier discussion, we further hypothesize that this effect is likely to be gendered. Having a male non-remitting migrant should lighten the social and economic support burden of the family, especially with regards to education resource allocation. A male, non-remitting migrant, implies few ties of obligation or reciprocity between migrant and family of origin and reduces future family obligations to invest in that male's education, freeing up resources for remaining, youthful family members.

We also hypothesize that greater proximity of schools, through the establishment of a nearby secondary school, will increase the chances that youth will have an opportunity to further their secondary education. Greater proximity of secondary schools to villagers' everyday lives should ease safety concerns about schooling (Knodel, 1997) and diminish its opportunity costs. This effect should be more pronounced for girls than for boys. Finally, village accessibility to the district town, through ease of transportation (better roads and shorter distances and times to markets) will also increase youth opportunities as parents and community members become more aware of the labor market returns to education. We expect that support for this hypothesis will show little, if any, gender differential.

DATA AND METHODS

Data and Measures

The data is a matched file of individuals, households, and villages from one district in Thailand – Nang Rong District in Buriram Province. The district had a population of about 200,000 people in 1990 and consisted of one municipality or town (also called Nang Rong) and more than 250 villages. The data on individuals comes from a complete household census conducted in 1984 in 50 villages.[6] The census included information about each household member's marital status, relationship to household head, educational attainment, migration status (temporary and/or remitting), and contraceptive behavior (for women between 15–49). In addition, data was collected about household assets. Further, there was an extensive community survey conducted with community leaders. A similar census was conducted in the same villages in 1994.[7] This census was considerably more detailed and complex, and included life history calendars, and information on all siblings and migration. The household data collected was also more complex, with information on land use and networks of social support.

Another community survey was conducted in all of the villages in Nang Rong ($N = 276$). The purpose of the studies in both periods was to examine demographic change. In 1984 the census was designed to provide a baseline for evaluating family planning interventions. In 1994 the census was designed to follow up on the family planning studies and to study migration. Although information about an individual's educational attainment was collected in both 1984 and 1994, this was not the focus of the survey. Schooling information was also collected at both time periods, but merely to develop contextual measures of economic and social infrastructure, not to evaluate school policy. Despite these limitations, the data provides an ideal opportunity to examine prospective education choices during a period of great economic and social change. It also includes information about migration, rarely available in most studies of education.

The 1994 household census includes those people who were present in the village during the 1984 survey as well as those who moved into the village since that time. In 1994, information was also gathered about people who were living in the village in 1984 but had since moved away. For this analysis, we constructed a subset of individuals who were 6–12 years old in 1984 and who had not completed more than primary school. At some point over the ten-year period, this group of individuals was faced with the decision of whether to continue on to secondary school. The matching of cases across the two panels is of relatively high quality, given the time lapse between the first and second round of the data. Of an initial sample of 6,652 in 1984, we lost 12% of the cases to sample attrition because entire households moved away and were not followed. The remaining sample of 5,837 was reduced by an additional 2.6% because of a lack of information about siblings needed for this analysis.[8]

We used a three-category measure of educational attainment. We measure whether youth, by 1994, had only completed compulsory education (six years), had attained some lower secondary schooling (7–9 years), or had attained at least some upper secondary schooling (10 or more years). We chose to focus on the transitions from primary to lower secondary, and the transition from lower secondary to upper secondary, rather than on a continuous measure of educational attainment. These are the critical decision points for young people and their parents when considering continued investment in education.

We include measures of sex (female=1, male=0) and birth cohort (1972–1974, 1975–1976, 1977–1978) in our data set and analyses, plus we test an interaction between sex and birth cohort. The interaction term provides an opportunity to model more accurately the observed trends of narrowing gender differences over time. We expect to see no male schooling advantages in the cohorts born between 1977–1978.

To help explain the gender gap and the narrowing of the gap, we also include measures of the number of siblings (0 siblings, 1 sibling, 2 siblings, 3 siblings, and 4 or more siblings) in 1984 and whether or not an additional sibling is added between 1984 and 1994. We chose to measure the number of siblings as a categorical variable because some evidence from other settings implies a curvilinear relationship (Morduch, 2000). Inequality of resource allocation may be lower in small families (with all children getting equal access to resources) and in large families (with all children getting few resources), but greater in middle-sized families (with some children getting more resources). Although our dependent variable is not a measure of inequality, we expect that a categorical measure of the number of siblings will do a better job of explaining gender differences in educational attainment.

Our measures of migration capture whether the family has some remitting temporary migrants or only non-remitting temporary migrants in 1984. Temporary migrants are those usual household members who have been gone from the household from 2 to 12 months prior to the date of the survey. As a result of the time lag between 1984 and 1994, we suspect that the effects of migration will be relatively attenuated. Unfortunately the measures of migration collected in 1994 do not allow us to adequately account for migration of all family members over the time period. The 1984 measure is the best we can do to ensure temporal ordering of events and to avoid problems of endogeneity. If anything, our measure of migration, despite the lagged effect, will reflect the perceptions of early adopters of migration as part of a family economy calculus. We decompose this measure further by the gender composition of migrants, including a measure of whether the family has any remitting female migrants and whether the family has only male, non-remitting migrants.

Our measures of school proximity and village accessibility include the respondent's village location in 1984 and in 1994 relative to the nearest secondary school and to the district town. Our measure of village accessibility or remoteness incorporates aspects of the difficulty of travel to the district town. These "obstacles" include the presence of a portion of the route to the district town that is a cart path (unpaved, rutted, and narrow); the lack of public transportation to the district town; travel time to the district town that takes an hour or more (as reported by a village headman or key informant); four or more months each year when travel from the village is difficult (this is also a measure of road conditions and susceptibility to flooding); and a distance of 20 or more kilometers to the district town. We recoded village remoteness as either not at all remote (0 obstacles), somewhat remote (1–2 obstacles), or very remote (3–4 obstacles).

School proximity is measured by the establishment date of a secondary school within a subdistrict. Subdistricts are small administrative governance units composed of a cluster of 10–20 villages in relatively close proximity to each other (within easy bicycling distance). This measure was constructed based on our knowledge of village locations, Ministry of Education administrative records, and brief interviews with local Ministry of Education officials in Nang Rong. We coded villages according to whether their subdistrict had no secondary school either in 1984 or 1994, whether one was established by 1994, and whether there was an established secondary school in 1984 and 1994. Unfortunately, our data does not include any other information about primary school or secondary school quality. We also do not include a measure of primary schools, since all villages had a primary school.

As control variables, we measure wealth and prior educational experiences of adult members. The wealth measures include land ownership (whether a family is practically landless, owning 10 or fewer rai[9] of land, 11–24 rai, or 25 rai or more) and ownership of a motorcycle. The prior adult educational experience measures whether there is an adult family member with less than primary schooling, or whether there are two or more adults with less than primary schooling. This is measured as fewer than four years of schooling, since laws expanding primary schooling to six years were passed in 1978, after most adults had completed their own schooling.

Description of Quantitative Analysis

Our analysis begins with two sets of bivariate comparisons. We use a chi-square statistic to evaluate the significance of the comparisons. In the first set of bivariate comparisons, we examine gender differences in schooling outcomes, compare cohort differences, and then compare cohort differences between boys and girls. In the second set of comparisons we examine schooling outcomes across the size and growth of the number of siblings, migration factors, school and village accessibility, land and motorcycle ownership, and prior adult education.

We then pursue a multivariate analysis of schooling outcomes, including all of the factors in a nonlinear regression estimation. We have described educational attainment as a non-linear distribution, and the data shows significant heaping tendencies around the transitions from primary to lower secondary and from lower secondary to upper secondary. Further, rather than estimating a typical ordered logistic model, we estimate a less constraining, multinomial logistic equation (Long & Freese, 2001). We have strong substantive reasons for doing so. An ordered logistic estimation assumes equal distance between categories, estimating a threshold coefficient. Instead, based on work by Knodel (1997) and our own fieldwork, we have reason to suspect that the conceptual distance between transitions is quite different.

The distance between primary schooling and lower secondary is significantly larger than the distance between lower secondary and upper secondary. Further, we suspect that the distance to the first transition is greater for girls than boys, but the distance to the second transition is likely to be lower for girls than boys. We further suspect that the influence of the factors in the models will not be the same in the equations for the transition from primary to lower secondary and the transition from lower to upper secondary. We empirically evaluated our substantive interpretation by estimating an ordered logistic equation and testing the parallel regression assumption (Long & Freese, 2001). For all of our estimated equations, the assumption was violated. For these reasons we chose to evaluate an unordered or multinomial logistic equation. Our model takes the following form:

$$\log\left(\frac{p(M_{ij}=k)}{p(M_{ihj}=1)}\right) = X_i b_k + \mathrm{Sib}_i \alpha_k + \mathrm{Mig}_i \eta_k + \mathrm{School}_i \delta_k + C_i \rho_k + m_j$$

The dependent variable is the log odds that an individual i in 1984 in village j gains lower secondary schooling or upper secondary schooling (k) relative to primary schooling (l) by 1994. The first term ($X_i b_k$) represents the vector of variables for individuals, i.e. sex and birth cohort. The second term ($\mathrm{Sib}_i \alpha_k$) represents the vector of sibling measures, the third term ($\mathrm{Mig}_i \eta_k$) represents the vector of migration measures, the fourth term ($\mathrm{School}_i \delta_k$) represents the vector of schooling measures, and the fifth term ($C_i \rho_k$) represents the vector of control variables. The sixth term is the estimate of the error for the equations. Given the clustering of individuals within villages, the observations are unlikely to be independent, resulting in an underestimate of the error terms associated with each coefficient. A standard cluster adjustment is made to the equation to correct the standard errors (Long & Freese, 2001).

Given that the literature review and our ethnographic fieldwork suggest that explanations for educational attainment may differ for boys and girls, we estimate the same equation separately for boys and girls. We also suspect that the importance of some explanatory factors have changed with time. To evaluate this hypothesis we estimate the same equation for each cohort. In the next section we review the results of our bivariate and multivariate analyses.

RESULTS

Gender and Cohort Differences in Educational Attainment

Educational attainment among 16–22 year olds in 1994 in Nang Rong is still relatively low. In Table 1, the distribution for the total sample across education categories shows that slightly less than 20% of youth had some lower secondary schooling (9.2%) and some upper secondary schooling (9.5%). These proportions are slightly lower for women; 8.4% had completed some lower secondary schooling and 8.7% had completed some upper secondary schooling. Among boys the

Table 1. Distribution of Educational Attainment by 1994 by Gender and Birth Cohort for 6–12 Year Olds in 1984 in Nang Rong, Thailand.

Variable	Primary (0–6) (%)	Lower Secondary (7–9) (%)	Upper Secondary (10 or more) (%)	All
Gender				
Young women	50.28	45.05	45.03	49.31
Young men	49.72	54.95	54.97	50.69
		$\chi^2 = 9.752$, df = 2, $p = 0.008$		
Birth cohort				
1972–1974	46.41	31.59	40.51	44.49
1975–1976	28.15	21.12	30.92	27.77
1977–1978	25.44	47.29	28.57	27.74
		$\chi^2 = 119.604$, df = 4, $p = 0.000$		
N	4,749	535	553	5,837
%	81.36	9.17	9.47	100.00
Gender and birth cohort				
Young women				
1972–1974 Cohort	47.07	32.37	35.34	44.82
1975–1976 Cohort	28.56	21.99	31.33	28.25
1977–1978 Cohort	24.37	45.64	33.33	26.93
		$\chi^2 = 61.216$, df = 4, $p = 0.000$		
N (Young women)	2,388	241	249	2,878
%	82.97	8.37	8.65	100.00
Young men				
1972–1974 Cohort	45.74	30.95	44.74	44.17
1975–1976 Cohort	27.74	20.41	30.59	27.31
1977–1978 Cohort	26.51	48.64	24.67	28.52
		$\chi^2 = 66.096$, df = 4, $p = 0.000$		
N (Young men)	2,361	294	304	2,959
%	79.79	9.94	10.27	100.00

Note: Values (except the *N* and % rows) represent percentages within the educational attainment category (column percentages).

proportions are higher; 9.9% had completed some lower secondary schooling and 10.3% had completed some upper secondary schooling. The top panel of Table 1 shows that the gender differences in educational attainment are statistically significant. Also, in the top panel of Table 1, younger cohorts of youth are observed to have greater access to secondary schooling than older cohorts of youth, and these differences are statistically significant. The oldest cohort of youth are much less likely to have completed any level of secondary education, and the youngest cohort is most likely to have completed some lower secondary schooling. The middle cohort is slightly more likely to have finished some upper secondary schooling.

These cohort patterns are not entirely similar for boys and girls (comparing the results in the second two panels in Table 1). In particular, the youngest cohort of girls are more likely to have completed some lower and some upper secondary schooling, whereas amongst boys the youngest cohort is only more likely to have completed some lower schooling. This suggests that among the younger cohort of youth, girls may be more likely to make the transition from lower to upper secondary schooling than boys. This may be a reflection of Knodel's (1997) and our field observations about parents' perception that girls are more studious than boys, combined with growing awareness of the returns to education in the labor market.

Siblings, Migration, School Accessibility, and Educational Outcomes

Table 2 displays the sample distributions for each of the other explanatory factors and their distributions across education categories. Most youth have four or more siblings, reflecting their parents' high fertility rates. Table 2 also shows that number of siblings is negatively associated with educational attainment. Fewer siblings increase youth opportunities for schooling. The addition of a sibling between 1984 and 1994 is relatively rare, but poses a significant deterrent to further education.

In 1984, almost 17% of households had at least one migrant, with slightly more than half remitting. In 1984 migration is still a relatively rare phenomenon among households in Nang Rong, most likely because this is the very beginning of the period of rapid economic expansion that drew migrants from the Northeast to the Bangkok metropolitan area. Not surprisingly, therefore, most households with migrants are more likely to have male migrants than female migrants. The bivariate relationship between migration and educational attainment appears complex (Table 2). Having at least one migrant in 1984 slightly deters continued education, but not significantly. General remittance patterns also show little relationship with education outcomes. However, when gender composition of migrants is taken into account, significant relationships emerge. Having male migrants in the household marginally improves a youth's educational opportunities. On the other hand, having at least one female remitting migrant significantly deters secondary education for other youthful members.

It would appear from Table 2 that improved school proximity is an important explanation for increased secondary education. Both the recent establishment of a

Table 2. Distribution of Sibling Characteristics, Access to Secondary Schools, and Other Independent Variables for 6–12 Year Olds in 1984, Nang Rong, Thailand, Across Educational Attainment by 1994.

Variable	Primary (0–6) (%)	Lower Secondary (7–9) (%)	Upper Secondary (10 or More) (%)	All
Sibship size				
No siblings	2.21	2.99	2.17	2.28
One sibling	7.64	14.02	12.12	8.65
Two siblings	18.76	22.62	27.85	19.98
Three siblings	19.48	19.44	20.25	19.55
Four or more siblings	51.91	40.93	37.61	49.55
		$\chi^2 = 84.295$, df $= 8$, $p = 0.000$		
Any additional siblings 1984–1994*	8.60	5.36	7.37	8.19
None	91.4	94.64	92.63	91.81
		$\chi^2 = 6.865$, df $= 2$, $p = 0.032$		
Migration				
At least one temporary migrant in 1984	17.06	15.51	15.19	16.74
None	82.94	84.49	84.81	83.26
		$\chi^2 = 1.871$, df $= 2$, $p = 0.392$		
By remittance				
Only remitting migrants	8.99	8.41	5.79	8.63
Only non-remitting migrants	6.82	6.17	7.96	6.87
Both remitting and non-remitting migrants	1.26	0.93	1.45	1.25
Neither	82.92	84.49	84.81	83.24
		$\chi^2 = 8.200$, df $= 6$, $p = 0.224$		
By sex				
Only female migrants	5.18	4.3	3.44	4.93
Only male migrants	8.76	9.91	9.58	8.94
Both male and female migrants	3.14	1.31	2.17	2.88
Neither	82.92	84.49	84.81	83.24
		$\chi^2 = 11.4980$, df $= 6$, $p = 0.074$		
Female migrants by remitting				
Only female remitting migrants	4.70	3.74	2.35	4.39
Only female non-remitting migrants	3.22	1.68	3.07	3.07
Both remitting and non-remitting female migrants	0.40	0.19	0.18	0.36
No female migrants	91.68	94.39	94.39	92.19
		$\chi^2 = 12.3458$, df $= 6$, $p = 0.055$		
Male migrants by remitting				
Only male remitting migrants	5.98	5.23	4.7	5.79
Only male non-remitting migrants	5.33	5.23	6.15	5.4
Both remitting and non-remitting male migrants	0.59	0.75	0.9	0.63
No male migrants	88.1	88.79	88.25	88.18
		$\chi^2 = 3.281$, df $= 6$, $p = 0.773$		

Table 2. *(Continued)*

Variable	Primary (0–6) (%)	Lower Secondary (7–9) (%)	Upper Secondary (10 or More) (%)	All
School accessibility				
No School in Subdistrict	38.66	36.45	29.48	37.59
Secondary school in 1994 only	39.17	39.25	45.39	39.76
Secondary school in 1984 and 1994	22.17	24.30	25.14	22.65
		$\chi^2 = 18.811$, df = 4, $p = 0.001$		
Remoteness				
Not at all remote in 1984	31.96	37.94	42.86	33.54
Somewhat remote village	51.36	54.58	48.28	51.36
Very remote	16.68	7.48	8.86	15.09
		$\chi^2 = 65.706$, df = 4, $p = 0.000$		
Controls				
Land ownership**				
10 or fewer rai	54.56	45.22	41.23	52.43
11–24 rai	22.14	24.20	25.50	22.65
25 or more rai	23.30	30.58	33.27	24.92
		$\chi^2 = 52.994$, df = 4, $p = 0.000$		
Household owns at least a motorcycle***				
Yes	4.47	11.92	26.35	7.35
No	95.53	88.08	73.65	92.65
		$\chi^2 = 292.479$, df = 2, $p = 0.000$		
Household education				
One adult with less than 4 years of school	23.33	19.81	15.73	22.29
Two or more adults with less than 4 years of school	9.35	7.85	5.24	8.82
No adult with less than 4 years of school	67.32	72.34	79.02	68.89
		$\chi^2 = 35.411$, df = 4, $p = 0.000$		
Household size in 1984	7.07 (2.20)	6.67 (2.25)	6.54 (2.10)	6.98 (2.20)
N	4,749	535	553	5,837

Notes: Values represent percentages within educational attainment categories, except the "Household size in 1984" row where the numbers are the means and standard deviations (in parentheses). For the asterisked items, *N* is different from the above, due to the different number of missing values.
* Primary: 4,594; lower secondary: 504; upper secondary: 529; all: 5,627.
** Primary: 4,729; lower secondary: 533; upper secondary: 553; all: 5,815.
*** Primary: 3,604; lower secondary: 428; upper secondary: 444; all: 4,476.

school by 1994 and the existence of a school in 1984 are significantly associated with youth opportunities for secondary schooling, relative to youth who live in villages where there is no secondary school. In addition, village remoteness from towns and markets significantly reduces youth opportunities for secondary schooling.

Finally, wealth and prior adult education are significantly associated with secondary education. Those youth who live in households with larger landholdings are more likely to have attained some secondary education. Households with motorcycles are also more likely to send their youth to secondary school. In addition, households where all adults have completed at least primary schooling are significantly more likely to have sent their children to secondary school.

Factors Narrowing the Education Gender Gap

Although the evidence from Nang Rong shows that there continues to be a gender gap in secondary schooling opportunities among 16–22 year olds (Table 1), the narrowing of the gender gap displayed in Fig. 1 can still be observed by combining measures of gender and birth cohort in one model. Table 3 displays multivariate, multinomial logistic regression results for a model that includes all hypothesized factors and controls.

To simplify our interpretation of the results for the gender and cohort effects, because of the interaction term, we have generated predicted probabilities for the secondary schooling outcomes, holding all other values at their means and only varying the values of gender and cohort. These results are shown in Fig. 2 and demonstrate dramatic increases in girls' secondary schooling opportunities, especially for the youngest cohort (1977–1978). Figure 2 also shows differences in the patterns of educational attainment for girls and boys, as well as shifts in the relative schooling advantages of boys versus girls.

The probabilities of only having completed some lower secondary schooling remain the same for the oldest and middle cohorts of girls (0.06), but more than double for the youngest cohort (0.14). A similar pattern is observed for the boys, but at slightly higher rates. For girls' upper secondary schooling opportunities, the probability of having completed some upper secondary schooling rises from 0.06 for the oldest cohort of girls to 0.11 for the middle cohort and stays at the same level for the youngest cohort.

The boys' pattern is different. The oldest cohort's upper secondary schooling probability is 0.11 and increases to 0.12 for the middle cohort, but then drops to 0.09 for the youngest cohort. This curvilinear pattern signals a reversal of boys' schooling advantage. These patterns, especially for the youngest cohort's upper secondary schooling probabilities should be cautiously considered, given that these youth are 16–17 years old in 1994. Although they are the appropriate age for having some upper secondary schooling, there may be some lagging students who have not yet completed the transition to upper secondary and still plan to make the transition. This lagging behavior may be related to gender, that is boys may be

Table 3. The Role of Gender, Birth Cohort, Sibship Size, Additional Siblings, Composition of Migrants With Respect to Remitting, School Accessibility, and Remoteness for Explaining Educational Attainment, Multinomial Logistic Regression Results (Odds-Ratios Presented).

Variable	Lwr vs. Prm	Upr vs. Lwr	Upr vs. Prm
Gender			
Young woman	0.814	1.547**	1.259
Young man	–	–	–
Birth cohort			
1972–1974	0.411***	2.823***	1.162
1975–1976	0.437***	2.950***	1.288
1977–1978	–	–	–
Gender and birth cohort interaction			
Young woman born in 1972–1974	0.907	0.409***	0.371***
Young woman born in 1975–1976	0.886	0.735	0.651
Young man or born in 1977–1978	–	–	–
Sibship size			
No siblings	2.432**	0.925	2.249*
One sibling	2.449***	1.083	2.653***
Two siblings	1.652***	1.373	2.269***
Three siblings	1.601**	1.219	1.953***
Four or more siblings	–	–	–
Additional siblings	0.647*	1.362	0.881
Composition of migrants with respect to remitting			
Some remitting migrants	1.520	0.877	1.333
Only non-remitting migrants	0.807	2.149	1.735
Neither	–	–	–
Composition of migrants with respect to gender and remitting			
Any remitting female migrants	0.579	0.843	0.488
No remitting female migrants at all	–	–	–
Non remitting male migrants only	2.373	0.530	1.259
Any other than non-remitting male migrants	–	–	–
School accessibility			
No secondary school in 1984 or 1994	–	–	–
Secondary school in 1994 only	0.921	1.402	1.291
Secondary school in both 1984 and 1994	0.853	1.217	1.038
Remoteness			
Not at all remote in 1984	–	–	–
Somewhat remote in 1984	0.919	0.795	0.731
Very remote in 1984	0.297***	1.302	0.387**

Table 3. *(Continued)*

Variable	Lwr vs. Prm	Upr vs. Lwr	Upr vs. Prm
Controls			
Land ownership			
10 or fewer rai	0.685**	0.891	0.611***
11–24 rai	–	–	–
25 or more rai	1.434***	0.945	1.356*
Household owns at least a motorcycle			
Yes	2.674***	2.565***	6.857***
No	–	–	–
Household education			
One adult with less than 4 years of school	0.674**	0.915	0.617***
Two or more adults with less than 4 years of school	0.822	0.827	0.679
No adults with less than 4 years of school	–	–	–
N		4311	
Log likelihood		−2432.85	
Ward X^2		4318.82***	
Pseudo R^2		0.10	

*$p \leq 0.1$.
**$p \leq 0.05$.
***$p \leq 0.01$.

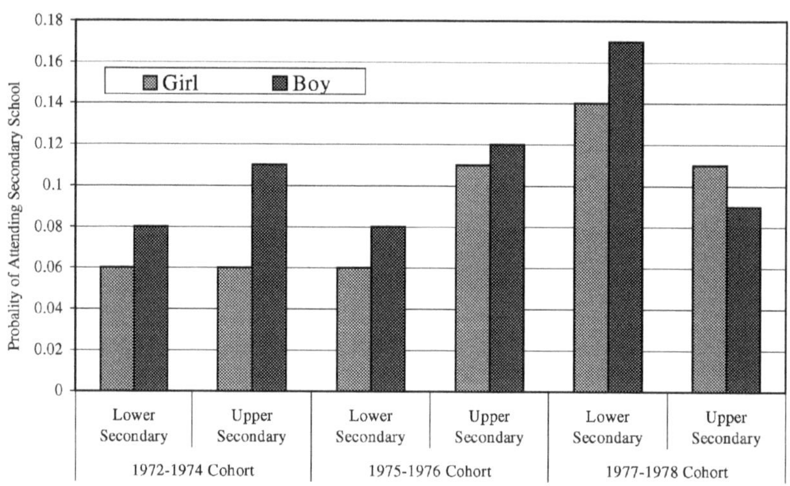

Fig. 2. Predicted Probabilities Estimating Secondary Education Outcomes For Girls and Boys Across Cohorts (Estimated from Results in Table 3).

more likely to lag behind in making transitions than girls, and therefore may not completely signal a reversal in boys' schooling advantage.

Before discussing additional explanations for the narrowing of the gender gap, we briefly discuss the remaining results in Table 3, which, although they do not explain away the effect of gender and cohort, provide additional reasons for secondary school advancement. Despite significant bivariate relationships (shown in Table 2), few of the other factors included in the multivariate model maintain much explanatory power. Number of siblings is still significantly and negatively associated with the transition from primary to lower secondary schooling; however, it is not significantly associated with the transition from lower to upper secondary. In other words, it is a significant barrier to secondary school, but not to continued schooling once a decision to enter secondary school has been made. Similarly, additional siblings reduce the odds of entering secondary school, but have no effect on the odds of continuing secondary school.

The relationship between migration and schooling is weak, at best. There are no statistically significant effects of migrants (remitting or non-remitting) upon educational attainment. The effect of gender composition of migrants, however, is just outside the margins of significance.[10] The effect of remitting females upon educational attainment supports a competing alternative explanation for the transition from primary to lower secondary school.[11] Remitting females reduce the odds of making the transition from primary to lower secondary school. Although not a statistically significant effect, remitting females also improve the odds of a school transition from lower to upper secondary school. Thus, some weak statistical evidence suggests that when the decision to make the transition from primary to lower secondary school is made, then competing alternatives (such as migration) diminishes youths' schooling options. However, when the transition to secondary school has already been made once, then remitting female migrants improve the odds of continued secondary schooling.

Weak statistical support for resource concentration through migration is also evident in the results. Coming from a family where there are only non-remitting male migrants increases the odds of secondary educational attainment.[12] When a migrant no longer remits earnings or goods back to the household of origin, this may be an indication of diminished or non-existent ties to the household. Resources that might have been expended upon the migrant may be redirected towards other youths and their schooling, producing a resource concentration effect rather than resource dilution.

Taken together, the migration effects in Table 3 provide weak statistical evidence for a family economy perspective, where competing alternatives and resource burdens are important considerations in deciding whether youth have opportunities to further their education. The importance of the family economy is particularly apparent for the transition from primary to secondary school and less *apparent for continued secondary schooling*.

Notwithstanding other factors, school establishment has little effect upon secondary schooling opportunities for youth. However, village remoteness from markets and towns significantly decreases youths' opportunities for secondary education. This effect is only important for the transition from primary to lower secondary school. Land ownership and adult education are also important explanations for transitions from primary to lower secondary. But neither has a statistically significant impact upon the decision to make the transition from lower to upper secondary. Motorcycle ownership significantly improves youths' opportunities for both lower and upper secondary education.

To see whether our full model works differently for boys and girls and if some factors matter more for older cohorts than younger cohorts, we estimate our equations on separate samples of young men and women, as well as separate samples of each cohort grouping. These results are displayed in Table 4 (for young men and women) and Table 5 (for each cohort).

The cohort patterns discussed earlier for Table 3 are also apparent in Table 4. Here, we focus on the difference in importance of number of siblings, migration, and school and village accessibility for young men and women's educational opportunities.

Although there is clearly a negative relationship between the number of siblings and educational attainment for both young men and women, the strength of the relationship is far greater for women than for men. For both young men and women, it is the transition from primary to lower secondary that defines the relationship, not the later transition to upper secondary school. However, the effect of an additional sibling does little to change a girl's schooling opportunities, but it does lower the odds of a boy's entry into secondary school.

At first glance, there are few results to report regarding the relationship between migration and educational attainment, insofar as the relationship differs across young men and women. However, a closer look at the *p*-values for the log-odds coefficients reveals effects just outside the margins of significance. These patterns then reveal differences between how migration differentially influences men and women's educational opportunities. For young women, there are marginal, statistically significant results supporting all of the migration hypotheses: remittance as investment, remittance as competing alternative, and resource concentration through migration. For young women, the odds of making the transition from primary to lower secondary schooling increases by 1.9 times when there is at least one remitting migrant. This suggests some support for remittance investment strategies with regards to education. Further, having only non-remitting migrants in the family improves the odds of

Table 4. The Role of Birth Cohort, Sibship Size, Additional Siblings, Composition of Migrants With Respect to Remitting, School Accessibility, and Remoteness for Explaining Educational Attainment, Multinomial Logistic Regression Results. Young Woman And Young Man Compared (Odds-Ratios Presented).

Variable	Young Men			Young Women		
	Lwr vs. Prm	Upr vs. Lwr	Upr vs. Prm	Lwr vs. Prm	Upr vs. Lwr	Upr vs. Prm
Birth cohort						
1972–1974	0.441***	2.572***	1.135	0.349***	1.190	0.416***
1975–1976	0.460***	2.769***	1.273	0.369***	2.222***	0.820
1977–1978	–	–	–	–	–	–
Sibship size						
No siblings	1.973	0.742	1.463	2.894**	1.095	3.169**
One sibling	2.723***	0.800	2.179**	2.236***	1.459	3.264***
Two siblings	1.739**	1.280	2.226***	1.549*	1.475	2.285***
Three siblings	1.350	1.001	1.351	2.121***	1.437	3.048***
Four or more siblings	–	–	–	–	–	–
Additional siblings	0.509*	1.851	0.942	0.784	1.034	0.811
Composition of migrants with respect to remitting						
Some remitting migrants	1.240	0.722	0.896	1.977	0.943	1.864**
Only non-remitting migrants	0.882	1.577	1.391	0.714	3.091	2.206*
Neither	–	–	–	–	–	–
Composition of migrants with respect to gender and remitting						
Any remitting female migrants	0.545	1.531	0.835	0.502	0.574	0.288*
No remitting female migrants at all	–	–	–	–	–	–
Non remitting male migrants only	2.479	0.521	1.292	2.100	0.576	1.209
Any other than non-remitting male migrants	–	–	–	–	–	–
School accessibility						
No secondary school in 1984 or 1994	–	–	–	–	–	–
Secondary school in 1994 only	0.719	1.628	1.170	1.280	1.148	1.469
Secondary school in both 1984 and 1994	0.700	1.595	1.116	1.087	0.845	0.918

Table 4. *(Continued)*

Variable	Young Men			Young Women		
	Lwr vs. Prm	Upr vs. Lwr	Upr vs. Prm	Lwr vs. Prm	Upr vs. Lwr	Upr vs. Prm
Remoteness						
Not at all remote in 1984	–	–	–	–	–	–
Somewhat remote in 1984	0.876	0.840	0.735	0.952	0.755	0.718
Very remote in 1984	0.289***	1.374	0.398**	0.288**	1.320	0.380*
Controls						
Land ownership						
10 or fewer rai	0.905	0.691	0.625**	0.435***	1.324	0.576***
11–24 rai	–	–	–	–	–	–
25 or more rai	1.146	1.277	1.463*	1.775***	0.697	1.237
Household owns at least a motorcycle						
Yes	3.518***	2.062***	7.253***	1.938***	3.385***	6.560***
No	–	–	–	–	–	–
Household Education						
One adult with less than 4 years of school	0.772	0.790	0.610**	0.544**	1.138	0.619**
Two or more adults with less than 4 years of school	0.892	0.711	0.634	0.714	1.065	0.760
No adults with less than 4 years of school	–	–	–	–	–	–
N		2214			2097	
Log likelihood		−1326.25			−1081.95	
Ward X^2		1660.30***			1465.92***	
Pseudo R^2		0.10			0.11	

*$p \leq 0.1$.
**$p \leq 0.05$.
***$p \leq 0.01$.

Table 5. The Role of Gender, Sibship Size, Additional Siblings, Composition of Migrants With Respect to Remitting, School Accessibility, and Remoteness for Explaining Educational Attainment, Multinomial Logistic Regression Results. Three Birth Cohorts Are Compared (Odds-Ratios Presented).

Variable	1972–1974 Birth Cohort Only			1975–1976 Birth Cohort Only			1977–1978 Birth Cohort Only		
	Lwr vs. Prm	Upr vs. Lwr	Upr vs. Prm	Lwr vs. Prm	Upr vs. Lwr	Upr vs. Prm	Lwr vs. Prm	Upr vs. Lwr	Upr vs. Prm
Gender									
Young woman	0.745	0.641	0.478***	0.727	1.117	0.812	0.798	1.559**	1.245
Young man	–	–	–	–	–	–	–	–	–
Sibship size									
No siblings	1.288	0.880	1.133	0.750	2.246	1.684	3.493***	1.431	4.999***
One sibling	4.506***	0.395**	1.779	1.835	1.383	2.536***	2.059**	2.503**	5.153***
Two siblings	2.031**	0.760	1.544**	0.966	2.677**	2.586***	1.834**	2.077**	3.809***
Three siblings	2.518***	0.585	1.472*	1.413	1.847*	2.609***	1.127	2.212**	2.492***
Four or more siblings	–	–	–	–	–	–	–	–	–
Additional siblings	0.674	0.805	0.543*	0.442	2.120	0.937	0.739	2.130*	1.573
Composition of migrants with respect to remitting									
Some remitting migrants	1.587	0.646	1.025	1.669	1.344	2.243*	1.493	0.886	1.323
Only non-remitting migrants	1.393	0.914	1.272	0.722	4.484	3.237**	0.327	2.188	0.716
Neither	–	–	–	–	–	–	–	–	–
Composition of migrants with respect to gender and remitting									
Any remitting female migrants	0.770	0.413	0.318	0.476	0.947	0.451	0.444	1.363	0.605
No remitting female migrants at all	–	–	–	–	–	–	–	–	–
Non remitting male migrants only	2.513	0.471	1.182	1.132	0.753	0.852	4.823	0.824	3.977
Any other than non-remitting male migrants	–	–	–	–	–	–	–	–	–
School accessibility									
No secondary school in 1984 or 1994	–	–	–	–	–	–	–	–	–
Secondary school in 1994 only	0.873	2.210***	1.929**	0.485***	1.953**	0.948	1.286	0.815	1.048
Secondary school in both 1984 and 1994	0.930	1.311	1.219	0.575	1.177	0.677	1.016	1.318	1.339

Table 5. *(Continued)*

Variable	1972–1974 Birth Cohort Only			1975–1976 Birth Cohort Only			1977–1978 Birth Cohort Only		
	Lwr vs. Prm	Upr vs. Lwr	Upr vs. Prm	Lwr vs. Prm	Upr vs. Lwr	Upr vs. Prm	Lwr vs. Prm	Upr vs. Lwr	Upr vs. Prm
Remoteness									
Not at all remote in 1984	–	–	–	–	–	–	–	–	–
Somewhat remote in 1984	0.911	0.809	0.737	0.768	0.866	0.666	0.977	0.763	0.745
Very remote in 1984	0.315**	1.439	0.454	0.191***	1.176	0.224**	0.335***	1.345	0.451
Controls									
Land ownership									
10 or fewer rai	0.667	1.017	0.678*	0.463**	1.369	0.633**	0.847	0.615*	0.521**
11–24 rai	–	–	–	–	–	–	–	–	–
25 or more rai	1.243	0.889	1.105	0.920	1.577	1.451**	2.162***	0.824	1.783*
Household owns at least a motorcycle									
Yes	2.435**	3.179***	7.741***	3.205***	1.897*	6.080***	2.694***	2.716***	7.317***
No	–	–	–	–	–	–	–	–	–
Household education									
One adult with less than 4 years of school	0.553*	1.315	0.727	1.111	0.512	0.569**	0.576**	0.881	0.508**
Two or more adults with less than 4 years of school	1.035	0.723	0.748	1.146	0.616	0.706	0.517*	1.045	0.540
No adults with less than 4 years of school	–	–	–	–	–	–	–	–	–
N		1807			1232			1272	
Log likelihood		−881.51			−671.80			−841.26	
Ward X^2		1408.16			547.22***			606.49***	
Pseudo R^2		0.11			0.10			0.09	

*$p \leq 0.1$.
**$p \leq 0.05$.
***$p \leq 0.01$.

lower to upper secondary schooling by 3.17 times[13] and increases the odds of completing some upper secondary schooling relative to primary schooling by two times.

Excluding the preceding migrant factors, if there are any remitting female migrants in the household, the odds that a young woman will make the transition from primary to secondary school are reduced by 55%.[14] This disadvantage is magnified to a 72% reduction in the odds of completing upper secondary rather than primary schooling. Thus, having female remitting migrants in a young woman's family presents an example of a competing alternative, rather than creating educational opportunities for that young woman. For men, none of these relationships are close to being statistically significant.

For both men and women, village accessibility and school proximity affect educational opportunities in the same way. School establishment in a subdistrict has little impact upon either group's access to secondary education. Rather, it is the remoteness of the village from town and markets that determines educational opportunities, particularly the transition from primary to lower secondary school. For both young men and women, decreased accessibility to the district town significantly lowers the odds of going to secondary school.

We now turn briefly to examine the results of the same equation estimated for cohort subgroups (Table 5). Given that the sample sizes diminish significantly, our interpretations of these results are tentative. Rather than discuss the gender and sibship size (number of children in a family) effects, we will only focus upon migration and school and village accessibility effects.

There are no significant migration effects for the oldest cohort of youth. For the middle cohort, migration of other household members positively influences educational opportunities, especially upper secondary schooling. Excluding migration, the competing alternatives hypothesis (female migrant remitters) or the reduced resource dilution hypothesis are not supported among the middle cohort. However, weak statistical support is found for these hypotheses among the youngest cohort. Competing alternatives (any female remitters) reduces the odds by 60% of having some lower secondary rather than primary schooling. Having non-remitting male migrants marginally increases the odds by 2.9 times of having some lower secondary schooling relative to primary schooling;[15] evidence in support of resource concentration through migration.

Shifting our attention to school proximity, school establishment is apparently much more important for the older cohorts of youth. These effects are significant for improving access to upper secondary schooling, rather than lower secondary schooling. Oddly, for the middle cohort, the establishment by 1994 of a secondary school reduces the odds of transitioning to lower secondary school. It may be that this effect reflects some endogeneity (reverse causality), insofar as lowered levels of transitions from primary to lower secondary school in a particular village or locality point to the need for the establishment of schools in that place.

Most of the school building occurred in the two years prior to the 1994 survey, which is after the middle cohort of youth were at risk of making a decision to go to secondary school. Nevertheless, for those youth in the middle cohort that had already made a decision to go to secondary school, school establishment by 1994 meant improved odds of continuing their schooling. Again, village remoteness from district markets and town significantly reduces the odds of lower secondary schooling across all three cohorts.

In the following discussion we summarize the findings of our analyses of both quantitative and qualitative data. We place these findings in perspective for understanding the Thai context, the role of migration and school accessibility in the literature on cross-national perspectives on stratification processes, and the limitations of this particular research project. We conclude with suggestions for future research.

DISCUSSION

The relationship between social and economic change, educational attainment, and inequality are puzzles that remain to be unraveled, despite significant research effort across many disciplines (Buchmann & Hannum, 2001). We pursue pieces of the puzzle with an analysis of educational attainment between 1984–1994 in rural Northeast Thailand. This is a period of rapid economic growth in Thailand and, during the latter part of the 10-year period, significant expansion of secondary schools. We build upon previous research by examining the role of gender, cohort, sibship size, migration, and school and village accessibility in explaining secondary schooling. Our analysis confirms what other researchers have observed in Thailand: the gender gap has narrowed significantly over the time period (Knodel, 1997; Knodel & Jones, 1996). But, there are several competing forces at work to both widen and narrow the gap.

The data we employ were not originally designed to study this research question, and as such, contain some inherent study design problems. There is no data on individual learning abilities, parental attitudes about schooling, school quality (either primary or secondary), and only limited information about migration. Nevertheless, the data offer opportunities, otherwise unavailable in Thailand (and to our knowledge elsewhere) to follow youth over time, to quantitatively assess explanations for the narrowing of the gender gap, evaluate the role of migration and migrant remittances, the impact of school establishment, the addition of siblings, and village accessibility to markets and towns.

In discussing our results, we first consider the dynamics of the gender differential in educational attainment. Next we discuss the importance of migration for studying educational attainment, and how transitions between levels of schooling vary in their difficulty. We conclude with directions for future research.

The evidence in the Nang Rong data shows a continued gender differential in secondary schooling. However, there is evidence of a narrowing of the gender gap when comparing educational attainment across cohorts. Birth cohort makes a significant difference for youth educational opportunities, particularly girls and young women. The youngest cohort of youth (born after 1976) gains significant advantage in schooling opportunities. Younger cohorts of girls are almost equally likely to go to secondary school as are boys, and they are more likely than boys to continue their secondary schooling.

In addition, other factors appear to diminish the educational differences between boys and girls. Having few or no siblings diminishes the gender difference (although it does not explain it away). Previous high levels of fertility among the mothers of this generation of youth are an important explanation for the very low levels of secondary schooling overall among youth in Nang Rong (less than 20%). The odds of education increase dramatically with each reduction in the number of siblings, suggesting that youth born to the next generation of mothers (among whom average fertility is fewer than two children) will likely benefit greatly in terms of educational opportunities from smaller family sizes. More importantly, the reduced fertility of younger mothers appears to be more beneficial for girls than for boys. Interestingly, additional siblings born at the time when secondary schooling decisions are made, although not disadvantaging girls, do disadvantage boys and helps to narrow the gap between boys and girls insofar as access to any secondary schooling.

Migration appears to narrow the gender differential under some circumstances. This works in two ways – migrant remittances provide families with a source of income for educational investment, and the act of migration helps to concentrate family resources. Having some remitting migrants (of either sex) increases a girls' secondary schooling opportunity, as does living in a household with only non-remitting migrants. Having non-remitting male migrants concentrates resources in favor of girls' continued secondary schooling. Further, once a girl has made a decision to enter secondary school, a female remitting migrant promotes her continued schooling, narrowing the male advantage. Finally, although we expected to find that school proximity would be more important for girls than boys, we found no evidence of such an effect.

Although there are powerful cohort effects that narrow the gender differential – in combination with dramatically smaller family sizes and some positive effects of migration towards educational investments in girls – there are also factors that maintain the male secondary school advantage or female disadvantage. Resource limitations, as expressed by large sibship sizes and landless or near landlessness households, significantly limit girls' secondary schooling but are less inhibiting of boys' education. In addition, limited educational experience among adult members of the household significantly widens the gender differential in schooling. Finally, even though having some remitting migrants increases girls' access to secondary schooling, having female remitting migrants diminishes a girls' access or entry into secondary school. This suggests that when there is evidence that female household members can earn money to support the household economy, they represent a competing alternative option to secondary schooling for the next female household member.

We hypothesized that migration might influence educational attainment in three different ways. First, that remittances sent from migrant household members might be used to invest in youth's education. Second, that migrant remittances, especially from women, might create a competing alternative to schooling. Successful remittance behavior might encourage parents to pursue migration as part of a family economy calculus, rather than invest in riskier educational investments. And third, that migration accompanied by non-remittance would increase educational opportunities, especially if the non-remitting migrants are male. Non-remitting male migrants indicate probable permanent movement out of the household and disassociation with the family economy. Given that there is a slight preference to invest in boys' education, this serves to concentrate education resources, rather than dilute them.

For the first hypothesis about migration, we found some qualitative evidence that migrant remittances do support other family members' educational opportunities, according to migrant accounts. For the second hypothesis, the competing alternatives, we found some support in the qualitative evidence, especially in accounts from parents and young women. We also found weak statistical support for this hypothesis in the quantitative analysis. For the third hypothesis regarding the positive impact of resource concentration, we did not find evidence in the qualitative data and only weak statistical support for the resource concentration hypothesis. The latter two hypotheses were better supported with evidence from the girls-only sample and the youngest cohort sample.

We suspect that the relationship between migration and education may be different at different points in the migratory and economic history of a particular community and a family's life cycle dynamic (along the lines of Kandel and Kao's (2000) logic and conclusions to their study). Poor, young families (such as many of those represented in the data from Nang Rong in the mid-1980s) are likely to view education as a risky investment, at least initially, but perceive migration as a less risky opportunity to smooth income and lighten family economy burdens. Initially, remittance income is used for family survival, to upgrade the rural quality of life, and in farming. Eventually as families become more economically comfortable and more is known about the labor market returns to education, remittances are more likely to be directed towards education investments. We find some evidence of this effect, especially with regards to continuing secondary schooling, once a decision to attend secondary school has been made. Unfortunately, evidence to evaluate this conjecture would only be apparent during the latter part of the 1990s, which is past the time this study was undertaken.

Even though school proximity shows a strong relationship with secondary schooling in the bivariate analysis (Table 2), the effect completely disappears in a multivariate analysis. It only reappears later among the oldest cohort of youth, promoting their completion of some upper secondary schooling. It could be that the association between school establishment and village accessibility to the district town, although not extreme, is high enough that village accessibility absorbs some of the effect of school establishment. It could also be that since most of the new secondary schools were only established between 1990 and 1994, and a high proportion only established in 1993 and 1994, that fewer youth were able to take advantage of the opportunities offered. Village accessibility to the district town is, indeed, an important factor explaining school opportunities. Limited road improvement efforts (besides main highways) over the last two decades are a significant deterrent to economic development, and they would also appear to be a deterrent of educational attainment.

We find that analyses of secondary education, especially in Thailand, must take into account the fact that some transitions are harder than others. In particular, the transition from primary to lower secondary involves greater barriers and is associated with different factors than is the transition from lower secondary to upper secondary. Attention to the differences in the conceptual distance between the two transitions should be of interest to both educational researchers and policy makers. Insofar as gender is concerned, the barriers girls face for the first transition are much higher than those faced by boys. However, the female disadvantage then becomes an advantage in making the transition from lower to upper secondary, especially among the youngest cohort of youth (born after 1976). Nevertheless, there are still significant barriers to girls' education that continue to maintain a slight male advantage in schooling.

In conclusion, no other studies have examined the role of migration, and very few sites offer opportunities to evaluate the impact of school establishments upon educational change. Although we can only offer tentative and weak quantitative evidence for their importance in future models of educational attainment, we did find strong evidence of the importance of migration in consideration of education investments in our qualitative data. We suspect that data from more recent time periods would reveal a stronger effect. Similarly, we suspect that the secondary school expansion program had not had a long enough impact within the communities we observed (at most four years and probably only two years) to influence the educational choices of youth in our data.

Our analysis suggests that there is theoretical and substantive reason to suspect the importance of both migration and school establishment for secondary schooling. Our analytic approach introduces elements of the dynamics of social change into prospective models of education. In so doing, our results and discussion demonstrate not only the potential for evaluating the impact of school establishment and migration for educational attainment, but also the potential importance of temporal depth for illuminating how schooling choices shift with the social, economic, and cultural changes occurring in a place. This inevitably places more demands on future data collection efforts and will result in more complex study designs.

NOTES

1. Kaufman et al. (1998) conduct a multilevel analysis but use a cross sectional database from South Africa.

2. Fieldwork was conducted during eight months in 1991, one month in 1993, three months in 1994, one month in 1996, one month in 1997, one month in 1998, one month in 2000. Fieldwork included in-depth interviews, observation, and focus group interviews on a variety of topics related to migration, education, farming, and livelihoods in Nang Rong with young people, parents, teachers, government workers, factory managers, and village leaders. The initial fieldwork in 1991 was used to establish a list of villagers that were then re-interviewed through either in-depth or focus group interviews in subsequent fieldwork. The villagers included in the in-depth interviews primarily came from one village in the district, but the focus group interviews came from 17 other villages in the district. During several of the fieldwork trips, migrants were interviewed in their place of destination, primarily in the Bangkok metropolitan area.

3. This is the national currency; worth 1/25 of a dollar in 1991.

4. During the 1991 fieldwork, parents often observed that girls are more diligent at their studies than are boys.

5. Compared with its Southeast Asian neighbors, Thailand had the highest rates of education among its civil servants as of 1986 (Rock, 2000).

6. Information about this survey and data are available from the following: http://www.cpc.unc.edu/projects/nangrong/

7. By 1994 the original 50 villages had been administratively split into 76 villages. Administrative divisions occur as the number of households and the population grows. In general, the preferred average village size is about 100 households. This is considered to be a manageable number of households for village headmen (usually men) to manage. For the purposes of this analysis we maintain the original 50 village distinction, since, from our experience, there is considerable social meaningfulness to these boundaries. In 1984 there were 10 villages that were very close and almost indistinct from each

other. But in each of these cases, there was a relatively long history of separate administration.

8. Most of the information about siblings came from a separate data collection instrument used in 1994, which asked about sibling age, sex, and location (line number in the household roster or residence in a district, province, or country). This instrument was applied to current household members in 1994 who were 18–35 years old – but to only one member of the sibling set. Among the sample used in this analysis 56.23% of the cases used sibling information from this source. Another 33% of the cases were migrants in 1994 and so were their siblings. Using information from the migrant portion of the data collection we were able to recover 70% of the sibling information for these respondents. Finally, for 8.4% of the cases we were able to reconstruct sibling structures using information collected on the household roster asking for mother and father's line number.

9. A rai is a square unit of land. Approximately 2.53 rai are equivalent to 1 acre.

10. Given that the measure of migration is taken only in 1984 and quite distant from outcomes considered in 1994, it is plausible to widen our consideration of what is a significant effect.

11. If a one-tailed z-test were used to evaluate significance of the relationship, then the p-value for the coefficient associated with remitting females would be 0.097.

12. If a one-tailed z-test were used to evaluate the significance of having only non-remitting male migrants, then the p-value would be 0.071.

13. The coefficient p-value is 0.188 for a two-tailed z-test statistic.

14. The coefficient p-value is 0.128 for a two-tailed z-test statistic.

15. The coefficient p-value is 0.219 for a two-tailed z-test statistic.

ACKNOWLEDGMENTS

Special thanks to the Institute for Population and Social Research, Mahidol University, Nakhom Prathom, Thailand, the CEP-CPC Project at the University of North Carolina for access to the data, a Mellon Foundation grant to the Center for Migration and Development, Princeton University, and continued institutional support from the Office of Population Research, Princeton University. Thanks also to Germán Rodríguez for valuable statistical advice, as well as Melanie Adams and Abigail Cooke for editorial and administrative assistance.

REFERENCES

Anh, T. S., Knodel, J., Lam, D., & Friedman, J. (1998). Family size and children's education in Vietnam. *Demography*, *35*, 57–70.

Appleton, S., & Collier, P. (1995). On gender targeting of public transfers. In: D. van de Walle & K. Nead (Eds), *Public Spending and the Poor* (pp. 555–581). Baltimore, MD: Johns Hopkins University Press.

Ashby, J. (1985). Equity and discrimination among children: Schooling decisions in rural Nepal. *Comparative Education Review*, *29*(1), 68–79.

Axinn, W. G., & Barber, J. S. (2001). Mass education and fertility transition. *American Sociological Review*, *66*, 481–505.

Axinn, W. G., & Yobiku, S. T. (2001). Social change, the social organization of families, and fertility limitation. *American Journal of Sociology*, *106*(5), 1219–1261.

Bakarr, F. K. (2000). *Factors that affect girls' access to basic education in the rural areas of the Gambia*. Dissertation Abstracts International: The Humanities and Social Sciences. Teachers College, Columbia University.

Behrman, J. R., Foster, A. D., Rosenzweig, M. R., & Vashishtha, P. (1997). Women's schooling, home teaching, and economic growth. Working Paper, University of Pennsylvania.

Bello, W., Cunningham, S., & Poh, L. K. (1998). *A Siamese tragedy: Development and disintegration in modern Thailand*. London: Zed Books.

Blake, J. (1989). *Family size and achievement*. Berkeley, CA: University of California Press.

Blossfeld, H.-P., & Huinink, J. (1991). Human capital investments or norms of role transition? How women's schooling and career affect the process of family formation. *American Journal of Sociology*, *97*(1), 143–168.

Buchmann, C. (1996). The debt crisis, structural adjustment and women's education: Implications for status and social development. *International Journal of Comparative Sociology*, *37*(1–2), 5–30.

Buchmann, C. (2000). Family structure, parental perceptions, and child labor in Kenya: What factors determine who is enrolled in school? *Social Forces*, *78*(4), 1349–1379.

Buchmann, C., & Hannum, E. (2001). Education and stratification in developing countries: A review of theories and research. *Annual Review of Sociology*, *27*, 77–102.

Chamratrithirong, A., Archavanitkul, K., Richter, K., Guest, P., Varachai, T., Boonchalaksi, W., Piriyathamwong, N., & Vong-ek, P. (1995). National migration survey of Thailand. Bangkok, Thailand: Institute for Population and Social Research, Mahidol University.

Chernichovsky, D. (1985). Socioeconomic and demographic aspects of school enrollment and attendance in rural Botswana. *Economic Development and Cultural Change*, *33*, 319–332.

Conley, D. (2000). Sibship sex composition: Effects on educational attainment. *Social Science Research*, *29*, 441–457.

Curran, S. R. (1996). Intrahousehold exchange relations: Explanations for education and migration outcomes. Seattle Population Research Center Working Paper No. 96–5.

Curran, S. R., & Saguy, A. C. (2001). Migration and cultural change: A role for gender and social networks. *Journal of International Women's Studies*, *2*(3), 54–77.

Durand, J., Parrado, E. A., & Massey, D. S. (1996). Migradollars and development: A reconsideration of the Mexican case. *International Migration Review*, *30*(2), 423–444.

Fry, G., & Kempner, K. (1996). A subnational perspective for comparative research: Education and development in northeast Brazil and northeast Thailand. *Comparative Education*, *32*(3), 333–360.

Fuller, B., & Liang, X. (1999). Which girls stay in school? The influence of family economy, social demands, and ethnicity in South Africa. In: C. H. Bledsoe, J. Casterline, J. Johnson-Kuhn & J. Haaga (Eds), *Critical Perspectives in Schooling and Fertility in the Developing World* (pp. 181–215). Washington, DC: National Academic Press.

Greenhalgh, S. (1985). Sexual stratification: The other side of "growth with equity" in east Asia. *Population and Development Review*, *11*(2), 265–314.

Hadden, K., & London, B. (1996). Educating girls in the third world: The demographic, basic needs, and economic benefits. *International Journal of Contemporary Sociology*, *37*(1–2), 31–46.

Itzigsohn, J. (1995). Migrant remittances, labor markets, and household strategies: A comparative analysis of low-income household strategies in the Caribbean basin. *Social Forces*, *74*(2), 633–655.

Kandel, W., & Kao, G. (2000). Shifting orientations: How U.S. labor migration affects children's aspirations in Mexican migrant communities. *Social Science Quarterly*, *81*(1), 16–32.

Kaneda, T. (1998). *The effects of gender composition and birth order of siblings on educational attainment: The Japanese case*. Annual Meeting of the Population Association of America, Chicago, IL, April 2–4.

Kaufman, C., Maharaj, P., & Richter, L. (1998). *Children's schooling in South Africa: Transitions and tensions in households and communities*. Annual Meeting of the Population Association of America, Chicago, IL, April 2–4.

Keyes, C. F. (1991). The proposed world of the school: Thai villagers' entry into a bureaucratic state system. In: C. F. Keyes (Ed.), *Reshaping Local Worlds: Formal Education and Cultural Change* (pp. 89–130). New Haven, CT: Yale University Press.

King, E. (1991). *Educating girls and women: Investing in development*. Washington, DC: World Bank.

King, E. M., & Hill, M. A. (1993). *Women's education in developing countries*. Baltimore, MD: Johns Hopkins University Press for the World Bank.

King, E., & Lillard, L. (1987). Education policy and school attainment in Malaysia and the Philippines. *Economic Education Review*, *6*, 167–181.

Kingdon, G. G. (1998). Does the labour market explain lower female schooling in India? *Journal of Development Studies*, *35*(1), 39–65.

Knodel, J. (1997). The closing of the gender gap in schooling: The case of Thailand. *Comparative Education Review*, *33*(1), 61–81.

Knodel, J., & Jones, G. (1996). Post-Cairo population policy: Does promoting girls' schooling miss the mark? *Population and Development Review*, *22*(4), 683–702.

Knodel, J., & Wongsith, M. (1991). Family size and children's education in Thailand: Evidence from a national sample. *Demography*, *28*(1), 119–131.

Kurz, K. M., & Prather, C. J. (1995). Constraints limiting girls' quality of life. In: K. M. Kurz & C. J. Prather (Eds), *Improving the Quality of Life of Girls* (pp. 9–29). New York, NY: UNICEF.

Lillard, L. A., & Willis, R. J. (1994). Intergenerational educational mobility: Effects of family and state in Malaysia. *Journal of Human Resources*, *29*(4), 1126–1166.

Lloyd, C. B., & Gage-Brandon, A. J. (1994). High fertility and children's schooling in Ghana: Sex differences in parental contributions and educational outcomes. *Population Studies*, *48*(2), 293–306.

Long, J. S., & Freese, J. (2001). *Regression models for categorical dependent variables using stata*. College Station, TX: Stata Press.

Malhotra, A., & Mather, M. (1997). Do schooling and work empower women in developing countries? Gender and domestic decisions in Sri Lanka. *Sociological Forum*, *12*(4), 599–630.

Massey, D. (1990). Social and economic origins of immigration. *ANNALS AAPSS*, *510*, 60–72.

Mensch, B., & Lloyd, C. (1998). Gender differences in the schooling experiences of adolescents in low-income countries: The case of Kenya. *Studies in Family Planning*, *29*(2), 167–184.

Mills, M. B. (1999). *Thai women in the global labor force: Consuming desires, contested selves*. New Brunswick, NJ: Rutgers University Press.

Ministry of Education. *Educational Statistics in Brief. 1984–1994*. Bangkok, Thailand: Ministry of Education.

Morduch, J. (2000). Sibling rivalry in Africa. *American Economic Review*, *90*(2), 405–409.
Ono, H. (in press). Are sons and daughters substitutable? Allocation of family resources in contemporary Japan. *Journal of the Japanese and International Economies*.
Parish, W. L., & Willis, R. J. (1993). Daughters, education, and family budgets: Taiwan experiences. *Journal of Human Resources*, *29*(4), 863–898.
Phongpaichit, P., & Baker, C. (1996). *Thailand's boom*! New South Wales, Australia: Allen and Unwin.
Pong, S. L. (1997). Sibship size and educational attainment in Peninsular Malaysia. *Sociological Perspectives*, *40*, 227–242.
Powell, B., & Steelman, L. C. (1993). The educational benefits of being spaced-out: Sibship density and educational progress. *American Sociological Review*, *58*(June), 367–381.
Reichert, J. S. (1982). Social stratification in a Mexican sending community: The effect of migration to the United States. *Social Problems*, *29*, 422–433.
Richter, K. (1989). *Transitions to adulthood in rural and urban Thailand*. Annual Meeting of the Population Association of America, Baltimore, MD, March 30–April 1.
Richter, K., & Pong, S. L. (1995). Schooling and work among Thai adolescents: Household dynamics under rapid economic and demographic change. Population Research Institute, Working Paper 95–11.
Rock, M. T. (2000). Thailand's old bureaucratic polity and its new semi-democracy. In: M. Khan & J. K. Sundaram (Eds), *Rents, Rent-Seeking and Economic Development: Theory and Evidence in Asia* (pp. 182–206). Cambridge, UK: Cambridge University Press.
Shavit, Y., & Blossfeld, H.-P. (1993). *Persistent inequality: Changing educational attainment in thirteen countries*. Boulder, CO: Westview Press.
Shavit, Y., & Pierce, J. (1991). Sibship size and educational attainment in nuclear and extended families: Arabs and Jews in Israel. *American Sociological Review*, *56*(June), 321–330.
Slagter, R., & Kerbo, H. (2000). *Modern Thailand: A volume in the comparative societies series*. New York: McGraw Hill.
Stark, O. J. (1991). *The migration of labor*. Cambridge, MA: Basil Blackwell.
Stark, O. J., Taylor, E., & Yitzhaki, S. (1988). Migration, remittances, and inequality: A sensitivity analysis using the extended Gini Index. *Journal of Development Economics*, *28*, 309–322.
Stash, S., & Hannum, E. (2001). Who goes to school? Educational stratification by gender, caste, and ethnicity. *Comparative Education Review*, *45*, 354–378.
Stromquist, N. P. (1990). Gender inequality in education: Accounting for women's subordination. *British Journal of Sociology of Education*, *11*(2), 137–153.
Stromquist, N. P. (1998). The institutionalization of gender and its impact on educational policy. *Comparative Education*, *34*(1), 85–100.
Subbarao, K., & Raney, L. (1995). Social gains from female education: A cross national study. *Economic Development and Cultural Change*, *44*(1), 105–128.
Summers, L. (1994). Investing in all the people: Educating women in developing countries. Economic Development Institute of the World Bank: EDI Seminar Paper Number 45.
Sussangkarn, C. (1993). Labour markets. In: P. G. Warr (Ed.), *The Thai Economy in Transition* (pp. 355–400). Cambridge, UK: Cambridge University Press.
Taylor, E. J. (1992). Remittances and inequality reconsidered: Direct, indirect, and intertemporal effects. *Journal of Policy Modeling*, *14*(2), 187–208.
Tindigarukayo, J. K. (1996). Gender differentials in education and labour force in Jamaica. *Canadian Journal of Development Studies*, *17*(3), 449–467.
Tsai, S.-L., Gates, H., & Chiu, H.-Y. (1994). Schooling Taiwan's women: Educational attainment in the mid-20th century. *Sociology of Education*, *67*(4), 243–246.

Tzannatos, Z. (1999). Women and labor market changes in the global economy: Growth helps, inequalities hurt and public policy matters. *World Development, 27*(3), 551–569.

United Nations Development Program (1994). *Human development report 1994*. New York, NY: United Nations.

Warr, P. (1993). *The Thai economy in transition*. New York: Cambridge University Press.

Yoddumnern-Attig, B., Richter, K., Soonthorndhada, A., Sethaput, C., & Pramualratana, A. (1992). *Changing roles and statues of women in Thailand: A documentary assessment*. Salaya, Nakhon Prathom, Thailand: Institute for Population and Social Research, Mahidol University.

IN PURSUIT OF COLLEGE QUALITY: MIGRATION DECISIONS AMONG COLLEGE STUDENTS IN JAPAN

Hiroshi Ono

ABSTRACT

The high value that Japanese place upon college prestige suggests that Japanese families will do whatever it takes to gain entry into the nation's top colleges, including paying the high costs of preparation, tuition, or relocation. Of all the costs confronting parents of college-bound students, the greatest is that of migration, or the cost of attending college away from home. I use a 1995 cross-sectional dataset to examine how the pursuit of college quality factors into migration decisions among college students in Japan. My findings clearly show that the difference in university resources across regions is an important factor in determining migration decisions, while financial considerations are secondary.

INTRODUCTION

In economic theory, migration is deemed a worthwhile investment that increases the returns to human capital if the benefits of migration outweigh the costs. In this paper, I apply the economics of migration framework to analyze the circumstances under which individuals choose to migrate for their university education.

Inequality Across Societies: Families, Schools and Persisting Stratification
Research in Sociology of Education, Volume 14, 103–123
(Formerly Research in Sociology of Education and Socialization)

ISSN: 1479-3539/doi:10.1016/S1479-3539(03)14005-0

I hypothesize that migration is an investment in human capital, and that the migration decision depends on the differences in university resources across regions.

Japan presents an interesting case for analysis mainly because college quality plays an important role in determining an individual's success and advancement (Ando, 1994; Ono, forthcoming; Rohlen, 1983). Both students and parents make considerable investments in their pursuit of college quality, and there is ample evidence suggesting that cost considerations are secondary to the ultimate goal of getting admitted to the *right* college, regardless of its geographical location. However, like all investments, investments in education are subject to financial constraints. Given the high cost of living in Japan, the cost of living away from home turns out to be greater than the cost of tuition. Migration is the *most expensive decision* that confronts parents who finance their children's college education.

Previous studies of advancement into higher education in Japan have shown that the financial well-being of the parents plays an important role in determining who goes to college and who does not (Ishida, 1993; Ono, 2001; Treiman & Yamaguchi, 1993). However, the fact that migration is the most expensive investment in college education is often overlooked in the literature. My research attempts to fill this void by identifying key factors that determine Japanese students' migration decisions. My results, based on empirical analysis using a 1995 cross-sectional dataset of men and women in Japan, show that students choose colleges located in other prefectures when there is a relative scarcity of high quality colleges in their home prefecture. The results also show that the influence of financial constraints on the migration decision is small.

BACKGROUND

The College Application Process in Japan

College acceptance in Japan requires that applicants successfully pass entrance examinations.[1] National and private universities require different examinations, and testing is specific to the department of the university to which students apply. Preparations begin early, as applicants must decide well in advance which field they wish to specialize in, and whether they will apply to a national or a private university.

There are over 600 colleges in Japan, so there are ample slots to accommodate all students who seek a college education. But the colleges are not all perceived as being of equal quality. Instead, they are ranked along some dimension of quality – reputation, prestige or other – such that the fierce competition to enter the schools at the upper end has come to be known as "examination hell."

Students who are motivated to endure examination hell believe that entry into the preferred institutions will result in greater benefits than into less preferred institutions, and that the potential benefits of examination hell are greater than the costs. The positive association between college quality and occupational outcomes in Japan has been documented in several studies (Ishida, Spilerman & Su, 1997; Iwamura, 1996; Ono, forthcoming). These findings support the claim that it matters *where* one goes to college, and not just how much college education one receives (Kingston & Lewis, 1990).

The time, money and energy families devote to examination hell are indeed substantial. Sakurai (1997) suggests that the supplementary education industry, which provides specialized training and preparation for college-bound students, grosses one percent of Japan's gross domestic product. The intensity of examination hell and the extreme measures taken by students and their parents have been documented by numerous ethnographic studies (Rohlen, 1983; Tsukada, 1991). Indeed, parental involvement and support are ingrained features of examination hell, as the parents themselves become consumed by the mission of sending their children to a prestigious college. Parental support for their children's college education is generous; studies have reported that Japanese parents finance over 80% of their children's college education (Ministry of Education, 1998; Nakata & Mosk, 1986).

Costs of College Education in Japan

Like their U.S. counterparts, college education is a private investment in Japan for which students are charged tuition. Financial aid and scholarships are rare. Approximately 10% of students receive some type of financial assistance, but this is only offered in the form of interest-free loans that require repayment.[2] Further, dormitory residences among Japanese universities remain few, so most students must live in rented apartments. It can be inferred, therefore, that a majority of Japanese students and their parents shoulder the full cost of college education.

Table 1 shows the comparison of annual tuition and living costs among Japanese college students for the year 1996 (Ministry of Education).[3] We observe that: (1) The cost of living for students who attended college away from home was more than 2.5 times as expensive as for students who attended college while living at home;[4] (2) Tuition was more than twice as expensive for students who attended private rather than national universities; and most importantly; and (3) The cost of living away from home was higher than tuition, which demonstrates that migration represents the biggest cost associated with college education in Japan.

Table 1. Annual Tuition and Living Costs Comparison Among College Students.

	Tuition	Living Costs		Total Costs	
		Home	Away	Home	Away
Mean	1,064.6	481.6	1,307.6	1,546.2	2,372.2
National	555.7	451.0	1,292.4	1,006.7	1,848.1
Private	1,222.5	488.2	1,319.5	1,710.7	2,542.0

Note: Unit: 1000 yen. *Source:* Ministry of Education 1996.

The costs of private/home students are not significantly different from national/away students (1.1 = 1,848.1/1,710.7). Moving away from home has almost the same effect in magnitude as attending a private (versus national) university. In contrast, the doubled cost of paying private tuition *and* moving away from home puts a very large financial burden on families. The comparison of the two extreme cases shows that costs for private/away students are 2.5 times higher than for national/home students. Thus, the total direct cost of a four-year college education in Japan ranges roughly from 4 million to 10 million yen.[5]

Regional Distribution of College Students in Japan

The Ministry of Education reports the distribution of college students using a regional classification system that includes the following divisions: Tokyo, the "10 prefectures," and "other prefectures."[6] The 10 prefectures are regions that are home to Japan's most prestigious national universities; six of the 10 prefectures are home to the former "Imperial" universities.[7] According to 1995 statistics, Tokyo and the "ten prefectures" attracted approximately three-fourths of all college students in Japan, a proportion that has changed very little since 1960. Granted that approximately half of all Japanese high school students reside in Tokyo and the ten prefectures, the pattern still holds that the net migration to these regions is positive.

The Ministry of Education estimates that the proportion of students attending colleges outside their prefecture of origin (prefecture at time of high school graduation) fluctuated little during the years 1975–1995, averaging about 60%. This percentage may be interpreted as the mobility rate of college students, but it is misleading to interpret it as the migration rate, because it does not account for the distance of migration.[8] Fully 60% should be interpreted as the upper bound of the migration rate. A finer measure of the migration rate that accounts for the distance of migration is estimated in the analysis section of this paper, and is found to be 41%.

THEORETICAL FRAMEWORK AND PREDICTIONS

In economic theory, migration is a worthwhile investment that increases the returns to human capital, if it is determined that the benefits (or the expected benefits) of migration outweigh the costs. In this tradition, migration is a process in which individuals maximize their utility subject to financial constraints. The theory has been applied to examine patterns of labor migration, and these studies have found that factors such as differences in wages and employment opportunities between sending and receiving regions are important determinants of migration (DaVanzo, 1981; Massey, 1990; Mincer, 1978; Sjaastad, 1962).

The economic theory of migration can be applied to analyze circumstances under which students migrate for their college education. We formulate a "decision rule" of migration among college students that captures the differences in university resources between sending and receiving regions.[9] We hypothesize that the relative scarcity of university resources between regions will be the driving force that compels individuals to migrate, and that this decision is subject to financial constraints. Individuals migrate to regions with higher university resources because they rationalize that so doing will increase their returns to human capital.

The critical link in the decision rule is the positive association between college quality and (expected) returns. Empirical studies in Japan and elsewhere have established that graduation from higher quality colleges leads to higher economic benefits, and we take this as a given.[10] We therefore start with the position that students will pursue higher quality colleges in expectation of higher returns. A mathematical formulation of the following predictions is provided in the Appendix.

The first and most important prediction of the decision rule is that students will migrate if they believe that the higher benefits associated with attending higher quality colleges away from home will compensate for the costs of migration. The propensity to migrate is determined by the relative scarcity of university resources between sending and receiving regions.

Second, if there is any concern for cost-minimization, then students who migrate will choose national over private universities. Recall from Table 1 that tuition for private universities is considerably more expensive than tuition for national universities, and that the cost of living away from home is considerably larger than the cost of living at home. Students who migrate may therefore be less likely to attend private universities in order to avoid having to pay for both private tuition and lodging.

And third, if students who migrate choose private over national universities, then they must boost their college quality more than they would had they chosen a national university. Students who take on bigger costs must consequently achieve bigger improvements in college quality in order to break even. Private university students who migrate must achieve benefits that can compensate for their increased financial burden. Their decision to migrate must be matched by an improvement in college quality large enough to cover both the costs of migration and the higher tuition at private universities.

DATA

The dataset used for the analysis here is the 1995 Social Stratification and Mobility National Survey (SSM) which consists of men and women between the ages of 20 and 69 residing in Japan in 1995. SSM is particularly suited for the purposes of the present research because it reports the name of the college for respondents who attended college. College quality was measured by mean scores on entrance examinations administered by each college as reported by the Obunsha publication in 1986 (see Appendix for description of coding procedure). Colleges refer to four-year universities, and do not include junior colleges.[11]

Father's occupational prestige and sibling size were used to control for socioeconomic status (SES) and family background.[12] Several other variables were also used to examine social origin effects – education of the mother, father, and the average of the two parents – but the analysis did not reveal significantly different results. Hence, I proceed by using father's occupational prestige and sibling size, in order to reduce the degrees of freedom.[13]

City size of origin refers to the size of the city where the respondent resided at the time of middle school graduation. Ideally, we would like to know the city of residence at the time of high school graduation, but this information was not available in the SSM survey data. The assumption here is that the respondents did not relocate to another region during their high school years. City size was constructed following the Ministry of Home Affairs classification of city size, and is coded from one to three in ascending order of city size. The current sample concerns college graduates only. After accounting for missing values, the sample size is 395. Descriptive statistics of the variables are reported in the Appendix.

ANALYSIS AND RESULTS

Patterns of Geographic Mobility

We begin the analysis by examining patterns of geographic mobility among SSM respondents as a function of the city size before and during college (Table 2). The pattern is intuitively clear. We observe a strong pattern of one-way mobility from low to high population areas, with over 90% of students attending colleges located in "cities" or "large cities." On the other hand, none of the students who lived in large cities attended colleges located in towns and villages.

We next estimate the proportion of individuals who moved away from home to attend college. The numbers reported so far show changes in regional distributions, but we do not have information on the number of individuals who actually migrated. For example, of the respondents who lived in "large cities" before and during college, some may have migrated from one large city to another (e.g. from Tokyo to Osaka). In order to capture migration patterns, I constructed the migration variable θ which takes a value of 0 if the respondent attended college from home, and 1 if the respondent attended college away from home. The coding procedure accounted for the approximate distance involved in the migration, and the mean migration rate is found to be 41%. (Details of the coding procedure are explained in the Appendix.) The right-hand column of Table 2 shows the proportion of students who migrated to attend college. There is a clear negative relationship between migration and city size: students living in small cities are significantly more likely to move away from home than students living in large cities.

Table 2. Patterns of Geographic Mobility by City Size.

City Size at the Time of Graduation from Mandatory Education	City Size of College			Proportion Attending College Away from Home[a]
	1: Towns and Villages	2: Cities	3: Large Cities	
1: Towns and villages	7.9	52.4	39.7	73.0
2: Cities	2.1	46.6	51.3	49.2
3: Large cities	0.0	28.0	72.0	8.4

[a] See Appendix for coding of home/away distinction.

The Migration Decision

If university resources are allocated equally across all regions, then we would expect equal proportions of students attending colleges regardless of city size or region. However, the data clearly shows that students attend colleges in urban areas in significantly higher proportions than in rural areas.

Does the unequal distribution of university resources compel students to migrate? Or do students migrate to urban areas for interests other than increasing their returns to human capital? We begin our empirical analysis by defining variables that capture the differences in university resources across regions.[14] I focus on three particular indices specific to each prefecture, and which are consistent with the process of college choice in Japan as described previously: number of university departments, average college quality and average competitiveness.[15]

Following the economics of migration literature, I hypothesize that the pursuit of college quality compels students to migrate to regions that are better endowed with respect to both the quantity and quality of university resources. The null hypothesis is therefore that migration is a random process, in which case we would observe no systematic variations in migration regardless of differences in university resources between sending and receiving regions.[16]

The variable, number of university departments (D), examines the effect of quantitative differences in university resources between sending and receiving prefectures. In the migration literature, this measure is analogous to opportunity differences between the two regions. Because Japanese university students must first decide on their major (or department) prior to entry, it makes sense that students will be more attracted to regions that offer a larger availability of resources specific to their area of study.

The variables, college quality (Q) and competitiveness (C), examine qualitative differences in university resources between sending and receiving regions. Competitiveness is the inverse of the acceptance ratio and is estimated as the number of applicants divided by the number admitted, i.e. the higher the competitiveness, the tougher the competition to get admitted. As argued elsewhere (Ono, 1999), the competitiveness measure can be used as a rough index of "popularity." For example, two universities may have the same Q, but differ with respect to C. In such cases, the university with the higher C can be deemed "more popular," by virtue of attracting a higher number of applicants and/or accepting a smaller number of applicants.[17]

Competitiveness is also specific to each university and was coded in the same manner as college quality. It can be argued that the higher quality colleges are also more popular, i.e. Q and C are positively correlated, and may pose problems of collinearity. However, the correlation between Q and C is 0.34, and diagnostics show that collinearity was not a problem in the estimations. Hence the variation between Q and C warrant the inclusion of both variables in the estimations.

Using the information provided in the SSM survey and the 1986 Obunsha publication, I created the following variables to examine differences in university resources between sending and receiving regions. The subscripts i, j, and k refer to the individual, university type (national or private), and college major, respectively. Measures for home prefecture are the following:

D^b_{ijk}	Total number of college departments in the home prefecture offering the same major of study as the respondent's college major
$\bar{Q}^b_{ijk}$	Mean measure of college quality for all colleges in the home prefecture
$\bar{C}^b_{ijk}$	Mean measure of competitiveness for all colleges in the home prefecture

Respective measures for the college attended by the respondent are:

D_{ijk}	Total number of college departments in the prefecture of destination offering the same major of study as the respondent's college major
Q_{ijk}	Quality of the college attended by the respondent
C_{ijk}	Competitiveness measure of the college attended by the respondent

The differences in university resources between sending and receiving regions are measured by $\Delta D = D_{ijk} - D^b_{ijk}$, $\Delta Q = Q_{ijk} - \bar{Q}^b_{ijk}$, and $\Delta C = C_{ijk} - \bar{C}^b_{ijk}$. Following the decision rule of migration, we predict that students will migrate when ΔD, ΔQ, and ΔC are positive and large enough to warrant undertaking the costs of migration.[18]

The logit equation expressing the propensity to migrate for each individual is:

$$\text{Logit}(\theta) = \alpha + \beta_1(\Delta D) + \beta_2(\Delta Q) + \beta_3(\Delta C) + \mathbf{Xf} + \varepsilon$$

where **Xf** represents the vector of other variables to be included in the regression, and ε is the error term.

The underlying logic here is simple: the three estimates are intended to capture the differences in university resources between sending and receiving regions. We would expect that the larger the differential, the greater the propensity to migrate to a different region to attend college. If individuals migrate from low-resource to high-resource regions, we would expect the β coefficients to be significant and positive.

We next consider the financial constraints of migration decisions. In my analysis, I use father's occupational prestige and number of siblings as family background variables to examine the effect of financial constraints on the migration decision. Because parents finance the largest share of college costs in Japan, I assume here that the family background can be used as reasonable proxies for the family's socioeconomic status (SES). If financial considerations factor into the migration decision, then we would expect a positive association between family background and migration. Further, following the decision rule for migration, we could postulate that conditional on choosing a private university, individuals would choose not to migrate in order to avoid both the higher costs of tuition and migration.

Table 3 shows the summary of the logit coefficients describing the determinants of moving away from home (θ).[19] The first model does not include city size and performs poorly. There is some evidence that women were less likely to move

Table 3. Logit Coefficients Describing Determinants of Moving Away From Home (θ).

	Model 1	Model 2	Model 3	Model 4
University resources				
ΔD			0.029^{**}	0.022^{**}
			(0.008)	(0.008)
ΔQ			0.109^{**}	0.105^{**}
			(0.020)	(0.020)
ΔC			0.293^{**}	0.244^{**}
			(0.065)	(0.065)
Private university dummy			-1.371^{**}	-0.818^{*}
			(0.302)	(0.345)
Social origin				
Father's occupational prestige	$0.015^{\dagger}$	0.026^{*}	0.001	0.010
	(0.009)	(0.010)	(0.011)	(0.012)
Sibship size	−0.028	−0.133	−0.043	−0.123
	(0.088)	(0.098)	(0.105)	(0.112)
Individual characteristics				
Sex	-0.486^{*}	$-0.472^{\dagger}$	−0.319	−0.249
	(0.244)	(0.286)	(0.302)	(0.340)
Age	0.005	0.011	−0.007	−0.003
	(0.010)	(0.012)	(0.012)	(0.013)
City size prior to university		-1.667^{**}		-1.409^{**}
		(0.203)		(0.225)
Constant	-1.233^{*}	1.672^{*}	0.077	2.162^{*}
	(0.613)	(0.806)	(0.750)	(0.876)
df	4	5	8	9
Log-likelihood	−262.5	−218.8	−198.8	−176.7
Pseudo R^2	0.013	0.177	0.253	0.336

Note: Standard errors are in parentheses and are White-corrected for individual-specific heteroscedasticity.

$^{\dagger}p < 0.10$.

$^{*}p < 0.05$.

$^{**}p < 0.01$.

away from home, but this effect diminishes after we control for the university resources in Models 3 and 4. The coefficient for age remains insignificant throughout all models, suggesting that mobility rates have remained stable over time. In Model 2, we confirm that city size of origin is a powerful predictor of moving away from home, a finding that is consistent with Table 2.

There is some evidence that family background matters, but this effect also disappears after controlling for differences in university resources, indicating that students from low SES families were just as likely to migrate as students from high SES families. These findings therefore suggest that the financial constraint is not the primary factor determining the migration decision.

Model 3 shows the results of the logit model, which includes the differences in university resources. The results are consistent with the predictions of the decision rule for migration. We find that students are more likely to migrate if: (1) the number of college departments offering the same major of study (*D*) is greater than their home prefecture; (2) the quality (*Q*) and competitiveness (*C*) of the college attended exceed the respective mean values of their home prefecture; and (3) they attended a national university. Finally, Model 4 results show that the differences in university resources remain highly significant even after we control for city size. These results suggest that migration decisions are dictated not simply by urban/rural differences, but by differences in university resources between the sending and receiving regions.

Findings (1) and (2) strongly suggest that there is a systematic pattern of migration towards regions with better college opportunities and resources. Finding (3) may reflect aversion from the doubled financial burden of attending private universities and living away from home. Parents may be willing to finance their children's tuition at a private university, or to pay for their living away from home, but not both.

Finally, we examine how differences in university resources factor into the migration decision when migration is categorized in ascending order of costs. Following the prediction of the decision rule, we expect students who take on bigger costs to be more concerned about improving college quality. For this analysis, I constructed four exclusive categories in ascending order of total college costs, of students who attended: (1) national universities from home; (2) private universities from home; (3) national universities away from home; and (4) private universities away from home.

Table 4 reports the results of the multinomial logit model used to predict the four outcomes, where the baseline category is (1) – students who attended national universities from home. None of the social origin variables were found to be significant (and suppressed from the output), supporting the prior finding that financial constraint was not a deciding factor in the migration decision.

Table 4. Multinomial Logit Coefficients Describing Determinants of Moving Away From Home.

	Vs Private/Home	Vs National/Away	Vs Private/Away
ΔD	0.045**	−0.024*	0.073**
	(0.014)	(0.010)	(0.013)
ΔQ	0.022	0.083**	0.138**
	(0.026)	(0.032)	(0.029)
ΔC	0.063	−0.032	0.378**
	(0.086)	(0.160)	(0.095)
City size	1.378**	−0.810*	−0.504†
	(0.296)	(0.348)	(0.303)

Note: Baseline category is respondents who attended national universities from home. df = 24, Log-likelihood = −341.6, Pseudo $R^2 = 0.304$. Standard errors are in parentheses and are White-corrected for individual-specific heteroscedasticity. Model controls for family background, sex and age.

†$p < 0.10$.
*$p < 0.05$.
**$p < 0.01$.

On the other hand, the university resource variables among the students who attended private universities away from home are all highly significant, and the coefficients are larger than the other two groups. These results suggest that differences in university resources were far more important in the migration decision for this group than for the other reference groups. In order to test the hypothesis derived from the decision rule for migration, I performed the same multinomial logit model setting the baseline category to be (3) – students who attended national universities away from home. The results (not shown here) are consistent with the predictions. The coefficients for the university resources variables for students in category (4) were all positive and significant.

In general, the findings suggest that the more expensive the decision becomes, the more serious the students become in their pursuit of college quality. Intuitively, this makes sense. Private university students are less likely to migrate, but when they do, it is because of their uncompromising desire to attend the better colleges. From the parents' perspective, we can conjecture that they may be willing to send their children to expensive colleges away from home, but it had better be for a good reason.

CONCLUSION

The pursuit of college quality among Japanese students and their parents suggests that families will do whatever it takes to gain entry into the nation's top colleges.

Individuals pursue college quality because they believe that the quality gains will lead to higher economic returns. Among the costs confronting the parents of college-bound students, the largest is the cost of migration. This paper has examined how the pursuit of college quality factors into the migration decision in the face of financial constraints. The findings clearly show that differences in university resources across regions is an important factor determining migration decisions among Japanese college students, while financial considerations were secondary in importance. These findings lend further support to the claim that what matters in Japan is not only how much college education one has, but where one attends college.

These findings are consistent with the predictions of the decision rule for migration, in which I claim that if students migrate for their college education, they do so because there is a relative scarcity of high-quality colleges in their home regions. The improvement in college quality obtained from migration subsequently leads to higher benefits, which is expected to be greater than the costs incurred from migration.

In an earlier study, I found that parent's socioeconomic status plays a decisive role in determining college advancement, but its role in sorting individuals into colleges of different rank is weak (Ono, 2001). My findings here lend further support to this claim, mainly that once students have decided to advance to college, the pursuit for college quality overrides cost considerations. Despite the fact that migration is the most expensive investment associated with college education, I find little evidence that the decision is constrained by the socioeconomic status of the family. Concerns over college quality between regions were found to be most important among the students in the most expensive category, attending private universities away from home. This finding suggests that the more expensive the migration decision becomes, the more serious the students and their parents become about their pursuit of college quality.

While migration is undeniably an expensive investment, these findings suggest that Japanese students and their parents will make the necessary sacrifices in their pursuit of college quality. But is it really worth the costs? Answering this question requires an analysis that examines both the costs and benefits involved in a college education. This paper has applied a cost-benefit approach to migration under the implicit assumption that the expected benefits were sufficient to motivate the students to invest in their education. In future research, we can relax this assumption by including actual earnings subsequent to graduation. An estimation of the net benefits of a college education in Japan that accounts for the costs of migration would further improve our understanding of the incentives underlying the pursuit of college quality in Japan.

In recent years, one-way out-migration of college students to urban centers has become a source of increasing concern in rural areas in Japan. Several prefectures have responded by opening their own local colleges to counter the outflow of students. While this may be part of the solution, my research has shown that the quality of the institution is a critical factor in the migration decision, and not just the quantity or availability of university resources. It is too early to judge the outcome of these recent efforts, but it is hasty to assume that "if you build it, they will come." Students may come, but only if the quality of the institution matches their expectations.

A natural extension to the current research would be to investigate patterns of migration among students after they graduate from university. Among students who migrated for their university education, a common pattern of employment migration following graduation is when they return to find work close to home. This pattern has become so much more frequent in recent years, that the media have now coined the expression "U-turn employment" to describe it. Based on the findings from the current research study and from the economics of migration framework, one future line of research would be to investigate how university resources and labor market conditions in sending and receiving regions influence employment migration decisions. A systematic analysis of employment migration in Japan has yet to be conducted, and research opportunities remain vast.

NOTES

1. In recent years, some universities have introduced recommendations as a new criterion to diversify their admission procedures. However, the proportion of students entering universities under this criterion remains small.
2. There are two types of scholarships available. The first is an interest-free loan, and is available to students of exceptional quality with financial problems. The second is an interest-bearing loan for other students who did not qualify under the first criterion. (Source: Japan Scholarship Foundation Homepage: http://www.ikuei.go.jp/).
3. Living costs include food, rent, utilities, medical care, amenities and recreation, and other expenses associated with daily life.
4. Ministry of Education statistics show that the ratio of total costs regarding living home versus away has remained unchanged in the last thirty years, averaging about 1.5.
5. The discussion here concerns direct costs only. For college students, indirect costs are their foregone earnings had they entered the labor force instead of advancing to college.
6. Following the reorganization of Japanese ministries in January 2001, the Ministry of Education is now called the Ministry of Education, Culture, Science, and Technology.
7. The ten prefectures include Hokkaido, Miyagi, Chiba, Kanagawa, Aichi, Kyoto, Osaka, Hyogo, Hiroshima, and Fukuoka. "Other prefectures" include the remaining 36 prefectures not listed in the other two categories.

8. Commuting across adjacent prefectures, e.g. from Kanagawa to Tokyo, is perfectly feasible.

9. The expression decision rule borrows from Willis (1986) in which he models college choice as a cost-benefit estimation.

10. See, for example, Brewer et al. (1999), James et al. (1989), Kingston and Smart (1990), Loury and Garman (1995) for studies on college quality and earnings in the U.S., and Ishida et al. (1997), Karabel and McClelland (1987), and Useem and Karabel (1990) for studies relating to college quality and promotions in the U.S. For studies on college quality and earnings in Japan, see, for example, Iwamura (1996), Nakata and Mosk (1986), and Ono (forthcoming).

11. The entrance examinations are different for junior colleges, so consistent comparisons cannot be made between junior colleges and colleges.

12. Father's occupational prestige is measured using the Japanese occupational prestige scores developed by the SSM research team (Naoi, 1994; Okamoto & Hara, 1994).

13. Another shortcoming is that the inclusion of the mother's and father's education results in a 17% reduction in the sample size due to missing cases.

14. Commonly used measures of college quality in the U.S. include per pupil expenditures, average faculty salary, and average educational attainment of faculty (Behrman & Birdsall, 1983; Johnson & Stafford, 1996; Morgan & Duncan, 1979; Solmon, 1975). However, these measures are not available at the level of desired specificity (i.e. by region, by university type, etc.) for Japanese universities.

15. I used the number of university departments instead of number of universities because students have decided on their intended field of study prior to applying.

16. Sjaastad (1962), Manski, and Wise (1983) and others have noted that the distance of migration factors into the migration decision because it is more costly to relocate to distant locations. However, because Japan is a small country with a well-developed transportation system, I assume here that the distance of migration does not influence the migration decision.

17. It can be argued that prefectures with more selective colleges are, by design, less able to accept more students. However, there are still ways in which this can work. Students apply to more than one school, which inflates C. The mean competitiveness of all colleges (according to the Obunsha data) is found to be 3.8, with min $C = 1.1$, meaning that all colleges attract more applicants than they accept. However, we do not have information on the percentage of accepted students that actually matriculate (which will always be smaller than 100). Unfortunately, without this missing link, the truth behind C cannot fully be revealed, hence the loose interpretation, "popularity." For an analysis of the relationship between C and Q in the U.S., see Monks and Ehrenberg (1999) who use the *U.S. News and World Report* ranking of U.S. colleges.

18. ΔD, ΔQ and ΔC must be positive, is a necessary but not sufficient condition. The benefits obtained from migration must be large enough to cover the costs of migration. Small differences in university resources between regions may not be sufficient to warrant migration. This relationship corresponds directly to Eq. (A.1′) in the Appendix.

19. Individuals are nested in prefectures so there is reason to suspect that the error terms may be systematically biased. I conducted several tests by relaxing the assumption of independence within groups, e.g. city size, prefecture, age cohort, but the results were not significantly different and are not reported here.

ACKNOWLEDGMENTS

This research was supported by grants from the Center for East Asian Studies at the University of Chicago, Japan-America Society of Chicago and the American Compensation Association. I am grateful to Mary Brinton, Gary Becker, and Kazuo Yamaguchi for comments on an earlier draft of the paper. I thank Lawrence Brown, Rosa Fernandez, Margaret Stevens, Kazuaki Uekawa, and to Bruce Fuller and the *RSOE* reviewers for their helpful criticisms and comments. I am grateful to Mary Brinton and the SSM Committee for granting me permission to use the 1995 SSM data, to Mr. Hisashi Arai of Obunsha for allowing me access to past issues of their publications, and to Takehiko Kariya for providing me access to the SSM occupational prestige scores.

REFERENCES

Ando, B. (1994). Gakureki shakai kasetsu no kento (Examining the educational credentialism hypothesis). In: K. Tominaga (Ed.), *Nihon no Kaiso Kozo* (pp. 275–292). Tokyo: University of Tokyo Press.

Behrman, J. R., & Birdsall, N. (1983). The quality of schooling: Quantity alone is misleading. *American Economic Review*, *73*, 928–946.

Brewer, D. J., Eide, E. R., & Ehrenberg, R. G. (1999). Does it pay to attend an elite private college? Cross-cohort evidence on the effects of college type on earnings. *Journal of Human Resources*, *34*, 104–123.

DaVanzo, J. (1981). Microeconomic approaches to studying migration decisions. In: G. F. De Jong & R. W. Gardner (Eds), *Migration Decision Making: Multidisciplinary Approaches to Microlevel Studies in Developed and Developing Countries* (pp. 90–129). New York: Pergamon Press.

Ishida, H. (1993). *Social mobility in contemporary Japan: Educational credentials, class, and the labour market in a cross-national perspective*. Stanford: Stanford University Press.

Ishida, H., Spilerman, S., & Su, K. (1997). Educational credentials and promotion chances in Japanese and American organizations. *American Sociological Review*, *62*, 866–882.

Iwamura, M. (1996). Koto-kyouiku no shiteki shuekiritsu (Private rate of return to higher education). *Kyouiku Shakaigaku Kenkyu*, *58*, 5–28.

James, E., Alsalam, N., Conaty, J. C., & To, D. (1989). College quality and future earnings: Where should you send your child to college? *American Economic Review*, *79*, 247–252.

Johnson, G. E., & Stafford, F. P. (1996). On the rate of return to schooling quality. *Review of Economics and Statistics*, *78*, 686–691.

Karabel, J., & McClelland, K. (1987). Occupational advantage and the impact of college rank on labor market outcomes. *Sociological Inquiry*, *57*, 323–347.

Kingston, P. W., & Lewis, L. S. (1990). Introduction: Studying elite schools in America. In: P. W. Kingston & L. S. Lewis (Eds), *High-Status Track: Studies of Elite Schools and Stratification* (pp. xi–xxxiv). Albany: State University of New York Press.

Kingston, P. W., & Smart, J. C. (1990). The economic pay-off of prestigious colleges. In: P. W. Kingston & L. S. Lewis (Eds), *High-Status Track: Studies of Elite Schools and Stratification* (pp. 147–174). Albany: State University of New York Press.

Loury, L. D., & Garman, D. (1995). College selectivity and earnings. *Journal of Labor Economics, 13*, 289–308.

Manski, C. F., & Wise, D. A. (1983). *College choice in America*. Cambridge: Harvard University Press.

Massey, D. (1990). The social and economic origins of immigration. *Annals of the American Academy of Political and Social Science, 510*, 60–72.

Mincer, J. (1978). Family migration decisions. *Journal of Political Economy, 86*, 749–773.

Ministry of Education (1998). *Monbu Tokei Yoran* (Statistical Abstract of Education, Science, Sport and Culture). Tokyo: Ministry of Finance Printing Bureau.

Monks, J., & Ehrenberg, R. G. (1999). U.S. News and world report's college rankings: Why they do matter. *Change, 31*, 42–51.

Morgan, J. N., & Duncan, G. J. (1979). College quality and earnings. *Research in Human Capital and Development, 1*, 103–121.

Nakata, Y., & Mosk, C. (1986). The demand for college education in postwar Japan. *Journal of Human Resources, 22*, 377–404.

Naoi, A. (1994). Shokugyoteki Chiishakudo no Kosei (The Construction of the Occupational Scale). In: K. Tominaga (Ed.), *Nihon no Kaiso Kozo* (pp. 434–472). Tokyo: University of Tokyo Press.

Okamoto, H., & Hara, J. (1994). Shokugyo no Miryoku Hyoka no Bunseki (The analysis of prestige evaluation of occupations). In: K. Tominaga (Ed.), *Nihon no Kaiso Kozo* (pp. 421–433). Tokyo: University of Tokyo Press.

Ono, H. (1999). *For what it's worth: The value of college education in Japan*. Ph.D. dissertation, Department of Sociology, University of Chicago.

Ono, H. College quality and earnings in the Japanese labor market. Forthcoming in *Industrial Relations*.

Ono, H. (2001). Who goes to college? Features of institutional tracking in Japanese higher education. *American Journal of Education, 109*, 161–195.

Rohlen, T. P. (1983). *Japan's High Schools*. Berkeley: University of California Press.

Sakurai, H. (1997). Japan's changing education market. *NRI Quarterly, 6*, 48–69.

Sjaastad, L. A. (1962). The costs and returns of human migration. *Journal of Political Economy, 70*(Supplement), 80–93.

Solmon, L. C. (1975). The definition of college quality and its impact on earnings. *Explorations in Economic Research, 2*, 537–587.

Treiman, D. J., & Yamaguchi, K. (1993). Trends in educational opportunities. In: Y. Shavit & H. Blossfeld (Eds), *Persistent Inequality: Changing Educational Attainment in Thirteen Countries* (pp. 229–249). Boulder: Westview Press.

Tsukada, M. (1991). *Yobiko life: A study of the legitimation process of social stratification in Japan*. Berkeley: University of California Press.

Useem, M., & Karabel, J. (1990). Pathways to top corporate management. In: P. W. Kingston & L. S. Lewis (Eds), *High-Status Track: Studies of Elite Schools and Stratification* (pp. 175–207). Albany: State University of New York Press.

Willis, R. J. (1986). Wage determinants: A survey and reinterpretation of human capital earnings functions. In: O. Ashenfelter & R. Layard (Eds), *Handbook of Labor Economics* (Vol. 1, pp. 525–602). Amsterdam: Elsevier.

APPENDIX

Constructing the Home/Away Variable (θ)

Table 1. Means and Standard Deviations of Variables.

Variable	Mean	S.D.
Home/away variable (θ) where $\theta = 0$ if attended college from home, $\theta = 1$ if attended college away from home	0.41	0.49
Difference in number of university departments between sending and receiving region (ΔD)	10.04	19.11
Difference in college quality between sending and receiving region (ΔQ)	3.78	8.86
Difference in competitiveness measure between sending and receiving region (ΔC)	0.75	2.26
Private university dummy (versus national university)	0.74	0.44
Father's occupational prestige	58.17	11.68
Sibling size	2.85	1.37
Women dummy (versus men)	0.26	0.44
Age	38.99	11.86
City size at origin	2.12	0.68

In order to analyze mobility patterns before and during college, I constructed a variable θ which takes the value of 1 if the respondent had moved to a different prefecture for college, and 0 if the respondent had remained in the same prefecture. The 47 prefectures in the SSM survey are coded using the numbering system established by the Ministry of Home Affairs. In general, the prefectures are numbered in order from north to south (from Hokkaido (1) to Okinawa (47)). I constructed a measure of distance (L) between the prefecture of residence at time of graduation from mandatory education (P_1) and the prefecture of the college attended (P_2), such that $L = |P_1 - P_2|$. I briefly summarize the θ coding procedure as follows: (1) Of the 395 college graduates in the SSM, 143 were cases where $L = 3$. These respondents were coded $\theta = 1$. (2) There were 164 cases where $L = 0$. These respondents were coded $\theta = 0$. (3) There were 54 cases where $L = 1$ suggesting that these respondents had moved to an adjacent prefecture to attend college. I reviewed P_1 and P_2 for each of these cases to examine whether these respondents were within reasonable commuting distance of their colleges. For example, if P_1 or P_2 was coded Tokyo (34 cases), then these individuals were coded $\theta = 0$. On the other hand, if P_1 or P_2 was coded Hokkaido or Okinawa (i.e. the island prefectures), then it was not reasonable to assume that these respondents had commuted by sea to attend college, and they were coded $\theta = 1$. (4) There were 34 cases where $L = 2$. Again, I reviewed P_1 and P_2 for each case to evaluate if they were within reasonable commuting range. Of these cases, 19 were in Tokyo, which implies that P_1 or P_2 for these respondents were either in Kanagawa or Saitama prefecture. These prefectures are within reasonable commuting distance from Tokyo and were coded $\theta = 0$. When the coding was completed in this way, there were 233 respondents coded $\theta = 0$, and 162 who were coded $\theta = 1$.

Coding College Quality

Obunsha, a publishing company located in Tokyo, tabulates and publishes results of entrance examinations and the competitiveness scores of Japanese colleges on an annual basis. Their publication, *Keisetsu Jidai*, is the Japanese equivalent of *Barron's Guide to American Colleges*, and ranks university departments based on results from the examinations administered in the previous year. Test scores are standardized across different universities and range from 30 to 80 (80 being the highest).

The "Decision Rule" for Migration

We start by formulating the relationship between college quality (Q), tuition (U), living costs (M), and the internal rate of return (IRR) for a college education. For simplicity, assume U differs only with respect to attendance at a private or national university, and M differs only with respect to the cost of migration versus the cost of commuting from home (the magnitude of the costs correspond directly to the costs described in Table 1). The *IRR* (or the expected *IRR*) equates the sum of the net present value of costs to the sum of the net present value of benefits, and is the benchmark measure that indicates whether the investment yields a positive or a negative return. We start with the condition, $\partial IRR/\partial Q > 0$, i.e. the change in *IRR* from investments in Q is positive, ceteris paribus. Since migration and attendance at a private university are costs (and not benefits), their direct effects on *IRR* are always negative, i.e. $\partial IRR/\partial M < 0$ and $\partial IRR/\partial U < 0$. Setting *IRR* as a function of Q, M and U, the total change in *IRR* from migration can be expressed:

$$\frac{d\,IRR}{dM} = \underset{(+)}{\frac{\partial IRR}{\partial Q}}\underset{(+)}{\frac{dQ}{dM}} + \underset{(-)}{\frac{\partial IRR}{\partial U}}\underset{(?)}{\frac{dU}{dM}} + \underset{(-)}{\frac{\partial IRR}{\partial M}} > 0 \tag{A.1}$$

Or

$$\frac{\partial IRR}{\partial Q}\frac{dQ}{dM} > \frac{\partial IRR}{\partial M} - \frac{\partial IRR}{\partial U}\frac{dU}{dM} \tag{A.1'}$$

which states that the benefit of migration (left-hand term) must be greater than the cost of migration (right-hand term). Equation (A.1′) is the decision rule for migration and points to several important predictions. First and most importantly, dQ/dM must be positive in order for this relationship to hold true, i.e. the improvement in college quality obtained from migration must always be positive, and sufficient to recover the costs of migration.

Second, if there is any concern for cost minimization, students who migrate will choose national over private universities. Why? Because if students who migrate choose private over national universities (if $dU/dM > 0$), then $(\partial IRR/\partial U)(dU/dM) < 0$, in which case the benefit of migration must be great enough to cover the cost of migration plus the cost of higher tuition. This relationship corresponds to the increased financial burden of private tuition and living away from home described in Table A.1.

And third, if students who migrate choose private over national universities, then from Eq. (A.1′) it can be shown that the following condition must hold true:

$$\text{If } \frac{dU}{dM} > 0, \quad \text{then } \left.\frac{dQ}{dM}\right|_{U=\text{private}} > \left.\frac{dQ}{dM}\right|_{U=\text{national}} \qquad \text{(A.2)}$$

If students who migrate choose private universities, then they must improve their college quality more than they would had they chosen a national university, in order to cover the cost of higher tuition.

Constructing the Variables Used for Analysis on Migration Decisions

The underlying assumption here is that college quality remains unchanged over time. This is not an unreasonable assumption given that Ishida, Spilerman and Su (1997), and also Ono (1999) examined the Obunsha data for various years and found only small fluctuations in college quality during the postwar period. Also, because the age of the respondents in the SSM survey ranges from 20 to 69, it would have been necessary to collect college quality data for all Japanese universities over a span of 50 years if this assumption was not made. Therefore, I used the college quality estimates provided in the 1986 Obunsha supplement to construct the data necessary for this analysis.

First, for each individual i, I constructed mean measures of college quality $\bar{Q}^b_{ijk}$ and competitiveness $\bar{C}^b_{ijk}$ at the prefecture of origin of the SSM respondents. The superscript b identifies the prefecture of origin which is proxied by the prefecture of residence at time of graduation from mandatory education. The subscript j identifies university type (national or private) and k identifies the college major.

Both were estimated using the following set of equations:

$$\bar{Q}^b_{j,k} = \frac{\sum_{m=1}^{M} Q^b_{j,k,m}}{M} \tag{A.3}$$

$$\bar{C}^b_{j,k} = \frac{\sum_{m=1}^{M} C^b_{j,k,m}}{M} \tag{A.4}$$

where M represents the total number of university departments of type k at prefecture b among university type j. For example, the mean college quality of humanities departments ($k = 1$) among national universities ($j = 1$) in Hokkaido prefecture ($b = 1$) is estimated by:

$$\bar{Q}^{b=1}_{j=1,k=1} = \frac{\sum_{m=1}^{M} C^{b=1}_{j=1,k=1,m}}{M}$$

Table A.2 shows the sample matrix of mean college quality by university departments by prefecture of origin among national universities ($j = 1$).

Next, in order to minimize changes in college quality over time, I replaced the individual-level college quality and competitiveness measures of the SSM respondents (i.e. Q and C of the college attended by respondents, denoted by Q_{ijk} and C_{ijk} respectively) with the 1986 data. Q_{ijk} and C_{ijk} therefore represent college quality and competitiveness measures of respondents had they attended their colleges in 1986. The subscripts j and k are retained to maintain consistency with the mean level measures.

The number of university departments must also contain the same parameters provided at the individual level. For each individual i, I constructed D^b_{ijk} to represent the number of university departments of university type j and department k at the prefecture of origin and D_{ijk} as the same number at the prefecture where the individual attended college.

Table A.2. Mean College Quality by University Departments by Prefecture of Origin Among National Universities ($j = 1$).

Prefecture of Origin (P)	University departments (k)				
	1 Humanities	2 Law	3 Economics	...	10 Phys Ed
1 Hokkaido	$\bar{Q}^{b=1}_{j=1,k=1}$	$\bar{Q}^{b=1}_{j=1,k=2}$	$\bar{Q}^{b=1}_{j=1,k=3}$	...	$\bar{Q}^{b=1}_{j=1,k=10}$
2 Aomori	$\bar{Q}^{b=2}_{j=1,k=1}$	$\bar{Q}^{b=2}_{j=1,k=2}$	...		⋮
⋮	⋮				
47 Okinawa	$\bar{Q}^{b=47}_{j=1,k=1}$	...			$\bar{Q}^{b=47}_{j=1,k=10}$

COMMENTARY: EDUCATIONAL STRATIFICATION IN ASIA

Emily Hannum and Bruce Fuller

INTRODUCTION

The papers in this section investigate a range of conventional educational stratification topics – gender inequality, class-based differences, and social mobility – as they relate to pre-primary through higher education in Asia. Yet, the authors are able to move beyond typical tests of stratification theories. While all of the papers are grounded in comparative frameworks, they also draw on the authors' deep, country-specific knowledge. This local knowledge enables authors to consider institutional organization, educational policy, and the cultural or economic context of schooling in their interpretation of results.

The China paper investigates social disparities in children's pre-primary experiences, including formal child care. The topic is timely, as preschooling is a rapidly emerging but poorly understood institution in China and in Asia. The Thailand and Korea papers investigate changing educational stratification regimes across periods of dramatic educational and economic development, and contribute significant new case studies to the growing comparative literature on development and stratification. Finally, the Japan paper offers an analysis of institutional attributes and college choice in a non-Western society, inspiring provocative questions about how institutionalized values of education may condition stratification mechanisms in culturally-specific ways.

Inequality Across Societies: Families, Schools and Persisting Stratification
Research in Sociology of Education, Volume 14, 125–137
(Formerly Research in Sociology of Education and Socialization)

ISSN: 1479-3539/doi:10.1016/S1479-3539(03)14006-2

Taken together, the papers yield four insights that are particularly helpful in considering future directions for comparative research on inequality. First, they suggest that attributes of institutional organization and quality – often obscured in the individual data that serves as the basis for many stratification studies – constitute critical elements of educational opportunity. Second, they show that stratification can emerge at different points in the school attainment process, and that particular mechanisms at each level are worthy of additional scrutiny. Third, they suggest that non-class-based inequalities can be highly culturally contextualized, and are thus more complex to characterize than class inequalities. A lack of focus on these other lines of inequality creates significant impediments to our understanding of global social stratification patterns. Fourth, the studies illustrate that while certain elements of educational inequality emerge across societies, some elements may emerge more strongly in particular nations or groups of nations. In the sections that follow, we first highlight key contributions made by each paper, then return to these four cross-cultural themes and their implications for the comparative study of educational stratification.

STRATIFICATION OF EARLY CHILDHOOD IN CHINA

Through the creative use of multipurpose survey data and in-depth interviews, Short and Sun present a pioneering analysis of access to formal child care within the context of a low-income country. Their paper addresses both the distribution of types of child care, including formal and non-formal care, and family perceptions of how child care affects children's development and subsequent schooling outcomes.

This topic has broad significance. In Asia, as in many parts of the world, organized care prior to primary school is a growing phenomenon. For example, between 1980 and 1997, pre-primary gross enrollment ratios grew from 13 to 29% in China, from 8 to 88% in Korea, from 10 to 75% in Thailand, and from 41 to 50% in Japan[1] (see Table 1).

This pattern of growth is likely to continue given recent trends in female employment. In Thailand and China, a high rate of female participation in the work force is an established tradition; in Korea and Japan, female participation is rising rapidly. According to United Nations estimates, the number of economically active women in China ages 25–29 grew from 87% in 1980 to hover in the low 90s through the year 2000; in Thailand, 83% of women were economically active throughout the same period. In Japan, the number of economically active women grew from 49% in 1980 to 70% by the year 2000; in Korea, corresponding figures were 38 and 58% (see Fig. 1). Despite broad social trends that continue to promote institutionalized preschooling, few comparative studies have considered

Table 1. Gross Enrollment Ratios by Level, China, Japan, Korea, and Thailand.

	Pre-Primary				Primary				Secondary				Tertiary			
	China	Japan	Korea	Thailand	China	Japan	Korea	Thailand	China	Japan	Korea	Thailand	China	Japan	Korea	Thailand
1980	13	41	8	10	113	101	110	99	46	93	78	29	2	31	15	15
1981	12	41	18	10	113	102	109	99	39	94	79	29	2	30	19	19
1982	14	41	21	11	114	103	107	98	36	93	81	30	2	30	23	21
1983	15	43	26	13	115	103	103	97	36	92	86	31	2	30	28	22
1984	17	45	33	14	120	103	100	97	37	93	89	31	2	29	31	20
1985	20	46	42	18	123	102	97	96	40	95	92	31	3	28	34	19
1986	22	46	48	28	126	100	97	97	43	96	94	29	3	28	35	17
1987	24	47	53	33	127	99	98	97	45	97	93	28	3	28	36	15
1988	23	48	54	40	127	99	100	98	46	97	92	28	3	29	36	15
1989	22	48	54	41	127	99	103	99	46	96	91	28	3	29	37	16
1990	23	48	55	43	125	100	105	99	49	97	90	30	3	30	39	–
1991	25	48	59	45	122	101	105	99	52	96	89	33	3	30	40	–
1992	26	49	65	50	119	101	103	97	55	96	91	37	3	31	44	19
1993	27	49	71	58	117	102	101	94	57	99	95	42	4	40	45	19
1994	28	49	80	63	117	103	98	91	61	100	98	48	5	41	48	19
1995	29	49	85	57	118	103	95	87	66	103	101	54	5	–	52	20
1996	29	50	88	63	120	102	94	87	69	–	102	56	6	–	60	22
1997	29	–	88	75	123	101	94	89	70	–	–	59	6	–	68	–

Source: UNESCO Institute for Statistics (2002). Indicators. Electronic database, http://www.uis.unesco.org/en/stats/centre.htm, accessed March, 2003.

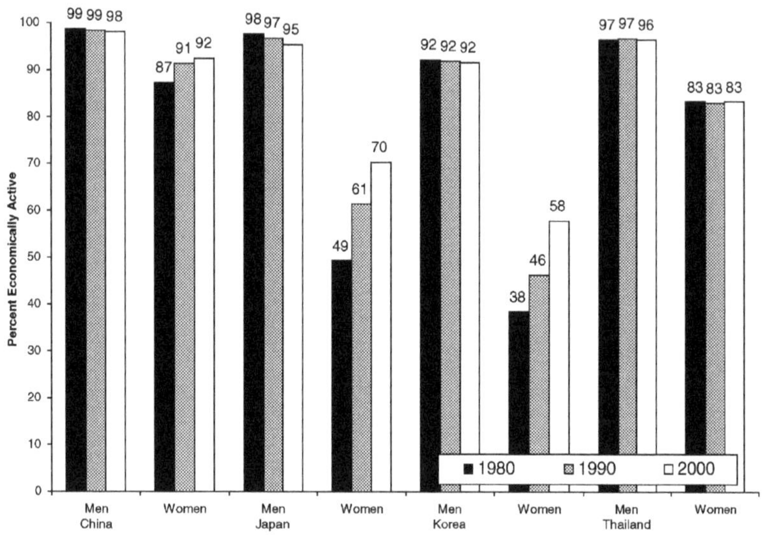

Fig. 1. Economic Activity Rates Among 25–29-Year-Olds by Sex and Year, China, Japan, Korea, and Thailand. *Source:* Calculated from United Nations, 2002. "United Nations Common Database," http://unstats.un.org, series 4270: Economic activity rate by sex, 13 age groups, 1950–2010 (ILO) [204 countries, 1950–2010], accessed March, 2003.

the distribution or impact of formal, organized child care as an element of social inequality.

That non-parental child care affects a significant proportion of Chinese children is highlighted in Short and Sun's data: about a quarter of children five years and under receive care outside the household, and about 65% of these receive care in a formal setting. Importantly, their analysis indicates that access to formal care is unequally distributed in ways that directly parallel results of studies of educational stratification at higher levels of schooling. First, there is an important spatial dimension to the distribution of child care, both due to cross-community differences and to differences across urban-rural lines. Second, among poor families, boys are favored. Studies among older children in China have similarly found that urban-rural residence and community of residence are important predictors of enrollment, and, in some cases, that gender gaps may emerge among impoverished families (Hannum, 2002a, b).

One question that arises from Short and Sun's analysis is whether disparity in access to formal care or preschooling matters from a stratification perspective. In other words, does access to formal care confer a long-term educational advantage? While Short and Sun are unable to directly assess the impact of child care on subsequent educational performance, they do investigate attitudes about the value of formal care in qualitative interviews with 48 mothers. They show that formal care is highly desirable through mothers' eyes, because it is widely perceived to confer real educational advantages. In interviews, parents talked of the utility of preschooling in terms of offering socialization, inculcating discipline, and contributing to school readiness. These findings suggest that the internal values and notions of merit inherent in modern schooling are seeping down to three- and four-year-olds in China.

To the extent that these perceptions represent accurate assessments of the value of formal care in China, Short and Sun's work suggests that patterns of educational advantage and disadvantage associated with location of residence, poverty, and gender may start much earlier in the schooling process than has been recognized. Such a conclusion would be consistent with findings from studies in the West that suggest that sharp inequalities emerge earlier than the primary years, as children enter school with dramatically different levels of preparedness (Fuller & Strath, 2001; Wrigley, 1999). Recent studies have suggested, for example, that access to high-quality child care or preschool prior to primary school confers significant educational advantages (West et al., 2000).

Together with evidence that preschooling is a growing global phenomenon and that it matters for subsequent educational achievement, Short and Sun's provocative analysis highlights the urgent need for more comparative research on early childhood schooling and educational stratification.

ECONOMIC DEVELOPMENT, SCHOOL EXPANSION, AND THE GENDER GAP IN THAILAND

Combining fieldwork and analysis of prospective survey data from Thailand, Curran, Chung, Cadge and Varangrat analyze changes in the gender gap during the 1980s and early 1990s, a period of rapid economic development and significant expansion of secondary education. The authors discuss the many social changes that have emerged over this period that may modify the value attached to schooling for girls. These changes include the rise of export manufacturing and the associated value attached to secondary schooling, and a growing service sector that may favor young females in the job market.

Consistent with earlier survey work in Thailand (e.g. Knodel, 1997; Knodel & Jones, 1996), Curran et al. show that the gender gap in the Nang Rong region narrowed significantly over this time period. Particularly interesting in their paper is the discussion of complex forces that have contradictory implications for the gender gap. Curran et al. characterize family relations in Nang Rong as being governed by bilateral inheritance, matrilineal residence preferences, and little or no son preference. They credit limited son preference to the family economy's traditional dependence on rice growing, and the value of women's labor and knowledge about land use and history.

However, by the 1980s, limited land availability and large family sizes made farming families increasingly reliant on cash income derived from labor migration. Many families perceived girls as being more diligent students than boys. Yet, in part because of their diligence, girls were said to need less education to become successful labor migrants, and were seen to be more reliable wage remitters. Girls' greater remittance to their natal homes and the reliability of their sending behavior were important considerations for parents in making educational decisions.

The paper offers several insights of broad significance. First, the mixed implications of labor market change in Thailand for children's schooling, and for the gender gap in schooling, are issues with implications for countries elsewhere in the developing world. In particular, the authors highlight important links between labor migration and education – links that had been studied very little in earlier work. Their fieldwork suggests that prospects for labor migration may influence the perceived value of schooling, and that remittances may influence schooling investments. Further, their fieldwork suggests that these influences may operate differently depending on the gender of the individuals involved, and depending on the migratory and economic history of a particular setting.

These points pertain to domestic labor migration in Thailand, but the educational issues raised by rural-urban migration patterns suggest important parallels in other less-developed countries where cross-border migration is common. With globalization, remittances sent home by international migrants have become a significant component of the economies of some countries. For example, according to United Nations estimates for the year 2000, remittances from abroad constituted more than 10% of the gross domestic product in several poor countries.[2] However, little is known about whether labor migration and remittances constitute significant educational resources or impediments for families in developing countries (for one significant exception, see Kandel & Kao, 2000). These issues are worthy of increased research attention.

Second, Thailand presents an interesting case in the study of gender and education. As reflected in available national gross enrollment ratios, Thailand's gender gap in education is small, and where gaps have existed, progress toward gender parity has been rapid (see Table 2). Highlighting trends of a declining gender gap in education in many regions of the world, including Thailand, Knodel and Jones (1996) have raised the provocative question of whether attention to gender inequalities is excessive, given that gender gaps seem to respond to development, while socioeconomic gaps persist.

Curran et al. concur with the view that attention to promoting girls' schooling might be better directed toward improving access for children of both genders from

Table 2. Female Gross Enrollment Ratios as a Percent of Male Gross Enrollment Ratios, China, Japan, Korea, and Thailand.

	Pre-Primary				Primary				Secondary				Tertiary			
	China	Japan	Korea	Thailand	China	Japan	Korea	Thailand	China	Japan	Korea	Thailand	China	Japan	Korea	Thailand
1975	–	101	83	95	88	100	101	92	52	101	74	80	57	49	41	63
1980	–	101	88	98	86	100	101	97	69	102	90	94	32	50	41	–
1981	–	101	90	–	84	100	101	–	69	102	91	–	33	51	35	–
1982	–	100	90	–	83	100	101	–	68	103	92	–	–	52	37	–
1983	97	101	92	–	83	100	102	–	69	103	95	–	37	53	38	–
1984	93	101	94	–	83	100	102	–	69	102	96	–	41	54	43	–
1985	96	101	96	–	86	100	102	–	71	102	98	–	44	56	49	–
1986	97	101	97	–	88	100	102	–	70	102	100	–	46	58	46	–
1987	95	101	97	–	89	100	101	–	74	102	97	–	50	61	46	–
1988	95	101	99	–	90	100	101	–	74	102	–	–	51	63	45	–
1989	95	101	98	–	91	100	101	–	75	103	–	105	51	65	46	–
1990	100	101	98	101	93	100	101	98	74	103	–	97	51	65	47	–
1991	98	101	100	101	94	100	101	98	75	103	–	97	53	71	49	–
1992	98	102	100	101	95	100	101	98	78	103	–	98	53	76	51	115
1993	98	102	100	–	96	100	101	–	79	102	90	–	52	81	58	–
1994	97	102	101	–	97	100	101	–	84	101	90	–	–	82	56	–
1995	98	102	100	–	99	100	101	–	87	111	–	–	–	–	57	–
1996	97	102	102	–	100	100	101	–	89	–	89	–	53	–	57	–
1997	–	–	103	–	100	100	101	–	90	–	–	–	–	–	62	–

Source: Calculated from UNESCO Institute for Statistics (2002). Indicators. Electronic database, http://www.uis.unesco.org/en/stats/centre.htm, accessed March, 2003.

poor socioeconomic backgrounds. Yet, their fieldwork highlights an interesting contradiction: even in a country where gender gaps have unambiguously narrowed and are now slight, parental attitudes about the utility of education for girls and boys in the labor market are still shaped by gender. These findings suggest that where gender differences in basic education access have narrowed, there may be potential value in shifting the lens to consider possible gender differences in the school-work nexus.

Finally, the paper emphasizes that some transitions are harder than others. In Nang Rong, the barriers girls face for the transition to lower secondary are much higher than the barriers faced by boys, but the female disadvantage then becomes an advantage in making the transition from lower to upper secondary, especially among the youngest cohort of youth. The difference in mechanisms of inequality embedded within institutions operating at different levels of schooling is a point highlighted in other papers, and one to which we will return in the discussion below.

SCHOOL EXPANSION AND INEQUALITY IN KOREA

Korea offers a fascinating case study of how remarkable school expansion can coincide with the persistence of stratification and allocation processes. Park's analysis of educational stratification in Korea contributes a new and convincing case to the growing body of research suggesting that educational expansion does not reduce the relative advantages of elite children over children from less-privileged backgrounds (for a review, see Hannum & Buchmann, 2003). He looks across 50 years of cohorts of males born between 1921 and 1970. His paper traces massive expansion at primary, middle, and secondary school levels across the period under study. Yet, strikingly, he shows little progress in reducing the effect of parents' background on children's attainment. In fact, he shows that father's occupation actually becomes a stronger predictor of university entry.

In interpreting his results, Park considers the effects of public policy, because the state's behavior has changed over time and varied across levels of the school system. While South Korea's policies have generally focused on expansion, certain shifts have left their mark. For example, Park notes that the abolition of entrance examinations facilitated rapid growth in middle school education. He attributes a decline in the importance of father's occupation for middle school completion among the youngest cohort in part to the dramatic increase in middle school education that resulted from the abolition of exams. In its careful treatment of policy, Park's study contributes to a growing number of comparative and international studies that have begun to link educational stratification not only to broad processes of development, but also to institutional structures such as explicit policy interventions and the organizational structure of schools.

Park's study also highlights the potential role of institutional organization in another way, by suggesting that the level and type of schooling are important. For example, the rising importance of father's education for university entrance does not apply to junior college transitions. Further, as Park acknowledges, there is some possibility that the risk pool of secondary graduates represents a changing mix of vocational versus academic students. This shifting mix might influence the observed portrait of unequal transitions to tertiary-level schooling. Park's findings hint that the type and quality of schools are probably crucial elements of stratification; they are particularly salient in Korea at the secondary and higher levels of schooling, where branching begins in earnest. Institutional attributes and mechanisms such as these are obscured by data constraints in many existing stratification studies and are deserving of further research.

Finally, as Park notes, the low level of female labor force participation in Korea precludes his use of a labor force survey to investigate either gender stratification trends or differences in the pattern of parental influence on children's schooling by gender. This data constraint is substantively important. Korea's female economic activity rate, while rising, remains substantially lower than those of any of the other Asian countries represented in this volume (Fig. 1). This pattern is striking in the context of virtually full enrollments at the primary and secondary levels in Korea and dramatic gains in tertiary enrollment. Korea's tertiary gross enrollment ratios rose from 15% in 1980 to a high of 68% in 1997. This latter figure places Korea first among the four countries examined in this volume (Table 1). Yet by 1992, the latest year for which gender-specific data for all four countries was available, Korea was last in terms of gender parity: women's tertiary gross enrollment ratio was just 51% of men's (Table 2).

This contradiction highlights some of the subtleties of gender differences that may persist even in the face of rapid economic growth, large-scale educational expansion, and widespread female access to basic and secondary education. In Korea, dramatic gender differences in the labor outcomes of schooling suggest that the purpose of schooling must also differ by gender, particularly beyond the stage of basic skill acquisition. As with the analysis by Curran et al., the case of Korea points to the need to pursue the relationship of schooling to employment when considering gendered forms of stratification.

COLLEGE CHOICE IN JAPAN

Ono argues that indicators of college quality and status help to predict how students select and migrate into "higher quality" universities. Family income does affect which students pursue university education. However, economic factors fade once the decision to attend is made, and the pursuit of college quality and status override cost considerations. This is a solid institutional story, as Ono argues that institutional reputation and "quality" are important drivers of individual decision making and migration.

Three interesting insights stem from Ono's line of analysis. First and most obviously, this paper focuses explicitly on an issue hinted at in the Park paper: that school type and quality are important elements of the stratification process at higher levels of schooling. Given that participation in tertiary education is increasingly widespread in Japan and the other Asian countries (Table 1), the nature of the institutions that students are enrolling in becomes increasingly important. Ono's work suggests the fruitfulness of reorienting strategies in social mobility research so as to explicitly consider quality measures and families' constructed meanings of institutional status.

Second, Ono's work is grounded in the notion that the obsession for college quality – a trait he considers particular to Japanese culture – drives his results. This interpretation underscores the potential role of culturally-specific factors as drivers of stratification. Yet, the degree to which cultural factors play a direct role in individual decisions about colleges is not fully clear. For example, perhaps the unrelenting pursuit of college quality stems not from a cultural orientation toward quality, but from accurately-perceived differences in the economic consequences of attending low- or high-status universities. In either case, Ono's work suggests the possibility that the value attached to institutional quality, whether by the labor market or by individuals seeking higher education, may vary significantly across national settings.

Finally, like the Curran et al. paper, Ono's work highlights the role of migration as an element of educational decision-making. Whereas Curran et al. make links between educational decisions at lower levels of schooling and labor migration, Ono highlights educational migration as an element of decision making for college students. These papers draw attention to the value of further study of migration-education linkages. They also point out that migration operates differently at different levels of education.

NEW AVENUES TO EXPLORE EDUCATIONAL INEQUALITY

Taken together, these four Asia-focused chapters offer novel insights for future directions in the comparative study of stratification. First, attributes of institutional organization and quality, invisible in many stratification studies, constitute critical elements of educational opportunity. Short and Sun's paper suggests the potential importance of knowing more about how fledgling systems of early education function as part of the stratification regime. Park's work suggests that data designed to better pick up the branching that occurs within secondary and higher education is essential for understanding changing inequalities in progress through the school system. Ono's work illuminates the potential theoretical leverage for stratification research that might emerge from increased attention to institutional quality and prestige at the tertiary level.

Together, these studies highlight the limitations imposed by the traditional individualistic focus that has characterized many stratification and mobility studies. They suggest the fruitfulness of increased attention to measuring aspects of institutions, along with individuals, to more fully understand systems of stratification and their changes.

A second contribution of these papers is to reiterate the finding that stratification can emerge at different points in the attainment process, in sometimes different and sometimes similar ways. The research of Curran et al. specifically finds that gender differences in transitions operate differently at different levels of schooling. Short and Sun's work posits the intriguing, and largely unexplored, possibility that some of the inequalities observed in basic education in China may have roots in the formal organization of early childhood. Park finds different trends in the effects of father's education and occupation at different levels of schooling, and Ono's work highlights educational migration as a unique element of school choice that comes into play at the tertiary level. These examples highlight the complexities of inequality across levels of schooling. They point to the value of fuller scrutiny of particular mechanisms or policies at each level for advancing theories of educational stratification.

A third insight that emerges from these papers is that inequalities other than those associated with socioeconomic status may operate very differently, and a lack of focus on these other lines of difference impedes our understanding of broader stratification patterns. Short and Sun's work highlights spatial dimensions of educational inequality, and an interaction between gender and poverty. Curran et al.'s fieldwork suggests that gender and socioeconomic status have quite distinct implications for families' educational decisions. Park's work, together with Korea's trajectory of educational expansion with persisting gender disparity at high levels of education and in the labor force, suggests that socioeconomic status and gender also operate differently in Korea. These examples reiterate that the focus on socio-economic status and mobility that characterizes much of the comparative stratification research does not necessarily generalize to other important stratifiers, such as location of residence within spatial hierarchies, gender, or by extension, ethnicity. These and other dimensions of inequality may be as fundamental as socioeconomic inequality in many societies, and are worthy of more determined attention within stratification research.

A final point illuminated by these studies is that, while certain dimensions of educational inequality emerge across societies, some dimensions emerge much more strongly in particular nations or groups of nations. As the preceding paragraph suggests, some of these differences emerge via national differences in fundamental dimensions of inequality. Also important is the potential for different considerations to influence educational choices across countries, an argument made by Ono in his discussion of Japan's obsession with college quality. Curran et al. also provide a persuasive example of the different considerations that may come into play in educational decisions across national settings. How family labor migration and the future migration of current students affect educational opportunities is a question of little relevance for many advanced industrial societies. However, labor migration is a potentially crucial element of the educational decision-making process for families in many impoverished developing countries. These examples, together with the other papers in this section, illustrate the larger point that cross-national similarities and differences in stratification systems are best revealed when authors are able to combine comparative paradigms and grounded knowledge of local societies.

NOTES

1. For Japan, the 50% figure represents 1996 data.
2. These countries include Albania, Bosnia and Herzegovina, Cape Verde, El Salvador, Jamaica, Jordan, Nicaragua, Samoa and Yemen (United Nations, 2003).

REFERENCES

Fuller, B., & Strath, A. (2001). The child-care and preschool workforce: Demographics, earnings, and unequal distribution. *Educational Evaluation and Policy Analysis*, *23*, 122–137.

Hannum, E. (2002a). Modernization versus market transition? Explaining educational gender inequality in reform-era rural China. Paper presented at the Annual Meetings of the American Sociological Association, Chicago.

Hannum, E. (2002b, forthcoming). Poverty and basic education in rural China: Communities, households, and girls' and boys' enrollment. *Comparative Education Review*.

Hannum, E., & Buchmann, C. (2003). *The consequences of global educational expansion: Social science perspectives*. Occasional Paper of the American Academy of Arts and Sciences Project on Universal Basic and Secondary Education, http://www.amacad.org/publications/monographs/Ubase.pdf

Kandel, W., & Kao, G. (2000). Shifting orientations: How U.S. labor migration affects children's aspirations in Mexican migrant communities. *Social Science Quarterly*, *81*(1), 16–32.

Knodel, J. (1997). The closing of the gender gap in schooling: The case of Thailand. *Comparative Education Review*, *33*(1), 61–81.

Knodel, J., & Jones, G. (1996). Post-Cairo population policy: Does promoting girls' schooling miss the mark? *Population and Development Review*, *22*(4), 683–702.

UNESCO Institute for Statistics (2002). Indicators. Electronic database, http://www.uis.unesco.org/en/stats/centre.htm accessed March 2003.

United Nations (2002). United Nations Common Database, http://unstats.un.org, series 4270: Economic activity rate by sex, 13 age groups, 1950–2010 (ILO) (204 countries, 1950–2010), accessed March 2003.

United Nations (2003). International Migration 2002. New York: United Nations Population Division, Department of Economic and Social Affairs. http://www.un.org/esa/population/publications/ittmig2002/Migration2002.pdf, accessed March 2003.

West, J., Denton, K., & Reaney, L. (2000). The kindergarten year. Washington, DC: National Center for Educational Statistics, Working Paper.

Wrigley, J. (1999). Hiring a nanny: The limits of private solutions to public problems. *Annals of the American Academy of Political and Social Science*, *563*, 162–174.

EGALITARIANISM VERSUS SOCIAL REPRODUCTION: STRATIFICATION IN EASTERN EUROPE

Raymond Sin-Kwok Wong

ABSTRACT

This study examines educational inequalities under socialism in Bulgaria, Czechoslovakia, Hungary, Poland, and Russia to assess the extent to which egalitarianism was achieved and whether there was restratification after the common retreat from egalitarian ideology and practices since the 1970s. Exploring the extent of parental influences in three key educational outcomes and their changes in four birth cohorts, the study finds remarkable stability across cohorts and across transitions. Contrary to expectation, the net effect of parental social capital (communist party membership status) is prominent only in the former Soviet Russia and Bulgaria, moderate in Czechoslovakia, and negligible in Hungary and Poland. On the other hand, the effect of parental cultural capital is consistently strong but its influence is somewhat weaker at higher transitions. Its inclusion also dramatically reduces the effect of parental education and father's occupation, suggesting that a significant extent of intergenerational transmission of educational inequality is mediated through parental cultural capital rather than human capital per se.

Inequality Across Societies: Families, Schools and Persisting Stratification
Research in Sociology of Education, Volume 14, 139–170
(Formerly Research in Sociology of Education and Socialization)

ISSN: 1479-3539/doi:10.1016/S1479-3539(03)14007-4

INTRODUCTION

Educational reforms were significant in almost every country after World War II, resulting in major expansions of educational institutions and increased opportunities for those previously excluded from the educational system. Such changes were particularly pronounced in state-socialist societies, where the educational system was used explicitly as a major vehicle to promote egalitarianism and induce changes in the social structure. In short, socialist education was designed, at least in theory, to be a "social leveler," part of a deliberate social engineering to pursue communist goals.

Driven by the Marxist ideals to realize human potential and eliminate class-based inequalities, as well as the practical need for an educated labor force to build communism, unified school systems (closely resembling the Soviet system) were instituted throughout Eastern Europe after World War II to provide all citizens with a free education. The new constitutions granted every citizen the same opportunity of education regardless of social origin, sex, nationality, or religion.

However, since schooling was seen as a vehicle to create greater mobility and equality, socialist ideology also justified regulating access to education. Thus, many socialist governments had programs or policies of active and explicit interventions in school admissions. Children from formerly privileged classes were often treated unfavorably in the higher education selection process despite academic achievement that equaled or surpassed that of other students. In fact, strong preference was usually given to children of workers and cooperative farmers. Such a "principled class approach" in educational selection embodied the socialist regime's drive towards egalitarianism, especially in the early years of socialist transition (e.g. see Ulč, 1978 and Szelényi, 1998 for a discussion of policies implemented in Czechoslovakia and Hungary).

Whether such efforts really led to more egalitarian educational attainment, however, is an open question.[1] It has been argued that the communist party's monopoly of power and active intervention in all aspects of social life made it a major stratifying agent and created a "new class" under socialism (Djilas, 1957). Furthermore, there was a general retreat from the "principled class approach" in most countries by the mid-1970s, significantly undermining the claim of socialist egalitarianism.[2] The abolition of reverse discrimination, together with market reforms and active recruitment of professionals and technical experts into the power structure, suggested the possibility of restratification in later periods even if a more egalitarian system was established earlier during the socialist transition (Kelley & Klein, 1977; Konrád & Szelényi, 1979; Matějů, 1993; Parkin, 1971; Szelényi, 1998; Szelényi & Aschaffenburg, 1993; Wong & Hauser, 1992).

With repeated deliberate and dramatic shifts, the socialist experiment in educational stratification left tantalizing questions about its effects and legacy. To what extent was egalitarianism achieved? Did restratification return, and did the degree of social reproduction increase after the retreat from egalitarian ideology and practices in the 1970s? These remain topics of contention years after socialism was all but abandoned. Central to these questions is the extent to which social origin continued to play a role in major educational transitions during different phases of socialism. While this issue has been explored fruitfully in some individual countries, it has yet to be addressed substantially in a comparative study of educational stratification under socialism.

This study offers such an investigation through a cross-national analysis that incorporates cross-cohort comparisons of educational transitions that are highly competitive and consequential.[3] It analyzes the effects of parental background in three key educational outcomes, and their changes in four birth cohorts, under five socialist regimes in Eastern Europe, namely, Bulgaria, Czechoslovakia, Hungary, Poland, and Russia.[4]

Besides the two commonly investigated outcomes (attendance in secondary educational institutions and entry into the tertiary level), the study also examines the differentiation of secondary curricula into vocational and academic tracks, with their consequential diploma and non-diploma outcomes. We factor this into our analysis of inequalities, because their differential outcomes perform an important gatekeeper role in the entry to tertiary education, one of the key competitive transitions. While a secondary diploma is a prerequisite for entry into tertiary education, in most East European countries there are still large numbers of people without one. Therefore, we also look at how social origins may affect earning a high school diploma, and what this tells us about the social reproduction of educational inequality under socialism.

In considering parental background, this study also goes beyond the variables commonly derived from status attainment literature to reflect its multidimensional nature. A typically omitted variable that has been shown in recent works to be significant in educational attainment is parental social capital, of which communist party membership is arguably the key element under socialism (Hanley, 2001; Wong, 1998). Given the party apparatus' prominence in all social institutions, an association with its organized networks would provide valuable resources for parents. Thus, party membership not only conferred power and privileges on the holders themselves, but could also secure benefits for the holders' offspring.

Another often overlooked variable is parental cultural capital, or activities parents provide their children that cultivate and foster values and cultural preparedness for educational success. Parental cultural capital provides critical educational resources that aid children's learning motivation, educational aspirations, and academic performance (see Bourdieu & Passerson, 1977; Lamont & Lareau, 1988; Lareau, 1987; Wong, 1998 for details),[5] and complements the familiar variables of parental education and occupation.

An expanded view of parental background, along with new data on the relative importance of these two components and how they have changed over time, will illumine not only the degree of egalitarianism but also how various forces of egalitarianism and social reproduction fared under socialism. For example, it is entirely plausible for some of the previously observed socioeconomic background effects to disappear or weaken considerably once other factors are studied simultaneously. Thus, the multidimensional conception of family background used in this study can cast a new light on previous findings about educational inequalities under socialism. By applying these measures consistently to all five countries, our analysis may reveal further similarities and country-specific differences in socialist educational stratification.

EGALITARIANISM UNDER SOCIALISM?

In an early affirmation of the achievement of socialist egalitarianism, Dobson (1977, p. 264) argued that despite the persistence of educational inequalities, access to higher education in Russia was considerably more egalitarian than in countries in Western Europe, and rather similar to the United States. This was challenged and refined in a particularly influential study by Simkus and Andorka (1982). Through an investigation of educational inequality in Hungary between 1923 and 1973, Simkus and Andorka found that the transition to socialism led to a decline in the effects of social origins on educational attainment primarily in the earlier educational transitions, but had relatively little effects on later transitions. They attributed the decline in earlier transitions to Hungary's aggressive and successful educational policies during the 1950s, particularly the "... effectiveness of both the elimination of a class-based dual structure of primary education and administrative control over the process of social selection as a means of substantially reducing socioeconomic inequalities in the allocation of schooling" (p. 740).

Later works found similar declining effects of social origins in earlier transitions (to cite a few, Matějů, 1986, 1993; Peschar & Matějů, 1988 for Czechoslovakia; Peschar & Popping, 1986; Szelényi, 1998; Szelényi & Aschaffenburg, 1993 for Hungary; Heyns & Białecki, 1993; Peschar, Popping & Mach, 1986 for Poland), but they tended to emphasize the remarkable stability over time in the transitions to higher levels of education. They pointed out that most of the changes at lower-level transitions could be attributed to the rapid expansion of slots at these levels, while relative educational opportunity remained stable throughout the socialist era.

That social origins not only continued to affect educational attainment but also found new channels of influence under socialism was suggested by Szelényi and Aschaffenberg (1993) and Szelényi (1998), who reported evidence of a resurgence of educational inequality in Hungary during the 1980s. Although the restratification process might have resulted from an early abandonment of the reverse discrimination policy in school admissions, Szelényi and her associates believed that the key might lie in the act of deliberate intervention itself. Specifically, state and party intervention created ample room for the "new class" to use informal ties, bribes, and other extra-legal activities to secure places for their children (see also Matějů, 1993). Bureaucratic measures that were originally designed to open up the educational system to talented children of workers and peasants soon became channels that enabled the new elites and their successors to circumvent meritocratic competition. Thus, access to higher education once again became ascriptive and dependent on the social capital of the family.

More recent works also appear to lend support to this argument. Wong (1998) found that after controlling for other measures of family environment – such as father's education, financial capital, and cultural capital – father's social capital communist party membership had a net positive influence on individual's educational attainment in the former Czechoslovakia. Similarly, Hanley (2001) found that having a father who was a communist party member greatly increased one's odds of attaining secondary education, though membership had little impact in the progression to the tertiary level. By studying inter-cohort changes, he further discovered that the impact of communist party membership in Czechoslovakia was stronger among those educated in the post-1968 era.

Noting that the social class composition of students at the secondary and tertiary levels had remained the same at various times, Hanley disputed the validity of earlier claims such as Simkus and Andorka's that the reduction in origin-based inequalities was due primarily to the effectiveness of class-based quota policies. Instead, he attributed the observed decline to changes in structural opportunities because of the rapid expansion in the secondary level. Finally, Gerber (2000) found that parental communist party membership in Russia played a significant role in the completion of secondary grammar education and entry at the tertiary level, not only for all post-World War II cohorts, but also in the contemporary post-communist setting.

Such continuing, and sometimes even increasing, importance of family background at higher educational transitions may seem peculiar and puzzling. It departs from the universal waning coefficient pattern found in other industrial societies, as documented in the 18 studies collected by Shavit and Blossfeld (1993), which show a decline across transitions in the logit coefficients of nearly every cohort in each country. However, it is entirely consistent with the maximally maintained inequality (*MMI*) thesis advanced by Raftery and Hout (1993) and Hout, Raftery and Bell (1993). Postulating that parental background may continue to be influential at certain critical competitive educational transitions, the *MMI* thesis can be interpreted as a variant of the universal waning coefficient pattern. It features a more dynamic conception of the relationship among educational expansion, social origins, and educational attainment.

The thesis has four major components. First, all things being equal, the expansion of secondary and higher education will reflect increased demand generated by two typical forces: population growth and social origin upgrading. Second, if for some reason educational opportunity expands faster than the demand attributable to social origin upgrading, then transition rates for all social origins increase, but the increase occurs in such a way that the class odds ratios in all the transitions are preserved. Third, if the completion of a given level of education becomes universal for upper-class individuals, then the effects of social background at that transition will decline over time. Finally, the falling effects of social background can be reversed if external conditions change (for example, the effects of social class can increase if public support for education is reduced, see Hout, Raftery & Bell, 1993 for details). This dynamic framework makes the *MMI* thesis very useful in explaining cross-cohort variation in social background effects, in both capitalist and socialist countries.

Under socialism, many Eastern European countries saw a vast expansion at the secondary and tertiary levels of education, but the rate of expansion in the former far outstripped the latter. As enrollments at the secondary level grew, they created a bottleneck at the transition to the tertiary level because it was not expanding fast enough to accommodate all qualified students. As a result, the effects of social origins on the transition may actually have increased over time at the tertiary level. This has indeed been documented by Gerber and Hout (1995) in the former Soviet Russia. Whether the same is true in other socialist countries has yet to be determined empirically.

As seen in the above discussion, past research on educational stratification under socialism mostly focused on a single country. This approach has enriched our knowledge of individual countries, but yielded only sketchy information about commonality and differences among the socialist regimes. Without a consistent framework of analysis, findings from studies of individual countries cannot be systematically compared to assess whether there are general characteristics and similar trends in socialist educational stratification.

The five-country study reported here attempts to fill in this gap in knowledge. By using a consistent framework to analyze the effects of parental background in three key educational transitions/outcomes for four birth cohorts under socialism in Bulgaria, Czechoslovakia, Hungary, Poland, and Russia, the study seeks to determine if and when egalitarianism was a significant feature of educational stratification under the various socialist regimes. It also investigates whether and how family background continued to affect educational attainment despite the attempt at egalitarianism. Building on previous findings from studies of individual countries, our analysis also specifically addresses whether parental membership in the communist party played a significant role in educational attainment under socialism. With comparable results from five countries, we would be in a better position to advance a general picture of the socialist educational stratification system.

DATA AND METHODS

The data for this study came from the 1993 survey of *Social Stratification in Eastern Europe After 1989 (SSEE)*, coordinated by Ivan Szelényi and Donald J. Treiman. Based on detailed individual histories, the study analyzes secondary and tertiary educational attainment of individuals aged 25–34 in 1960, 1970, 1980, and 1988.[6] It includes data on four birth cohorts (1926–1935, 1936–1945, 1946–1955, and 1956–1963) that completed their primary education during the following time periods: 1940–1949, 1950–1959, 1960–1969, and 1970–1977. Occasionally there is a slight variation in the actual time frame in cases where the educational structure was changed. For instance, the length of primary education in Czechoslovakia was nine years between 1948 and 1974, but only eight years after 1974. Most respondents were educated under the socialist regime, except those who were less educated in the oldest cohort in Bulgaria, Czechoslovakia, Hungary, and Poland.

An individual's ultimate educational attainment is not used to construct the dependent variables because it may understate the effectiveness of socialist educational policies. Socialist citizens often improved their education over time while working full-time in the labor force. This was particularly true of citizens who experienced the socialist transition. The underlying causes of additional education might reflect sponsored mobility by the government or the communist party, individual efforts to increase the chances of upward mobility, or simply individual interest in intellectual pursuits.

Given that most sponsored mobility occurred during the early years of an individual work career, an assessment of individual educational attainment at an early age (mid-20s and early-30s) should maximize the effects of deliberate state policies as vehicles in promoting university attendance among students from working and other underprivileged backgrounds. The present treatment would also reduce biases due to the privileged classes' ability to obtain tertiary education once discriminatory policies were either relaxed or no longer enforced years later.

(see Deng & Treiman, 1997 for the experience of China, which may serve as a useful illustration.)

The following variables are used to indicate respondent's family environment: (1) the maximum of father's and mother's education (measured in years);[7] (2) father's occupation at age 14 (measured in international socioeconomic index, ISEI); (3) whether either parent was self-employed at age 14; (4) whether either parent had joined the communist party; and (5) a composite measure of parental cultural capital, which is derived from eight indicators measuring how often the respondent's parents participated in the following activities when the respondent was growing up: (a) visiting art museums or art exhibits (PMUSEUM); (b) attending ballet, opera, theater, or concert (PPERF); (c) listening to classical music at home (PMUSIC); (d) reading serious books such as history, biography, science, or literature (PREAD); (e) going to the library (PLIB); (f) having a dictionary or encyclopedia at home (PDICT); (g) having atlases at home (PATLAS); and (h) number of books at home (PBOOKS).

Results from principal component factor analysis indicate that only one factor can be extracted from the eight indicators (using eigenvalues greater than 1 as the cutoff). The factor loadings are 0.716, 0.719, 0.606, 0.733, 0.549, 0.599, 0.537, and 0.767, respectively, and are used to construct factor scores of parental cultural capital. To maximize the utility of the constructed variable, an imputation method is used to assign values to those cases that have missing values, using father's education, mother's education, father's occupation, and their missing dummies as predictors. About 18.4% of the sample has imputed values of cultural capital. The measure is then standardized to have a mean of 0 and a standard deviation of 1 within each country.[8]

Other independent variables include female, number of siblings, cohorts (with the 1926–1935 cohort as the reference category), and secondary grammar education (useful only in the last transition, university attendance).[9] It should be noted that the inclusion of secondary grammar or *gymnasium* education into the statistical modeling dramatically improved the goodness-of-fit of the models in all countries.[10] Once secondary grammar education is controlled, the effect of female generally becomes negative, except for Czechoslovakia (reduced) and Russia (no change).

This should not be surprising, given the widespread phenomenon of the "feminization of the gymnasia," which means that there were more qualified women than men to enter university but the gender composition of university entrants did not reflect the composition of the pool. For those variables that have missing values (such as father's and mother's education), the mean substitution method is used, with dummy variables indicating their missing status entered into the statistical models as well.[11] Appendix A lists the total number of valid cases for each transition, as well as the descriptive statistics of the variables used in the analysis.

Logistic regression models are applied to each educational outcome and to each individual country separately. The following strategy is used to facilitate the search for the best model for each outcome: first, the main effects model is estimated; interaction terms are then added one by one to the model and the results compared; those interactions that are significant at the 0.10 level or lower are added simultaneously into the model; and, finally, all non-significant interaction parameters are deleted in a stepwise fashion using the backward selection strategy. In addition, the *BIC* statistic (Raftery, 1995) is used to decide whether particular interaction effects should be omitted. Given that the *BIC* statistic penalizes models with greater complexity relative to sample size, this is a conservative strategy. At the same time, we do not want to capitalize on chance when the sample size is relatively large. Interactions pertaining to gender and cohort differences, as well as interactions among parental characteristics are considered (Gerber & Hout, 1995).

GENERAL EDUCATIONAL TRENDS IN EASTERN EUROPE

Before we investigate how family environment affected educational inequality in the five East European countries, Table 1 summarizes the educational attainment of men and women aged 25–34 in 1960, 1970, 1980, and 1988. The results confirm our observation about universal educational upgrading in all five countries. In 1960, a substantial proportion of individuals had only a primary education or less (49%, 68%, 39%, 66%, 52% in Russia, Bulgaria, Czechoslovakia, Hungary, and Poland, respectively) and, except in Poland, less than 10% received post-secondary training. The situation improved dramatically over time. By 1988, less than 20% of Bulgarians and Hungarians had primary or less education, whereas the proportion in Russia, Czechoslovakia, and Poland was about 10%. Much of the educational upgrading, however, was at the secondary but not tertiary level. Although the proportion of individuals with post-secondary education doubled since 1960, the increase occurred mainly during the 1970s and had either remained relatively stable (Russia and Poland) or had stable growth rates (Bulgaria and Czechoslovakia).

Growth in secondary education, on the other hand, was phenomenal. The expansion path, however, shows considerable variation across countries: in Russia, there was significant expansion of secondary academic education; in Bulgaria and Czechoslovakia, expansion was more notable in technical secondary education; whereas in Hungary and Poland, there was considerable expansion of both vocational (non-diploma) and technical (diploma) secondary education.

Table 1. Individual Educational Attainment for Ages 25–34.

	1960		1970		1980		1988	
	N	%	*N*	%	*N*	%	*N*	%
(a) Russia								
Primary-incomplete	186	30.34	71	9.57	45	4.26	16	1.91
Primary-complete	114	18.60	135	18.19	139	13.15	69	8.25
Vocational	58	9.46	83	11.19	91	8.61	78	9.33
Secondary-technical	123	20.07	150	20.22	235	22.23	174	20.81
Secondary-academic	53	8.65	140	18.87	281	26.58	290	34.69
Post-secondary	79	12.89	163	21.97	266	25.17	209	25.00
Total	613	100.00	742	100.00	1057	100.00	836	100.00
(b) Bulgaria								
Primary-incomplete	181	24.49	93	12.05	62	6.49	23	3.52
Primary-complete	320	43.30	264	34.20	207	21.65	98	15.01
Vocational	31	4.19	89	11.53	106	11.09	54	8.27
Secondary-technical	37	5.01	111	14.38	278	29.08	251	38.44
Secondary-academic	101	13.67	115	14.90	137	14.33	102	15.62
Post-secondary	69	9.34	100	12.95	166	17.36	125	19.14
Total	739	100.00	772	100.00	956	100.00	653	100.00
(c) Czechoslovakia								
Primary-incomplete	152	10.08	58	3.37	28	1.17	9	0.56
Primary-complete	439	29.11	359	20.87	346	14.47	151	9.38
Vocational	546	36.21	695	40.41	1029	43.04	662	41.14
Secondary-technical	144	9.55	307	17.85	530	22.17	427	26.54
Secondary-academic	78	5.17	102	5.93	144	6.02	86	5.34
Post-secondary	149	9.88	199	11.57	314	13.13	274	17.03
Total	1508	100.00	1720	100.00	2391	100.00	1609	100.00
(d) Hungary								
Primary-incomplete	220	40.00	79	11.35	29	3.31	14	2.24
Primary-complete	146	26.55	207	29.74	210	23.97	102	17.03
Vocational	88	16.00	178	25.57	270	30.82	223	37.23
Secondary-technical	34	6.18	88	12.64	153	17.47	117	19.53
Secondary-academic	29	5.27	72	10.34	125	14.27	53	8.85
Post-secondary	33	6.00	72	10.34	89	10.16	90	15.03
Total	550	100.00	696	100.00	876	100.00	599	100.00
(e) Poland								
Primary-incomplete	102	14.76	10	1.39	8	0.72	4	0.49
Primary-complete	256	37.05	254	35.23	209	18.78	82	10.10
Vocational	75	10.85	109	15.12	305	27.40	290	35.71
Secondary-technical	75	10.85	128	17.75	247	22.19	200	24.63
Secondary-academic	70	10.13	59	8.18	83	7.46	47	5.79
Post-secondary	113	16.35	161	22.33	261	23.45	189	23.28
Total	691	100.00	721	100.00	1113	100.00	812	100.00

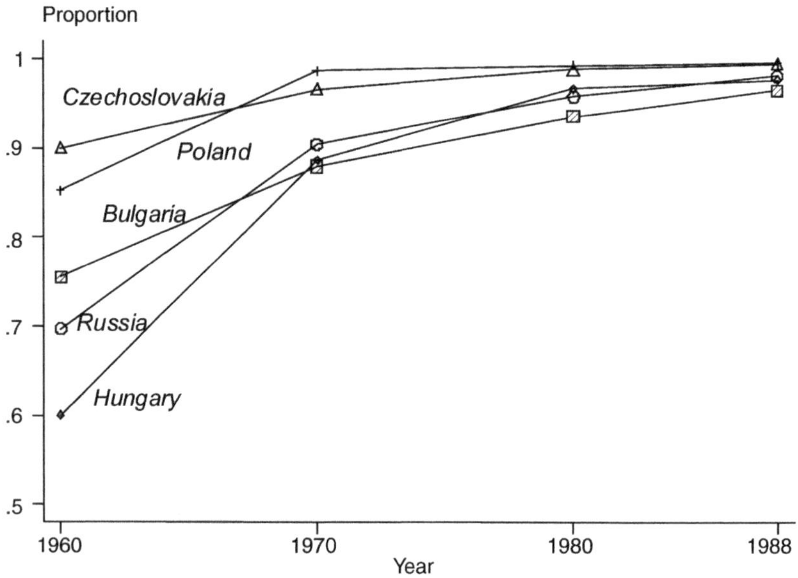

Fig. 1. Proportion of Completed Primary.

Despite such variation, it is obvious that in all five countries, the pace of expansion at the secondary level far outstripped expansion at the tertiary level, thereby creating severe bottlenecks for qualified individuals and consequently making tertiary and (in some countries) academic secondary training highly competitive.

Figures 1–4 summarize the trends in transition rates of various educational outcomes for the four birth cohorts in 1960, 1970, 1980, and 1988. While the proportion of the population that had at least completed primary education differed widely among the countries initially (90% in Czechoslovakia, 85% in Poland, 75% in Bulgaria, 70% in Russia, and 60% in Hungary), the gaps narrowed considerably over time (see Fig. 1). By 1988, the completion rate was almost universal (over 92%). The improvement was particularly dramatic for Hungary. Since the completion rate was close to saturation and socioeconomic differentials would probably be relatively minor, there will be no further examination of this particular educational outcome.

Similar cross-national convergence is also observed in the transition from completed primary to attended secondary. Secondary school transition rates improved dramatically in all five countries over time (Fig. 2). This is, of course, due to the rapid expansion of slots at the secondary level. Among those who completed

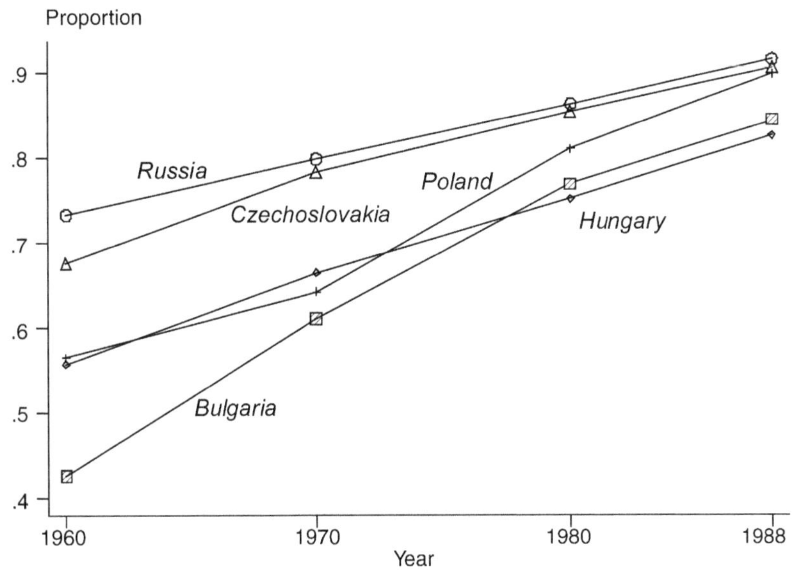

Fig. 2. Proportion of Attended Secondary.

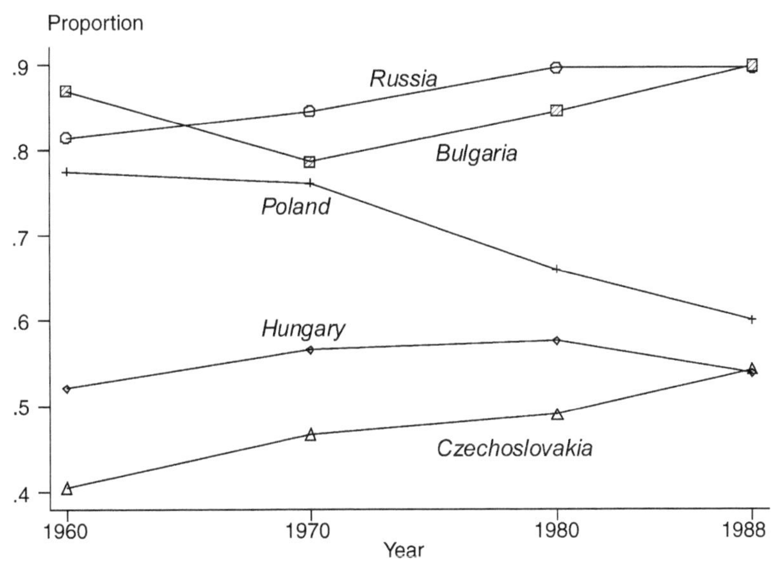

Fig. 3. Proportion of Diploma Secondary.

primary education, however, secondary attendance was still not universal. For the oldest (1926–1935) cohort, transition rates were the highest in Russia and Czechoslovakia (high 70s and low 80s), medium in Hungary and Poland (55), and the lowest in Bulgaria (43). For the youngest (1956–1963) cohort, the transition rates were between 75 and 88%. Thus, a sizable proportion of socialist citizens still started to work immediately after completing primary schooling.

Those who attended secondary schools faced alternative tracks: vocational without diploma, vocational (or technical) with diploma, and secondary grammar (or *gymnasium*) with diploma. Since only diploma holders could apply for university admission, the distinction between diploma and non-diploma secondary education was critical. So was the distinction between vocational with diploma and secondary grammar education, since the latter conferred greater success in university attendance, as our statistical analyses later show. Unlike the two educational outcomes discussed above, the pattern of secondary track assignments varies considerably across countries.

As Fig. 3 illustrates, an overwhelming majority of Bulgarians and Russians received diploma (vocational or academic) rather than non-diploma education, while the proportions were substantially lower in Czechoslovakia, Hungary, and Poland. In the latter three countries, the relative share of diploma education even shows a decreasing trend. Considering that close to three-quarters of Polish secondary students received a diploma in 1960 and 1970 but only 60–65% did in the 1980s, the Polish government appears to have increased the number of seats in non-degree vocational and technical tracks in order to deal with the severe labor shortage and demand for unskilled and semi-skilled workers created by a rapid push toward industrialization. With an increasing number of individuals completing primary and attending secondary education, the rate of expansion of secondary diploma education certainly did not keep pace with increasing demand in Czechoslovakia, Hungary, and Poland.

Transition rates at the university level also show considerable cross-national variation (see Fig. 4). In Poland, university transition rates remained relatively stable across birth cohorts at slightly over 43%. But given the decline over time in the pool of qualified students (the proportion with secondary diploma education), the university population in Poland was actually not expanding as fast as those in the other East European countries. For the other four countries, the university transition trend was generally downward, with minor increases for the youngest cohort in Hungary and Czechoslovakia in 1988. Although the increase in Hungary may appear large, it is partly due to a decline in the qualified pool (see Fig. 3) combined with an expansion at the tertiary level.

In sum, the trend clearly indicates a bottleneck created by a rapid expansion at the secondary level. The cross-national variation in the proportion of secondary

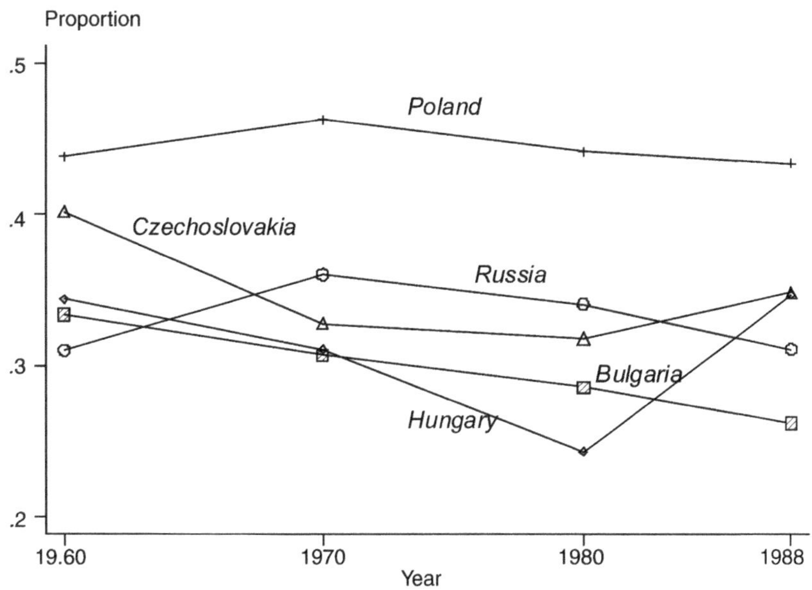

Fig. 4. Proportion of Attended University.

education diplomas further hints that these may have become a key competitive prize in Czechoslovakia, Hungary, and Poland. If the *MMI* thesis is correct, one would expect the influence of family background in this educational attainment to be particularly strong in these three countries.

EDUCATIONAL INEQUALITIES IN RUSSIA

The results of our analyses for Russia are shown in Table 2. Russian women were under-represented in secondary schooling in all cohorts: the odds for a Russian woman to attend secondary education was only about 0.41 times that of her male counterpart and this disadvantage persisted across cohorts. Only women with well-educated parents were able to circumvent the gender disadvantage in receiving education beyond the primary level. Each additional year in parental education increased the odds of women's secondary attendance by 13%. For those who did receive some form of secondary training, Russian women were 1.39 times as likely as men to receive diploma rather than non-diploma secondary education. However, among those eligible for tertiary training, there was no gender disparity in attendance.

Table 2. Logistic Regression of Educational Transitions in Russia.

Independent Variable	Dependent Variable: Attended Secondary	Diploma Secondary	Attended University
Intercept	1.387***	0.668#	−3.320***
Female	−0.893***	0.326**	0.044
Sibling	−0.027	−0.013	−0.044
Parent education (years)	−0.006	0.023	0.074***
Father occupation	−0.001	0.021**	0.019***
Parent self-employed	−0.139	0.009	−0.177
Parent cultural capital	0.288***	0.558***	0.462***
Parent party Member	0.244	0.357#	0.535***
Cohort 2	0.262#	0.109	−0.198
Cohort 3	0.554***	0.389*	−0.668***
Cohort 4	1.004***	0.323	−0.993***
Secondary grammar			2.086***
Interactions			
Female × parent education	0.122***		
Parent cultural Capital × cohort 2			−0.497***
Sample size	2930	2473	2163
Log-likelihood	−1170	−852	−1038
Model χ^2	196	163	672
df	14	13	15
Pseudo-R^2	0.078	0.087	0.244

#$p < 0.10$; *$p < 0.05$; **$p < 0.01$; ***$p < 0.001$, two-tailed test.

While parental education (for Russian men), father's occupation, and parental self-employment status had negligible influences on secondary attendance, some of these factors were significant for the other two educational outcomes. Father's occupation played an important role in university admission and the types of secondary education received, whereas parental education was significant for university attendance. Given that a sizable proportion of Russian men and women attended secondary grammar education, this finding is consistent with the *MMI* thesis, which postulates that parental influences will persist and even increase in key competitive educational outcomes.

It is worth noting that if parental cultural and social capital are both omitted from the analysis, the effects of parental education and father's occupation become much stronger and attain statistical significance in university attendance, and particularly diploma secondary education. This clearly indicates that the conventional status attainment approach masks the fact that a substantial degree of familial influences are mediated largely through parental cultural capital, thus overstating the importance of its socioeconomic background measures. More importantly, the finding illustrates that, though highly related, parental education is not synonymous with parental cultural capital and each can have independent influence on individual educational attainment. In some cases, the latter's influence was stronger and more prominent.[12]

A resilient influence is found for parental cultural capital in all three educational outcomes. One standard deviation change in parental cultural capital increased the odds for secondary attendance by 33% and the odds for a secondary diploma by 75%. Though slightly weaker, its influence in university attendance was still substantial (59% for cohort 1, 3, and 4). Interestingly, its influence in the 1936–1945 cohort was almost zero. While it may be tempting to attribute this inter-cohort change to policies instituted during the Stalinist era to penalize the intelligentsia, the persistently strong and stable effects of other parental measures across birth cohorts caution us against a simple interpretation of the effectiveness of particular policies.

The effect of parental party membership clearly indicates how social connections and networks can enhance the importance of parental background in educational attainment under socialism. Although parental party membership did not have any significant effect on secondary attendance, it was moderately influential in the types of secondary education received, and significant in university admission. Children of party members were 43% more likely to attend a diploma secondary school and 68% more likely to attend university than non-members. The finding is consistent with that reported in Gerber (2000).

Instead of a waning coefficient pattern, many of the measures of family background hardly exhibit any perceptible trend of declining influence across the three educational outcomes. Their effects are relatively stable across cohorts. In the case of parental education and party membership, the influence has even increased significantly for the two competitive outcomes. Generally speaking, then, the overall degree of stability and limited range or lack of intercohort changes raise questions about the effectiveness of socialist policies to reduce intergenerational transmission of inequality in education. However, it may not be appropriate to draw any conclusions about policy effectiveness from the results obtained here, since most of Russia's "revolutionary" transformations took place before the period studied. With this in mind, we turn our analysis to the other four countries, which established socialist rule in the late 1940s.

EDUCATIONAL INEQUALITIES IN BULGARIA

The experience of Bulgarian women in educational stratification was identical to that of their Russian counterparts: they were under-represented in secondary

Table 3. Logistic Regression of Educational Transitions in Bulgaria.

	Dependent Variable		
Independent Variable	Attended Secondary	Diploma Secondary	Attended University
Intercept	−0.231	1.130***	−1.926***
Female	−0.623***	0.520***	0.146
Sibling	−0.064*	−0.112**	−0.070
Parent education (years)	0.081***	0.117***	0.084***
Father occupation	−0.002	0.004	−0.000
Parent self-employed	−0.049	0.146	0.024
Parent cultural capital	0.773***	0.462***	0.476***
Parent party member	0.590***	0.372#	0.083
Cohort 2	0.547***	−0.736**	−0.187
Cohort 3	1.092***	−0.542*	−0.386#
Cohort 4	1.399***	−0.160	−0.645**
Secondary grammar			0.818***
Interactions			
Female × parent education	0.089**		
Sample size	2761	1872	1592
Log-likelihood	−1341	−684	−826
Model χ^2	789	211	261
df	14	13	14
Pseudo-R^2	0.227	0.134	0.137

#$p < 0.10$; *$p < 0.05$; **$p < 0.01$; ***$p < 0.001$, two-tailed test.

education. Those with well educated parents, however, could significantly increase their odds of attending secondary schools, leaving women from poor socioeconomic backgrounds as the most disadvantaged group. Among those who did receive secondary education, a disproportionate number received diploma rather than non-diploma education. And, as in Russia, there was gender parity in university attendance (Table 3).

Overall, socioeconomic influences on educational attainment in Bulgaria came not from father's occupation and parental self-employment status, but through parental education, cultural capital, and communist party membership. The effects of parental education were positive and significant in all outcomes, and particularly on obtaining a secondary diploma. Its influence on university attendance was slightly weaker than on diploma secondary education, but was virtually identical to that in secondary attendance: each additional year in parental education improved the odds by close to 9%, less than the 12% observed in diploma secondary. Coupled with an absence of any significant intercohort changes, this indicates a stable and persistent influence of parental education in educational stratification in Bulgaria.

Parental cultural capital was extraordinarily influential in secondary attendance. Everything else being equal, one standard deviation change in parental cultural capital improved the odds of secondary attendance to almost 2.2 times. The effects were considerably weaker for the other two outcomes but similar to that observed in Russia (about 1.6 times). As to parental social capital, the Bulgarian experience departed significantly from the Russian experience: whereas parental social capital was critical at the higher end of the educational hierarchy in Russia, it was most prominent at the lower end in Bulgaria. In particular, the odds for the offspring of communist party members to receive some form of secondary education were 1.8 times that of children of non-members; and the advantage dropped to 1.45 times (significant only at the 0.10 level) for diploma versus non-diploma education. This advantage did not change across cohorts.

In sum, educational stratification in socialist Bulgaria was very similar to that of Russia. No dramatic changes were observed during the transformation into socialism, nor was there any restratification later. The effects of family background remained remarkably stable across transitions as well as across cohorts. Thus, socialism in Bulgaria did not appear to have dramatically changed the mechanism of intergenerational transmission of educational inequality.

EDUCATIONAL INEQUALITIES IN CZECHOSLOVAKIA[13]

Because of its long and strict adherence to the socialist ideology, one would expect a higher degree of egalitarianism in Czechoslovakia. Surprisingly, not only do we find parental education and father's occupation still highly influential in all educational outcomes, but there are few notable intercohort changes. In the case of diploma secondary, the effect of parental education has even increased dramatically in the youngest cohort, suggesting a movement toward inequality rather than egalitarianism. Only in the case of secondary attendance do we find the effect of parental education reduced almost to zero for the 1946–1955 cohort. Nonetheless, there are limited signs of socialist influence in that individuals from self-employed origins were penalized in secondary attendance (77% as likely as those from non-self-employed origins). However, this disadvantage did not carry forward to other more competitive outcomes (Table 4).

Of the two unconventional measures of socioeconomic background, only parental cultural capital had prominent and important effects in all three outcomes. For diploma secondary, its influence was particularly strong in the two oldest cohorts, which correspond roughly to those completing primary education before 1961. Its influence declined somewhat in the two youngest cohorts, but

Table 4. Logistic Regression of Educational Transitions in Czechoslovakia.

	Dependent Variable		
Independent Variable	Attended Secondary	Diploma Secondary	Attended University
Intercept	0.189	−1.354***	−2.684***
Slovakia	0.340***	0.885***	0.490***
Female	−1.280***	−0.204	−1.059***
Sibling	−0.108***	−0.136***	−0.032
Parent education (years)	0.148***	0.044*	0.070***
Father occupation	0.016***	0.019***	0.014***
Parent self-employed	−0.266*	0.110	0.138
Parent cultural capital	0.632***	0.728***	0.338***
Parent party member	0.003	0.128#	0.052
Cohort 2	0.427***	−0.213#	−0.058
Cohort 3	1.910***	−0.380***	−0.125
Cohort 4	1.225***	−1.870***	0.309#
Secondary grammar			1.847***
Interactions			
Sibling × cohort 34	−0.092**		
Parent education × cohort 3	−0.107**		
Female × cohort 234		0.842***	
Parent education × cohort 4		0.149***	
Parent cultural capital × cohort 34		−0.217**	
Slovakia × cohort 4			−0.658**
Sample size	6981	5686	2754
Log-likelihood	−2674	−3357	−1389
Model χ^2	1350	1163	752
df	16	17	16
Pseudo-R^2	0.202	0.148	0.213

#$p < 0.10$; *$p < 0.05$; **$p < 0.01$; ***$p < 0.001$, two-tailed test.

remained strong and positive (one standard deviation change in parental cultural capital improved the odds for diploma secondary to 1.7 times in the 1946–1955 and 1956–1963 cohorts rather than 2.1 times in the 1926–1935 and 1936–1945 cohorts).

Unlike what Hanley (2001) found, our results do not show any significant influence of a parental party member on secondary attendance or any intercohort changes. While we see some evidence of parental party membership having an effect in the youngest cohort, the improvement in the *BIC* statistic is small and the possibility of chance due to the large sample size cannot be ruled out. Some evidence of the importance of parental social capital is also found in diploma secondary. For individuals with either parent being members of the communist party, the odds to receive a diploma secondary education was about 14% higher than that for the offspring of non-member. This evidence, however, is still inconclusive since the coefficient is only significant at the 0.10 level.

The extent of gender inequality in Czechoslovakia is very similar to that in Russia and Bulgaria, with two notable exceptions. First, the oldest cohort (1926–1935) of Czechoslovak women did not enjoy greater representation in diploma secondary. Second, Czechoslovak women were grossly underrepresented in university attendance. Everything else being equal, Czechoslovak women were only 35% as likely as their male counterparts to enter a university.

In sum, educational inequalities remained entrenched in Czechoslovakia in many respects, despite its rhetorical claim to be one of the few countries achieving socialism. Many measures of family background continued to play important roles in educational attainment. There were no dramatic changes in the effects due either to socialist transformation in the early period or the reintroduction of reverse discrimination policies in 1971. If one of the purposes of the reintroduction was to reduce parental influences in education, our results clearly show it to be ineffective. Finally, insofar as a waning logit coefficient pattern is observed, it is limited to parental cultural capital only.

EDUCATIONAL INEQUALITIES IN HUNGARY

Similar to the case in Czechoslovakia, both parental education and father's occupation played a role in educational stratification under socialism in Hungary. Here, however, their contributions are complementary: while parental education was instrumental in secondary and university attendance, father's occupation was important in diploma secondary, with no notable intercohort changes.[14] As expected, the effect of parental cultural capital was strong and significant in all three outcomes, but declined considerably from secondary to university attendance. For example, one standard deviation change in parental cultural capital improved the odds of secondary attendance to 2.7 times, but only 2.0 and 1.3 times for diploma secondary and university attendance, respectively. The decline is likely to have resulted from a more complete transfer of parental cultural capital to individual cultural capital. It is also the only parental background variable that displays a waning coefficient pattern (Table 5).

Contrary to the prediction of Szjona Szelényi and her associates, parental party membership had no impact on educational outcomes and cohort variation. The experience of Hungary is thus quite distinctive from the socialist countries discussed so far. One reason lies perhaps in the relative success of the Hungarian

Table 5. Logistic Regression of Educational Transitions in Hungary.

	Dependent Variable		
Independent Variable	Attended Secondary	Diploma Secondary	Attended University
Intercept	0.426	−0.841**	−1.876***
Female	−0.956***	0.893***	−0.729***
Sibling	−0.030	−0.119***	−0.063
Parent education (years)	0.106***	0.038#	0.099**
Father occupation	0.002	0.023***	0.004
Parent self-employed	−0.107	0.240	−0.433#
Parent cultural capital	0.978***	0.692***	0.224*
Parent party member	−0.112	−0.053	−0.224
Cohort 2	0.610***	−0.125	−0.243
Cohort 3	1.068***	−0.209	−0.712*
Cohort 4	1.535***	−0.458*	−0.045
Secondary grammar			1.161***
Interactions			
Sibling × cohort (linear)	−0.106***		
Sample size	2379	1714	953
Log-likelihood	−1074	−980	−500
Model χ^2	671	394	161
df	14	13	13
Pseudo-R^2	0.238	0.167	0.139

$^{\#}p < 0.10$; $^{*}p < 0.05$; $^{**}p < 0.01$; $^{***}p < 0.001$, two-tailed test.

Communist Party in recruiting the intelligentsia into its own rank (Wong, 1996), who tend to transmit inequality effectively irrespective of party membership status. Also, gender inequality in Hungary follows a pattern similar to that in Russia and Bulgaria. The only difference is that Hungarian women were under-represented in university attendance once we appropriately control for secondary grammar education. Far fewer women in the eligible pool had the same chance to enter university as their male counterparts, an experience also shared by women in Czechoslovakia.

EDUCATIONAL INEQUALITIES IN POLAND

Both parental education and father's occupation played a significant role in educational stratification in Poland. The effect of father's education even increased in university attendance: each additional year in parental education raised the odds

Table 6. Logistic Regression of Educational Transitions in Poland.

	Dependent Variable		
Independent Variable	Attended Secondary	Diploma Secondary	Attended University
Intercept	0.239	0.644#	−3.389***
Female	−0.148	1.063***	−0.671***
Sibling	−0.083***	−0.218***	−0.008
Parent education (years)	0.068***	0.010	0.121***
Father occupation	0.012*	0.024***	0.014*
Parent self-employed	−0.049	0.395***	0.316*
Parent cultural capital	1.036***	0.746***	0.329***
Parent party member	0.217	0.047	0.164
Cohort 2	0.102	−0.828***	1.706***
Cohort 3	0.830***	−2.600***	0.457*
Cohort 4	1.489***	−2.510***	0.259
Secondary grammar			2.146***
Interactions			
Sibling × cohort 23		0.163**	
Parent education × cohort 34		0.126***	
Father occupation × cohort 2			−0.033***
Parent cultural capital × cohort 3			−0.377**
Sample size	3213	2412	1618
Log-likelihood	−1382	−1190	−838
Model χ^2	845	654	550
df	13	15	15
Pseudo-R^2	0.234	0.216	0.247

#$p < 0.10$; *$p < 0.05$; **$p < 0.01$; ***$p < 0.001$, two-tailed test.

of university attendance by 13%, substantially greater than the 7% in secondary attendance. In the case of diploma secondary, parental education had negligible influence for the two oldest cohorts, but for the two youngest cohorts, the increase in odds was also 13% for each additional year, virtually identical to university attendance. There is thus clear evidence that the influence of parental education has increased in Poland (Table 6).

The effects of father's occupation remained strong and significant in all three outcomes for all cohorts, except in university attendance for the second (1936–1945) cohort, where it turned negative. For all other cohorts, the odds for an individual of professional origin (ISEI = 70) to attend university was 1.6 times that for an individual of skilled manual worker origin (ISEI = 38); but for this particular cohort, the odds were reversed to 1.8 times in favor of the latter. This indicates clearly the fervor of reverse discrimination policies in Poland during the early years of socialism. However, this policy effect was short-lived. Furthermore, contrary to expectation, having self-employed parents actually increased one's odds of receiving a secondary diploma as well as attending a university. Since a majority of the self-employed in Poland are small farmers, they comprise a larger proportion of those whose children received a secondary diploma than might be predicted by their low socioeconomic status. What is unclear is whether this is also the result of deliberate social promotion by the socialist government or simply self-selectivity.

Consistent with our findings on the other four countries, parental cultural capital played a critical role in all three outcomes, but its importance declined precipitously across transitions. The evidence suggests that parental cultural capital was insignificant for the third cohort in university attendance (that is, those about to enter university from the mid-1960s to mid-1970s), due perhaps to increasing political pressure from the communist party. The role of parental party membership was weak, and none of the coefficients reaches statistical significance. Finally, the pattern of gender inequality in Poland is similar to that in Hungary: women were over-represented in diploma secondary and under-represented in university attendance. There was, however, gender parity in secondary attendance.

DISCUSSION

This study examines the pattern of educational inequalities over time in five East European countries under socialism to determine whether the socialist regimes succeeded in instituting a more egalitarian educational stratification system. The analyses specifically address the following: (1) whether the egalitarian policies implemented in the early years were successful and had lasting impact; (2) whether the influences of family background remained stable, declined, or increased over time; (3) whether the influences of family background exhibited a waning pattern across educational transitions or remained stable or even increased at key competitive transitions; and (4) whether the communist party became an important stratification agent under socialism, with parental party membership playing a significant role in educational attainment.

Regarding the first question, the findings here afford only a tentative answer. While there is some evidence from Russia and Poland that the influence of parental background was distinctive in the second cohort, the so-called revolution effect was rather sporadic and inconsistent. In other words, there is no clear indication that the socialist revolution was successful in fundamentally transforming the nature of the educational stratification system in the five socialist societies studied. The influences of parental education, occupation, and cultural capital tended to remain strong throughout the socialist era. In addition to the stability across cohorts, there was also considerable stability in these coefficients across educational transitions.

Of the various measures of family background, only parental cultural capital displays the familiar waning coefficient pattern in some but not all countries. It is important to note that some of the conventional measures of parental background variables indeed exhibit a waning coefficient pattern across transitions when parental cultural and social capital variables are omitted in the analyses. But when both these two measures are included, their significance either remains the same or increases at higher transitions. Thus, with proper consideration of the multi-dimensional influences of the family, the patterns displayed here are generally supportive of the arguments of the maximally maintained thesis, particularly its postulation of resilience against change in key competitive transitions.

On the question of the communist party becoming a new stratification agent under socialism, our findings suggest that the significance of parental party membership in educational inequality has perhaps been overstated. Much of its influence, if existent, was in secondary education. The only exception is in Soviet Russia, where parental party membership affected university attendance as well. According to Gerber (2000), the effect of parental party membership extends even beyond the socialist era to contemporary Russia, largely because of the continued utility of the deeply entrenched networks rather than membership per se. Interestingly, political/social capital in the form of communist party membership played no role in the educational stratification of the country with the most inclusive communist party, Hungary. It may be precisely because of the Hungarian Communist Party's inclusive strategy of recruiting technocrats and the intelligentsia class into its own rank that party membership was not so important in educational inequality there.

The study finds that despite deliberate socialist egalitarian practices, the forces of social reproduction remained highly effective in structuring educational inequalities in five Eastern European countries. However, the fact that no significant or long-lasting effect of socialism is found here does not mean that we can completely rule out the impact of socialist egalitarian policies. While the present research offers an improvement over previous research by refining the measure of educational attainment to those aged between 25 and 34 at four time points, it is vulnerable to the critique that using inter-cohort changes to index temporal changes may gloss over fine and subtle changes over a relatively short period of time. An alternative approach is to incorporate the time factor explicitly in statistical modeling. This powerful and flexible method to detect temporal changes would also enable a close correspondence to historical changes within individual countries, an issue left largely unexplored in the present comparative framework.

While the finding of continuity rather than interruptions in educational stratification is largely consistent with and confirms previous findings on Eastern Europe, it contrasts rather sharply with recent findings on another communist society, China, where periodic shifts in state policies seem to have direct effects on the life chances of individuals from various social and class backgrounds (Deng & Treiman, 1997; Zhou, Moen & Tuma, 1998; Zhou, Tuma & Moen, 1996). Deng and Treiman (1997) and Zhou, Moen and Tuma (1998), for instance, both found that under the more radical and egalitarian education policies instituted during the Cultural Revolution, well-educated and upper-class individuals were clearly penalized in educational attainment.

These different findings, however, are not necessarily contradictory, as there are several key differences between China and Eastern Europe. First, there is the difference between an "indigenous" revolution with broad-based support, and an "imposed" revolution under the shadow of Soviet power. In addition, there was in China the presence and continuity of a charismatic political leader in Mao Zedong. In his strict pursuance of a philosophy of continuous revolution, Mao initiated numerous rounds of collective movement (such as the Great Leap Forward and the Cultural Revolution) to eliminate remnants of capitalistic elements in the Chinese society, penalizing the bourgeoisie and intelligentsia. Thus, except for several brief calm years, China has witnessed almost 30 years of uninterrupted revolution since 1945.

In contrast, many of the "reverse discrimination" policies started to fade away rapidly in Eastern Europe, some as early as the 1960s. Indeed, many programs did not see full implementation before they were abandoned. There is, then, no comparison between the Chinese and the East European experience in terms of the scope and intensity of egalitarian policies. The Russian experience, of course, was not comparable either since its revolution occurred more than 30 years earlier. Also, considering that the Cultural Revolution was probably the most drastic intervention in human history to reduce intergenerational transmission of inequality, its impact was hardly exceptional. Empirical findings show that its egalitarian effects did not last long and rapidly waned after the policies were terminated. According to Deng and Treiman (1997), educational stratification returned to its usual trend within seven short years. Similarly, Zhou, Moen and Tuma (1998) found a surge in importance of parental background in the post-Cultural Revolution era.

From the Chinese experience, it is plausible to conjecture that egalitarian policies in Eastern Europe may have been effective in creating short-run openness in educational attainment. That we cannot locate any distinctive pattern here is probably because our observation point is too far removed from when the changes occurred, aside from the problem of the intercohort approach discussed earlier. To address the issue adequately, we need to use more sensitive models and combine older data with new data. Several large-scale national surveys are available for thorough analyses of the experience in Czechoslovakia, Hungary, and Poland. For comparative purposes, studies of educational inequality in contemporary socialist countries such as Vietnam, North Korea, and Cuba will also be valuable, though data availability may pose a major problem. In sum, with further vigorous comparative and trend analysis, it may be possible to arrive at a more refined picture of the tug-of-war between egalitarianism and social reproduction in educational stratification under socialism than the broad pattern of stability found in the current study.

NOTES

1. The discussion here pertains only to available literature on Eastern European countries. Recent findings from socialist China are not entirely consistent with East European experiences (Deng & Treiman, 1997; Zhou, Moen & Tuma, 1998; Zhou, Tuma & Moen, 1996). This will be addressed later.

2. Czechoslovakia was perhaps the only exception. It reintroduced the reverse discrimination policy in 1971, shortly after the unsuccessful Prague Spring uprising, and left the policy largely intact until the fall of communism in 1989.

3. The educational transitions approach (see Mare, 1980, 1981) differs significantly from the traditional linear regression framework that measures education in terms of years of schooling. It treats education as a series of transition or school continuation decisions, since students can choose when to continue or end their formal education. With years of schooling as the dependent variable, this approach argues, the OLS coefficients reflect not only the level of association but also the variance of educational attainment. Since the latter has changed over time due to the universal expansion of educational systems, especially at the elementary and middle levels, comparisons of OLS coefficients across different cohorts or countries will not reveal whether the structural parameters governing the process of educational attainment truly differ from each other. This is of particular importance to cross-national and cross-cohort research because the effects of social background on educational attainment can differ over time and across societies, and we would like to separate changes in available positions from changes in the association between origins and destinations.

4. There are plenty of important works about educational inequality in these countries except Bulgaria. To cite a few, in Czechoslovakia (Hanley, 2001; Matějů, 1993; Matějů & Peschar, 1990; Wong, 1998), in Hungary (Ganzeboom, De Graaf & Róbert, 1990; Hanley & McKeever, 1997; Peschar & Popping, 1986; Róbert, 1991; Simkus & Andorka, 1982; Szelényi, 1998; Szelényi & Aschaffenburg, 1993), in Poland (Heyns & Białecki, 1993; Peschar, Popping & Mach, 1986); and in Russia (Dobson, 1977; Gerber, 2000; Gerber & Hout, 1995).

5. Parental education is sometimes used as a proxy for cultural capital. While the two variables are highly correlated, they are not identical, either theoretically or empirically.

6. In 1988, only those aged between 25 and 32 were selected. It is also important to note that the samples of individuals in 1960, 1970, and 1980 might not be representative of the

target population at the time because of selective out-migration and differential mortality. This is a common problem of retrospective data, besides data reliability.

7. Different strategies were used to check which measure of parental education provides the best result. They include separate measures of father's and mother's education and the maximum of their education (measured either in years of schooling or in educational dummies). Using the *BIC* statistic (Raftery, 1995) for model selection, the maximum of parental education in years of schooling provides the best result in terms of model accuracy and scientific parsimony. The choice of measures did not affect the interpretation of results and decision to include particular interaction effects. These results are available from the author upon request.

8. The self-reported responses of parental cultural activities can be subjected to recall errors or response biases. However, unless the errors are systematic, the potential biases and errors should not affect the results in any meaningful manner, especially when several important correlates of such biases and errors are also included in statistical modeling. Of course, further research to address the reliability issue would be useful in the future.

9. There is no statistical control for the urban/rural differentiation. Although the original survey collects detailed information on residential history, it does not provide any mapping of the regional codes to the size of residence, except for current residence.

10. According to the differences in the model chi-square statistics, the improvement was 126% in Poland, 93% in Czechoslovakia, 59% in Russia, 52% in Hungary, and 21% in Bulgaria.

11. The mean substitution method may artificially deflate the variance of the estimates, but the introduction of missing dummies in the regression models should minimize its influence. Other statistical procedures such as the multiple imputation method generally provide superior results (Little & Rubin, 1987; Schafer, 1997) but they tend to be computationally intensive.

12. The same observation applies to the other countries studied: the inclusion of parental cultural and social capital weakens considerably the effects of parental education and father's occupation. While the influence of parental education and father's occupation still maintains statistical significance in most cases, it diminishes to non-significance in several instances.

13. Since our primary interest is how various measures of family background affect the chances of attaining specific educational outcomes, regional variation and their changes across birth cohorts will not be discussed.

14. If parental cultural and social capital were omitted, the effects of parental education and father's education would be significant in all three outcomes except for father's occupation in tertiary attendance.

ACKNOWLEDGMENTS

Earlier versions of this paper were presented at the Research Committee on Social Stratification and Mobility (RC28) of the International Sociological Association at Mannheim, Germany, April 26th–28th, 2001, and the Annual Meeting of the American Sociological Association at Chicago, Illinois, August 15th–19th, 2002. I thank Peter Chua and Ming-Yan Lai for assistance. The research received partial funding from a grant by the Institute for the Social, Behavioral, and Economic Research at the University of California, Santa Barbara.

REFERENCES

Bourdieu, P., & Passerson, J.-C. (1977). *Reproduction in education, society, and culture*. Beverly Hills, CA: Sage.

Deng, Z., & Treiman, D. J. (1997). The impact of the cultural revolution on trends in educational attainment in the People's Republic of China. *American Journal of Sociology*, *103*(2), 391–428.

Djilas, M. (1957). *The new class*. New York: Harcourt Brace Jovanovich.

Dobson, R. (1977). Social status and inequality of access to higher education in the U.S.S.R. In: J. Karabel & A. H. Halsey (Eds), *Power and Ideology in Education* (pp. 245–275). New York: Oxford University Press.

Ganzeboom, H. B. G., De Graaf, P. M., & Róbert, P. (1990). Reproduction theory on socialist ground: Intergenerational transmission of inequalities in Hungary. In: A. L. Kalleberg (Ed.), *Research in Social Stratification and Mobility* (Vol. 9, pp. 79–104). Greenwich, CT: JAI Press.

Gerber, T. P. (2000). Educational stratification in contemporary Russia: Stability and change in the face of economic and institutional crisis. *Sociology of Education*, *73*(4), 219–246.

Gerber, T. P., & Hout, M. (1995). Educational stratification in Russia during the Soviet period. *American Journal of Sociology*, *101*(3), 611–660.

Hanley, E. (2001). Centrally administered mobility reconsidered: The political dimension of educational stratification in state-socialist Czechoslovakia. *Sociology of Education*, *74*(1), 25–43.

Hanley, E., & McKeever, M. (1997). The persistence of educational inequalities in Socialist Hungary: Trajectory vs. counter-selection. *Sociology of Education*, *70*(1), 1–21.

Heyns, B., & Białecki, I. (1993). Educational inequalities in postwar Poland. In: Y. Shavit & H.-P. Blossfeld (Eds), *Persistent Inequality: Changing Educational Attainment in Thirteen Countries* (pp. 303–336). Boulder, CO: Westview Press.

Hout, M., Raftery, A. E., & Bell, E. O. (1993). Making the grade: Educational stratification in the United States, 1925–1989. In: Y. Shavit & H.-P. Blossfeld (Eds), *Persistent Inequality: Changing Educational Attainment in Thirteen Countries* (pp. 25–49). Boulder, CO: Westview Press.

Kelley, J., & Klein, H. S. (1977). Revolution and the rebirth of inequality: A theory of stratification in postrevolutionary society. *American Journal of Sociology*, *83*(1), 78–99.

Konrád, G., & Szelényi, I. (1979). *The Intellectuals on the Road to Class Power*. New York: Harcourt Brace Jovanovich.

Lamont, M., & Lareau, A. (1988). Cultural capital: Allusions, gaps, and glissandos in recent theoretical developments. *Sociological Theory*, *6*(2), 153–168.

Lareau, A. (1987). Social class differences in family-school relationship: The importance of cultural capital. *Sociology of Education*, *60*(2), 73–85.

Little, R. J. A., & Rubin, D. B. (1987). *Statistical Analysis with Incomplete Data*. New York: Wiley.

Mare, R. D. (1980). Social background and school continuation decisions. *Journal of the American Statistical Association*, *75*(370), 295–305.

Mare, R. D. (1981). Change and stability in educational stratification. *American Sociological Review*, *46*(1), 72–87.

Matějů, P. (1986). Demokratizace vzdělání a reprodukce vzdělánstní struktury v CSSR ve světle mobilitních dat. (Democratization of Education and the Reproduction of the Educational Structure of Czechoslovakia Using Mobility Data). *Sociologický casopis*, *22*(2), 131–152.

Matějů, P. (1993). Who won and who lost in a Socialist redistribution in Czechoslovakia. In: Y. Shavit & H.-P. Blossfeld (Eds), *Persistent Inequality: Changing Educational Attainment in Thirteen Countries* (pp. 251–72). Boulder, CO: Westview Press.

Matějů, P., & Peschar, J. L. (1990). Family background and educational attainment in Czechoslovakia and the Netherlands: The analysis of cultural and economic sources of inequality in comparative perspective. In: M. Haller (Ed.), *Class Structure in Europe: New Findings from East-West Comparisons of Social Structure and Mobility* (pp. 121–45). Armonk, NY: Sharpe.

Parkin, F. (1971). *Class inequality and political order*. London: McGibbon and Kee.

Peschar, J. L., & Matějů, P. (1988). Levels and opportunities in Czechoslovakia and the Netherlands. Paper presented at the International Sociological Association Research Committee on Social Stratification, Madison, WI.

Peschar, J. L., & Popping, R. (1986). Educational mobility in Hungary and the Netherlands: A log-linear comparison. *Research in Sociology of Education and Socialization*, *6*, 45–78.

Peschar, J. L., Popping, R., & Mach, B. W. (1986). Educational mobility in Poland and the Netherlands. *Netherlands Journal of Education*, *1*, 119–139.

Raftery, A. E. (1995). Bayesian model selection in social research. In: P. V. Marsden (Ed.), *Sociological Methodology* (Vol. 25, pp. 111–164). Washington, DC: American Sociological Association.

Raftery, A. E., & Hout, M. (1993). Maximally maintained inequality: Expansion, reform, and opportunity in Irish education, 1921–1975. *Sociology of Education*, *66*(1), 41–62.

Róbert, P. (1991). Educational transition in Hungary from the post-war period to the end of the 1980s. *European Sociological Review*, *7*(3), 213–236.

Schafer, J. L. (1997). *Analysis of Incomplete Multivariate Data*. London: Chapman & Hall.

Shavit, Y., & Blossfeld, H.-P. (Eds) (1993). *Persistent Inequality: Changing Educational Attainment in Thirteen Countries*. Boulder, CO: Westview Press.

Simkus, A., & Andorka, R. (1982). Inequalities in education in Hungary 1923–1973. *American Sociological Review*, *47*(6), 740–751.

Szelényi, S. (1998). *Equality by Design: The Grand Experiment in Destratification in Socialist Hungary*. Stanford, CA: Stanford University Press.

Szelényi, S., & Aschaffenburg, K. (1993). Inequalities in educational opportunity in Hungary. In: Y. Shavit & H.-P. Blossfeld (Eds), *Persistent Inequality: Changing Educational Attainment in Thirteen Countries* (pp. 273–302). Boulder, CO: Westview Press.

Ulč, O. (1978). Some aspects of Czechoslovak society since 1968. *Social Forces*, *57*(2), 419–435.

Wong, R. S.-K. (1996). The social composition of communist parties of Czechoslovakia and Hungary in the 1980s. *Social Forces*, *75*(1), 61–90.

Wong, R. S.-K. (1998). Multidimensional influences of family environments in education: The case of socialist Czechoslovakia. *Sociology of Education*, *71*(1), 1–22.

Wong, R. S.-K., & Hauser, R. M. (1992). Trends in occupational mobility in Hungary under socialism. *Social Science Research*, *21*(4), 419–444.

Zhou, X.-G., Moen, P., & Tuma, N. B. (1998). Educational stratification in urban China, 1949–1994. *Sociology of Education*, *71*(3), 199–222.

Zhou, X.-G., Tuma, N. B., & Moen, P. (1996). Stratification dynamics under state socialism: The case of urban China. *Social Forces*, *74*(3), 759–796.

APPENDIX A
SUMMARY STATISTICS OF DEPENDENT AND INDEPENDENT VARIABLES

Description	Attended Secondary		Diploma Secondary		Attended University	
	Mean	S.D.	Mean	S.D.	Mean	S.D.
(A) Russia						
Transition	0.844	0.363	0.875	0.331	0.331	0.471
Female	0.591	0.492	0.589	0.492	0.600	0.490
Sibling	2.296	1.932	2.226	1.881	2.174	1.855
Parent education	8.264	3.936	8.592	3.885	8.855	3.860
Father occupation	36.871	13.506	37.343	13.845	38.084	14.184
Parent self-employed	0.033	0.179	0.033	0.178	0.033	0.179
Parent cultural capital	0.000	1.000	0.076	1.010	0.155	1.015
Parent party member	0.266	0.442	0.285	0.451	0.305	0.461
Cohort 2	0.229	0.420	0.217	0.412	0.209	0.407
Cohort 3	0.345	0.476	0.353	0.478	0.362	0.481
Cohort 4	0.280	0.449	0.304	0.460	0.311	0.463
Secondary grammar					0.654	0.476
Sample size	2930		2473		2163	
(B) Bulgaria						
Transition	0.678	0.467	0.850	0.357	0.289	0.453
Female	0.485	0.500	0.490	0.500	0.514	0.500
Sibling	1.882	1.626	1.682	1.539	1.590	1.468
Parent education	6.743	4.050	7.868	3.848	8.286	3.757
Father occupation	31.718	12.714	33.756	13.813	34.616	14.221
Parent self-employed	0.194	0.395	0.147	0.355	0.145	0.352
Parent cultural capital	0.000	1.000	0.265	1.049	0.368	1.061
Parent party member	0.208	0.406	0.261	0.439	0.282	0.450
Cohort 2	0.246	0.431	0.222	0.415	0.205	0.404
Cohort 3	0.324	0.468	0.367	0.482	0.365	0.482
Cohort 4	0.228	0.420	0.284	0.451	0.300	0.459
Secondary grammar					0.475	0.500
Sample size	2761		1872		1592	

Description	Attended Secondary		Diploma Secondary		Attended University	
	Mean	S.D.	Mean	S.D.	Mean	S.D.
(C) Czechoslovakia						
Transition	0.814	0.389	0.484	0.500	0.340	0.474
Female	0.474	0.499	0.426	0.495	0.497	0.500
Sibling	2.391	1.992	2.201	1.821	1.895	1.595
Parent education	10.079	2.611	10.376	2.635	11.111	2.866
Father occupation	35.212	13.149	36.454	13.553	40.298	15.060
Parent self-employed	0.087	0.282	0.069	0.254	0.055	0.228
Parent cultural capital	0.000	1.000	0.132	0.998	0.481	1.025
Parent party member	0.232	0.422	0.247	0.431	0.289	0.453
Slovakia	0.445	0.497	0.441	0.497	0.473	0.499
Cohort 2	0.238	0.426	0.229	0.420	0.221	0.415
Cohort 3	0.338	0.473	0.355	0.478	0.359	0.479
Cohort 4	0.229	0.420	0.255	0.436	0.286	0.452
Secondary grammar					0.367	0.482
Sample size	6981		5686		2754	
(D) Hungary						
Transition	0.720	0.449	0.557	0.497	0.297	0.457
Female	0.450	0.498	0.400	0.490	0.491	0.500
Sibling	2.388	2.120	2.018	1.810	1.742	1.607
Parent education	8.656	3.431	9.391	3.406	10.239	3.541
Father occupation	33.695	13.143	35.413	13.954	38.891	15.885
Parent self-employed	0.165	0.371	0.142	0.349	0.138	0.345
Parent cultural capital	0.000	1.000	0.238	1.009	0.578	1.031
Parent party member	0.171	0.376	0.189	0.392	0.217	0.412
Cohort 2	0.259	0.438	0.239	0.427	0.243	0.429
Cohort 3	0.356	0.479	0.372	0.483	0.384	0.487
Cohort 4	0.246	0.431	0.282	0.450	0.272	0.445
Secondary grammar					0.490	0.500
Sample size	2379		1714		955	
(E) Poland						
Transition	0.751	0.433	0.677	0.468	0.443	0.497
Female	0.478	0.500	0.473	0.499	0.541	0.498
Sibling	2.614	1.958	2.387	1.832	2.126	1.683
Parent education	9.121	3.732	9.850	3.617	10.628	3.738
Father occupation	34.444	13.502	36.313	14.381	39.061	15.499
Parent self-employed	0.395	0.489	0.342	0.474	0.312	0.464

APPENDIX A *(Continued)*

Description	Attended Secondary		Diploma Secondary		Attended University	
	Mean	S.D.	Mean	S.D.	Mean	S.D.
Parent cultural capital	0.000	1.000	0.223	1.003	0.474	1.023
Parent party member	0.175	0.380	0.206	0.404	0.229	0.420
Cohort2	0.221	0.415	0.189	0.392	0.213	0.410
Cohort 3	0.344	0.475	0.371	0.483	0.362	0.481
Cohort 4	0.251	0.434	0.301	0.459	0.267	0.443
Secondary grammar					0.494	0.500
Sample size	3213		2412		1633	

PARENTS, PARTNERS, AND CREDENTIALS: SELF-EMPLOYMENT MOBILITY IN THE UNITED STATES AND GERMANY

Patricia A. McManus

ABSTRACT

This research compares the effects of career credentials and family factors on self-employment careers in the United States and Western Germany. In Germany, both general education and vocational credentials structure self-employment, primarily at entry. In the United States, general education alone structures self-employment, primarily by stabilizing the self-employment careers of workers with higher credentials. Intergenerational transmission of self-employment is more prominent among men, while spousal transmission of self-employment status is more prominent among women. In the United States, but not in Germany, there is evidence of a "caretaker" pathway that brings mothers of young children into self-employment for short periods of time.

INTRODUCTION

The transition from industrial to post-industrial economy is marked by a pervasive shift in the structure of organizations, labor markets, and the careers of workers (Aronowitz & Cutler, 1998; Block, 1990; Piore & Sabel, 1984; Smith, 1997).

Inequality Across Societies: Families, Schools and Persisting Stratification
Research in Sociology of Education, Volume 14, 171–200
(Formerly Research in Sociology of Education and Socialization)

ISSN: 1479-3539/doi:10.1016/S1479-3539(03)14008-6

One component of this shift is a departure from the long-term secular decline in self-employment that marked the industrial era. Outside of agriculture, self-employment rates in North America and Western Europe have hovered at roughly one-tenth of total employment in recent decades (OECD, 1998), and in some countries self-employment rates have risen, fueled by a rapid increase in self-employment participation among women (McManus, 2001).

Despite the relatively small numbers of self-employed, the sector carries great symbolic significance. Self-employment once seemed out of place in an industrial-era landscape dominated by mass-production, a throwback to the dawn of capitalist development. More recently, self-employment has emerged as an integral feature of postindustrial economies. This new face of self-employment is not without controversy. On the one hand, economic development organizations eagerly embrace self-employment as an engine for growth in the new economy, claiming, for example, that "the countries best equipped to exploit future opportunities will be characterized by dynamic entrepreneurship" (OECD, 1998). Others worry that the post-industrial economy produces a disproportionate share of "bad jobs" with no job security, few benefits, and unstable earnings (Kalleberg, Reskin & Hudson, 2000).

These analysts see the resurgence of self-employment as symptomatic of this disturbing trend away from standard employment relations. Debates on the nature and quality of this "new self-employment" are exacerbated by the recent increase in self-employment among women in many post-industrial economies. The rise in female self-employment may indicate the expansion of opportunities for women accompanied by a breakdown of gender barriers in the labor market, or it may be interpreted as the expansion of poor quality, sex-segregated labor into the self-employment sector (McManus, 2001).

If any of these scenarios carries weight, the "new self-employment" presents challenges to the institutional processes that structured mobility during the golden age of industrialism. Different as they are, each conceptualization of self-employment implies the emergence of new career pathways into self-employment in post-industrial labor markets. This suggests a weakening of conventional pathways into self-employment, as new forms of self-employment replace the old. The mechanisms that govern these new pathways may bear little resemblance to the mechanisms that governed self-employment entrance and stability throughout much of the twentieth century; indeed, there may be little structure at all in the new self-employment.

This analysis contributes to these debates on the nature of the new self-employment by investigating pathways into self-employment among men and women in two post-industrial economies. Although the prominence of any one pathway varies cross-nationally, depending on other institutional features of the labor market, the traditional pathway into self-employment is through intergenerational transmission of self-employment from parent to child. Formal pathways into self-employment developed in industrial labor markets, through occupational qualification or accreditation. I investigate the persistence of these two mechanisms for self-employment mobility, and consider new mechanisms for family transmission of self-employment. The analyses compare self-employment mobility in the United States and Germany, countries with similar positions in the global economy yet with very different labor market institutions.

This analysis addresses four questions:

(1) Do parental self-employment and career credentials continue to facilitate self-employment entry and stabilize self-employment careers?
(2) Are new pathways emerging from family institutions or educational institutions?
(3) Are there gender differences in self-employment pathways?
(4) Are there cross-national differences in self-employment pathways, and can these differences be explained by cross-national differences in institutional arrangements?

The answer to these questions will enhance current knowledge about comparative social stratification processes in the new economy. A better understanding of mobility processes in the self-employment sector can also shed light on the relationship between family institutions, educational institutions, and labor market outcomes in advanced capitalist economies.

PATHWAYS INTO SELF-EMPLOYMENT

The traditional pathway into self-employment is through ascription, or inheritance of a family tradition of self-employment. The rise of managerial capitalism in the 20th century coincided with a long-term decline in both farm and non-farm self-employment. At mid-century, Daniel Bell described the demise of family capitalism,

> ... a social system wherein power has been transmitted through the family, and where the satisfactions of ownership lay, in part, in the family name, by which the business enterprise was known (Bell, 1960, p. 39).

But even as family capitalism ceded to large-scale conglomerates as the dominant form of enterprise, the strong association between parental self-employment and self-employment among their adult children persisted (Dunn & Holtz-Eakin, 2000; Hout & Rosen, 2000; Wong, 1992).

The resilience of traditional intergenerational links among the self-employed may be attributed to the difficulties of creating and maintaining the kind of organizational infrastructure that most employees take for granted. Building a firm typically requires financial capital, and the capital resources which contribute to a successful entry into self-employment are often found first in the family. New entrepreneurs with self-employed parents are privileged with additional advantages. First, they may inherit the material and financial capital invested in the family business, avoiding the startup costs of a new enterprise. Second, children of self-employment parents can develop specialized skills by interacting with parents on business matters or simply by working at the family firm. Finally, parental self-employment can be an important source of social capital via the intergenerational transmission of reciprocal obligations with vendors and clients: the son (typically) inherits the good reputation and client list of his father (Blau & Duncan, 1967).

An alternative pathway into self-employment relies on formal educational institutions rather than family institutions. Structural theories of career mobility assert that educational and occupational credentials can structure labor market mobility in the self-employment sector just as they do in wage and salary labor markets (Rosenfeld, 1992). From a skills or resources/rewards perspective, the human capital gained through formal education and training can facilitate the transition into self-employment, just as it facilitates upward mobility in the wage and salary sector. Educational and occupational credentials also provide a reassuring "market signal" to prospective customers, clients, and vendors who may be uncertain about the competence and reliability of a business owner (Spence, 1973). Market signals are used in the wage and salary sector, for example, when prospective employers prefer a candidate who has a secondary school degree to a candidate without a degree for a job that requires minimal skills. Likewise, the practice of hanging framed diplomas and certificates is common among self-employed professionals and skilled craftsmen. The signal value of credentials may be especially useful in the self-employment sector, since many self-employment jobs lack the formal screening procedures typically used in the wage and salary sector.

In some cases credentials are not only useful, they are essential. Institutional rules limit access to certain occupations by requiring specific credentials. These rules structure career pathways in the labor market, constraining mobility across occupations while facilitating mobility between firms or across the boundary between the wage and salary sector and the self-employment sector and back again. Occupational labor markets can operate either at the aggregate level, as in the case of the labor market in Germany (Kalleberg, 1988) or primarily within specific occupations or clusters of occupations, for example, medical professions in the U.S. (Althauser, 1989). Indeed, those occupations boasting the highest self-employment rates in both Germany and the United States include the highly regulated liberal or "free professions" of medicine, law, architecture, and engineering.

POSTINDUSTRIAL PRESSURES AND NEW OPPORTUNITIES

The postindustrial shift from capital-intensive manufacturing industries to labor-intensive service industries provided a favorable competitive environment for small firms, and the explosion of information technologies facilitated the growth of new forms of small-scale businesses (Aronson, 1991; Steinmetz & Wright, 1989). At the same time, larger firms faced new competition in an increasingly global marketplace. Employers met these competitive pressures with a demand for greater labor market flexibility, tighter controls over fringe benefits, and an increased reliance on workers with non-standard employment relations such as part-time work, short-term contracts, and independent contractors – many of who are self-employed consultants (Hinrichs, 1991; Kalleberg et al., 2000; Rodgers & Rodgers, 1989). In short, the erosion of the "standard" employment contract coincided with the expansion of self-employment opportunities and a decline in start-up costs (Carré et al., 2000). By the end of the 20th century, the tradeoff between wage work and self-employment was more favorable to self-employment than it had been a quarter-century before.

The post-industrial shift seemingly bodes well for both male and female self-employment. The erosion of the gender gaps in educational attainment, labor force participation, and control over household financial resources greatly enhances women's access to forms of self-employment long dominated by men. More so than ever before, daughters and sons may stand an equal chance to inherit the family firm. However, the relevance of traditional self-employment pathways is not at all assured in this new economic terrain. Parental transmission of self-employment is likely to be weakened by simple demography: the share of workers with self-employed parents declined steadily throughout the last century.

Moreover, the material, human, and social capital that self-employed parents bequeath to their children may be less advantageous during an era of rapid structural change than in less turbulent times. Rapid social and technological change also threatens the effectiveness of school-to-work linkages that previously provided a structured pathway into self-employment. Ongoing educational expansion throughout the latter half of the 20th century was met by an increasing diversity of academic and vocational credentials tailored towards both general and specific skills (Shavit & Müller, 1997). However, if the pace of structural change outpaces the adaptive capacity of the institutional rules that match occupations with appropriate vocational training, credentials will be less useful as mechanisms to foster self-employment entry and stabilize self-employment careers.

Alternative pathways into self-employment may be emerging in post-industrial economies, but persistent gender differences in work careers suggest that these pathways are also likely to be strongly gendered. Women are more likely than men to experience interrupted work careers, so for many women the tradeoff between non-employment and self-employment is as salient as the tradeoff between wage work and self-employment. Employed women are also more likely than employed men to see themselves as primary caretakers and secondary breadwinners in the family, and they may be more willing to give up job security in favor of job flexibility.

The rise in dual-earner households suggests that spousal self-employment may provide an important new family-based pathway into a self-employment career. A successful business run by just one partner may eventually draw in a spouse, in much the same way that parents formerly drew their children into the family firm. Although ostensibly women and men alike may originate a family business, the primacy of men's careers among most married couples suggests that spousal transmission of self-employment is a more important pathway into self-employment among women than among men. Using the same gender reasoning, it is reasonable to expect that the stabilizing effect of spousal self-employment is likely to be greater among self-employed women than among self-employed men.

To the extent that men and women do not share their self-employment careers, a narrowing gender gap in self-employment can be accompanied by a widening gap in the *types* of self-employment jobs held by men and women. The explosion of personal-service businesses in the United States illustrates this point. Rising female labor force participation was accompanied by a transformation of unpaid household labor into a marketplace commodity, as childcare, elder care, pet care, housecleaning, plant care, and gardening are widely available for a fee. These tasks are gendered in the labor market just as they were traditionally gendered in the household, and the increased demand for these services is associated with the rise in female self-employment (Arum, 1997; Carr, 1996; Connelly, 1992). Indeed, gender differences in self-employment outcomes are well documented. Self-employed women earn less than self-employed men; women are more likely than men to engage in part-time self-employment, to have unstable self-employment careers, and to be engaged in personal services in both the United States (e.g. Arum, 1997; Carr, 1996; Devine, 1994) and in Germany (Jungbauer-Gans, 1999).

Some of the gender disparities in self-employment can be explained by the disproportionate share of women who are engaged in the growing market for childcare, eldercare, housecleaning, and other domestic services, and the low value assigned to "women's work" (England et al., 1994; Folbre, 2001). But in part, these gendered outcomes also reflect gendered, socially structured career choices and a gendered pathway into self-employment. Married women with young children may choose self-employment because it allows them to participate in paid work without making a commitment to a job that compromises their primary responsibilities in the home (Carr, 1996; Connelly, 1992; Devine, 1994). This "caregiver" pathway is likely to be unstable, since part of the attraction of self-employment for these mothers is the ease of exit.

COUNTRY DIFFERENCES IN INSTITUTIONAL ARRANGEMENTS

The strength of each pathway into self-employment depends on the institutional context, and although the United States and Germany occupy similar positions in the world economy, the two countries have very different labor market institutions, school-to-work linkages, and family employment patterns.

School-to-Work Linkages and Labor Market Institutions

Weak school-to-work linkages, loosely structured labor markets, and highly decentralized wage mechanisms in the United States foster higher levels of voluntary job mobility, often associated with earnings growth (Topel & Ward, 1992). Job structures in the U.S. wage and salary sector are less fettered by institutional constraints than in the German labor market, and work careers are marked by greater uncertainty and greater flexibility. The rapid pace of technological change spurred a surge in independent contractors in recent years, many of whom provide services that might otherwise be provided by regular employees. Independent contractors typically are self-employed with no employees. This group accounted for roughly the same proportion of the U.S. labor market as the regular self-employed by the mid-1990s (Polivka, Cohany & Hipple, 2000). Workers with specialized knowledge and skills are often able to negotiate favorable compensation packages by bidding up competing offers from potential employers and potential clients simultaneously.

Few self-employment activities in the United States are closely monitored, regulated, or protected by the state or industry associations. The primary exceptions can be found among the liberal professions comprising medicine, law, architecture, and related occupations. Entrance into these occupations is restricted to those holding appropriate credentials, and members of the liberal professions are subject to alternate governance structures, either through specific legal requirements or through regulations specified through professional associations that effectively formalize the rules for professional self-employment (Freidson, 1986). Many states specify a distinct organizational form for self-employed professionals, and apply stricter regulations than apply to other legal forms of self-employment. For example, the law governing professional service corporations in New York restricts the establishment and transfer of such organizations to licensed professionals, typically "accountants, architects, chiropractors, lawyers, physicians, podiatrists, psychologists, and architectural, electrical, industrial, mechanical, and structural engineers" (Freidson, 1986, p. 128).

Professional certification requires an advanced tertiary degree, but vocational training in the United States is typically associated with the vocational-track secondary schools that enroll less than 1% of students in public secondary education (National Center for Education Statistics, 2001). Although post-secondary vocational training is widely available, vocational training has a poor reputation in the United States, and formal company-based training is far less prevalent than in Germany (Winkelmann, 1997). Surprisingly, however, a substantial number of Americans hold specific post-secondary credentials, and many who engage in vocational training that is not sponsored by their employer report that they do so to retain occupational competitiveness (Elman & O'Rand, 1998). In a turbulent self-employment market (McManus, 2000), post-secondary vocational training may stabilize the careers of non-professional entrepreneurs.

In contrast with the United States, Germany has tight school-to-work linkages characterized by a dual system of classroom-based academic training in conjunction with company-based apprenticeships (Müller, Steinman & Ell, 1997). Labor market mobility in Germany is strongly linked to occupational certification (Blossfeld, 1986, Carroll & Mayer, 1986), constraining voluntary job mobility by effectively limiting the set of jobs demanding specific credentials. The German labor market is also characterized by the neocorporatist wage-setting institutions found in many European countries (Goldthorpe, 1984). Although there is no formal minimum wage law, a hierarchical web of industry-level agreements between unions and employer associations effectively establish a standard workweek and an earnings floor for full-time workers which is well above the poverty level (Lange, Wallerstein & Golden, 1995). Centralized wage-setting practices imply not only an earnings floor but an implicit ceiling on job remuneration. The net effect is to reduce both career uncertainty and career mobility in the wage and salary labor market (see Allmendinger, 1989 for a comparison of mobility in the U.S. and Germany), and these effects carry over into mobility into and out of self-employment.

As in the United States, self-employment in the liberal professions is highly regulated. Professionals are marked by status distinctions which carry over into specialized pension structures within the system of national social insurance (International Social Security Association, 1982), and institutional restrictions on the establishment and transfer of professional self-employment organizations is closely tied to occupational privileges. Credentialed self-employment in Germany extends well beyond the professions, however. German laws regulating artisans restrict self-employment entry in the craft sector as well. The *Handwerksrecht* specifies 125 trades, including butchers, bakers, hairdressers, and dispensing opticians, which are legally restricted to certified artisans.

The law specifies the training and certification necessary to engage in these trades, and it mandates the membership of artisan firms in regional bodies which support the trade through training programs and by bringing legal proceedings against uncertified individuals and firms engaging in the trade (Grant & Streeck, 1985). Business owners in the craft sector must either hold the required occupational certificate or employ someone who holds such a certificate. By definition, entry into self-employment in these occupations is restricted to workers with the highest educational and training credentials. The institutionalization of the occupations transcends organizational form. By definition, then, the formal criteria governing labor market mobility in the wage and salary sector also govern mobility into these forms of self-employment.

Rapid technological change in recent years raised concerns about skill mismatch in the vocational training system and inadequate provision for continuing vocational training over the course of workers' careers (Müller, Steinman & Ell, 1997). These factors alone may weaken the traditional pathway from vocational credential to self-employment, and in recent years the credential pathway may have been further weakened by the challenges of a sluggish economy, high unemployment rates, and the ongoing efforts to synchronize institutional arrangements in the East and West. Despite these problems, the system of occupational credentials continues to provide far more structure in the German labor market than is found in the U.S. market. Career credentials are likely to be a more prominent pathway to self-employment in Germany than in the United States.

Family Institutions and Gender

While there is no a priori reason to think that parental resources are more or less useful to self-employment in the U.S. and Germany, the more fluid labor market in the United States provides more alternative avenues for mobility into and out of self-employment. This suggests that the *relative* advantages of parental self-employment may be stronger in Germany, so parental resources may be more effective at facilitating entry and stabilizing careers in Germany than in the United States.

Cross-national differences are likely to be more prominent for newer family-based pathways into self-employment. Female labor force participation is substantially lower in Germany than in the United States, German women are less likely than women in the United States to be in paid employment when their children are very young, and German women are more likely to work part-time when they are employed (Drobnic, Blossfeld & Rohwer, 1999). This suggests that the spousal transmission of self-employment status in Germany is likely to be more strongly gendered than in the United States, with men drawing their wives into the family business rather than the reverse.

More importantly, while the German and U.S. welfare states are distinctive for their failure to play a strong role in providing personal social services like day care and elder care, the household response is very different in each country. Households seeking help must turn to the private sector, or to churches and other non-profit organizations. In Germany, relatively low rates of maternal employment allow many households to continue to rely solely on unpaid household labor. In the United States, high rates of maternal employment, flexible market institutions, and minimal regulations all contribute to a flourishing market for commodified household labor. The market for personal services is less well-developed in Germany, which implies that the "caregiver" pathway into self-employment will be substantially stronger in the United States than in Germany.

METHODS AND DATA

The empirical analyses are designed to investigate whether traditional intergenerational transmission of self-employment is still evident in German and U.S. labor markets; the extent to which career credentials structure self-employment; whether there is evidence of spousal transmission of self-employment; and whether there is evidence for a "caretaker" pathway that moves mothers into self-employment. To recap the earlier discussion of gendered self-employment pathways, I expect that career credentials matter more for men's self-employment careers than for women's, and spousal self-employment matters more for women's self-employment careers than for men's. Career credentials should be a more prominent pathway to self-employment in Germany than in the United States, and spousal transmission of self-employment should be more prominent and more gender-neutral in the United States than in Germany. Finally, I expect the "caregiver" pathway for mothers to be more prominent in the United States than in Germany.

To test these hypotheses, I use longitudinal data from each country to construct measures for alternative pathways to self-employment. The empirical analyses use conventional discrete time event history methods to assess whether each set of measures increases, decreases, or has no effect on the risk of self-employment mobility among men and women in each country. The event history analyses include models for entry into self-employment as well as models for self-employment exit. Both analyses are crucial because self-employment pathways are characteristic of careers, acting to facilitate entry, to stabilize the self-employment spell, or both. For example, in a volatile self-employment market with low start-up costs, many workers might "try" self-employment and "fail" in short order. In such a market, the advantages of a traditional pathway such as parental self-employment might be obscured at the time of entry, but a significant source of self-employment stability.

There are two distinct risk sets for entry into self-employment. A worker can move into self-employment from a wage and salary job or from a position outside the workforce. Over the course of any given observation period, a wage worker can either stay put, take a job with a new employer, leave the workforce, or enter self-employment. Likewise, a respondent who does not hold a job can remain out of the workforce, move into a wage and salary job, or enter self-employment. Since self-employment is one of several potential job mobility outcomes for respondents at risk, I use multinomial logit models to estimate the conditional annual probability of becoming self-employed as opposed to experiencing each alternative outcome.

To facilitate the presentation, entry results are shown only for the contrast between job changes that result in a new self-employment job and job changes that result in a new wage and salary employer (other results are available on request). The exit analyses do not distinguish between alternative outcomes for those who leave self-employment, allowing the use of binary logit event history models to estimate the impact of alternative pathways on self-employment stability. To avoid problems with left-censoring, the exit analyses were limited to the self-employment spell that began during the observation period.

The data for the analyses draws primarily on 14 consecutive annual interviews of households and individuals in each country. The German data comes from the first fourteen waves (1984–1997) of the German Socio-Economic Panel (SOEP). The U.S. sample comes from waves XVII–XXX (1984–1997) of the Panel Study of Income Dynamics (PSID), with matched data on respondents' father's self-employment drawn from waves II–XXX (1969–1997). Both surveys were initially conducted on national probability-based samples with oversamples of target populations of interest (a poverty subsample in the U.S., and an ethnic minority subsample in Germany), requiring the use of sample weights in the analyses. The U.S. data excludes the Latino subsample added to the PSID in 1990, and a refresher sample added in 1997. The German data excludes the subsample of households from the former East Germany and the immigrant subsample begun in 1994.

Sample restrictions were designed to ensure comparable samples of prime working-age men and women who participated in work during the observation period. The sample includes observations on men and women aged 25–54 who were interviewed as sole heads of household or as partners in couple-headed households for at least two consecutive waves, and who were self-employed or in paid employment at the time of at least one interview during the fourteen-year observation period. Respondents who were not sample members were excluded from the sample, as were respondents and/or their partners who reported employment as farmers at any time during the observation period. Missing data (primarily on the education variables) accounted for less than 5% of the sample in each country.

MEASURES

The dependent variables for the analyses are employment transitions. Detailed information on job characteristics was collected each year on all adult household members in the SOEP, and on household heads and their partners in the PSID. Respondents were queried about current work status and job changes during the course of the previous calendar year, and the responses to these questions were used to code spells of employment (including marginal or irregular employment) and non-employment (including temporary layoffs and family leave). Respondents to the PSID were coded as self-employed if they reported that they were currently employed and that they worked primarily for themselves on their main job. In the GSOEP, job spells were classified as self-employment spells if any of the following conditions were met: (1) respondent reported a shift into self-employment at the start of the spell; (2) at any time during the spell, respondent reported being self-employed in response to a question on establishment size or type of employment contract; or (3) respondent reported more months of self-employment income than wage and salary income during the spell, or at least 24 months of self-employment income. The working definition of self-employment in this study includes own-account workers, employers, and unpaid family workers in incorporated and unincorporated businesses. Each spell of employment or non-employment was observed annually at the time of each interview, and if a spell ended between the time of two interviews, a transition was recorded.

The key independent variables for the transition analyses are measures of self-employment pathways. Measures for each of the pathways identified are as follows:

Intergenerational Transmission of Self-Employment. Parental self-employment is measured using data on father's occupational status, since previous research indicates that maternal self-employment has no effect on adult children's self-employment outcomes (McManus, 2001). Household heads in the PSID who reported that their father was a "self-employed businessman" were coded as having a self-employed parent. Respondents were also matched to their parent's interviews dating back to 1968, and respondents whose father reported being self-employed during at least three interviews, were coded as having a self-employed parent.[1] In Germany, father's occupational status was recorded in a biographical interview that captured substantial detail about parental occupation. Respondents who reported that their father was self-employed as a free-lance professional, a proprietor, or an unpaid family worker were coded as having a self-employed father.

Career Credentials. Career credentials are captured through combined indicators of academic degrees and vocational certificates. In Germany, respondents reported both their highest academic degree and their highest vocational qualification. This data was then coded using a modified CASMIN scheme of comparative educational categories, designed to capture educational expansion in Europe during the last decades of the 20th century, and especially the growing number of adults with upper secondary degrees (e.g. *Abitur*) who do not enroll in university, and who often go on to receive additional vocational training (Brauns & Steinmann, 1999).

The modified scheme, The CASMIN categories are (1a) No school degree; (1b) Lower secondary degree (*Hauptschulabschluß, Volkschulabschluß*); (1c) Lower secondary with apprenticeship; (2a) Intermediate secondary degree (*Realschulabschluß*) with apprenticeship or intermediate vocational credential; (2b) Intermediate secondary degree; (2c_gen) Upper secondary, general maturity certificate (*Abitur*); (2c_voc) Upper secondary degree with a vocational credential; (3a) Lower tertiary technical colleges (*Fachhochschule, Ingenieurschule*); (3b) University degrees. In this data, category (2b) was very sparse, so it was collapsed with category (2c_gen).[2]

The great majority of German workers hold some form of occupational credential, but a substantial number of workers report a mismatch between their vocational training and their current job. The variable Credential Fit was created as an indicator of those respondents in Germany who reported that the self-employment job they are working at is the job they trained for. This measure is only available for Germany. Including it, the exit analyses (see Table 6) leads to some loss of comparability with the results for the United States. However, employment credentials are an extremely important part of the German labor market, and a very weak part of the U.S. labor market, so the bias introduced by the omitted variable in the United States is likely to be minimal.

The CASMIN scheme is especially useful for capturing variation in educational qualifications in European countries with strong vocational training institutions (Braun & Müller, 1997), but an adaptation of the CASMIN scheme was developed here in order to assess the impact of post-secondary vocational training on self-employment mobility. Beginning in 1985, respondents to the PSID were asked if they had completed a certificate or obtained a degree from a vocational school, a training school, or an apprenticeship program[3]. Respondents who did not go to college but did complete a certificate or non-academic degree were coded as having a vocational credential, and this measure was combined with traditional academic degrees to produce eight categories of credentials. These are not intended to be directly comparable to the German data, but they are coded in accordance with the CASMIN principle of distinguishing between general and vocational credentials, and they effectively capture the variation in education and vocational training in the United States: (1) Less than high school; (2) Less than high school with a vocational credential; (3) High school and a vocational credential; (4) High school degree; (5) Some college; (6). Some college and a vocational credential; (7) Bachelor's degree; (8) Advanced tertiary degree, e.g. masters or doctoral degree.

Caregiver Responsibilities. To test whether there is a gendered, domestic pathway into self-employment, a variable is included to indicate whether there is at least one child in the household under the age of six.[4]

Spousal Transmission of Self-Employment. Spousal self-employment is measured with a variable that indicates whether or not the respondent was living with a spouse or cohabitant who was self-employed in his or her main job at the onset of the risk period. This measure misses some closely spaced spells of spousal self-employment, but this loss is compensated for by the reduction in ambiguity between sequential and joint spells of self-employment.

Controls

The transition analyses include controls for age (centered at age 25), employer tenure or duration in non-employment, and an indicator for respondents who are neither married nor living with a cohabiting partner.[5] The entry analyses are structured so that the intercept, when exponentiated, can be interpreted as the odds that a married, 25-year-old respondent with no young children, no job tenure, and the lowest credentials will end up in self-employment, given that he or she is making a job shift.

RESULTS

Career Credentials and Family Characteristics of the Self-Employed

As a basic comparison, Table 1 shows sectoral differences in the career credentials and family characteristics of employed men and women in the United States. Self-employed men have higher levels of general education than wage workers, with two-thirds of self-employed men in the U.S. reporting at least some college education, as compared to somewhat more than half of wage workers. The disparity increases with level of education, so that self-employed workers are twice as likely as wage workers to have earned a master's or doctoral degree. But among men with less than a tertiary degree, vocational credentials are less prevalent among the self-employed than among wage workers in the United States.

Table 1. Education and Family Status, Employed Men and Women 25–54, United States.

	Men		Women	
	Wage & Salary (%)	Self-Employed (%)	Wage & Salary (%)	Self-Employed (%)
(1) Less than high school	6.5	5.7	8.0	7.3
(2) Less than high school with vocational credential	2.9	2.0	1.8	1.5
(3) High school and vocational credential	14.9	11.0	14.9*	21.2
(4) High school	20.6*	14.5	24.9	21.3
(5) Some college	14.2	17.6	15.0*	9.8
(6) Some college and a vocational credential	9.3	7.6	10.7	9.4
(7) Bachelor's degree	23.6	24.6	17.8	18.8
(8) Advanced degree	7.9*	17.0	7.1	10.7
Father self-employed	12.7*	19.1	13.0*	17.6
No partner	24.9*	19.5	37.4*	22.5
Partner self-employed	6.7*	17.9	9.2*	30.3
Child under 6 in household	26.9	24.6	21.9*	29.3
N (persons)	2851	757	3404	705

Note: asterisk indicates significant differences between wage & salary and self-employed at $p < 0.05$. Percentages for education categories do not always total 100% because of rounding errors. Includes left-censored self-employment spells that are excluded from transition analyses. Some sample members with multiple spells may contribute to both wage and salary distributions and self-employed distributions.

The opposite is true for women. Self-employed women in the United States are not significantly more educated than women in wage work. They are somewhat more likely to have a bachelor's or advanced degree but also somewhat more likely to have no college education at all. Instead, self-employed women with less than tertiary schooling are more likely to earn a vocational credential than women in wage work.

In contrast with the United States, the credential profile among self-employed men and women in Germany is strikingly similar, despite higher levels of education and training among men. Table 2 shows that both self-employed men and women in Germany have more general education than wage workers. Well over half of self-employed men and women hold at least an intermediate-level qualification, as compared to roughly 45% of wage workers. Self-employed men are half again as

Table 2. Education and Family Status, Employed Men and Women 25–54, Germany.

	Men		Women	
	Wage & Salary (%)	Self-Employed (%)	Wage & Salary (%)	Self-Employed (%)
(1a) No degree	4.9	3.5	4.7	1.7
(1b) Lower secondary	8.5	4.0	16.8	12.9
(1c) Lower secondary and vocational credential	45.4*	36.0	34.0	32.0
(2a) Intermediate secondary and vocational credential	16.1	21.1	22.9	21.3
(2bc_gen) Upper secondary/intermediate secondary	3.0	4.4	5.3	4.4
(2c_voc) Upper secondary and vocational credential	5.9	6.9	6.3	10.1
(3a) Technical college	4.9*	8.3	1.8*	7.1
(3b) University degree	11.4	15.9	8.1	10.6
Credential fit	55.5*	63.9	48.9	44.6
Father self-employed	8.9*	23.9	13.2*	19.6
No partner	24.7*	33.0	32.0*	24.9
Partner self-employed	2.6*	15.3	3.7*	25.5
Child under 6 in household	20.0	17.8	13.2*	18.4
N (persons)	3604	468	2839	417

Note: Asterisk indicates significant differences between wage & salary and self-employed at $p < 0.05$. Percentages for education categories do not always total 100% because of rounding errors. Includes left-censored self-employment spells that are excluded from transition analyses. Some sample members with multiple spells may contribute to both wage and salary distributions and self-employed distributions.

likely to have a degree from a technical college or university as their counterparts in wage work, and self-employed women twice as likely to have a tertiary degree as women in wage work. The share of workers with high-level occupational training in the form of a degree from a technical college is significantly higher in the self-employment sector, but even those self-employed with less than a tertiary degree are more likely to hold vocational credentials than are wage workers.

Despite higher overall education levels, self-employed women are likely to be working in an occupation for which they do not have specific training. The gender gap in career credentials is most evident with respect to the "fit" between occupation and training. The majority of working men are employed in the occupation they trained for, and self-employed men are significantly more likely to have a credential fit than wage workers. Fewer than half of all women trained in their current occupation, and there are no significant differences in credential fit for self-employed women.

The descriptive statistics also show that the family characteristics of the self-employed are significantly different from the family characteristics of wage workers. Aside from German men, the self-employed are significantly more likely than wage workers to be married or cohabiting. Self-employed men and women in both countries are significantly more likely to have a self-employed partner, and to have a father who was self-employed. The primary gender difference in both countries is that links to the conjugal family are especially powerful among self-employed women, and self-employed women are significantly more likely to have young children in the home than are women who hold wage and salary jobs. There is no difference in parental status for self-employed men in either country.

Pathways Into Self-Employment

The descriptive statistics strongly suggest the persistence of intergenerational linkages in the self-employment process. There is also descriptive evidence of linkages to credentials, especially among men, and linkages to the conjugal family, especially among women. The transition analyses investigate these linkages for new entrants into self-employment during the 1980s and 1990s.

The first set of event history analyses model the effect of career credentials and family characteristics on labor influence mobility rates into alternative labor market positions. The primary interest here is in the effect of the pathway variables on the probability that a job changer will end up in self-employment instead of a wage and salary job. These results are presented in Tables 3 and 4.

Table 3 shows the results of the analysis of pathways into self-employment for men and women in the United States. The first and third columns show results

Table 3. Multinomial Logit Event History Analysis for Transitions Into Self-Employment vs. Transitions to New Wage and Salary Employers, United States 1984–1997.

	Men		Women	
	Employed	Not Employed	Employed	Not Employed
Tenure/duration	0.04^{*} (0.017)	0.09 (0.092)	0.03 (0.026)	0.01 (0.031)
Age	0.03^{**} (0.010)	0.02 (0.014)	0.02 (0.011)	0.02^{*} (0.010)
Education & Credentials				
Less than HS + vocational credential	−0.47 (0.379)	0.09 (0.421)	0.17 (0.606)	−0.27 (0.443)
High school + vocational credential	-0.54^{*} (0.275)	−0.23 (0.378)	0.12 (0.367)	−0.18 (0.232)
High school degree	-0.56^{*} (0.274)	0.38 (0.309)	0.02 (0.358)	−0.38 (0.220)
Some college	−0.03 (0.265)	−0.45 (0.378)	0.004 (0.376)	-0.57^{*} (0.270)
Some college + vocational credential	−0.56 (0.308)	−0.64 (0.484)	−0.28 (0.395)	−0.34 (0.280)
Bachelor's degree	−0.22 (0.247)	−0.44 (0.383)	−0.11 (0.372)	−0.40 (0.279)
Advanced degree	0.07 (0.302)	0.41 (0.520)	1.24^{***} (0.375)	-0.94^{*} (0.438)
Family				
Father self-employed	0.37^{*} (0.175)	0.86^{**} (0.267)	−0.02 (0.219)	0.18 (0.197)
No spouse or partner in HH	−0.18 (0.163)	−0.06 (0.238)	−0.15 (0.172)	−0.17 (0.160)
Spouse self-employed	0.43 (0.242)	0.69 (0.461)	0.85^{***} (0.228)	1.03^{***} (0.190)
Children under 6 in HH	0.08 (0.168)	0.07 (0.270)	0.48^{**} (0.176)	0.41^{**} (0.151)
Constant	-2.01^{***} (0.282)	-1.77^{***} (0.376)	-2.79^{***} (0.360)	-1.48^{***} (0.243)
Wald chi-square (df = 13)	58.04	26.66	75.79	47.33
Observations (Person-years)	19700	2581	21951	9400
Self-employment events	371	227	244	488

Note: Numbers in parentheses are standard errors. Omitted category for credentials is less than high school.
$^{*}p < 0.05$.
$^{**}p < 0.01$.
$^{***}p < 0.001$.

Table 4. Multinomial Logit Event History Analysis for Transitions Into Self-Employment vs. Transitions to New Wage and Salary Employers, Germany, 1984–1997.

	Men		Women	
	Employed	Not Employed	Employed	Not Employed
Tenure/Duration	0.04 (0.030)	−0.05 (0.169)	−0.04 (0.095)	−0.05 (0.046)
Age	0.01 (0.023)	0.05* (0.021)	−0.05* (0.018)	0.04** (0.012)
Career credentials				
[1b] Lower secondary	0.28 (0.736)	−1.47 (0.992)	2.58 (1.358)	0.13 (0.491)
[1c] Lower secondary + vocational credential	0.55 (0.552)	−0.20 (0.809)	1.44 (0.996)	0.55 (0.463)
[2a] Intermediate + vocational credential	1.27* (0.572)	0.74 (0.944)	1.62 (1.004)	0.19 (0.496)
[2bc_gen] Upper secondary/intermediate secondary	−0.47 (0.842)	0.70 (0.882)	2.24* (1.023)	1.49* (0.644)
[2c_voc] Upper secondary + vocational credential	1.18 (0.661)	0.24 (0.899)	2.52* (1.075)	0.92 (0.739)
[3a] Technical college	1.38* (0.647)	−0.14 (1.308)	2.92* (1.232)	1.03 (0.713)
[3b] University	0.77 (0.608)	1.87* (0.917)	1.16 (1.098)	0.92 (0.583)
Family				
Father self-employed	−0.08 (0.443)	1.19* (0.487)	−1.90* (0.702)	0.87** (0.290)
No spouse or partner in HH	0.15 (0.334)	−0.50 (0.475)	−0.35 (0.487)	−0.13 (0.316)
Spouse self-employed	0.07 (0.894)	1.38* (0.685)	1.24* (0.547)	1.60*** (0.263)
Children under 6 in HH	0.19 (0.329)	1.04* (0.531)	−0.17 (0.532)	0.35 (0.212)
Constant	−3.32*** (0.577)	−3.05*** (0.840)	−3.49*** (0.959)	−2.94*** (0.464)
Wald chi-square (df = 13)	24.96	38.62	37.99	108.33
Observations	23371	1653	15338	7399
Events	143	74	64	258

Note: Numbers in parentheses are standard errors. Omitted category for credentials is (1a) no degrees or qualifications.
*$p < 0.05$.
**$p < 0.01$.
***$p < 0.001$.

from the analysis of employed men and women, respectively, and the second and fourth columns show results from the analysis of men and women who do not hold a job at the onset of the risk period.

It is important to remember that each of the results for career credentials is interpreted with respect to the omitted category for education, which is also the lowest category, comprising those with less than a high school degree. There are two noteworthy findings on career credentials in the results for men. First, the highest rates of self-employment are observed among men with the least and greatest qualifications. Advanced degree holders and those with no credentials are equally likely to leave wage work for self-employment (column 1), and both groups enter at significantly higher rates than those with a high school degree. Among new entrants (column 2), advanced degree holders are significantly more likely to enter self-employment than those with some college or a bachelor's degree. Second, the net effect of vocational credentials is to inhibit self-employment among those with less than a tertiary degree.

The same findings on career credentials apply to women. The effect of career credentials is also curvilinear for women, but in contrast with men, most women enter self-employment from positions outside the workforce. Among employed women, self-employment rates are undifferentiated by credential except at the very highest level. The odds of entering self-employment are roughly $3\frac{1}{2}$ times greater for women with advanced degrees as compared to women with no qualifications, women with a high school degree, or women with a bachelor's degree. Among women outside the workforce, women with advanced degrees are the least likely to enter self-employment, and the highest rates of entry into self-employment are observed among women with no degrees or credentials. In contrast to the descriptive statistics, the results show no evidence that vocational credentials provide a career pathway into self-employment for women with less than tertiary education. Taken together with the results for men, the findings provide mixed evidence that career credentials structure self-employment in the United States.

However, there is evidence of both traditional and emerging family pathways to self-employment careers in the United States. Intergenerational pathways still have significant "pull" over men in the United States, whether they are employed in the wage and salary sector (column 1) or especially if they are out of the workforce at the start of the risk period (column 2). Spousal transmission also appears to be an important pathway into self-employment for men, although the results are only marginally significant ($p = 0.07$ and $p = 0.14$).[6]

The findings for women's family pathways are consistent for women in the workforce and those outside. Surprisingly, given the evidence that men are still influenced by parental self-employment, father's self-employment has no effect on women's entrance into self-employment. Instead, these results confirm the conclusion that women's self-employment is more strongly linked to the conjugal family. Women with a self-employed spouse have two to three times the odds of entering self-employment as compared to women married to a man with a wage job, all else being equal. Mothers of young children have odds half again as large as women without young children. These effects hold for women who are employed, and for women who are not.

The analysis of pathways into self-employment in Germany is presented in Table 4, and the omitted category for career credentials is again those with no qualifications. The results for men (columns 1, 2) show that the rate of transition into self-employment increases with qualifications. Men with upper tertiary degrees are most likely to enter self-employment directly from positions outside the workforce. Even among employed men, however, those with tertiary degrees have the highest rates of transition while men with lower secondary education have low rates of mobility into self-employment. The results also show that vocational credentials are as important to self-employment mobility in Germany as is general education. Men with intermediate and upper-level general qualifications, especially, are significantly more likely to enter self-employment if they also hold a vocational qualification.

Women's self-employment mobility in Germany is both less differentiated than men's and less strongly tied to vocational credentials. The results in column 3 show that women with any educational qualifications are significantly more likely to enter self-employment than women with no qualifications, but there are no significant differences between CASMIN categories, nor are there differences by vocational credentials. The transition rates are substantively the same for women in CASMIN (1a), with only a lower secondary degree, and women in CASMIN (2c_voc), with both an upper secondary degree (*Abitur*) and vocational qualifications. Among women moving into the workforce, only women in CASMIN (2c_gen) are significantly more likely to become self-employed than women with no academic or vocational credentials.

The results for the effect of family characteristics on self-employment mobility in Germany are striking because the pathways operate very differently depending on whether the origin state is within or outside the workforce. Among employed German men, family characteristics have no effect at all on self-employment mobility (Table 4, column 1). However, both traditional and new family pathways structure men's entry into the workforce. Among German men moving into the workforce, father's self-employment increases the odds of self-employment entry threefold, spousal self-employment increases the odds by a factor of four, and, surprisingly, men with young children and no job also have a higher risk of moving into self-employment. This result cannot reasonably be interpreted as a "caregiver" pathway among men. It may reflect a life course effect among university graduates in the liberal professions, or possibly the effect of family pressures in pushing unemployed men into self-employment.

For women in Germany, as for men, father's self-employment is a significant pathway into self-employment, but only among women outside the workforce. Women in wage and salary jobs are significantly *less* likely to move into self-employment if they have a self-employed father. Two other results underscore gender differences and cross-national differences in self-employment. First, spousal transmission of self-employment is more prominent among women than among men in Germany, increasing the odds of self-employment entry among women who hold wage jobs as well as women who are just entering the workforce. Second, the results do not support the hypothesis that a "caregiver" pathway into self-employment exists among mothers in Germany.

Self-Employment Stability

The traditional pathway into self-employment, by inheriting the family firm, was a source of career stability as well as career direction. In the next set of analyses, I ask whether intergenerational pathways, career credentials, spousal self-employment, and domestic responsibilities stabilize, destabilize, or have no effect on the careers of new entrants into self-employment. The exit analyses model the duration of the employment spells that began during 1985–1996 in each country, and which were observed as events in the transition analyses.[7] It is worth noting that in all of these results, the best predictor of self-employment stability is simple endurance: the longer the spell of self-employment lasts, the more likely that it will endure another year.

Table 5 shows that career credentials do stabilize self-employment careers in the United States. The high entry rates into self-employment among workers with no high school degree or vocational training is matched by a high exit rate, while the high rates of entry among advanced degree holders result in the most stable self-employment spells. The effects of general education are fairly linear and progressive for both men and women. Yet while men gain no additional advantages from vocational credentials, there is some evidence that vocational credentials stabilize the self-employment careers of women. Women with a high school degree are somewhat less likely to exit self-employment if they hold an additional vocational credential. These women may be the licensed beauticians and hairdressers who account for a substantial share of female self-employment.

Family characteristics have no impact on self-employment stability among men in the United States, except that unmarried men are more likely to exit self-employment jobs, just as unmarried men are more likely to exit wage and

Table 5. Event History Analysis for Transitions Out of Self-Employment Men and Women Aged 25–54, United States 1985–1997.

	Men	Women
Tenure/duration	-0.18^{***} (0.027)	-0.20^{***} (0.028)
Age	-0.01^{**} (0.010)	−0.01 (0.009)
Career credentials		
Less than HS + vocational credential	0.19 (0.269)	−0.17 (0.274)
High school + vocational credential	−0.34 (0.236)	-0.55^{**} (0.211)
High school degree	−0.32 (0.224)	−0.37 (0.208)
Some college	-0.65^{**} (0.239)	-0.49^{*} (0.231)
Some college + vocational credential	-0.68^{**} (0.239)	-0.56^{*} (0.249)
Bachelor's degree	-0.56^{*} (0.231)	-0.90^{***} (0.226)
Advanced degree	-0.89^{**} (0.275)	-0.99^{***} (0.258)
Family		
Father self-employed	−0.25 (0.150)	−0.29 (0.163)
No spouse or partner in HH	0.45^{**} (0.147)	0.07 (0.138)
Spouse self-employed	−0.25 (0.177)	-0.30^{*} (0.129)
Children under 6 in HH	0.18 (0.161)	0.37^{**} (0.132)
Constant	-0.54^{***} (0.250)	0.12^{***} (0.237)
Wald chi-square (df = 13)	109.52	111.12
Observations (person-years)	2703	2234
Exit events	581	697

Note: Numbers in parentheses are standard errors. Omitted category for credentials is less than high school.

$^{*}p < 0.05$.

$^{**}p < 0.01$.

$^{***}p < 0.001$.

salary jobs. In contrast with men, family pathways continue to influence women's self-employment careers after entry. Self-employed women are less likely to exit if their partner is also self-employed. Although it is not possible to discern whether these partners are jointly running a family business, it seems likely that many self-employed couples are doing just that. The results for women provide additional support for the development of a "caretaker" pathway into self-employment. Self-employed women who started their spell with a young child in the household have higher rates of exit than do other self-employed women.

The results for Germany in Table 6 show that career credentials are an important source of self-employment stability to the extent that they provide a match between vocational training and occupational destination. The stabilizing effect of credential "fit" is similar for men and women. Once this credential match

Table 6. Event History Analysis for Transitions out of Self-Employment Men and Women Aged 25–59, Germany 1985–1997.

	Men	Women
Tenure/Duration	−0.20* (0.094)	−0.19** (0.057)
Age	−0.08* (0.031)	0.01 (0.016)
Career credentials		
[1b] Lower secondary	0.84 (0.869)	0.48 (0.591)
[1c] Lower secondary + vocational credential	0.66 (0.718)	0.34 (0.527)
[2a] Intermediate + vocational credential	0.60 (0.739)	0.32 (0.548)
[2bc_gen] Upper secondary/intermediate secondary	0.32 (0.837)	0.76 (0.655)
[2c_voc] Upper Secondary + vocational credential	2.04* (0.885)	−1.06 (0.690)
[3a] Technical college	0.54 (0.789)	0.65 (0.682)
[3b] University	1.48 (0.787)	0.71 (0.607)
Credential Fit	−0.85* (0.352)	−0.88** (0.260)
Family		
Father self-employed	−0.02 (0.297)	−0.51 (0.333)
No spouse or partner in HH	0.16 (0.310)	0.27 (0.341)
Spouse self-employed	−0.26 (0.446)	0.02 (0.255)
Children under 6 in HH	0.46 (0.333)	0.33 (0.253)
Constant	−1.23 (0.803)	−1.35 (0.550)
Wald chi-square (df = 14)	55.66	52.05
Observations (person-years)	947	991
Exit events	126	222

Note: Numbers in parentheses are standard errors. Omitted category for credentials is (1a) no degrees or qualifications.

*$p < 0.05$.

**$p < 0.01$.

has been accounted for, there is little demarcation of self-employment stability by career credentials or family self-employment. The absence of any strong relationships between career credentials and exit rates in Germany may also be an artifact of the more structured pathway into self-employment. In the more stable labor markets of Germany, resource stratification at entry appears to minimize resource stratification at exit.

DISCUSSION

Parental self-employment and career credentials continue to play a role in self-employment careers in the United States and Germany. At the same time, the changing gender composition of the workforce, and the rise in dual earner households has fostered new pathways into self-employment. The institutional source of these new pathways is not the educational system, but the family. Spousal transmission of self-employment is an important pathway in both countries, and there is evidence of a "caretaker" pathway into self-employment in the United States.

The results show important gender differences. Education and vocational training provide mobility pathways for women as well as men, but in both countries, men's self-employment careers are more clearly delineated by career credentials than women's self-employment careers. As expected, the results confirm that career credentials are less important to women's self-employment mobility than family pathways. Women's self-employment careers are more sensitive to characteristics of the conjugal family – especially to partner's self-employment – than are men's self-employment careers.

The evidence also points to cross-national differences in self-employment mobility. As expected, entrance into self-employment in Germany is strongly tied to career credentials. Both general qualifications and vocational training are important at entry, and self-employment is stabilized by training that matches the self-employment occupation. Career credentials are less important at entry into self-employment in the United States, and despite the prevalence of post-secondary credentials, vocational training does not foster entrance into self-employment. Instead, mobility into self-employment is highest among the least educated and the most educated, while there is a strong, linear effect of education on self-employment stability.

These differences may be interpreted in light of institutional arrangements in each labor market. In Germany, career pathway into self-employment remains highly structured even in an economy under pressure. Once entry has been accomplished, self-employment careers are relatively stable, and credential fit is the primary sorting process. The lack of occupational credentials as "gatekeepers" in the United States means that sorting takes place *after* self-employment entry, resulting in the much stronger relationship between academic qualifications and exit rates in the United States. The results also suggest that much of the volatility of the self-employment sector in the United States can be attributed to "churning" among the low-skilled self-employed, who enter more readily and exit more rapidly than skilled workers.

The institutional embeddedness of self-employment careers is also evident in the cross-national differences in the relationships between gender, family, and self-employment outcomes. Family pathways structured self-employment entry in both countries, but although these effects were found among jobholders and new entrants alike in the United States, the effects of family were largely confined to the transition *into* the workforce in Germany. Among men, especially, the structured labor market in Germany may buffer workers' careers from family influences once they have achieved "insider" status, while flexible labor markets in the United States remain permeable to family influences.

Not all of the family effects were expected. The expectation that women would have access to traditional family resources via the intergenerational transmission of self-employment was borne out only in Germany. And although I expected the "caregiver" pathway to self-employment to be less well-developed in Germany, support for this pathway was found only in the United States. Moreover, while findings supported the prediction that men and especially women who live with a self-employed partner are more likely to become self-employed themselves, the evidence for spousal transmission of self-employment from wives to husbands was stronger in Germany than in the United States. This result is surprising, but it should be interpreted with caution because it reflects self-employment entry among the handful of men who were married to a self-employed wife but reported not having a job themselves. In the larger sample of German men who held a job at the onset of the risk period, the effect of spousal self-employment is both statistically insignificant and close to zero in magnitude.

A possible explanation for these unexpected findings may be that self-employment is more strongly sex-segregated in the United States than in Germany. If so, gender differences in self-employment careers in Germany may arise less from sex-segregation of self-employment occupations than from gender differences in employment participation and hours worked. Women in Germany may participate in the family business and run it alone if necessary, and women may also be more likely to work part time or leave the business for extended periods. Women in the United States also participate in their partner's business, but many self-employed women are providing childcare and other low-paid domestic services that offer poor prospects for a joint family business.

Although this research lays out some important gender differences in self-employment mobility patterns, future research should address the implications of these gender differences. Two outcomes are of special interest. First, research on the occupational destinations of self-employed women and men is necessary to provide a context for the interpretation of cross-national differences in self-employment mobility. Second, future research should address the implications of gendered patterns of self-employment on gender inequality in income, both within the context of individual spells of self-employment and over the course of men's and women's careers.

This research extends comparative research on labor market dynamics by demonstrating that in the self-employment sector, as in the wage and salary sector, cross-national differences in job mobility can be attributed to differences in educational systems and institutional arrangements in the labor market. The research also shows that conventional resources/rewards explanations of mobility dynamics are seriously limited by their neglect of family processes in the labor market. These findings are limited to the self-employment sector, but they show that family arrangements help to explain men's mobility, and they are essential for explaining women's careers. Incorporating family processes into comparative research will also provide a more complete explanation for cross-national differences in labor market outcomes.

NOTES

1. Matching parental records greatly increased the proportion of respondents who were coded as having a self-employed father. All of the PSID respondents in the subsample used in these analyses were in sample households in 1969, or were born into sample households after that time. Respondents who could not be matched were coded using only the family background data.
2. These observations were included for completeness, and coded to reflect the absence of vocational training. Results were substantively the same when these observations were dropped altogether.
3. The sample begins in 1984, but all sample respondents in 1984 were also interviewed in 1985, so the 1985 data were used to fill in values for 1984.
4. A more inclusive measure of caregiving would account for care of non-children in the household. There are questions on the health of household members in both the GSOEP and the PSID, however the questions are not strictly comparable, and the wording of the PSID variable changed over time. The presence of young children in the household measures most, but not all caregiving responsibilities, and the measure is the same in the German and the U.S. data.
5. Cohabitants in these data are heterosexual partners, and in the PSID only partners who have been together for two interviews are classified as cohabitants. In the remainder of the paper, references to "marriage" and "spouses," etc. will be used to refer to both marital and cohabiting relationships.
6. The coefficients for spousal self-employment are large, indicating that spousal self-employment might increase men's odds of becoming self-employed by a factor of one and a half to two, and the large standard error is likely due to the heterogeneity of women's self-employment.
7. The entry analysis includes self-employment spells that occurred in 1997, but only spells beginning before 1997 could be observed to "fail."

ACKNOWLEDGMENTS

Earlier versions of this paper were presented at the Spring, 2000 meeting of the Research Committee on Social Stratification and Mobility of the International Sociological Association, in Libourne, France and at the GSOEP 2000 Conference in Berlin, Germany. I am grateful to Jack L. Thomas for assistance with data preparation, and to Richard Arum, Mariah Evans, Walter Müller, Sylvia Luber, Henning Lohmann, two anonymous reviewers, and the editors of *Research in the Sociology of Education* for providing helpful comments on earlier drafts. I thank the Deutsches Institut für Wirtschaftsforschung for providing access to the German Socio-Economic Panel (SOEP), and the Cross-National Equivalent File (CNEF) project at the College of Human Ecology at Cornell University, Ithaca, NY, for providing access to harmonized data from the SOEP and the Panel Study of Income Dynamics.

REFERENCES

Allmendinger, J. (1989). *Career mobility dynamics: A comparative analysis of the United States, Norway, and West Germany*. Berlin: Max Planck Institut für Bildungsforschung.

Althauser, R. P. (1989). Internal labor markets. *Annual Review of Sociology*, *15*, 163–186.

Aronowitz, S., & Cutler, J. (Eds) (1998). *Post work: The wages of cybernation*. New York: Routledge.

Aronson, R. L. (1991). *Self-employment: A labor market perspective*. Ithaca, NY: ILR.

Arum, R. (1997). Trends in male and female self-employment: Growth in a new middle class or increasing marginalization of the labor force? *Research in Social Stratification and Mobility*, *15*, 209–238.

Bell, D. (1960). *The end of ideology: On the exhaustion of political ideas in the fifties*. Glencoe, IL: Free Press.

Blau, P. M., & Duncan, O. D. (1967). *The American occupational structure*. New York: Wiley.

Block, F. L. (1990). *Postindustrial possibilities: A critique of economic discourse*. Berkeley: University of California Press.

Blossfeld, H. P. (1986). Career opportunities in the FRG: A dynamic approach to the study of life-course, cohort, and period effects. *European Sociological Review*, *2*, 208–225.

Braun, M., & Müller, W. (1997). Measurement of education in comparative research. *Comparative Social Research*, *16*, 163–201.

Brauns, H., & Steinmann, S. (1999). Educational reform in France, West-Germany, the United Kingdom, and Hungary. Updating the CASMIN Educational Classification. ZUMA-Nachrichten 23.

Carr, D. (1996). Two paths to self-employment? *Work and Occupations*, *23*, 26–53.

Carré, F., Ferber, M. A., Golden, L., & Herzenberg, S. A. (Eds) (2000). *Nonstandard work: The nature and challenges of changing employment relations*. Champaign, IL: Industrial Relations Research Association.

Carroll, G. R., & Mayer, K. U. (1986). Job shift patterns in the Federal Republic of German: The effects of social class, industrial sector, and organizational size. *American Sociological Review*, *51*, 323–341.

Connelly, R. (1992). Self-employment and providing child care. *Demography*, *29*, 17–29.

Devine, T. J. (1994). Changes in wage-and-salary returns to skill and the recent rise in female self-employment. *American Economic Review*, *84*, 108–113.

Drobnic, S., Blossfeld, H. P., & Rohwer, G. (1999). Dynamics of women's employment patterns over the family life-course: A comparison of the United States and Germany. *Journal of Marriage and the Family*, *61*, 133–146.

Dunn, T., & Holtz-Eakin, D. (2000). Financial capital, human capital, and the transition to self-employment: Evidence from intergenerational links. *Journal of Labor Economics, 18*, 282–305.

Elman, C., & O'Rand, A. (1998). Midlife entry into vocational training: A mobility model. *Social Science Research, 27*, 128–158.

England, P., Herbert, M. S., Kilbourne, B. S., Reid, L. L., & Megdal, L. M. (1994). The gendered valuation of occupations and skills: Earnings in 1980 census occupations. *Social Forces, 73*, 65–100.

Folbre, N. (2001). *The invisible heart: Economics and family values*. New York: New Press.

Freidson, E. (1986). *Professional powers: A study of the institutionalization of formal knowledge*. Chicago: University of Chicago Press.

Goldthorpe, J. H. (1984). The end of convergence: Corporatist and dualist tendencies in modern Western societies. In: J. H. Goldthorpe (Ed.), *Order and Conflict in Contemporary Capitalism* (pp. 315–343). Oxford: Oxford University Press.

Grant, W., & Streeck, W. (1985). Large firms and the representation of business interests in the U.K. and West German construction industry. In: A. Cawson (Ed.), *Organized Interests and the State* (pp. 145–173). London: Sage.

Hinrichs, K. (1991). Irregular employment patterns and the loose net of social security: Some findings on the West German development. In: M. Adler, C. Bell, J. Clasen & A. Sinfield (Eds), *The Sociology of Social Security* (pp. 110–127). Edinburgh: Edinburgh University Press.

Hout, M., & Rosen, H. S. (2000). Self-employment, family background and race. *Journal of Human Resources, 35*, 671–692.

International Social Security Association (1982). *The social protection of self-employed workers*. Report of the European Regional Meeting on the Social Protection of Self-Employed Non-Agricultural Workers, Paris 4–6 November 1981. International Social Security Association, Geneva.

Jungbauer-Gans, M. (1999). The wage gap between female and male self-employed and employed persons in West Germany Der Lohnunterschied zwischen Frauen und Männern in selbständiger und abhängiger Beschäftigung. *Kölner Zeitschrift für Soziologie und Sozialpsychologie, 51*, 364–390.

Kalleberg, A. (1988). Comparative perspectives on work structures and inequality. *Annual Review of Sociology, 14*, 203–225.

Kalleberg, A. L., Reskin, B., & Hudson, K. (2000). Bad jobs in America: Standard and nonstandard employment relations and job quality in the United States. *American Sociolocial Review, 65*, 256–278.

Lange, P., Wallerstein, M., & Golden, M. (1995). The end of corporatism? Wage setting in the Nordic and Germanic countries. In: S. Jacoby (Ed.), *The Workers of Nations: Industrial Relations in a Global Economy* (pp. 76–98). New York: Oxford University Press.

McManus, P. (2000). Market, state, and the quality of new self-employment jobs among men in the United States and Western Germany. *Social Forces, 78*, 865–905.

McManus, P. (2001). Women's participation in self-employment in western industrialized nations. *International Journal of Sociology, 31*, 70–97.

Müller, W., Steinman, S., & Ell, R. (1997). Education and labor market entry in Germany. In: Y. Shavit & W. Müller (Eds) *From School to Work: A Comparative Study of Educational Qualifications and Occupational Destinations* (pp. 243–297). New York: Clarendon.

National Center for Education Statistics (2001). *Statistics in brief. Overview of public elementary and secondary schools and districts: School year 1999–2000*. Washington, DC: U.S. Department of Education, Office of Educational Research and Improvements.

Organization for Economic Cooperation & Development (1998). *Fostering entrepreneurship*. Paris: OECD.

Piore, M. J., & Sabel, C. F. (1984). *The second industrial divide*. New York: Basic Books.
Polivka, A. E., Cohany, S. R., & Hipple, S. (2000). Definition, composition, and economic consequences of the nonstandard workforce. In: F. Carré, M. A. Ferber, L. Golden & S. A. Herzenberg (Eds), *Nonstandard Work: The Nature and Challenges of Changing Employment Arrangements* (pp. 41–94). Champaign, IL: Industrial Relations Research Association.
Rodgers, G., & Rodgers, J. (1989). *Precarious jobs in labour market regulation: The growth of atypical employment in western Europe*. Geneva: International Labour Organization.
Rosenfeld, R. A. (1992). Job mobility and career processes. *Annual Review of Sociology, 18*, 39–61.
Shavit, Y., & Müller, W. (Eds) (1997). *From school to work: A comparative study of educational qualifications and occupational destinations*. Oxford: Clarendon.
Smith, V. (1997). New forms of work organization. *Annual Review of Sociology, 23*, 315–339.
Spence, M. A. (1973). Job market signaling. *The Quarterly Journal of Economics, 87*, 355–374.
Steinmetz, G., & Wright, E. O. (1989). The fall and rise of the petty Bourgeosie: Changing patterns of self-employment in the postwar United States. *American Journal of Sociology, 94*, 973–1018.
Topel, R. H., & Ward, M. P. (1992). Job mobility and the careers of young men. *The Quarterly Journal of Economics, 107*, 439–479.
Winkelmann, R. (1997). How young workers get their training: A survey of Germany versus the United States. *Journal of Population Economics, 10*, 159–170.
Wong, R. S. K. (1992). Vertical and nonvertical effects in class mobility: Cross-national variations. *American Sociological Review, 57*, 396–410.

HEATING UP THE ASPIRATIONS OF ISRAELI ARAB YOUTH

Gad Yair, Nabil Khattab and Aaron Benavot

ABSTRACT

An empirical study of the aspirations of Israeli Arab high school students shows that in comparison with the low educational and occupational attainments of their predecessors, Israeli Arab high school students hold unrealistic, highly optimistic views regarding their future educational and occupational destinations, irrespective of their social origins. These findings contradict extant sociological perspectives, which view the gap between aspirations and destinations as improbable, and to the extent that this gap exists, as an expression of naiveté, ignorance, or non-rationality. The puzzling gaps between aspirations and destinations among Israeli Arab adolescents led to a new model of the production of minority aspirations. This model suggests that high aspirations among minority youth are produced by converging expectations of local community leaders, school personnel, and parents, who actively heat up future aspirations amongst young cohorts. The paper concludes with proposals for comparative studies of minority aspirations in different societies.

> The cooling-out process in higher education is one whereby systematic discrepancy between aspiration and avenue is covered, and stress for the individual and the system is minimized . . . The general result of cooling-out processes is that society can continue to encourage maximum effort without major disturbance from unfulfilled promises and expectations (Clark, 1960, p. 576).

Inequality Across Societies: Families, Schools and Persisting Stratification
Research in Sociology of Education, Volume 14, 201–224
(Formerly Research in Sociology of Education and Socialization)

ISSN: 1479-3539/doi:10.1016/S1479-3539(03)14009-8

INTRODUCTION

Studies seeking to explain educational inequalities between minority and majority students have traditionally relied on the Wisconsin model (Sewell & Hauser, 1980), which highlights how educational and occupational aspirations mediate the relationship between social origins and occupational destinations (Jencks, Crouse & Mueser, 1983). Most of the theoretical statements in the sociology of education predict that majority students receive supportive messages from parents, teachers, and peers, thereby enhancing their aspiration levels. In contrast, it was theoretically conjectured that the less enthusiastic interpersonal experiences of minority students result in "cooled out" aspirations. Whether viewed as a consequence of the normative pressures of significant others or of their own accompanying rational calculations (Morgan, 1998), minority students are expected to exhibit lower levels of educational and occupational aspirations.

However, several empirical shortcomings have been identified in this theoretical tradition. First, the vast majority of empirical research testing the "cooling-out" thesis has employed evidence from a single case that is, in many respects, unusual: the USA (Buchmann & Dalton, 2002). Second, the widely-held prediction that aspirations among minority youth will be lower than those of majority youth is contradicted in recent studies (Buchmann & Dalton, 2002; Kao & Tienda, 1998). Most importantly, given the apparent tendency for minority youth to develop surprisingly high aspirations in diverse educational contexts, few convincing theoretical explanations have been put forward to account for this puzzling phenomenon.

This paper proposes to contribute theoretical clarity to the literature of minority adolescent aspirations by broadening its comparative study through a systematic analysis of several Israeli-Arab sub-group populations. Furthermore, we propose an alternative theoretical explanation for the formation of aspirations among minority youth. Empirically, the study compares the educational and occupational aspirations of Christian, Moslem, and Druze adolescents in Israel. The results show that Arab adolescents espouse to very high educational and occupational goals, which are not only weakly related to their social background but also stand in stark contrast to their probable future destinations in the labor market. This gap between aspirations and destinations – conventionally depicted as problematic, dysfunctional, and/or non-rational in sociological literature – is analyzed in the latter part of the paper.

In proposing an alternative theoretical explanation for minority youth aspirations, we argue that it is not only important to enlarge the range of educational contexts in which the antecedents and consequents of minority aspirations are examined, but also to widen the scope of social structures and agents involved in their production. We suggest that in certain societies, members of minority communities actively produce high future aspirations among their youth, thus minimizing the effects of social background on aspirations (Marjoribanks, 2002). Ideally, comparative studies should be able to show the conditions under which, and the mechanisms through which, minority youth aspirations are either "cooled-out" or "warmed-up." In the case of Arab adolescents in Israel, the evidence suggests that local politicians, principals, and parents intentionally heat up student aspirations in order to advance collective as well as personal aims. Thus, our call in support of comparative studies is intended to reorient analytical models to examine in which societies, and among which minority groups, adolescent aspirations result from differential "cooling-out" or "warming-up" processes.

THEORETICAL BACKGROUND

High school majority student aspirations and expectations are conventionally regarded as among the most significant contributors to eventual educational and occupational attainments (Schneider & Stevenson, 1999). This relationship has been consistently confirmed by a wealth of studies, particularly for students belonging to majority and dominant groups (see, for example Armer & Sewell, 1972; Ayalon & Yuchtman-Yaar, 1989; Hanson, 1994; Hao & Bruns, 1988; Hauser & Anderson, 1991; Sewell & Hauser, 1980; Stanton-Salazar & Dornbusch, 1995).

By contrast, the study of minority student aspirations is mired with puzzling contradictions. Supporting lay expectations and theoretical conjectures, many studies have previously recorded low educational and occupational aspirations among students belonging to ethnic or cultural minorities (Alexander & Cook, 1979; Gibson & Ogbu, 1991; Hanson, 1994; Hauser & Anderson, 1991; Kerckhoff, 1976; Marjoribanks, 1988; McLeod, 1987; McNair & Brown, 1983; Mickelson, 1990; Sewell & Shah, 1968; Solorzano, 1992; Stanton-Salazar & Dornbusch, 1995). However, growing empirical literature indicates that minority students actually exhibit very high educational and occupational aspirations (Ford & John, 1996; Goyette & Xie, 1999; Kao & Tienda, 1998; Morgan, 1996) with many having aspirations similar to – and at times even higher than – those held by majority students (Marjoribanks, 2002).

These "surprising" results emanate from theoretical commitments which led most scholars to assume that students align their aspirations with extant societal conditions. These commitments are apparent in different levels of analysis or causal factors proposed – all deemed to be gradually working to cool out students' educational and occupational aspirations.

Beginning at the individual level, many scholars expect to find large between-group inequalities in students' educational and occupational aspirations. More specifically, noting the lower position of minority groups in prevailing labor markets, scholars expect that minority student aspirations will reflect these social inequalities, and eventually reproduce them (Bourdieu, 1988; Bourdieu & Passeron, 1977, 1979). Thus, students' socioeconomic background is predicted to affect their aspirations. Similarly, it is expected that student-level attributes such as gender and religious affiliation will affect educational and occupational aspirations. The Wisconsin tradition suggests that parental expectations are also likely to affect students' aspirations (Buchmann & Dalton, 2002; Sewell & Hauser, 1980).

The literature further suggests that contextual variables may also affect students' educational and occupational aspirations. There is considerable evidence that students' institutional location in school affects their aspirations (Buchmann & Dalton, 2002). Similarly, students' academic success in school also affects their aspirations. It is also probable that school climate and teachers' support may affect students' future aspirations. Specifically, it is proposed that students' positions in a lower track in high school should cool out their aspirations (Friedkin & Thomas, 1997; Gamoran, 1986). The fact that minority students are concentrated in lower tracks (Page, 1991) and are the target of differential expectations by teachers (Yair, 1997) reduces the few grains of optimism they might have had otherwise. Finally, there is some evidence that community variables may also affect students' aspirations, because locales differ in labor market opportunities and the returns for education (Beattie, 2002).

While the theoretical discussion of student aspirations has diversified during the past three decades and become more critical, most of the theoretical statements in the sociology of education still predict minority students to evince low aspirations – even when this has been shown empirically not to be the case. Thus, while diverging in orientations and premises, extant theories hypothesize that minority students should evince lower aspirations relative to majority students. They further define rationality in terms of functional congruence between aspirations and reality. Students are said to be realistic (i.e. rational) if they closely align their educational and occupational aspirations with the objective distribution of adult attainments in society.

These theoretical presuppositions produce problematic interpretations of reported empirical findings. First, when minority groups exhibit similar aspirations to those of majority youth, the former are interpreted as having "over-shot" their aspirations (Kao & Tienda, 1998), while high aspirations among majority students are viewed uncritically as "natural" (Breen & Goldthorpe, 1997). Secondly, in testing extant theories of student aspirations, empirical studies seem predisposed to focus on social inequalities even when equality is actually apparent (Kao & Tienda, 1998).

This theoretical commitment creates significant conceptual enigmas: (1) What social conditions and mechanisms are actually producing the reported high aspirations espoused by minority students? and (2) Why are socioeconomic inequalities in student aspirations and expectations so much smaller than generally anticipated? The following empirical study makes a small step towards providing an answer to these pertinent questions.

The study uses a national representative sample of Arab high school students in Israel to investigate the educational and occupational aspirations of these students against the background of the limited opportunities that await them a few years hence. Diverging from similar efforts to compare majority-minority differences in aspirations (Seginer, 1988a, b), the present research focuses solely on Arab minority students while "dividing" the concept of "Arab minority" into the different religious groups that comprise this category: Christian, Moslem, and Druze.

THE CONTEXT OF THE STUDY

Israel is a bi-ethnic state where Jews (81%) and Arabs (19%) share the same geographical region, yet live mainly in separate localities (Central Bureau of Statistics, 2000: Table 2.1b; at www.cbs.gov.il). The Arab minority is residentially segregated from the Jewish majority and subordinate to it in many respects (Lewin-Epstein & Semyonov, 1994). About 85% of the Arabs in Israel live in segregated Arab locales in three regions: The Galilee, the Little Triangle, and the Negev, while about 15% live in mixed Arab-Jewish cities (e.g. Jaffa). The residential segregation of Arabs in Israel is partly a result of national and cultural factors (Lewin-Epstein & Semyonov, 1994), but no less importantly a product of historical and political factors (Rosenfeld, 1997).

Israeli Arabs suffer from extremely limited employment opportunities, high unemployment rates, and latent job discrimination. Based on legally binding security rationales, Arabs have been historically barred from jobs in government ministries and the public sector. Consequently, Arabs have historically been situated at the bottom of the labor ladder, employed in service provision, agriculture, construction, and manual labor in low-paying industries (Lewin-Epstein & Semyonov, 1994). The easing of restrictions and economic growth has not significantly altered the labor market position of Arabs. Even highly qualified university graduates (e.g. lawyers, physicians, engineers, scientists) encounter considerable difficulties and discrimination when seeking suitable positions in the dominant Jewish labor market, leaving them little choice but to pursue employment in ethnic Arab enclaves (Semyonov & Cohen, 1990; Shavit, 1992). "Blocked" labor market opportunities channel many highly educated Arabs into specialized occupational niches, especially the teaching profession (Al-Haj, 1995). Furthermore, since Arab society maintains traditional customs, women are extremely underrepresented in the labor market, with only 19% actually in the labor force.

Internally, Arab society is divided into distinct subgroups. The most prominent division is according to religion: Moslems comprise 75% of the Israeli-Arab population, Christians 16%, and Druze 9%. These subgroups also differ in terms of demographic characteristics, labor market employment, and their relations with the Jewish majority. While most Muslims and Druze live in villages, Christians are mostly urban. The latter also have lower fertility rates and higher educational and occupational attainments than Muslims and Druze. Furthermore, since 1956, Druze males have been conscripted into the Israeli military, a service which entitles them to certain benefits (Al-Haj, 1995).

The internal religious division is also reflected in the organization of Israeli-Arab education. For the most part, Moslem students attend Moslem schools, Druze attend mostly Druze schools, and Christians attend Christian schools (Mazawi, 1996). In fact, two national administrative bodies oversee the educational affairs of the Arab population: one public system mainly caters to Moslem students, while another public system assists Druze students. Christian students mostly attend elite private schools.

Arab schools are separated from Jewish schools both geographically and administratively, yet lack political autonomy: the funding, governance, and curricula of public Arab schools are tightly controlled by the State (Benavot & Resh, 2001). Compared to schools in the Jewish sector, schools in the public Arab sector are underfunded, vocational programs and tracks are conspicuously absent, and school counselors and psychologists are extremely rare (Al-Haj, 1995; Mazawi, 1994). Nevertheless, the two systems are similar in curricular demands, and students in both attend the 12th grade matriculation exams.

Dropout rates in Arab secondary schools are high. By the 9th grade, 15% of the cohort drops out, reaching up to 35% by the 11th grade, and 40% by the 12th grade. Furthermore, most Arab adolescents are enrolled in academic tracks which, in principle, enable them to sit for national matriculation exams and thus qualify for higher education (the Arab sector has very few vocational schools and programs, as these cost more and require constant updating of equipment and curricula). This study shows that almost 90% of Arab 11th graders are taught in academic tracks.

Despite their enrollment in academic tracks, Arab students rarely succeed in the national matriculation exams. For example, in 1995 only 20% of all Arab 18-year-olds received the matriculation certificate necessary for higher education in Israel. Of these, only 30% actually entered one of the major universities, which helps to explain why only 8.7% of all students in Israeli higher education institutions are non-Jewish (Israel Statistical Yearbook, 1999: Table 22.34).

Sociological studies of Israeli-Arab high school students are few and, for the most part, based on non-representative samples. Previous research on student aspirations tended to highlight Arab-Jewish differences, but ignored differences between Arab Moslem, Christian, and Druze students (Seginer, 1988a, b; Seginer & Halabi, 1991). Thus, the present study is the first nationally representative investigation of Israeli-Arab adolescents which allows for between-group comparisons within the Arab sector. Some of the prior studies also ignored gender differences, which in a traditional society should be of prime importance. Furthermore, while the literature suggests that schools may affect students' aspirations, not one of the available studies in Israel has focused on the differences between private and public schools, a topic comprehensively studied elsewhere (Bryk, Lee & Holland, 1993; Coleman & Hoffer, 1987; Coleman, Hoffer & Kilgore, 1982; Cuyck-Remijssen & Dronkers, 1990; Dijkstra & Dronkers, 2000; Dronkers, 1996).

THE STUDY

To compensate for these omissions in the study of Arab adolescents in Israel, the empirical objective of this study was to provide a valid representative picture of the educational and occupational aspirations of Moslem, Christian, and Druze boys and girls in public and private schools. We use this empirical investigation of minority aspirations to criticize extant theories in the sociology of education. Specifically, using the quantitative study, we test whether Arab adolescent aspirations are indeed cooled-out as theoretically expected. Having found that this is not the case, we conducted interviews with school principals, who helped to interpret the puzzling results. Their views – supporting a heating-up thesis – are presented in the latter part of the paper.

Sample

In order to ensure representation of major subgroups within the Arab population – i.e. by religion (Moslem, Christian, and Druze), socioeconomic status, school type (public and private schools), and locale (village, large city, etc.) – 27 sociodemographic profiles of all schools were constructed. These profiles were based on three community-level variables: (1) the average per capita income; (2) total fertility rate of women; and (3) proportion of women aged 30–34 possessing at least 10–12 years of formal schooling. Three levels of each variable were established, resulting in 27 possible combinations ($3 \times 3 \times 3$).

Approximately half of the schools in each stratum were randomly selected for the study. In each of the 42 selected schools, up to four classrooms in the 9th and 11th grades were chosen. This strategy resulted in a total sample of 213 classrooms in which all attending students filled out the questionnaire. A total of 5,281 students or 96% of those attending school that day provided usable questionnaires (approximately 16% of all the Arab students in Israel at each of the grade levels).

The high dropout rates mentioned previously produce a sample selection bias in our study, which precludes firm generalizations from the sample to the population of Israeli-Arab students. Sample attrition may produce over-estimation of students' educational and occupational aspirations, and – to the extent that boys drop out more than girls, and Moslems more than Christians – it may also distort estimates of religion and gender differentials. Thus, the estimated models in this paper represent a subsection of the student body, comprised by the higher-achieving students who are most likely to finish school. In other words, we may suspect that cooling-out mechanisms do work in Arab high schools and communities, leading to high dropout rates in the community.

However, this process is independent from heating-up mechanisms which may affect those remaining in school. We should mention, though, that the inclusion of a locale-level dropout rate variable to the regression models had no consistent or strong effects on students' aspirations, suggesting that – if they are present – sample biases are of minor substantive significance. However, future studies should take care to follow dropping-out students in order to correct for this sample bias.

Questionnaire and Variables

Cross-sectional data on students' educational and occupational aspirations, school experience, and background information was collected using closed-item questionnaires. Some schooling variables are derived from students' reports. This fact might confound some of the variables, cautioning us from making sweeping generalizations.

Dependent Variables

Educational Aspirations

Students indicated the level of education they believed they would attain in the future. An eight-point scale was used, ranging from 1 (incomplete high school education) through 8 (Ph.D. degree). Answers were recoded to reflect the number of years of schooling.

Occupational Aspirations
Students indicated in an open-ended question the field of employment or profession they planned to enter. Responses were coded into an Israeli scale of occupational prestige (see Kraus, 1981), ranging from 10 to 97. (An alternative 9-point ordinal scale of occupational prestige based on categories used by the Israeli Central Bureau of Statistics produced virtually identical distributions and did not significantly alter the study's main findings.)

Independent Variables

Background Variables
Gender was measured by a dichotomy with Boys = 1 and Girls = 0. Religious background was measured by dummy variables which were used to estimate the effect of being Muslim or Christian, relative to the Druze. Family's SES was estimated as an index of father's education and occupation ($\alpha = 0.78$).

Parental Variables
Parental Expectations were measured through students' reports of the educational level each of their parents wished them to obtain on a 7-point scale ranging from 1 (do not expect me to study) through 7 (expects me to study at a university). This variable is an index of the two items and its Alpha reliability is 0.91. Parental involvement was measured through the frequency of parents' discussing the following issues with the student: (1) Things students learned at school; (2) Post high-school plans; and (3) Grades at school ($\alpha = 0.70$).

School-Related Variables
Academic ability was measured by the grade point average the student received in four required subjects: Arabic, Hebrew, English, and Mathematics ($\alpha = 0.82$). School type was measured with a dummy variable, with public school = 0 and private school = 1. Curricular track (only relevant for 11th grade) was measured using a set of dummy variables to record academic-science track, academic-humanities track, and vocational track. School climate was measured through students' appraisal of their school's climate (see Appendix for details). Alpha reliability of this variable is 0.80. School experience was measured by an index of five items that indicated the student's school experience (see Appendix). Alpha reliability of this variable is 0.55. Teachers' support was measured by

students' reports of the extent to which teachers were a source of information for them. School contribution is an index of 13 items that had an Alpha reliability of 0.93. This variable indicates the extent to which the school has contributed to the student in terms of a number of relevant issues (see Appendix).

Community Variables

Dropout rate was measured using a continuous variable indicating the rate of those aged 18–24 in 1995 that dropped out of school before completing the 11th grade. This variable was measured at the locality level. Enclave Region was measured by using a dichotomous variable indicating whether students reside in: (1) an enclave economy community; or (0) in more integrated communities (based on Lewin-Epstein & Semyonov, 1994).

DISCUSSION

Analyses are conducted in two complementary steps. First, we report students' overall educational and occupational aspirations, and compare these with existing distributions of Arab adults by educational attainment and occupational position (comparing aspirations to reality). Second, we use OLS regression to assess the extent of social inequality in educational and occupational aspirations by focusing on gender and religious differences in Arab students' aspirations.

Gaps Between Aspirations and Avenue

Table 1 provides a breakdown of students' educational aspirations over gender and religious affiliation. It also provides a benchmark to assess these distributions: the distribution of years of schooling amongst the youngest cohort (25–34) of Arabs.

Overall, Table 1 shows that Israeli-Arab youth are very optimistic, expressing extremely high levels of educational aspirations. In fact, 75% plan to complete educational achievements beyond high school. These high levels of aspiration contrast sharply with the contemporary educational attainments of Arab young adults. While most high school students plan to enroll in higher education institutions, only 19% of Arab young adults actually took this route a decade earlier, suggesting that it is very likely that only a small minority of the student sample will actually fulfill their aspirations. Especially telling are figures regarding graduate studies: overall, 28% of Arab adolescents aspire to an academic degree beyond the undergraduate level (16 + years of schooling), whilst only 8% of young Arab adults have actually reached this educational level.

Table 1. Students' Educational Aspirations and Adult Educational Attainments (Percentages).

Years of Schooling	Adult Arabs						Total Population	25–34
	Muslim		Christian		Druze			
	Boys	Girls	Boys	Girls	Boys	Girls		
10	11	9	7	2	7	7	18	21
11–12	16	18	16	7	21	19	28	32
13–15	42	50	45	53	38	49	8	11
16+	31	22	32	37	33	25	4	8
N	1,484	1,937	407	471	311	351	58%	72%
Chi-square	40.0**		31.3**		8.46*			

Note: Adult figures are based on data provided by the Israeli Central Bureau of Statistics. The percentages do not add up to 100%, as many adults did not reach the 10th grade level.
Source: Israel Statistical Yearbook (1996), Central Bureau of Statistics: Tables 22.1a–22.1c.
*$p < 0.05$.
**$p < 0.01$.

The portrayed large gap between educational aspirations and probable destinations may be criticized by arguing that the past decade has drastically altered educational provision and returns to education, so that what students aspire to would be very much their real future a decade later. This interpretation is overly optimistic, though. Figure 1 shows the gap between 11th grade students' educational aspirations and their actual matriculation attainment two years after the study. It clearly shows that less than 50% of Muslim boys and girls attain matriculation, which is a prerequisite for higher education. Druze students evince very similar patterns, with only Christian students both aspiring to higher levels and fulfilling the prerequisites for enrollment in post-secondary institutions. However, since Muslims constitute most of the students, it is clear that most Arab students do not attain the minimal conditions which are necessary for reaching their educational aspirations. Similar results appear when we compare the results for students at the 9th grade level and the cohort's actual completion rates in the year 2000 (the year of their matriculation).

While these results point to a large gap between aspirations and reality, Table 1 and Fig. 1 nonetheless suggest that students partly respond to their probable educational destinations. Religion and gender do make a difference, though a modest one. Christian students, especially girls, display the highest aspirations. In comparison, being members of highly traditional, familial, and male-dominated groups, Muslim and Druze girls evince lower educational aspirations than boys, reflecting their delimited participation in extra-familial roles and public domains.

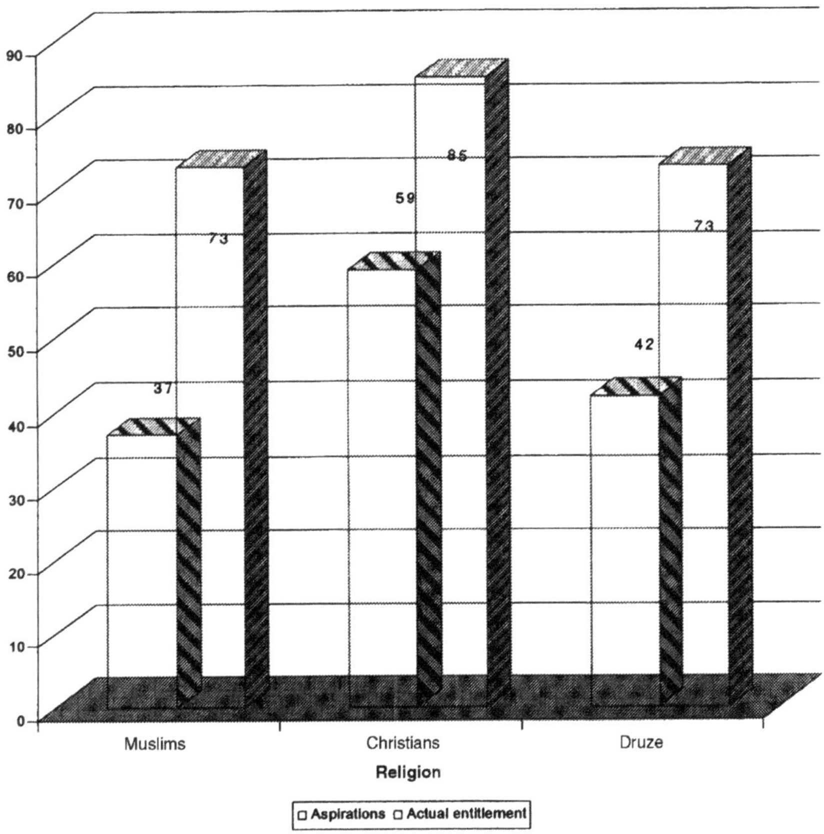

Fig. 1. Percentage of 11th Grade Students Who Aspire to Gain Matriculation and Beyond in 1997, Contrasting With the Percentage of those Who Matriculated from the Same Age Cohort in 1998 by Religion. *Note:* Entitlement percentages refer to the number of students who matriculated in 1998 divided by the total number of the 12th grade students. *Source:* Israeli Central Bureau of Statistics, 2000, Table 22.21.

Table 2 portrays similar gaps between students' occupational aspirations and their probable destinations in the labor market. It shows that the vast majority of Arab adolescents aspire to work in academic and liberal professions (e.g. teachers, nurses, photographers, accountants). Over two-fifths (41%) of the students aspire to the highest occupational category – academic professions, while 34% hope to enter a liberal profession. By comparison, the actual distribution of Israeli-Arabs in academic and liberal professions is 6 and 8%, respectively. Occupational destinations of younger cohorts are not significantly different from the total for the adult

Table 2. Students' Occupational Aspirations and Adult Occupational Attainments (Percentages).

Occupation	Muslim		Christian		Druze		Adult Arabs Total
	Boys	Girls	Boys	Girls	Boys	Girls	
Academic occupations	42	39	44	55	43	34	5.6
Liberal professions	25	43	27	31	20	49	8.4
Managers and clerical workers	7	9	5	9	6	11	7.7
Agents, salespeople, and services	9	7	11	5	21	4	12.3
Agriculture, industry, construction	16	2	14	0	10	1	66.0
N	1,135	1,662	339	415	238	300	252,700
Chi-square	242.57^{**}		71.27^{**}		87.90^{**}		

Note: Adult figures are based on data provided by the Israeli Central Bureau of Statistics.
Source: Israel Statistical Yearbook (1996), Central Bureau of Statistics: Table 12.14.
$^{*}p < 0.05$.
$^{**}p < 0.01$.

population. Similar "disjuncture" between occupational aspirations and probable destinations is also apparent at the lower end of the occupational scale. Students express an aversion to positions in agriculture, industry, or construction, with only 8.5% of the respondents choosing this category. This figure is negligible when compared to the 66% of all Arab adults who presently occupy such positions in the labor market.

These general trends conceal some religious and gender differences. Again, Christian students are more ambitious, especially due to the high aspirations of Christian girls. On the other hand, amongst Arabs generally, only boys see manual jobs as an option to aspire to, while girls' ambitions are highly skewed towards the upper echelon of the labor market. These high aspirations again contrast with Arab women's position in the labor market, with currently 80% of adult women actually absent from participation in paid markets, as they are required by their patriarchal male society to remain at home (Khattab, 2002).

All these results add up to the simple conclusion, namely that Arab students aspire to occupational statuses far removed from the lower rungs of the labor market, currently the typical destination of most Arab adult workers. To the degree that existing opportunity structures continue in the near future, it is clear that most Arab students will not realize their occupational aspirations, especially girls and Moslems.

Seen together, the results provide clear evidence of wide gaps between students' educational and occupational aspirations and their probable destinations. The results clearly show that Israeli-Arab students do not align their educational and occupational aspirations with their probable future destinations. Clearly, most Arab students have not "cooled out" their educational and occupational aspirations – even as close as two years prior to their actual matriculation from high school.

The Norm of Social Equality

Table 3 reports results obtained by regressing students' educational and occupational aspirations onto background, parental, school, and community

Table 3. Regression of Students' Educational and Occupational Aspirations, Background, Parental, School, and Community Variables.

Independent Variables	9th Grade		11th Grade	
	Educational Aspirations	Occupational Aspirations	Educational Aspirations	Occupational Aspirations
Background variables				
Muslims	−0.03	−0.03	0.05**	0.05
Christians	−0.02	−0.02	0.03	0.00
Boys	0.06**	−0.13**	0.08**	−0.15**
Family SES	0.07**	0.03	0.09**	0.07**
Parental variables				
Parental expectations	0.32**	0.19**	0.30**	0.16**
Parental involvement	0.09**	0.07**	0.06**	−0.01
Schooling variables				
Academic ability	0.32**	0.30**	0.31**	0.24**
Private school	0.05*	0.03	−0.01	−0.06*
Science track			0.17**	0.26**
Humanities track			0.03	0.19**
School climate	0.03	0.04	0.04	0.01
School experience	0.04*	0.03	0.04	0.04
Teachers' support	−0.01	0.01	0.01	0.11**
School contribution	0.02	0.00	0.05*	0.01
Community variables				
Dropout rate	0.01	0.03	−0.01	−0.01
Enclave community	−0.03	−0.02	−0.04	−0.03
Constant	4.59	6.61	5.47	15.29
Adjusted R^2	0.40	0.25	0.44	0.21

$^{*}p < 0.05$.
$^{**}p < 0.001$.

characteristics. Given the large sample size, even small parameters may be statistically significant. Consequently, interpretation of results focuses on substantive significance, expressed in terms of the relative size of the standardized coefficients in the regression model.

Table 3 reports four models for the two dependent variables, broken by grade level, since the tracking variables are only relevant at the 11th grade.

The results show that controlling for the other variables, religious background has no substantive effect on students' educational or occupational aspirations. In other words, when their schooling experiences are taken into account, differences between Moslem, Christian, and Druze students are proven to be negligible and inconsistent, with religious affiliation explaining almost none of the variation in the dependent variables. Students' socioeconomic status also has a very modest effect on their educational and occupational aspirations. Furthermore, boys have somewhat higher educational aspirations and lower occupational aspirations than girls, but controlling for the other variables, gender explains only 1–2% of the variation.

While the categorical ascriptive variables have minimal effects on students' future aspirations, parental expectations and involvement with students' educational experiences in school do have a strong effect on aspirations. The higher the parental expectations, and the more parents who are involved in students' schooling, the higher are students' educational and occupational aspirations (with the exception of 11th grade occupational aspirations). These results suggest that religious and gender inequalities are completely mediated by respondents' familial expectations and behavior vis-à-vis their schooling lives.

The lower section of Table 3 shows that school variables also significantly affect students' aspirations. First, students reporting higher school grades express higher educational and occupational aspirations. Second – and controlling for student achievement – those studying in the academic-science track have higher aspirations than their peers in the humanities and vocational tracks. Third – and contradicting our expectations – there is no consistent indication that students in private schools have higher educational aspirations than their peers in public schools.

Finally, the bottom section of Table 3 proves that living in an enclave community seems to have no effect on student aspirations; no effect is found for community-level dropout rates either.

These results exhibit relative social equality in Arab students' educational and occupational aspirations. Controlling for parental expectations, students' achievements, and their track position in high school, differences in students' educational and occupational aspirations are found to be minimal and inconsistent. In reality, students from diverse social backgrounds and communities exhibit similar and high educational and occupational aspirations.

These results suggest that students' visions of their futures are apparently "decoupled" not only from objective conditions of previous cohorts, but also from their own social backgrounds and their imminent future. The fact that high school students are decoupled from their social background contrasts sharply with the strong impact of social background on the educational and occupational attainments of prior cohorts, who are highly stratified according to religious affiliation, gender, and SES. In contrast, the future aspirations of Arab students are influenced by their institutional locations within school and their academic achievements. These latter variables account for up to 44% of the variation in students' educational aspirations, and up to 25% in occupational aspirations, while almost fully mediating the effects of background variables on these outcomes.

The Production of High Minority Aspirations: A New Explanation

A central finding of our study is that most Israeli-Arab high school students aspire to educational levels and occupational statuses far beyond their grasp. A logical conclusion is to characterize these aspirations as overly optimistic – even irrational – especially when compared with the actual destinations of young Arab adults in Israel. In addition, important social distinctions within the Arab community had little impact on students' aspirations. These findings, when placed together with recent evidence from comparative studies of minority youth (Kao & Tienda, 1998; Marjoribanks, 2002), point to fundamental weaknesses in existing theoretical models which rarely predict such significant "disjuncture" or "gaps" between aspirations and likely destinations.

The relatively high aspiration levels of minority youth challenges existing theoretical models, and underscores not only the need for more nuanced comparative approaches, but also alternative analytical accounts of this puzzling reality. With this in mind, we suggest a different starting point. Instead of viewing high aspirations as naturally given for majority youth and then cooled-out for minority youth, we find the production of student aspirations problematic and seek to discover the conditions under which, and the social forces by which, minority youth aspirations are actually heated-up. Drawing upon the present investigation, extant literature, and interviews with high school principals, we provide a new explanation for the production of Arab minority aspirations.

To begin with, Arab communities have traditionally ascribed respect to educated adults. Indeed, the reputation of families is enhanced when their members attend institutions of higher education. In recent years, as opportunities for Arab students in higher education have begun to increase, parental pressures and expectations have undoubtedly intensified. As one school principal explained:

> In looking for the causes of students' high aspirations, one should look for community and parental expectations and aspirations, as they put tremendous pressures on students. The high status and esteem that the family enjoys when one of its members attains higher education diplomas, causes the Arab family to develop high aspirations amongst students.

Institutional arrangements represent a second heating-up mechanism. For example, school systems employing rigid selection criteria (Kerckhoff, 2001) create high dropout rates, which in the classic "frog-pond thesis" (Davis, 1966) tend to enhance the aspirations of those remaining in school. As discussed earlier, schools in the Arab sector in Israel are characterized by high dropout rates, reaching 40% by the 12th grade. Those students who remain in school express extremely high aspirations, with few traces of any cooling-out process. Moreover, the predominance of academic tracks in Arab high schools means that students experience a non-differentiated track structure which, in their view, enhances their life chances. As one school principal commented,

> Many students, especially those who study in the academic tracks, will not be subjugated to an institution or an organization; they will be independent. They don't need the State (of Israel) in looking for jobs.

To sum up, the institutional arrangements commonly experienced by Arab youth in school, work conjointly to heat up their future aspirations.

The third factor that heats up students' aspirations results from teachers' expectations. Sociological research has shown that teachers' control of their classrooms is influenced by their students' attitudes towards school (Waller, 1932; Yair, 1997). To ensure that instructional tasks are completed, teachers seek to engender pro-school attitudes among their students. There is little doubt that schools work more efficiently with motivated, optimistic students. If teachers were to convey to minority students their probable destinations, for example, low-status positions in agriculture, construction, or shop-keeping, then the perceived rationale of academic instruction would become undermined, resulting in recalcitrant, disobedient, or rebellious behavior (Willis, 1977; Yair & Khatab, 1995). Thus, for reasons of organizational control, teachers have a clear interest in enhancing minority students' aspirations and constructing optimistic future scenarios. As one of the principals in our sample stated:

> We are well aware of the fact that our students have very high aspirations. We by policy encourage them to aspire to attain higher education diplomas and seek academic jobs. For there cannot be a situation for us to teach when students lack expectations or have low aspirations.

This quote conveys the reluctance of Arab teachers to discuss salient constraints on their students' future destinations, of which they are all too aware. Acknowledging market realities and explaining the basic incompatibility of school attainments on occupational destinations would, in their view, exacerbate problems of classroom order. As a result, teachers cling to the meritocratic ideal and shy away from realistic discussions of discrimination and segregation.

The fourth factor which raises students' aspirations results from the messages conveyed by local elites. Dissatisfied with their communities' marginal socioeconomic standing and limited occupational opportunities, Arab politicians and leaders call for the improvement of the Arab educational system (Abu-Asbah, 1998). As they champion the perceived benefits of schooling, they demand from the state more educational resources to raise achievement levels and prevent students from dropping out of school. These demands are widely perceived, both inside and outside the community, as legitimate concerns and policy targets for redressing existing inequalities. In speech and deed, they spread the belief that education is the best way for the community, families, and individual students to overcome the social handicaps that constrain their lives (Haidar, 1997). By propagating to students the myth of an open society, minority communities heat up educational and occupational aspirations, thereby weakening the impact of social background on students' aspirations. As one Arab leader stated a few years ago:

> If we fail to find a basic and appropriate solution to the problems of Arab education, the current state of affairs will bring about a total failure of the Arab educational system. This will fail the Arab population as a society and, in the long run, undermine its bases of existence (Almadi, 1996).

To conclude, we suggest that this study of minority Arab high school students in Israel exemplifies a society where all the above-mentioned factors work jointly to heat up students' aspirations. Further comparative studies are needed to assess under what conditions these factors explain empirical reality and, alternatively, under what conditions a cooling-out model explains students' aspirations.

Without overstating the example, we think that between-group and within-group analyses of student aspirations need to consider the four factors outlined in our model. In some cases, they may converge to form an additive effect; in others, they may conflict. Future empirical work should assess the utility of this model of aspiration production in other contexts, especially where migration creates and changes the social position of different minority groups in society (Dale, Shaheen, Kalra & Fieldhouse, 2001; Eldering, 1997; Gilborn, 1997).

This study suggests that widely-held sociological assumptions derived from the cooling-out thesis need to be reevaluated. Couched in "balance" terminology, these approaches expect a match between extant social conditions and student aspirations. Current conditions are overly emphasized as "objective" or as "social facts" that strongly influence human action and future orientations. By contrast, the present study suggests that rationality cannot be exclusively understood as a functional congruence between aspirations and reality. Under certain conditions, unusually high (but mostly unrealizable) aspirations may serve the collective interests of specific minority communities, while also serving the organizational agenda of schools. Conceiving gaps between aspirations and reality as non-rational is an a-priori theoretical construct of both judgment and social practice. A non-critical acceptance of a congruence model represents an ideological orientation, which may inadvertently reproduce the conditions for marginality (e.g. employing school counselors to inform students about their likely positions or, in other words, to cool them out).

We propose a more dialectic approach, one where aspirations that are non-congruent with current realities may produce paradoxical outcomes and actually bolster social change. We suggest that the concept of "hope" needs to be salvaged from a-priori designations of irrationality. Dreams (sometimes referred to as wishful thinking) can act as a catalyst for social change, and for some minority groups represent a potent, non-violent means for fighting prejudice and discrimination.

High future aspirations among Arab adolescents in Israel may be interpreted as individual and collective investments nurtured under conditions of high risk and uncertainty. Theoretically these conditions necessitate high levels of trust or hope. Such a positive attitude toward possible alternative futures acts as a precondition for attaining some of what minority groups desire. Although utopian visions usually go unrealized, such aspirations nonetheless fuel and give direction to social change and collective advancement. In the absence of such aspirations, minority groups would find themselves entangled in a myriad of unintended consequences, which simply result from a realistic acknowledgement of reality. For minority groups, then, it is often irrational to be rational.

In the Israeli-Arab case, we might have some indications that such hope and optimism do change reality. Indeed, during the past few years, several Arab high schools have sent shocks throughout the Israeli school system, leading the national matriculation "league table" and receiving national coverage in the media. These schools – some of which are located in extremely poor and marginal communities – exhibited very high success rates in the prestigious matriculation exams, leaving renowned Jewish high schools lagging behind. Having suffered collective marginalization and discrimination in the Israeli society, these schools are indeed breaking the mold. We suggest that these surprising results may derive from systematic forces which crystallize in the heating up of the educational and occupational aspirations of Arab students, motivating a greater number of them to push against all odds and succeed in otherwise extremely unfavorable circumstances. While such incidents go beyond our data, they do suggest that high aspirations may be realized – under some conditions – even among minority, disadvantaged groups.

ACKNOWLEDGMENTS

This study was supported by grants from the Truman Institute for the Advancement of Peace, the National Council of Jewish Women Research Institute in Education, and the Brookdale Institute. These foundations are not responsible for the arguments advanced herein. John Meyer and several reviewers provided insights and suggestions for which we are grateful. An earlier version of this paper was presented at the annual meeting of the American Sociological Association, San Francisco, August 1998.

REFERENCES

Abu-Asbah, K. (1998). *Arab children and youth in Israel: From current situation toward an agenda for the future*. Jerusalem: Brookdale (in Hebrew).

Alexander, K. L., & Cook, M. (1979). The motivational relevance of educational plans: Questioning the conventional wisdom. *Social Psychology Quarterly*, *42*, 202–213.

Al-Haj, M. (1995). *Education, empowerment, and control: The case of Arabs in Israel*. Albany: State University of New York Press.

Almadi, R. (1996). The creativity project: Existing models of education versus alternative models in the Arab educational system. Paper presented at the Special conference on Arab Children and Youth in Israeli Society, Qiryat Anavim, Israel.

Armer, M., & Sewell, W. H. (1972). High school context and college plans: A comment. *American Sociological Review*, *37*, 637–639.

Ayalon, H., & Yuchtman-Yaar, E. (1989). Educational and occupational aspirations: A two-dimensional approach. *Sociology of Education*, *61*, 191–210.

Beattie, I. R. (2002). Are all adolescent econometricians created equal? Racial, class, and gender differences in college enrollment. *Sociology of Education*, *75*, 19–43.

Benavot, A., & Resh, N. (2001). *Governance and curriculum implementation: Uniformity and diversity among Jewish and Arab schools in Israel*. Unpublished manuscript, Jerusalem.

Bourdieu, P. (1988). *Homo Academicus*. Stanford, CA: Stanford University Press.

Bourdieu, P., & Passeron, J. C. (1977). *Reproduction in education, society and culture*. London: Sage.

Bourdieu, P., & Passeron, J. (1979). *The inheritors*. Chicago: University of Chicago Press.

Breen, R., & Goldthorpe, J. H. (1997). Explaining educational differentials: Towards a formal rational action theory. *Rationality and Society*, *9*, 275–305.

Bryk, A. S., Lee, V. E., & Holland, P. B. (1993). *Catholic schools and the common good*. Cambridge, MA: Harvard University Press.

Buchmann, C., & Dalton, B. (2002). Interpersonal influences and educational aspirations in 12 countries: The importance of institutional context. *Sociology of Education*, *75*, 99–122.

Clark, B. R. (1960). The cooling-out function in higher education. *American Journal of Sociology*, *66*, 569–576.

Coleman, J. S., & Hoffer, T. (1987). *Public and private high schools: The impact of communities*. New York: Basic Books.

Coleman, J. S., Hoffer, T., & Kilgore, S. (1982). *High school achievement: Public, Catholic, and private schools compared*. New York: Basic Books.

Cuyck-Remijssen, A. v., & Dronkers, J. (1990). Catholic and Protestant schools, a better choice in the Netherlands? *School Effectiveness and School Improvement, 1*, 211–220.

Dale, A., Shaheen, N., Kalra, V., & Fieldhouse, E. (2001). *Routes into education and employment for young Pakistani and Bangladeshi women in the U.K.* Unpublished manuscript, Manchester.

Davis, J. (1966). The campus as a frog pond: An application of the theory of relative deprivation to career decision of college men. *American Journal of Sociology, 72*, 17–31.

Dijkstra, A. B., & Dronkers, J. (2000). Education between state and private delivery: Civil society as equilibrium: The Dutch case. In: J. L. Peschar & M. v. d. Wal (Eds), *Education Contested. Changing Relations between State, Market and Civil Society in Modern European Education* (pp. 105–120). Lisse: Swets & Zeitlinger.

Dronkers, J. (1996). Dutch public and religious schools between state and market. A balance between parental choice and national policy? *Zeitschrift fur Padagogik, 35*, 51–66.

Eldering, L. (1997). Ethnic minority students in the Netherlands from a cultural-ecological perspective. *Anthropology & Education Quarterly, 28*, 330–350.

Ford, D. Y., & John, J. H. (1996). Perceptions and attitudes of black students toward school, achievement, and other educational variables. *Child Development, 67*, 1141–1152.

Friedkin, N. E., & Thomas, S. L. (1997). Social positions in schooling. *Sociology of Education, 70*, 239–255.

Gamoran, A. (1986). Instructional and institutional effects of ability grouping. *Sociology of Education, 59*, 147–159.

Gibson, M. A., & Ogbu, J. U. (1991). *Minority status and schooling: A comparative study of immigrant and involuntary minorities*. New York: Garland.

Gilborn, D. (1997). Ethnicity and educational performance in the United Kingdom: Racism, ethnicity and variability in achievement. *Anthropology and Education Quarterly, 28*, 375–393.

Goyette, K., & Xie, Y. (1999). Educational expectations of Asian American youths: Determinants and ethnic differences. *Sociology of Education, 72*, 22–36.

Haidar, A. (1997). *The Palestinians in Israel and the Oslo agreement*. Beirut: Institute for Palestine Studies.

Hanson, S. L. (1994). Lost talent: Unrealized educational aspirations and expectations among U.S. youths. *Sociology of Education, 67*, 159–183.

Hao, L., & Bruns, M. B. (1988). Parent-child differences in educational expectations and the academic achievement of immigrant and native students. *Sociology of Education, 71*, 175–198.

Hauser, R. M., & Anderson, D. K. (1991). Post high-school plans and aspirations of black and white high school seniors: 1976–1986. *Sociology of Education, 64*, 263–277.

Jencks, C., Crouse, J., & Mueser, P. (1983). The Wisconsin model of status attainment: A national replication with improved measures of ability and aspiration. *Sociology of Education, 56*, 3–19.

Kao, G., & Tienda, M. (1998). Educational aspirations of minority youth. *American Journal of Education, 106*, 349–384.

Kerckhoff, A. (1976). The status attainment process: Socialization or allocation? *Social Forces, 55*, 368–381.

Kerckhoff, A. C. (2001). Education and social stratification processes in comparative perspective. *Sociology of Education, Extra Issue*, 3–18.

Khattab, N. (2002). Ethnicity and female labour market participation: A new look at the Palestinian enclave in Israel. *Work, Employment & Society, 16*, 91–110.

Lewin-Epstein, N., & Semyonov, M. (1994). Sheltered labor markets, public sector employment, and socioeconomic returns to education of Arabs in Israel. *American Journal of Sociology, 100*, 622–651.

Marjoribanks, K. (1988). Family background, social and academic capital, and adolescents' aspirations: A mediational analysis. *Social Psychology of Education, 2*, 177–197.

Marjoribanks, K. (2002). Family background, individual and environmental influences on adolescents' aspirations. *Educational Studies, 28*, 33–46.

Mazawi, A. (1994). Palestinian Arabs in Israel: Educational expansion, social mobility and political control. *Compare, 24*, 277–284.

Mazawi, A. (1996). *The structure of equality of educational opportunities in the Arab educational system in Israel*. Unpublished manuscript, Tel Aviv.

McLeod, J. (1987). *Ain't no makin' it*. London: Tavistock.

McNair, D., & Brown, D. (1983). Predicting the occupational aspirations, occupational expectations and career maturity of black and white, male and female tenth graders. *Vocational Guidance Quarterly, 32*, 29–36.

Mickelson, R. A. (1990). The attitude-achievement paradox among black adolescents. *Sociology of Education, 63*, 44–61.

Morgan, S. L. (1996). Trends in black-white differences in educational expectations, 1980–1992. *Sociology of Education, 69*, 308–319.

Morgan, S. L. (1998). Adolescent educational expectations: Rationalized, fantasized or both? *Rationality and Society, 10*, 131–162.

Page, R. N. (1991). *Lower-track classrooms: A curricular and cultural perspective*. New York: Teachers College Press.

Rosenfeld, M. (1997). *Ways of life, division of labor and social roles of Palestinian refugee families: The case of Dheisheh refugee camp*. Unpublished Ph.D. dissertation, Hebrew University of Jerusalem, Jerusalem.

Schneider, B., & Stevenson, D. (1999). *The ambitious generation: America's teenagers, motivated but directionless*. New Haven: Yale University Press.

Seginer, R. (1988a). Adolescents facing the future: Cultural and socio-political perspectives. *Youth and Society, 19*, 314–333.

Seginer, R. (1988b). Adolescents' orientation toward the future: Sex role differentiation in a sociocultural context. *Sex Roles, 18*, 739–757.

Seginer, R., & Halabi, H. (1991). Cross-cultural variations of adolescents' future orientation: The case of Israeli druze versus Israeli Arab and Jewish males. *Journal of Cross-Cultural Psychology, 22*, 224–237.

Semyonov, M., & Cohen, Y. (1990). Ethnic discrimination and the income of majority-group workers. *American Sociological Review, 55*, 107–114.

Sewell, W. H., & Hauser, R. M. (1980). The Wisconsin longitudinal study of social and psychological factors in aspirations and achievements. *Research in Sociology of Education and Socialization, 1*, 59–99.

Sewell, W. H., & Shah, V. P. (1968). Social class, parental encouragement, and educational aspirations. *American Journal of Sociology, 73*, 559–572.

Shavit, Y. (1992). Arabs in the Israeli economy: A study of the enclave hypothesis. *Israel Social Science Research, 7*, 1–2.

Solorzano, D. G. (1992). An exploratory analysis of the effects of race, class, and gender on student and parent mobility aspirations. *Journal of Negro Education, 61*, 30–43.

Stanton-Salazar, R. D., & Dornbusch, S. (1995). Social capital and the reproduction of inequality: Information networks among Mexican-origin high school students. *Sociology of Education, 68*, 116–135.

Waller, W. (1932). *The sociology of teaching*. New York: Wiley.

Willis, P. (1977). *Learning to labour*. Hants: Saxon House.

Yair, G. (1997). Teachers' polarisation in heterogeneous classrooms and the social distribution of achievement: An Israeli case study. *Teaching & Teacher Education*, *13*, 279–293.
Yair, G., & Khatab, N. (1995). Changing of the guards: Teacher-student interaction in the intifada. *Sociology of Education*, *68*, 99–115.

APPENDIX

School Climate

The students were asked to appraise their school's climate using a 6-point scale, indicating to what extent they agreed with the following items (1 = completely disagree; 6 = completely agree):

(1) Students get along well with teachers.
(2) The school's academic atmosphere is good.
(3) The school's rules are fair.
(4) The teaching at the school is good.
(5) When I work hard on school work, my teachers praise my effort.

School Experience

An index of five items was used to measure the student's total school experience. Factor analysis of these five items revealed one variable with Alpha reliability of 0.55. These items were also measured using a 6-point scale (1 = completely agree; 6 = completely disagree):

(1) In class I often feel bored.
(2) Other students often disrupt class without being punished.
(3) I don't feel safe at school.
(4) In class I often feel "put down" by other students.
(5) If I had the choice, I would not attend school.

School Contribution

An index of 13 items were factor analyzed with Alpha reliability of 0.93. This variable indicates the extent to which the school has contributed to the student in terms of a number of relevant issues. The students were asked to appraise their school's contribution using a 5-point scale (1 = did not contribute; 5 = a very significant contribution):

(1) To understand what is going on around me.
(2) To plan for my future.
(3) To understand the political system in my country.
(4) To explore the opportunities for higher education.
(5) To explore what are the occupations available for me.
(6) To achieve general knowledge.
(7) To understand my culture and heritage.
(8) To learn about interesting subjects.
(9) To obtain useful knowledge.
(10) To obtain a suitable job for the future.
(11) To fulfill my aspirations and dreams.
(12) To address attractive subjects.
(13) To have a chance for self-expression.

Note: Some of the variables were recoded.

EDUCATIONAL PATHWAYS INTO THE EVOLVING LABOUR MARKET OF WEST AFRICA

Stephen L. Morgan and William R. Morgan

ABSTRACT

This case study of Kano, Nigeria, examines changes over the past four decades in an education and labor market relationship that has evolved since the 10th century. We first offer an analysis of the historical origins of Kano's current three-layered segmented labor market and its corresponding three distinct, but increasingly overlapping, educational pathways. We then compare the labor market entry pathways reported in 1974 and 1992 by two cohorts of young adult males, the respondents having first been surveyed as 17-year-olds in 1965 and 1979.

Despite higher levels of modern secular education in 1992 for males in all occupational destinations, apprenticeship participation was significantly lower in 1992 only for young men who entered the professional and clerical positions that dominate Kano's public sector. Islamic training remained universal, and in fact increased significantly in years of participation across all occupational destinations. We next show that the jointly educated young men who were part of the first, more traditional sector of the labor market, were less seriously impacted in their earnings by Nigeria's turbulent end-of-the-century economy. Finally, we discuss the possible advantages of an

Inequality Across Societies: Families, Schools and Persisting Stratification
Research in Sociology of Education, Volume 14, 225–245
(Formerly Research in Sociology of Education and Socialization)

ISSN: 1479-3539/doi:10.1016/S1479-3539(03)14010-4

apprenticeship system coupled to modern secular education for moderating social inequality and stabilizing economic development in sub-Saharan Africa and other less-developed regions.

INTRODUCTION

At least five interrelated causal narratives for the rapid expansion of modern secular education[1] in developing countries can be found in the literature: (1) An international social movement for Western education led by a transnational cadre of Western-trained educational experts (Boli, Ramirez & Meyer 1985); (2) capitalism's quest for expanded consumer markets (Chase-Dunn, 1982; Sklair, 1991); (3) local demand from political elites seeking equity and universal access for their regional constituents (Fuller & Rubinson, 1992); (4) the belief of national governments that attitudinal modernity in the populace is a critical precondition for economic growth (Inkeles & Smith, 1974); (5) the need for an efficient system of selection and allocation into a division of labor of growing complexity (see Foster, 1987; Smelser & Lipset, 1966).

All five of these explanations have received empirical support in at least some countries. But because the expansion of modern secular education cannot be linked to the economic prospects of a large number of developing countries, especially those in sub-Saharan Africa (see Collier & Gunning, 1999; Freeman & Lindauer, 1999), a case can be made that the first four narratives have the most power.

The challenge for future research is to help generate more empirical support for the fifth narrative, by developing research programs that demonstrate when institutions develop in ways that promote the societal welfare and economic prospects of developing countries and when they do not. In Nigeria, and we suspect in other sub-Saharan African countries, this new research agenda must focus on the relationships between modern secular education, traditional apprenticeship training, and the local labor market.

Partly as a result of the preoccupation with explaining the world-wide expansion of Western-style education, sociologists have given too little attention to pre-existing forms of apprenticeship training.[2] Where substantial attention has been registered (e.g. Hoselitz, 1966), it has faded over the past 40 years. This has occurred for no apparent reason other than that the "replacement" hypothesis (i.e. increases in the institutional provision of modern secular education lead to a symmetrical decline in the need for and take-up of traditional forms of education) is only partly true, and not nearly as theoretically exciting as the intellectual agendas associated with the political economy literature of underdevelopment (e.g. Wallerstein, 1974) and the world polity literature (e.g. Meyer, Ramirez & Soysal, 1992).

In this article, we first offer a brief historical analysis of the institutional context of our case study of the labor market of Kano, Nigeria, reviewing the development of its 1000-year-old marketplace economy and its educational pathways. We then present findings on the persistence and modifications of these educational and occupational linkages, using second-round data on young adult males from the longitudinal, two-cohort Kano Youth Survey. Comparing survey data from 1974 and 1992, we examine pathways from coexisting traditional and modern forms of education to labor market destinations in an occupational group hierarchy, the origins of which lie in an historically rooted three-layered segmented labor market. This conceptualization permits a more accurate interpretation of our findings than formal-informal labor market characterizations that are more typically employed in similar case settings, and allows us to show that pathways from each form of education to established occupational destinations have remained surprisingly stable even though the earnings from those occupations have not.

THE HISTORICAL DEVELOPMENT OF PATHWAYS TO POSITIONS IN KANO'S SEGMENTED LABOR MARKET

Two pre-colonial institutions continue to shape the occupational destinations of Kano's youth. The ancient *Kurmi* market and its associated system of trade and craft occupations remains the foundation of Kano's labor market. This commercial sector is complemented by a distinct set of religiously legitimated occupations with origins in the rise of an Islamic theocracy in the 19th century. Historically, these two sectors were dominated by separate ethnic groups, with the indigenous Hausa controlling the positions associated with trade and craft work, and with the conquering Fulani controlling the positions associated with religious and governmental authority. Before detailing the impact of colonialism and 20th century capitalism on Kano's labor market, we first describe the origins of the traditional institutions at the center of these complementary sectors.

Kano was built upon economic activity that is now often conceptualized as informal. European explorers traveling through Hausaland in the 19th century provided some of the first outsider accounts of the city's prominence. Writing on his entry into the walled city, Englishman Hugh Clapperton admits:

> I had no sooner passed the gates than I felt grievously disappointed; for from the flourishing description of it given by the Arabs, I expected to see a city of surprising grandeur (Denham & Clapperton, 1826, p. 238).

Kano's grand reputation, Clapperton later realized, was based on the economic prominence of *Kurmi* market rather than its aesthetic charm. Based on his travels, Clapperton came to recognize that "there is no market in Africa so well regulated," as it was divided into sections by craft and product, carefully managed by a central market authority, and was "crowded from sunrise to sunset every day" (Denham & Clapperton, 1826, pp. 253–256). Leather workers, tanners, blacksmiths, textile workers, and basket makers all produced items of exceptional quality, sought after by traders throughout much of North and West Africa. Lovejoy (1980, p. 66) insists that Kano "had a concentration of craft industry unrivaled in African history."

To support this ancient marketplace economy, the Hausa developed an apprenticeship system to train each new generation of craft workers. The system became an integral part of Kano's pervasive patron-client social structure, serving as the commercial derivative of the Hausa patrilineal kinship system of exchange. When acting as a marketplace patron, a Hausa enterprise owner would award apprenticeship positions to the clients of the patrons whom he sponsored. However, when then acting as a household patron seeking apprenticeship opportunities for his own sons and "adopted" sons, the same enterprise owner would attempt to locate even better positions from the more highly regarded marketplace patrons who sponsored him.

Through the 18th century, the craft industry associated with *Kurmi* market grew within the Hausa quarters surrounding the central city market. In the 19th century, the Fulani jihadists entered Kano, established an Islamic theocracy, and settled to the south in the quarters surrounding the institutions that they developed and staffed: the Emir's palace, city mosque, prison, and Islamic courts.

The Fulani were not city dwellers by custom, having descended from nomads and shepherds, and they initially abstained from profit seeking in the profane marketplace economy. As a consequence, they were less invested in the apprenticeship system and the encompassing patronage networks surrounding *Kurmi* market. Instead, the Fulani established Islamic brotherhoods to provide Islamic instruction and to prepare individuals for positions in the newly consolidated Emirate theocracy (see Clarke & Linden, 1984). More than venues for religious fellowship, these brotherhoods also served as arenas for achievement. Status depended on more than just inherited social rank and could be earned through advanced Islamic learning and skilled practice of sacred but public ritual. Thus, for those young Fulani men who could not expect to inherit an Emirate title, Islamic learning became a pathway through the brotherhood networks to a prestigious position as a teacher, scholar, or judge in the Emirate system.

By the end of the 19th century, cultural assimilation had weakened the Hausa/Fulani division of labor. The language of Hausa, always dominant in the *Kurmi* market, was accepted as the official language for government and Islamic court proceedings. Newly-reformed Islamic brotherhoods became important arenas for inter-ethnic association (Paden, 1973), and the Fulani could no longer abstain from the commercial opportunities offered by the marketplace economy. Accordingly, joint participation in the apprenticeship system and in Islamic education became increasingly common among both the Hausa and Fulani. As a result, possession of Islamic knowledge created a new source of trust within the marketplace trading networks, and marketplace skills and patronage connections generated additional streams of income for government and judicial functionaries.

A third segment of the labor market emerged during the British colonial rule from 1901 to 1960. Like the Fulani before them, the British accepted Hausa as the *lingua franca* but transcribed it for their own use from Arabic to Roman script. Their strategy of indirect rule required a trained and loyal indigenous staff to channel colonial policy through the existing Emirate system. The British introduced modern secular education to train the future traditional rulers of Kano in the ways of the British empire.

Offended by the introduction of the new schools, the Hausa-Fulani elite refused to send their children for instruction. Concurrently, the Emir founded the Kano Law School to train even more experts in Islamic law. This cool reception was a demonstration of elite opinion that, despite the needs of the bureaucratic colonial regime, Western-style education was neither appropriate nor necessary for the maintenance of the traditional, religiously legitimated authority of the Emirate system. And, as a result, Islamic education continued to dominate throughout the early colonial era. Official Kano State enrollment figures for 1937 claim 49,123 Islamic education pupils compared to 1,178 government primary school pupils and 131 government secondary school pupils (Bray, 1981, p. 44).

A new threat brought change. Gradually, the ruling elite of Kano came to recognize that the preservation of their unique cultural identity within the new political construction called "Nigeria" would depend to a large extent upon the future economic prominence of their city. As a result, the importation of skilled southern Nigerians – previously educated and converted by Christian missionaries – to meet the labor demands of the colonial civil service and British commodity export businesses, aroused a sense of regional competitiveness that led Kano's traditional rulers to support modern secular education as an important pathway toward new and important occupational destinations. Enrollment in government-sponsored modern secular education gradually increased, resulting in a doubling of primary schools between 1940 and 1950 (Bray, 1981).

In summary, the ancient Hausa trading and craft economy centered around the *Kurmi* market (and now also around its satellite markets) is the foundation of Kano's current labor market. In the 19th and 20th centuries, first with the Fulani conquest and introduction of an Islamic theocracy and then with the British conquest and introduction of a colonial bureaucracy, new labor market segments were superimposed upon this foundation. These three labor market segments have retained their separate identities through the maintenance of distinct educational pathways to separate occupational destinations. What changed with time were recruitment patterns from diverse social origins. By recognizing and following the proper pathways, the Hausa broke into the Fulani theocracy, and the Hausa-Fulani broke into and captured the colonial bureaucracy.

As will be evident from our survey data, the current representations of the three pathways that are described next continue to provide entry into an occupational group hierarchy that is in part defined by this three-part legacy but that has also continued to evolve with changing political and economic realities of the post-independence era.

CURRENT EDUCATIONAL PATHWAYS

Apprenticeship Education

Apprenticeships continue to provide a vital flow of new labor to the craft industries and trading venues associated with Kano's central marketplace. There have never been uniform rules governing these apprenticeships. Their decentralized and particularistic nature has permitted the development of a labor force of differentially skilled workers. On-the-job training, in exchange for food and lodging, is typical.

Entry into this system varies as well. The most common, though perhaps declining, arrangement is for sons to become apprentices to their own fathers and thereby "inherit" their occupations. Smith (1959) notes the higher status that is accorded to those individuals of each occupational group whose fathers formerly held the same positions. However, since the supply of labor must respond to technological progress and variable demand for goods, other arrangements are common as well. Fathers also seek apprenticeships for their sons with other master craftsmen and traders, especially more highly regarded patrons in the marketplace economy.

Islamic Education

Methods of Islamic education in Kano have remained relatively unchanged since the Fulani conquest of 1807. Most children are still placed by their fathers under the instruction of a local Islamic teacher known as a *mallam* by the age of five or six. Primary Islamic education consists of the memorization and recitation of the *Qur'an* and lasts on average for six years, depending on standards and skills. In the language of Hausa, primary Islamic education is *makarantar allo*, translated as "board schools," referring to the wooden tablets on which students learn to write *Qur'anic* verses in Arabic and *Ajami* (Hausa in Arabic script).

Once a student learns to recite the *Qur'an*, he or she moves on to secondary Islamic education, or *makarantar ilmi*, which consists of further study of the *Qur'an*, religious commentaries, Islamic jurisprudence, and some science. Most Hausa men and many Hausa women pursue secondary Islamic education, some for only a few years and others for 10 or more since there are no age restrictions on participation. Adults often return from work in the market or elsewhere and, after evening prayers, study by candlelight with a *mallam* well into the night (Bray, 1981; Clarke & Linden, 1984; Ozigi & Ocho, 1981).

Modern Secular Education

The introduction in 1976 of universal primary education to Kano and the rest of the northern region rapidly expanded participation levels beyond the elite youth normally expected to move into government civil service and other bureaucratic positions. It also greatly increased the demand for secondary education among the growing number of youth who aspired to public sector employment. Employers from all sectors, however, soon realized that the basic literacy and numeracy skills which developed from modern secular education provided human capital that could be broadly utilized, giving all segments of the labor market increased capacity to perform in the modernizing economy.

More recently in Kano as across sub-Saharan Africa, government-supported modern secular education is in a state of acute deterioration, suffering from insufficient instructional materials and a shortage of qualified teachers (see Bradshaw, 1993; Buchmann, 1999). At least in Nigeria, all families who can afford to do so now educate their children in private schools. Yet, because of the general decline in the well-being of middle-income Nigerians over the past two decades, the proportion of families who can afford to opt out of the faltering public education system remains quite small.

KANO YOUTH SURVEY, 1965–1992

Sample

The Kano Youth Survey (KYS) consists of random area samples of two cohorts of young men born in 1947 and 1961 and first interviewed as 17-year-olds in 1965 and 1979, respectively. For each cohort, a second round of interviews was conducted in 1974 and 1992, when they were respectively 26 and 30 years old. The permission and support of local authorities to conduct the surveys precluded the inclusion of young women in the study. For all rounds of the survey, respondents were interviewed by indigenous Hausa speakers.

The survey of the first cohort had 591 baseline respondents, of which 401 were located and re-interviewed in 1974. The survey of the second cohort, using the identical random area sampling design, yielded 632 baseline respondents, of which 525 were located for the second round in 1992. Of these, 276 were reinterviewed, and for the remainder, basic education and occupation data were obtained from the heads of their wards and family members.[3] Tests for possible bias in the cohort comparisons due either to the age difference between the two groups in their respective second round interviews or possible systematic differences in attrition patterns were negative, as explained in the Appendix.

Variables

Each respondent's self-reported educational attainments in apprenticeship, Islamic, and modern secular forms were measured in total years engaged in each form by 1974 or 1992, respectively. As our data will show, these three forms of education are often pursued simultaneously.

Occupational attainment was derived from survey responses coded first into detailed occupations and then assigned to one of five groups corresponding to the traditional prestige hierarchy. These included professional and clerical office workers (government bureaucrats, accountants, university lecturers, bank clerks, etc.), teachers (primary and secondary school teachers, school principals), traders (import-export businessmen, foreign exchange traders, retail goods traders, etc.), skilled workers and artisans (blacksmiths, shoemakers, leather tanners, motor mechanics, etc.), and unskilled workers and drivers (laundry men, factory workers, laborers, taxi cab drivers, minibus drivers, etc.).[4] For the earnings differences reported in the last table, we subdivide unskilled workers and drivers into separate categories.

Finally, self-reported weekly earnings were initially recorded in the local currency (the Naira). The earnings reported in 1974 were converted to 1992 earnings, using a multiplier of 35.4 based on annual changes in the consumer price index reported by the International Monetary Fund (IMF, 1964–1992).

PATTERNS OF JOINT EDUCATION

Comparing the participation rates of respondents from each cohort indexes the pattern and degree of educational change in northern Nigeria since independence

Table 1. Joint Participation Rates for Apprenticeship, Islamic, and Modern Secular Education.

	1974	1992
Apprenticeship with		
Islamic only	23.2%	4.3%
Modern secular only	0.7%	0.0%
Islamic and modern secular	24.5%	30.6%
Subtotal[a]	48.4%	34.9%
No apprenticeship		
Islamic only	14.5%	2.3%
Modern secular only	0.7%	0.0%
Islamic and modern secular	36.5%	62.8%
Subtotal	51.7%	65.1%
Total	100.0%	100.0%
N	310	258

[a] Decline in rate of apprenticeships across cohorts is significant at $p < 0.01$, using a two-sample test of equality of proportions.

in 1960. As discussed earlier, the educational expansion literature posits that modern secular education expands in developing countries under increasing government provision, gradually replacing all traditional forms of education (Hoselitz, 1966). Contrary to this expectation, Table 1 demonstrates continued participation in traditional forms of education, despite increased participation in modern secular education.

Table 1 presents all possible joint participation rates for Kano's three available forms of education. Approximately 85% of first cohort respondents and 98% of second cohort respondents pursued more than one type of education. Islamic education remained universal from 1974 to 1992; modern secular education became nearly universal; and apprenticeships declined 14 percentage points, pursued by just over a third of the 1992 cohort. In both cohorts the most prevalent combination was Islamic with modern secular education, followed by apprenticeships with Islamic and modern secular education. These two combinations accounted for 61% of the types of educational attainment obtained by the young men in 1974, and 96% of the young men in 1992.

Participation rates only indicate utilization of each form of education. As participation and attainment in modern secular education increased, average attainment in one or the other forms of traditional education might have decreased despite continued joint participation by the majority of respondents. Table 2 addresses this issue with correlation coefficients between years of each form of

Table 2. Correlations Among Respondents' Years of Each Form of Education in 1974 (Below Diagonal) and 1992 (Above Diagonal).

		1992		
		Modern Secular	Islamic	Apprenticeship
1974	Modern secular	–	0.136*	−0.235***
	Islamic	−0.114*	–	0.030
	Apprenticeship	−0.352***	−0.003	–

Note: Numbers of respondents vary by correlation coefficient, ranging from 312 to 328 for the 1974 cohort and from 258 to 259 for the 1992 cohort.

*$p < 0.05$.

***$p < 0.001$.

education for both cohorts. The correlation coefficient between modern secular and apprenticeship education is moderately negative for both cohorts, indicating a stable tendency for increasing amounts of modern secular education to decrease the likelihood of starting and completing apprenticeship training. Similarly, modern secular education was weakly negatively related to Islamic education in the first cohort. For the second cohort, however, this relationship was reversed.

Equally revealing is the shift in the marginal distributions for these relationships. While pursuing an apprenticeship did continue to decrease the total years of modern secular education, apprentices who undertook modern secular education in 1992 on average obtained double the total years compared to apprentices who undertook modern secular education in 1974 (11.5 years compared to 5.6 years, significant at $p < 0.001$).

Thus, we have only limited support for the replacement hypothesis. Despite rapid expansion of modern secular education, the two traditional forms of education remained important. Participation in traditional apprenticeships did decrease as pursuit of modern secular education increased, and apprentices in 1992 had substantially more years of modern secular education. However, participation in Islamic education remained universal, and attainment levels for Islamic and modern secular education became positively related. A more detailed analysis of this new complementarity, conceptualized as structural accommodation, has been presented in earlier reports from the first rounds of these data (Morgan & Armer, 1988, 1991, 1992).

Clearly, traditional education is still relevant in post-independence Kano. But some important questions remain unresolved. Against the background of Nigeria's faltering economy, to be detailed below, it remains an open question whether or not, in hindsight, apprenticeship education can continue to provide skills that are valued in Kano's segmented yet continually changing labor market. To begin to address a question such as this one, we must first determine whether or not apprenticeship education retained substantial relevance for labor market allocation processes.

EDUCATIONAL PATHWAYS IN THE MARKETPLACE ECONOMY

Given that both cohorts in our survey participated in all three forms of education, the interest now is the extent to which their selection into Kano's post-independence occupational group hierarchy was guided by their training. Toward this end, we examine for each cohort the educational profiles of the five main occupational groups presented earlier in the description of the Kano Youth Survey data.

Table 3 reports apprenticeship, Islamic, and modern secular educational attainments for each occupational group, decomposed into rates of participation and mean years completed by participants, with values for the full samples of both cohorts also reported. Significance tests are presented for cohort differences in these occupation-specific attainments, since the key issue is whether there has been change or stability in the educational patterns of the successive incumbents of each occupational destination.

Most striking is that the significant overall 14-point decline from 1974 to 1992 in apprenticeship participation was restricted to the single occupational category of professional and clerical office workers. In all other groups, apprenticeship participation was essentially unchanged. Similarly, participation in Islamic education remained unchanged across all occupational groups – it remained universal within each group. This pattern of stability for traditional education participation is even more remarkable when viewed against the significant participation increase in modern secular education across all occupational categories (except among teachers, whose participation levels had already peaked by 1974).

This pattern of robust trends for participation in traditional education is also apparent when viewing duration of participation. Apprenticeships averaged two years longer, although the increase was significant for traders only. For Islamic education there was an average increase of seven years, significant in all occupational groups. Keeping in mind the joint nature of the contemporary Kano educational system, it is still remarkable that both duration increases occurred even though the duration of modern secular education also increased by five years, a universal increase that was also significant for all occupational groups.

Across occupational groups, the variation in educational attainment was as expected. Participation in apprenticeships was greater for skilled workers and artisans, traders, and unskilled workers and drivers for both cohorts. Participation in modern secular education was higher for professionals and clericals and for

Table 3. Cohort Differences in Educational Attainments, by Occupation.

	Participation Rate		Mean of Years Completed for Participants	
	1974	1992	1974	1992
Professional and clerical office workers				
Apprenticeship education	30.3%	13.5%**	5.0	5.9
Islamic education	98.5%	100.0%	11.6	19.5***
Modern secular education	95.2%	100.0%*	9.7	13.9***
Teachers				
Apprenticeship education	13.0%	27.3%	9.7	8.8*
Islamic education	100.0%	100.0%	10.8	19.9***
Modern secular education	100.0%	100.0%	11.1	12.9*
Traders				
Apprenticeship education	50.5%	46.6%	6.2	8.7*
Islamic education	98.9%	100.0%	14.6	20.5***
Modern secular education	58.5%	87.9%***	4.8	11.5***
Skilled workers and artisans				
Apprenticeship education	66.7%	81.5%	6.5	7.4
Islamic education	100.0%	100.0%	13.5	19.4***
Modern secular education	53.4%	84.2%**	5.5	10.3***
Unskilled workers and drivers				
Apprenticeship education	60.7%	47.6%	6.9	9.4
Islamic education	98.3%	100.0%	11.1	15.3**
Modern secular education	25.4%	81.0%***	4.4	10.2***
Full sample				
Apprenticeship education	49.4%	35.8%**	6.4	7.9**
Islamic education	99.0%	100.0%	12.8	19.4***
Modern secular education	61.2%	93.3%***	7.1	12.5***

Note: Significance tests for across-cohort occupational differences in participation rates are based on coefficients and standard errors estimated from a dummy variable logistic regression equation for each form of education, with $N = 647$. Significance tests of across-cohort occupational differences in years of participants' education are based on a dummy variable OLS regression for each form of education, with $N = 271$, 520, and 480 for the apprenticeship, Islamic, and modern secular equations, respectively. Full sample tests use standard two-sample z-tests of equality of proportions and t-tests of equality of means.

*$p < 0.05$.

**$p < 0.01$.

***$p < 0.001$.

teachers in the first cohort. In the second cohort, when modern secular education became universal, these two groups obtained, on average, three more years of secular education than the other groups.

Islamic education, which for both cohorts was universally obtained in all occupational groups, showed occupational variation only in duration of participation. In the first cohort, the two marketplace occupational groups of traders and skilled workers and artisans had three more years of Islamic education than the other three groups. In the second cohort, professionals and clericals as well as teachers had caught up to the two marketplace groups in years of Islamic education. Only unskilled workers had less Islamic education – on average four years less than the other groups.

In summary, when viewing cohort changes in education within specific occupational destinations, the joint nature of Kano's educational system is elaborated further. Apprenticeship training remained important in 1992, especially for occupations in the marketplace economy, and the training became longer. Islamic education remained universally valued to an increasing degree, in that young men in all occupational groups pursued it longer. At the same time, modern secular education became increasingly critical for entry into the professional and clerical office and teaching occupations, but was obtained in increasing amounts across all occupations.

EARNINGS IN THE MARKETPLACE ECONOMY

Given that the educational pathways each evolved in service of a different segment of Kano's historic labor market, the gradual elimination of boundaries to participation in each pathway has resulted in the universal participation across occupational groups in two of the pathways, and for the marketplace occupations with substantial apprenticeships, in all three. Of interest now is how the jointly educated incumbents of each occupational group were affected in their earnings by the severe economic decline of the 1980s that devastated Nigeria and the rest of sub-Saharan Africa (Mills & Sahn, 1995; Schultz, 1999). Over this time period the real wages of civil servants have fallen and the number of positions in the formal bureaucratic labor market, primarily in the public sector, have also decreased (Collier & Gunning, 1999; Freeman & Lindauer, 1999). Kano's segmented labor market was not impervious to these trends.

Table 4 presents median weekly earnings for the five occupational groups as before, except that drivers are analyzed separately from the other unskilled workers. Across occupations there were, in fact, variable shifts in earnings levels. Most dramatic was the absolute and relative decline in the wages of professional

Table 4. Median Weekly Earnings in the Marketplace Economy.

	Median in 1974	Median in 1992	Change in Median	Bootstrapped 95% Confidence Interval for Change in Median
Professional and clerical office workers	354	163	-191^{***}	(−256.8, −125.4)
Teachers	460	154	-306^{***}	(−378.6, −234.1)
Traders	177	300	123	(−25.0, 270.9)
Skilled workers and artisans	248	175	−73	(−157.6, 11.9)
Drivers	248	300	52	(−433.6, 537.9)
Unskilled workers (not drivers)	212	138	-74^{*}	(−117.1, −31.8)

Note: $N = 546$. Weekly earnings adjusted for inflation to 1992 Naira. Significance tests and confidence intervals for differences are estimated from a dummy variable median regression with bootstrapped standard errors.

$^{*}p < 0.05$.

$^{***}p < 0.001$.

and clerical workers and of teachers, and secondarily of the unskilled workers. By contrast, the occupations central to the marketplace economy – traders, skilled workers and artisans – did not share in this decline.

To some degree this differential impact of the 1980s' economic decline can be traced to varying strengths and opportunities in the local economy. To a larger degree, however, the variable impact can be related to the selective availability of local buffering influences, including the institution of apprenticeship.

ADJUSTMENTS IN THE LOCAL ECONOMY

Throughout the economic decline, currency devaluation and an associated decline in indigenous industrial output generated new opportunities for black market trading in hard currency, gasoline, and scarce imported goods. At the same time, consumption of the traditional goods manufactured by skilled workers and craftsman remained stable, since currency devaluation made the purchase of foreign-produced goods prohibitively expensive. And the virtual disappearance of private ownership of cars and motorcycles by the cash-starved lower-income segment of Nigerian society, coupled with long periods of gasoline shortages, generated new sources of revenue for low-skilled taxi, minibus, and motorcycle drivers with access to black market-traded gasoline. In response to these changes, the weekly earnings of traders and drivers have fared well, the decline in earnings of skilled workers was not significant, and only the unskilled workers of the marketplace economy suffered a significant drop in median earnings.

By contrast, the Nigerian federal government agreed to the International Monetary Fund's mandates for structural adjustment in response to its economic crisis, and the result was a freeze in the wages of public sector employees. This, coupled with rampant inflation, caused the significant wage declines reported in Table 4, all falling within the three occupational categories most engaged in the public sector. A more detailed analysis and explanation of this decline was presented in an earlier report (Morgan & Morgan, 1998).

APPRENTICESHIP AS A SOCIETAL INSTITUTION

Given that apprenticeship education remained most prevalent among workers in the relatively less impacted marketplace economy, the remaining issue is how this traditional institution may have helped buffer the impact of the economic decline. It is certainly possible that this form of workplace education offers a more general and fungible preparation for coping with economic uncertainties that will continue to be prevalent in Nigeria and other developing societies. If so, the comprehensive nature of apprenticeship training needs further elucidation.

More than job training, the premodern apprenticeships we have observed in the Kano marketplace provide communal socialization. Each apprentice begins a process of integration into the community of adult workers through the acquisition of skills and competencies that can be labeled, if one so desires, as cultural and social capital. The cultural capital with widest local currency is Islam, and the social capital that envelops the marketplace community is patron-clientage.

In the strong Islamic culture of Kano, one's status is dependent in no small part on how well one practices the religion, particularly its more public aspects. Use of the proper Islamic greetings and invocations in the workplace is a practiced art that can take years to develop, yet can be critical for one's acceptance as a mature workplace equal. Similarly, knowing how to disengage from work in order to perform the mandatory midmorning and afternoon prayers and then casually re-engage represents a cultural skill that distinguishes novices from veteran workers. The ability to practice Islam in the workplace is a cultural expectation, and if it is done properly it suffuses the most menial occupation with a sacred presence respected universally. These workplace skills presuppose but are distinct from formal Islamic education, since they develop best through practice in the actual workplace under the watchful eye and guidance of one's master. Over time the respect and approval an apprentice receives for his Islamic propriety builds status, and this improved status position signals one's readiness to move into a network of adult relations.

Beyond the development of this form of sacred and relatively diffuse cultural competence, the observance of Islamic ritual in the context of one's apprenticeship can be important for more directly securing a favorable position in the all-encompassing patron-client network of the marketplace. Market relationships are carefully circumscribed by these social networks. For successful activation of these networks, one needs to be well-placed, but just as importantly, one needs to learn the position of others in order to relate to them properly.

To the extent that apprenticeship is preparation for clientage and eventually patronage, apprenticeships serve as a structural mechanism for the maintenance of patron-client relations. Some may see this as a mixed blessing. The standard Marxist position is that patron-clientage hinders the development of class solidarity. Naive developmental theorists see patron-clientage as both a barrier to democratization and a legitimation of the corruption that prevents external assistance from stimulating economic development. Perhaps more realistic is the position that patron-clientage is a critical transition structure in the aftermath of traditional rule and before modern state bureaucracy has become legitimate. As such it brings to new nations an important degree of social integration and stability.

When viewing apprenticeship education in this way – as an institution capable of much more than simply providing skills relevant for successful performance in narrowly defined task niches – we can now characterize our findings in a more general way. We have suggested that a premodern form of apprenticeship education endures in Kano because of its utility in preparing and selecting new recruits into the complex patron-client network through which business is conducted in the local marketplace economy. The important change in this institution over the past 30 years is that young persons who enter apprenticeships and pursue advanced Islamic studies now also undertake modern secular schooling. This provision of multiple forms of education complies with national educational guidelines, which are heavily influenced by broad goals for modern nation-building and democratic citizenship. At the same time, this menu of educational opportunities remains consistent with the development of Kano's economic and political institutions and, as in the 19th century, affords young persons the opportunity to move away from the marketplace economy and into other sectors of the occupational structure. For an example from the KYS, Table 3 shows that in the second cohort a substantial number of former apprentices moved into primary school teaching.

Furthermore, during the period of economic stagnation, the increased duration of apprenticeships suggests that this institution, within the context of patron-clientage, served as a way station as well as a pathway, providing a subsistence livelihood for young workers in the absence of any formal unemployment insurance program. The maintenance of these young workers retains the future marketplace labor force that will be necessary if and when economic recovery fully takes hold.

Of course, a similar interpretation can be offered for the increased duration of modern secular education, in that this education could also operate – whether by design or simply by practice – as a holding ground for the growing number of young persons for whom work is unavailable. The major difference is that young persons who are in prolonged apprenticeships are coupled to an actual work experience, and usually also further modern secular education; young persons who are prolonging their modern schooling are likely to have only work aspirations, possibly unrealizable ones.

What is happening in Kano and elsewhere in modernizing Africa is quite different, of course, from the standardized apprenticeship-based vocational training of industrialized nations, Germany in particular (see Blossfeld, 1992; McKernan, 1994). Its further analysis will require a better understanding of productive business relations which are built on patron-client foundations, and in turn an assessment of the viability of both patron-clientage and diffuse apprenticeships as institutions that will inevitably need to respond to the pressures and demands of the global economy. One could predict, for example, that apprenticeships will founder if they operate contrary to new international child labor standards, resist the emerging egalitarian demands of women throughout the Third World, or if they should be reinstated as alternatives to modern secular schooling rather than as supplements. Conversely, if a global postmodern society seeking alternatives to materialist-based status structures is indeed emerging, Africa's signal contribution may be its communal apprenticeship institutions.[5]

CONCLUSION

In conclusion, our speculation on the future of premodern diffuse apprenticeships has moved us to an institutional perspective on the viability of the local economy. If the demise of this traditional pathway would endanger the local economy centered in and around the Kurmi market, more attention needs to be given to the premise that the restoration of this market economy will be facilitated by a reinvigorated apprenticeship pathway that supplements but does not replace modern secular education. Conversely, apprentices must continue to have equal opportunity to pursue a modern secular education, in order both to enhance their apprenticeship skills as broadly outlined here and to acquire more universal knowledge transferable across occupations should their particularized niche in the marketplace economy falter.

It would be counterproductive if the current, internationally supported drive for further expansion of modern secular education in developing countries resulted in the total obliteration of apprenticeship training in sub-Saharan Africa. And, it would be ironic, since industrialized societies have just begun to seriously explore alternatives for the reintroduction of workplace-centered apprenticeship training as a means for more effectively solving the problems inherent in the school-to-work transitions of post-industrial societies.

NOTES

1. We use the phrase "modern secular education" throughout this article to refer what is often labeled "Western education," in deference to our Nigerian colleagues' preference for "modern" to "Western," and their dislike for the implication that what is not "Western" is somehow "non-modern."

2. Anthropological research on apprenticeship training is substantial (e.g. Coy, 1989; Goody, 1982; Lave, 1977; Lave & Wenger, 1991). However, beyond meticulous accounts of master/apprentice relations, anthropologists have paid relatively little attention to patterns of selection into apprenticeships and subsequent employment allocation.

3. Fieldwork for the two rounds of the first cohort was directed by Armer (1968, 1970). Fieldwork for the first round of the second cohort was directed by W. R. Morgan (Morgan & Armer, 1988, 1991, 1992). S. L. Morgan directed the second round (Morgan, 1993; Morgan & Morgan, 1998), with support from colleagues at Bayero University Kano for both second cohort surveys.

4. We exclude from analysis all *mallams*, farmers, and students. Not only are there few such respondents, but their labor force participation patterns are only weakly tied to Kano's market economy on which we focus in this article.

5. Kano's apprenticeship system, at least in spirit, closely matches the policy dreams of James S. Coleman and the 1974 President's Science Advisory Committee (see Coleman et al., 1974). Coleman and his colleagues argued for the creation of government supported institutions in the United States that offer workplace education in age-heterogeneous groupings. He believed such institutions could provide more than just on-the-job training and could offer more effective workplace socialization than stand-alone vocational programs. This line of argument is an early example of what Coleman later referred to as the "rational reconstruction of society" (see Coleman, 1993).

ACKNOWLEDGMENTS

Data collection in 1992 was supported by grants to S. Morgan from the Harvard Institute for International Development, the Center for International Affairs, and the Committee on African Studies. Fieldwork in 2001 was supported by funds provided by the College of Arts and Sciences, Cornell University. None of these supporting agencies bear any responsibility for the conclusions contained herein.

REFERENCES

Armer, J. M. (1968). Intersociety and intrasociety correlations of occupational prestige. *American Journal of Sociology*, *74*, 28–36.

Armer, J. M. (1970). Formal education and psychological malaise in an African society. *Sociology of Education*, *43*, 143–158.

Blossfeld, H.-P. (1992). Is the German dual-system a model for a modern vocational training system? *International Journal of Comparative Sociology*, *3*, 168–181.

Boli, J., Ramirez, F., & Meyer, J. W. (1985). Explaining the origins and expansion of mass education. *Comparative Education Review*, *29*, 145–170.

Bradshaw, Y. W. (1993). State limitations, self-help secondary schooling, and development in Kenya. *Social Forces*, *72*, 347–378.

Bray, M. (1981). *Universal primary education in Nigeria: A study of Kano State*. London: Routledge & Kegan Paul.

Buchmann, C. (1999). The state and schooling in Kenya: Historical developments and current challenges. *Africa Today*, *46*, 95–117.

Chase-Dunn, C. (1982). The uses of formal comparative research on dependency theory and the world-system perspective. In: H. Makler, A. Martinelli & N. Smelser (Eds), *The New International Economy* (pp. 117–140). Beverly Hills: Sage.

Clarke, P. B., & Linden, I. (1984). *Islam in Modern Nigeria: A study of a Muslim community in a post-independence state 1960–1983*. Mainz: Grunewald and Kaiser.

Coleman, J. S. (1993). The rational reconstruction of society. *American Sociological Review*, *58*, 1–15.

Coleman, J. S., & members of the President's Science Advisory Committee (1974). *Youth: Transition to adulthood*. Chicago: University of Chicago Press.

Collier, P., & Gunning, J. W. (1999). Why has Africa grown slowly? *Journal of Economic Perspectives*, *13*, 3–22.

Denham, D., & Clapperton, H. (1826). *Narrative of travels and discoveries in northern and central Africa*. London: John Murray.

Foster, P. (1987). The contribution of education to development. In: G. Psacharopoulos (Ed.), *Economics of Education* (pp. 93–100). New York: Pergamon.

Freeman, R. B., & Lindauer, D. L. (1999). Why not Africa? National Bureau of Economic Research Working Paper No. 6942, Cambridge, MA.

Fuller, B., & Rubinson, R. (1992). Does the state expand schooling? In: B. Fuller & R. Rubinson (Eds), *The Political Construction of Education* (pp. 1–30). New York: Praeger.

Goody, E. N. (Ed.) (1982). *From craft to industry: The ethnography of proto-industrial cloth production*. Cambridge: Cambridge University Press.

Hoselitz, B. F. (1966). Interaction between industrial and preindustrial stratification systems. In: N. J. Smelser & S. M. Lipset (Eds), *Social Structure and Mobility in Economic Development* (pp. 177–193). Chicago: Aldine.

International Monetary Fund (1964–1992). *International financial statistics, 17–45*. Washington, DC: International Monetary Fund.

Inkeles, A., & Smith, D. H. (1974). *Becoming modern: Individual change in six developing countries*. Cambridge: Harvard University Press.

Lave, J. (1977). Cognitive consequences of traditional apprenticeship training in West Africa. *Anthropology and Education Quarterly*, *8*, 177–180.

Lave, J., & Wenger, E. (1991). *Situated learning: Legitimate peripheral participation*. Cambridge: Cambridge University Press.

Lovejoy, P. E. (1980). *Caravans of Kola: The Hausa Kola Trade 1700–1900*. Zaria, Nigeria: Ahmadu Bello University Press.

McKernan, J. R., Jr. (1994). *Making the grade: How a new youth apprenticeship system can change our schools and save American jobs*. Boston: Little, Brown.

Meyer, J. W., Ramirez, F., & Soysal, Y. (1992). World expansion of mass education. *Sociology of Education*, *65*, 128–149.

Mills, B. F., & Sahn, D. E. (1995). Reducing the size of the public sector workforce: Institutional constraints and human consequences in Guinea. *Journal of Development Studies, 31*, 505–528.
Morgan, S. L. (1993). *Labor market change and occupational aspirations in a turbulent economy: Kano, Nigeria, 1965 to 1992*. Unpublished B.A. Thesis, Harvard University.
Morgan, W. R., & Armer, J. M. (1988). Islamic and western educational accommodation in a west African society: A cohort-comparison analysis. *American Sociological Review, 53*, 634–639.
Morgan, W. R., & Armer, J. M. (1991). Structural accommodation and cultural duality: The northern Nigerian education system. *International Education, 21*, 41–48.
Morgan, W. R., & Armer, J. M. (1992). Western versus Islamic schooling: Conflict and accommodation in Nigeria. In: B. Fuller & R. Rubinson (Eds), *The Political Construction of Education* (pp. 75–88). New York: Praeger.
Morgan, S. L., & Morgan, W. R. (1998). Education and earnings in Nigeria, 1974–1992. *Research in Social Stratification and Social Mobility, 16*, 3–26.
Ozigi, A., & Ocho, L. (1981). *Education in Northern Nigeria*. London: George Allen & Unwin.
Paden, J. N. (1973). *Religion and political culture in Kano*. Berkeley: University of California Press.
Schultz, T. P. (1999). Health and schooling investments in Africa. *Journal of Economic Perspectives, 13*, 67–88.
Sklair, L. (1991). *Sociology of the global system*. Baltimore: Johns Hopkins Press.
Smelser, N. J., & Lipset, S. M. (Eds) (1966). *Social structure and mobility in economic development*. Chicago: Aldine.
Smith, M. G. (1959). The Hausa system of social status. *Africa, 29*, 239–251.
Wallerstein, I. (1974). *The modern world system I*. New York: Academic Press.

APPENDIX

We assessed the robustness of the cohort comparison central to our analysis for possible biases from the age difference of the cohorts and differences in attrition levels. Because of a four-year difference in the time lag of the two follow-up surveys, respondents from 1974 were 26 and 30 in 1992. This difference did not affect participation rates, and the cohort differences in years of participation were only negligibly biased upward. The amount of this bias can be assessed reasonably accurately by knowing how many respondents from the first cohort were still educationally active when surveyed at age 26.

A total of 11.7% of these respondents reported they were currently pursuing modern secular education as a primary or subsidiary activity (a primary activity for 8% in various post-primary programs, subsidiary for the other 3.7% in literacy class); 8.2% were continuing their Islamic education (a primary activity at the advanced level for 1.7%, a subsidiary activity at the primary level for 6.5%); and 1.2% were doing apprenticeships. A plausible upper-bound estimate of bias would be to recompute the mean years of attainment for the 1974 cohort, assuming each of the active respondents were to complete the maximum of four additional years of education possible between ages 26 and 30. Upper-bound estimates for average years of education among participants are 7.86 years for modern secular education (up 0.76 years from the value in Table 3), 13.13 years for Islamic education (up 0.33 years from the value in Table 3), and 6.5 years for apprenticeships (up 0.10 years from the value in Table 3).

The age difference could bias the cohort differences in median earnings that were reported only if the older cohort also had on average more years of full-time labor force participation. In fact, given that across the three forms of education the second cohort averaged an additional five years over the first cohort, their being four years older helped remove this source of bias.

Since attrition matters only if the attriters are substantially different from the retained sample, we used background data from the first rounds of both cohorts in order to compare attriters and completers. The differences were small, and what differences did exist were similar across cohorts, and so would be unlikely to bias the cohort differences reported.

For example, the proportion with fathers who were professional/clerical, skilled/artisan, or unskilled differed on average from the baseline proportions for each by only 3 percentage points. In the second cohort, the participation rate in post-secondary education differed by one percentage point between the sample of 276 who were reinterviewed and used in the analysis, and the located but not reinterviewed sample of 204 on whom informant data was available. Further details of this analysis, including the estimation of a selection bias equation and a robust regression to check for outlier effects for earnings changes similar to those modeled in Table 4, are available in a prior report (Morgan & Morgan, 1998, pp. 19–22).

UNEVEN INROADS: UNDERSTANDING WOMEN'S STATUS IN HIGHER EDUCATION

Karen Bradley and Maria Charles

ABSTRACT

Growth in female tertiary enrollment has been accompanied by persistent gender differentiation within systems of higher education worldwide. We identify three dimensions of female "status" in higher education – overall female enrollments, sex segregation across tertiary levels, and sex segregation across fields of study – and we offer a conceptual framework for understanding cross-national similarity and variability on these dimensions. Commonalities across countries reflect the interaction of global pressures for expansion and democratization of education with persistent cultural representations of "gender difference." Variability can be attributed, in part, to the different ways in which global cultural and structural pressures have been manifested within particular socio-historical settings.

INTRODUCTION

Access to higher education has long been considered an essential prerequisite to improving the social and economic status of women. Today, female representation in colleges and universities reaches or exceeds gender parity in many industrialized

Inequality Across Societies: Families, Schools and Persisting Stratification
Research in Sociology of Education, Volume 14, 247–274
(Formerly Research in Sociology of Education and Socialization)

ISSN: 1479-3539/doi:10.1016/S1479-3539(03)14011-6

nations. Distributions within and across the institutions that comprise national tertiary systems differ strongly by sex, however. This distributional inequality, or "sex segregation," takes the form of female overrepresentation in lower-status institutions (Charles & Bradley, 2002; Jacobs, 1996; Karen, 2002; Kelly, 1991; OECD, 1997, p. 67) and in fields such as humanities, arts, social sciences, education, and health (Barber, 1995; Bradley, 2000; Jacobs, 1995; Persell et al., 1999). The male domination of engineering and information technology programs is particularly conspicuous. These seemingly universal forms of sex segregation are receiving increased attention from advocates for gender equality and from policymakers concerned about potential labor shortages in science and technology fields (National Research Council, 1992; United Nations, 1995; European Union Commission, 2000). Scholars on the other hand, have not yet made much effort to reconcile uneven patterns of female participation in higher education with standard unidimensional theories of "women's status." Moreover, cross-national differences in levels and patterns of tertiary gender stratification have been neither empirically nor theoretically assessed in any comprehensive fashion.

In this article, we propose a conceptual framework for understanding both cross-national commonalities and cross-national differences in sex segregation in higher education. We begin by identifying three dimensions of gender stratification within higher education: overall access, sex segregation by field of study, and sex segregation by level of degree attainment. As we will show, disentangling these constituent elements of women's "status" in higher education is the essential starting point for meaningful theoretical and empirical analyses. Our argument, in short, is that the diffusion of universalistic ideals of educational democratization has contributed to erosion of some but not all forms of gender inequality within higher education. This is because pressures for universalism have emerged in a cultural context in which distinct male and female "natures" and dispositions continue to be taken for granted by the vast majority of citizens. Modern patterns of gender stratification in tertiary education – i.e. high levels of overall female enrollment and strong gender differentiation within systems – thus result from the interaction of universalistic mandates for gender equality with persistent and deeply institutionalized ideologies of gender difference (see also Charles & Grusky, in press). Furthermore, we argue that global trends toward structural differentiation of higher education (i.e. expansion of junior colleges and short-term vocational programs) have exacerbated sex segregation by field of study and by institution type.

Previous attempts to explain female underrepresentation in elite fields and levels have tended to prioritize individual-level factors, such as self-esteem (Berryman, 1983), role modeling/teacher encouragement (Hatchell, 1998), attitudes (Catsambis, 1994; Hanson, 1996; Shamai, 1996), and the existence of a "chilly climate" toward women (Hall & Sandler, 1982). Authors of these studies generally acknowledge the limits of a strictly micro-level framework and emphasize the importance of the social and cultural context in which educational choices unfold. No comprehensive approach has yet been advanced, however, that considers the effects of macro-level factors on patterns of gender stratification within higher education.

This article is divided into three analytical sections. First, we draw upon data from 26 industrial and newly industrializing countries to examine patterns of similarity and difference in overall enrollment rates, segregation by level (i.e. degree attainment at the non-university, university, and postgraduate levels), and segregation by field of study.[1] In the second and third sections, we develop frameworks for understanding the observed international similarities and differences, respectively.

THE MULTIDIMENSIONALITY OF TERTIARY GENDER STRATIFICATION: SOME EVIDENCE

Descriptive data on women's percentage share of graduates at three different tertiary levels and in two highly gender-typed fields of study are shown in Table 1. Figures are for 1995 and are based on information published in the 1997 and 1998 editions of UNESCO's *Statistical Yearbook*. Included here are all industrialized countries and "countries in transition" for which detailed data were available. We present data on graduates, rather than enrolled students, because reliable information on individuals' fields of study often becomes available for the first time at graduation.[2]

Women's overall share of tertiary graduates is shown in the first column of Table 1. Country values range from 36% in Switzerland to 62% in Poland. Although cross-national variability is substantial, it is notable that women's presence in higher education is within 14 points of gender parity (50%) in all 26 countries. The international mean of 53% suggests a strong global tendency toward gender parity, if not female advantage, in higher education (see Bradley & Ramirez, 1996).

The second, third, and fourth columns of Table 1 show women's share of graduates within the three tertiary levels distinguished by UNESCO. The non-university level houses a heterogeneous collection of academic and vocational programs, all of which culminate in an "award not equivalent to a first university degree." University-level institutions award degrees roughly equivalent to the U.S. bachelor's degree, although duration of study varies across countries. The postgraduate level encompasses programs of study beyond the first university degree that culminate in advanced professional or academic degrees. In a pattern reminiscent of the well-documented "glass ceiling" phenomenon in modern labor markets, we find declining female representation as we move up the hierarchy of levels. On average, women made up about 58% of lower-level graduates, 51% of university graduates, and 41% of graduates from postgraduate programs in 1995.

Table 1. The Multiple Dimensions of Women's Status in Higher Education: Female Share of Graduates (%), 1995.

	1 Tertiary Education Overall	2 Non-University Level (ISCED Level 5)	3 University Level, 1st Degree (ISCED Level 6)	4 University Level, Postgraduate (ISCED Level 7)	5 Humanities Field (All Levels)	6 Engineering Field (All Levels)
Austria	51.8	73.1	45.3	28.9	61.3	16.2
Belgium	51.2	57.8	45.4	36.6	62.9	17.5
Canada	49.7	47.3	58.3	47.4	59.8	12.7
Chile	51.8	53.6	51.6	39.9	68.9	17.6
Croatia	52.4	47.0	56.2	44.3	56.7	24.5
Czech Republic	56.4	68.0	51.5	26.2	53.6	26.8
Denmark	50.6	37.3	55.4	39.1	79.8	21.7
Finland	57.6	65.7	52.4	46.1	72.0	14.4
France	53.8	55.8	52.5	47.2	72.6	17.6
Germany	45.3	55.1	41.6	31.5	70.0	8.7
Hong Kong	42.5	41.6	45.4	35.6	75.5	6.0
Ireland	48.6	44.6	52.4	46.1	61.5	10.6
Italy	56.1	63.6	53.5	42.9	85.5	10.5
Japan	50.9	68.8	31.9	17.0	82.8	12.2
Korea (Rep.)	45.3	54.3	41.9	26.8	61.4	15.1
New Zealand	57.6	65.1	57.2	46.9	64.6	14.0
Norway	54.4	54.8	59.4	40.3	63.4	18.6
Poland	61.8	79.4	51.7	58.4	70.4	15.7
Slovenia	57.7	59.4	59.8	42.6	73.2	23.2
South Africa	53.8	54.9	53.9	49.5	62.1	7.6
Spain	56.5	50.3	57.5	39.3	64.2	18.6
Sweden	57.3	67.7	53.9	49.0	61.6	19.8
Switzerland	36.0	63.4	35.7	29.6	55.8	4.2
United Kingdom	53.6	63.6	50.7	48.0	62.9	15.0
United States	55.2	58.3	54.6	51.7	59.2	14.5
Yugoslavia (Rep.)	55.9	64.2	53.0	41.0	77.8	34.5
Mean (Std. Dev.)	52.5 (5.5)	58.3 (9.9)	50.9 (7.0)	40.5 (9.4)	66.9 (8.5)	16.1 (6.7)

Correlations	1	2	3	4	5	6
1. Overall	1.00					
2. Level 5	0.43	1.00				
3. Level 6	0.64	−0.24	1.00			
4. Level 7	0.56	−0.02	0.71	1.00		
5. Humanities	0.15	−0.01	−0.10	−0.07	1.00	
6. Engineering	0.54	0.10	0.44	0.05	0.02	1.00

Note: ISCED (International Standard Classification of Education) level 5 includes "programs leading to an award not equivalent to a first university degree;" level 6 includes "programs leading to a first university degree or equivalent qualification;" and level 7 includes "programs leading to a postgraduate university degree or equivalent qualification."

Sources: UNESCO *Statistical Yearbook* 1997, 1998, Table 3.12. Data are for 1995, or as close thereto as available (1994 for Canada, Finland, Hong Kong, Japan, Poland, South Africa; 1993 for Belgium, France, and Switzerland, 1996 for Korea and Ireland).

Research conducted in a variety of national settings suggests that this form of sex segregation has long-lasting negative effects on women's social and economic opportunities – most importantly because completion of higher-level degrees results in greater economic and non-economic payoffs to educational investments (Arum & Hout, 1998).

Statistics in Table 1 also point to important cross-national differences in the gender composition of graduates at each tertiary level. At the postgraduate level, women's share of degree recipients ranged from 17% in Japan to 58% in Poland, while the corresponding range at the non-university level was 37% (in Denmark) to 79% (in Poland). Variability in female representation is much more pronounced for specific levels than for higher education overall: the standard deviation for higher education overall is 5.5, but it is 9.9 at the non-university level, 7.0 at the university level, and 9.4 at the postgraduate levels. This confirms that a great deal of information about women's relative status in higher education is lost when researchers and policy makers rely on statistics that aggregate across levels.

Comparing values in the last two columns of Table 1, we find considerable sex segregation across fields of study as well. On average, 67% of humanities graduates but only 16% of engineering graduates were female in these 26 countries. This striking difference is consistent with previous research suggesting historical persistence of sex segregation by field despite dramatic increases in overall female enrollment rates (Barber, 1995; Bradley, 2000). Again, strong cross-national variability is evident, with women making up only about 4% of Swiss engineering graduates but nearly 35% of their Yugoslavian counterparts in 1995. In the humanities, we find similarly large differences – this time in the degree of women's overrepresentation, with women's share of graduates ranging from 54% (Czech Republic) to 86% (Italy).

Sex segregation by field of study is also likely to have important material consequences for women because credentials in male-dominated fields such as engineering, business, and the natural sciences provide access to jobs with significantly higher starting salaries than do those in such female-dominated fields as education and the humanities (see Davies & Guppy, 1997; Grubb, 1997; Jacobs, 1995; Rumberger & Thomas, 1993; Vincens, 1995).[3] In addition, female-typed fields of study appear to be of lower social status than those that are male typed.[4] Given growing shortages of qualified engineers, natural scientists, and information technology personnel in many countries, the persistent underrepresentation of women in technical fields of study is increasingly recognized as a significant socioeconomic problem as well (European Commission, 2000; National Science Foundation, 2000; Rosser, 1995).[5]

Table 1 also provides information on the relationships among the three dimensions of female tertiary status. Zero-order correlations indicate that female representation is only weakly correlated across tertiary levels, across fields of study, and between levels and fields (see correlation matrix columns 2 through 5).[6] Among the "level" variables, the only high positive correlation (0.71) is between the university and postgraduate levels. This is to be expected, since access to postgraduate institutions almost always requires a first university degree. We find a negative correlation (−0.24), however, between women's presence in the non-university and university sectors (levels 5 and 6), suggesting that two-year colleges and vocational institutions are not generally being used by women as stepping stones to higher levels of the tertiary system. This negative association is also consistent with the notion that university and non-university institutions serve distinct clienteles by providing different types of credentials. It is furthermore noteworthy that female representation in engineering programs and female representation in the postsecondary sector – arguably two important indicators of women's relative position in higher education – are virtually uncorrelated with one another ($r = 0.05$).

These data confirm the multidimensionality of female status within modern systems of higher education, and underscores the importance of moving away from unidimensional understandings and monocausal accounts of gender inequality (see also Charles & Bradley, 2002; Charles & Grusky, in press). We argue that the lack of covariation among our three status dimensions reflects the sector-specific (i.e. systemic, field- or level-specific) effects of modern cultural and structural pressures on female representation. We also note that both global and local contexts matter. International cultural mandates, such as the highly normative programs and policies promulgated by UNESCO, OECD, and the World Bank, have interacted with local contexts to produce cross-nationally variable effects (Pieterse, 1995 refers to this process more generally as hybridization).

In the following sections, we develop a conceptual framework for understanding the cross-national commonalities and differences revealed in Table 1. We begin by considering similarities.

UNDERSTANDING CROSS-NATIONAL SIMILARITIES

Normative Mandates for Equality

The global expansion and democratization of education since World War II has been spurred by dual rationales, each observable in national and individual-level practices. First is the widespread belief that education brings social, economic, and cultural advancement by enhancing workers' productivity. This investment argument has long been advanced by neoclassical economists and modernization theorists, who posit a strong positive association between human capital and socioeconomic progress (see Schultz's (1961) Presidential Address to the American Economic Association). Whether or not an actual association exists, the highly institutionalized belief in a cause-and-effect relationship has no doubt acted as a powerful "rational myth" that has propelled educational expansion (e.g. Chabbott & Ramirez, 2000; Meyer et al., 1977).

The second expansionary rationale derives from the rising popular notion that all persons ("individuals") should be accorded a set of universal rights, which include equal access to education. Education was formally proclaimed to be a fundamental human right in the original charter of the United Nations (1946), and it is increasingly treated as such in the discourse of citizens and policy makers worldwide, (see the "Declaration of Education for All," endorsed by over 150 countries in 1990 (UNESCO, 1995)). The idea that "education is a right" is strongly emphasized in neoinstitutionalist accounts of educational expansion (Ramirez & Cha, 1990; Thomas et al., 1987).

The incorporation of "human rights" and "human capital" justifications into national and international educational policy making is illustrated in the following statement from the 1963 Robbins Committee report, which played a significant role in shaping educational policies within the United Kingdom.

> Throughout our Report we have assumed as an axiom that courses of higher education should be available for all those who are qualified by ability and attainment to pursue them and who wish to do so ... Conceiving education as a means, we do not believe that modern societies can achieve their aims of economic growth and higher cultural standards without making the most of the talents of their citizens. This is obviously necessary if we are to compete with other highly developed countries in an era of rapid technological and social advance ... To realize the aspirations of a modern community as regards both wealth and culture, a fully educated population is necessary (Robbins Committee, 1963, as cited in Byrne, 1978, p. 184).

Around the globe, arguments of this sort continue to resonate with policy makers intent on advancing the prosperity and international standing of their countries and with individuals seeking to improve their own social positions.

Political activists and policy makers have drawn upon the same two themes in advocating increased female access to education. During the International Decade for Women (1976–1985), a far-reaching global effort to elevate women's status was initiated by numerous international organizations, including the United Nations, the World Health Organization, UNESCO, The World Bank, and the OECD. Equity in educational opportunity was identified as the primary mechanism by which women's overall status would be improved. Advocates of female educational access effectively redefined women as an underutilized productive resource, while emphasizing basic rights to educational access for girls and women (Berkovitch & Bradley, 1999).[7]

Underlying political efforts to expand and feminize education were liberal individualistic ideals, specifically the notion that women, like men, are individuals capable of reason who should have the same opportunities as men for education (Beasley, 1968; Berkovitch & Bradley, 1999; Chaton, 1968). Progress toward this goal was generally measured by comparing overall national enrollment rates of men and women. By this standard, considerable progress was made, with women's share of higher education enrollments increasing worldwide from 27% in 1965 to 40% in 1985, at the end of the International Decade (Bradley & Ramirez, 1996).

This trend lends itself to interpretation within the frameworks of three different theoretical paradigms, at three different levels of analysis. From a neoclassical economic perspective, increased female participation in higher education represents the outcome of individual-level decisions, with rational women pursuing expanding market opportunities through increased investment in human capital (e.g. Polachek, 1978). Modernization theory argues that the structural shift from traditional to bureaucratically organized industrial society would diminish use of ascriptive characteristics within the labor market in favor of merit-based criteria (Goode, 1963; Inkeles & Smith, 1974; Kerr et al., 1960). Thus, educational systems, themselves increasingly bureaucratically organized, expanded to meet the needs of the evolving occupational structures of industrial society, incorporating women in the process (Jackson, 1998). Neoinstitutional theory treats gender-role convergence as a cultural phenomenon, with global mandates for universal human rights working to delegitimize and erode gender-based inequalities (Berkovitch & Bradley, 1999; Ramirez, 1987). While overall enrollment trends seem to support these "gender-role convergence" theories, the persistence of extreme sex segregation within systems of higher education and variation in the degree of sex segregation among industrialized countries is difficult to reconcile with these accounts.

Despite growing cultural and institutional provisions to insure women's tertiary access, male and female students continue to make very different programmatic choices. Unless we are prepared to ascribe sex segregation solely to the innate tastes and preferences of individual men and women, analysts seeking to understand this phenomenon must consider the cultural and structural contexts in which preferences are developed and curricular choices unfold – in particular, the ways in which characteristics of educational systems interact with taken-for-granted norms concerning women's and men's roles in society.[8] We begin by considering how the process by which educational systems expanded their enrollments may have affected women's status – and their choices – within modern tertiary systems.

Segregative Structural Pressures

To accommodate expansionary demands during the second half of the twentieth century, systems of higher education throughout the world underwent a process of "massification" whereby governments increased enrollments, broadened curricular scopes, and created new types of institutions. Structural diversification, which has most often occurred through expansion and proliferation of non-university institutions, was intended to democratize higher education and to better meet the needs of the labor market, consistent with the two rationales discussed above (Clark, 1996; Meek & Goedegebuure, 1996; Van Nught, 1996). In the process, diversification became an end unto itself, a symbol of modern educational practices within a global environment in which increased access to higher education was normatively mandated (Sirowy & Benavot, 1986). As the organizational model (i.e. tertiary diversification) diffused throughout the world, modified systems were created that reflected the specific policy priorities and social contexts of adoptive countries. This has resulted in national-level variations on a common theme – in other words, in differences among "mass" systems with regard to the specific structural models and institutional practices adopted (Heidenheimer, 1997; Windolf, 1997).

As structural diversification increased, so did possibilities for stratification within tertiary systems. While the selectivity and prestige of short-cycle programs varies among countries, these programs are generally less prestigious than those in the university sector. Indeed, less selective tertiary sectors were arguably created in some countries to allow for growth in overall enrollment while preserving the status of elite institutions (Fujimura-Fanselow, 1988; Meek & Goedegebuure, 1996; Neave, 1985; Sirowy & Benavot, 1986).

The following excerpt from the 1973 OECD Report on the "problem of post-secondary education structures" underscores the tension underlying tertiary expansion in many countries.

> Few concepts in the field of education encounter such general acceptance as that of diversification of post-secondary education. Diversification is advocated as a remedy to almost every problem faced by existing higher education systems, whether in the field of curriculum reform, methods of study, degree structure, organization of courses or institutional framework. Many see diversification as an objective in itself consequent on the acceptance of a pluralistic society; others tend to see it as a protective measure for shielding elite institutions from the onslaught of mass higher education (OECD, 1973, p. 35).

Processes of diversification and structural change in higher education have helped to create and reinforce gender differentiation in a variety of ways, some unexpected and some not. During the first phase of expansion, in the 1970s, the reclassification in many countries of such female-dominated programs as nursing and teacher-training from a secondary or interstitial level to "higher education" had the statistical effect of increasing female enrollments without effecting any qualitative changes in the content of women's programs or in women's occupational options (e.g. see Elgqvist-Saltzman, 1988 on Sweden; Fjelde, 1991, on Norway; Teichler, 1996 on Germany).[9]

In many countries, growing demand for female access has been accommodated through establishment or expansion of female-labeled programs and institution types. Gender-specific modes of tertiary "democratization" have been especially evident in Japan, where junior college advancement rates of women increased tenfold between 1955 and 1975, while growth in higher education for men was concentrated almost completely at the university level (Brinton & Lee, 2001). In Japan, transfer from junior college to university is rare, and much of the curriculum at junior colleges is geared toward preparing women for future domestic roles. In 1989, for example, 91% of students studying at Japanese junior colleges were female; 28% of these women were studying home economics (Research Institute for Higher Education, 1992; Windolf, 1997 presents similar statistics for 1992).

Although Japan represents an extreme case, we have already established that distributional inequality by field and level exists in all industrialized and industrializing countries. This sex segregation is not surprising given the ideological context of expanding female enrollments. In addition to the human-capital and rights-based justifications for educating women, educational analysts and policy makers (and some feminist advocates) have often expounded on the benefits to society of having better educated mothers (Berkovitch & Bradley, 1999; Murphy, 1995; UNESCO, 1975). Universalistic mandates thus promote growing female access to tertiary education at the same time that essentialist stereotypes about men's and women's "natural" aptitudes and dispositions help to create and reinforce gender distinctions within the system.

As educational reform unfolded within specific country contexts, a presumption remained among some policy makers that women would continue to exhibit gender-typed educational choices – and that they would be inclined to choose fields and programs that are easily reconciled with their future domestic roles, that train them for female-typed occupations, or that are congruent with their purportedly natural predisposition for caring and interpersonal relations. The authors of the aforementioned Robbins Report, for example, clearly expected continuing gender differentiation in higher education in the United Kingdom:

> Training for many of the occupations open to girls does not at present fall within the definition of higher education adopted in our Report. But rising professional requirements may in future lead to more girls entering those occupations by means of full-time courses in higher education . . . such as new language courses that may prove particularly attractive to girls (cited in Jones & Castle, 1986, p. 291).

Gender essentialism has thus proven to be extremely resilient, even in highly universalistic cultural contexts (see also Charles & Grusky, in press). The tension in modern institutions between taken-for-granted ideologies of gender difference and normative mandates for "gender equality" is hardly surprising, however. It can, in fact, be found within the feminist movement itself – with liberal feminists tending to equate equality with "sameness" and others preferring to celebrate difference by promoting "separate but equal" roles for women and men (e.g. see Epstein, 1999 and Williams, 2000 on the gender-difference debate). We see little evidence to suggest that gender-egalitarian cultural mandates have begun to seriously undermine sex segregation within tertiary institutions. Whether or not such internal differentiation represents a permanent feature of modern educational systems, or merely a traditional artifact, remains to be seen. In any case, the persistence of particularist ideologies within increasingly liberal, universalistic cultural contexts has not yet received the theoretical attention it deserves by proponents of the gender-convergence accounts reviewed above.

Thus far, we have described global processes underlying a cross-nationally common pattern of gender stratification. We have argued that this common pattern – namely high overall tertiary enrollment rates of women combined with strong sex segregation across fields and levels – reflects the interaction of liberal ideals of universal citizenship with highly institutionalized beliefs about the natural differences between men and women (see also Berkovitch, 1999, pp. 12–14 on interaction of gender and citizenship). Essentialist stereotypes have thus helped shape the new institutions and programs that were developed to accommodate universalistic demands for educational expansion and democratization. They have also influenced women's choices among a growing array of fields and institutions, as we discuss further on.

Although previous research has identified important common trends worldwide, it is also important to attend to the considerable *variation* that exists among countries. On the following pages, we explore some macro-level factors that may underlie patterns of cross-national difference. We focus attention on variability across countries in: (1) the salience and prevalence of gender-egalitarian cultural norms; and (2) structural features of educational systems. While this is by no means an exhaustive account, attention to these key factors can considerably improve our understanding of cross-national variability in women's position within systems of tertiary education.

UNDERSTANDING CROSS-NATIONAL VARIABILITY IN FEMALE TERTIARY STATUS

Despite global pressures for expansion, democratization, and feminization of higher education, countries continue to differ with regard to the influence of gender-egalitarian ideals and with regard to the structure and size of their tertiary

Table 2. Accounting for Cross-National Variability in Women's Tertiary Status: Selected Cultural and Structural Effects.

	Female Representation in Tertiary Education Overall	Female Representation in Elite Tertiary Levels (Universities, Grad. Schools)	Female Representation in Historically Male Fields of Study
1. Gender egalitarianism			
a. Cultural egalitarianism	+	++	+
b. Structural egalitarianism	+	+	++
2. Educational structure			
a. Size of nonelite level ("Tertiary Differentiation")	+	–	–
b. Tertiary system size	+	0/–	0/–
c. Secondary differentiation	0	0	–
d. Centralization of authority	+	+	0

Notes: "0" denotes no effect. Positive and negative effects are indicated by "+" and "–" signs, respectively. Stronger positive effects are denoted by "++"; relative effect sizes reflect comparisons within, not across, rows.

systems. We maintain that these cultural and structural differences are key to understanding patterns of cross-national variability in gender stratification within higher education. Table 2 summarizes our arguments regarding effects of these variables on overall female access (i.e. women's share of all tertiary graduates), on sex segregation by tertiary level (i.e. female representation in elite tertiary levels), and on sex segregation by field of study (i.e. female representation in historically male-typed fields of study). Although the relationships posited in Table 2 are not directly tested in this paper, we do draw upon existing empirical studies, including our own 12-country study (Charles & Bradley, 2002), to bolster many of our claims. We discuss each in greater detail below.

Gender-Egalitarian Norms and Structures

Previous research has represented educational choices as a function of societal norms and stereotypes concerning women's and men's roles in society (e.g. see Correll, 2001; Shamai, 1996). Since most of these studies restrict attention to single national settings, it has not been possible to directly test the relationship between educational outcomes and societal gender norms. This represents an important gap in the literature on educational choice – one that can be partially filled through cross-national comparative research.

Although universalistic and gender-egalitarian discourse has been on the rise in all industrialized societies since the 1960s, countries vary considerably in the extent to which such principles have been internalized by the population-at-large and translated into practice through official policies and social arrangements (Alwin, Braun & Scott, 1992; Charles, 1998; Hakim, 1991; Haller & Hoellinger, 1992). This variability has been attributed to different historical traditions, socioeconomic circumstances, and interpersonal practices.[10]

In order to understand the effects of gender-egalitarian principles on concrete outcomes (e.g. gender distributions within higher education), it is useful to distinguish between the attitudinal and structural manifestations of these ideals. For present purposes, "cultural egalitarianism" (item 1a in Table 2) refers to the degree to which the liberal principles of gender equality that have been endorsed by international organizations and by women's movements have been incorporated into the mindsets of individual citizens. "Structural egalitarianism" (item 1b) here refers to the extent to which a gender-neutral division of family labor is facilitated by prevailing social and organizational provisions. Although cultural and structural egalitarianism are related reciprocally,[11] they exert independent effects on female public-sphere aspirations and opportunities at any given point in time.

Internationally standardized attitudinal surveys, such as the World Values Survey and the International Social Survey Program, provide the most direct gauge of cross-national variability in the salience and pervasiveness of gender-egalitarian cultural ideals. Despite steady increases in the percentage of national citizens professing egalitarian beliefs, pronounced cross-national differences remain (Charles, 1992, 2003; Inglehart, 1997). For example, among 14 of the countries included in Table 1, the percentage of national respondents who in 1994 claimed to disagree with the statement that "the household is the wife's job" ranged from 25% in the Czech Republic to 67% in Norway.[12] Evidence of strong intercorrelations among different measures of gender egalitarianism and of high intertemporal correlations on individual attitudinal indicators support our conceptualization of gender egalitarianism as a stable cultural attribute of national societies (see Charles & Bradley, 2002, on correlations across attitudinal indicators and over time).[13]

Entries in line 1a of Table 2 suggest that cultural egalitarianism is positively related to all three dimensions of women's status in higher education: female representation in tertiary education overall, in elite tertiary levels (i.e. universities and graduate schools), and in historically male-dominated fields. Drawing upon arguments by neoinstitutionalists and other scholars, we posit that educational aspirations and student choices are less sex-typed in contexts where gender-egalitarian principles are more salient and more pervasive (Jackson, 1998; Ramirez, 1987; see also Shu & Marini, 1998 on occupational aspirations).

We expect cultural effects to be uneven, however. Results of our recent 12-country analyses suggest that cultural egalitarianism more strongly undermines the legitimacy of gender segregation across tertiary levels ("vertical segregation") than segregation across fields of study ("horizontal segregation") (Charles & Bradley, 2002). We attribute this unevenness to the resilience of essentialist cultural stereotypes about gender difference (see also Charles, 2003; Charles & Grusky, in press). While field-specific distributions can be reconciled with a "different but equal" conceptualization of women's status, overt gender hierarchies (i.e. sex segregation by level) are more clearly at odds with liberal egalitarian principles. Our two-dimensional account differs from modernization and neoinstitutionalist formulations by allowing for variability across status dimensions in the rate of gender convergence – as opposed to uniform, across-the-board improvements in women's status. In Table 2, we have accordingly entered "++" (rather than "+") in the "levels" column of row 1a to indicate a relatively strong effect on this status dimension.[14]

Cross-national variability in structural egalitarianism varies as a function of differences in public and private childcare provisions, primary school schedules, family and employment policies, and tax laws, among other things. These organizational arrangements vary widely, even among countries with similar socioeconomic systems (Den Dulk, 2001; Gornick, Meyers & Ross, 1997; Kilkey, 2000). Differences in the social organization of children's lives are particularly striking. In 1991, for example, 98% of French three-year-olds but only 1% of their Irish counterparts were enrolled in public- or privately-funded preschools (Charles, 2002). Other research has documented strong cross-national variability in the compatibility of primary school schedules and shop opening hours with parental employment, and in provisions for parental leave (Buchmann & Charles, 1995; Van Dijk, 2001).

Neoclassical economic theory suggests that wives' and mothers' willingness to invest in education depends upon their rational assessment of the marginal costs and benefits of market work (e.g. Becker, 1991; Polachek, 1978; see also Charles et al., 2001; Trappe & Rosenfeld, 2001). If women indeed tend to make larger educational investments when they foresee a more continuous market career, prevailing social arrangements that affect the compatibility of work and family roles should influence female representation in tertiary education in general and in longer-cycle (i.e. university- and graduate-level) programs in particular. To the extent that male-dominated fields (e.g. physical science and engineering) require more time or effort, the neoclassical argument would also imply a positive relationship between structural egalitarianism and female representation in gender-atypical fields of study.[15] Because "normative alternatives" to a primary market role (e.g. a less demanding job, or full-time domesticity) are more available to women than to men, structural barriers to combining market and family roles may disproportionately affect women's willingness to invest in education (e.g. see Fiorentine, 1987).

Entries in line 1b of Table 2 imply that structural egalitarianism will most strongly influence female representation in mathematical and technical fields of study. The strength of this effect (relative to others in the same line) is represented by "++" in the third column. We posit this strong effect based upon previous research findings suggesting that girls' and women's disinclination to choose and complete quantitative majors reflects perceived characteristics of science and engineering careers, including their incompatibility with family life and/or motherhood (e.g. Donaldson & Dixon, 1995; Erwin & Stewart, 1997; Morgan, 1992; Seymour & Hewitt, 1997; Stolte-Heiskanen et al., 1991; Waite & Berryman, 1985).[16]

To the extent that egalitarian structural arrangements help bolster and spread the underlying cultural principles (e.g. the idea that women and men are equally entitled to participate in all aspects of public life), a generally integrative effect of structural egalitarianism would be predicted by institutionalist, as well as neoclassical and modernization scholars.

Educational Structure

Like the rise of egalitarian cultural mandates, the restructuring of higher education (e.g. expansion, diversification, democratization) has occurred in different ways and to different degrees cross-nationally (Shavit & Müller, 1998; Windolf, 1997). Many structural innovations were put into place during the 1970s, amid optimistic predictions about their effects. Although scholars have begun to examine the effects of structural arrangements on educational trajectories, little attention has been given to their gender-differentiated effects.[17]

As can be seen in Table 2, we have identified four specific features of national tertiary systems that may be relevant in this regard: (a) the relative size of the non-university level; (b) the absolute size of the tertiary system; (c) curricular differentiation within secondary education; and (d) centralization of educational authority. Although these features sometimes vary within nation states, cross-national variability is clearly more substantial.

We have described above how structural diversification of higher education (i.e. the expansion of vocational colleges and two-year institutions) has contributed to growth in overall female tertiary enrollment rates throughout the world. Our arguments imply a cross-sectional relationship as well, with women making up a larger share of tertiary graduates in countries with more diversified systems.[18] Results of our recent comparative study also suggest segregative effects, namely a tendency for weaker female representation at advanced levels and in traditionally male-dominated fields of study in more structurally diversified systems (Charles & Bradley, 2002). These relationships are represented in line 2a of Table 2.

Structural diversification may have some unanticipated negative effects on women's status within higher education. We have argued that opportunities for shorter, vocationally-oriented tertiary programs may divert university-qualified women (or potentially university-qualified women) from more elite forms of higher education (see Clark, 1960; Finley, 1992 on the "cooling-out effect" of non-elite educational programs; see also Karen, 2002). Due to actual or anticipated work-family conflicts, girls and women may be more susceptible than their male counterparts to such diversionary pressures (e.g. see Fiorentine, 1987).

Furthermore, we argue that structural diversification effects changes in the cultural meaning of higher education in general, and that it thereby contributes to a weaker female presence in male-typed fields of study. As the non-university sector grows in relative size, the overall status of tertiary education (and of tertiary students) tends to decline. In highly diversified systems, women may therefore enter tertiary education without enjoying the empowerment associated with acquisition of an elite identity (e.g. see Della Fave, 1980; Gecas, 1991 on the relationship between elite status and self-esteem). This is relevant to the question at hand because it implies that the average female student in structurally diversified systems will less often possess the sense of self-efficacy and self-esteem required for transgressing norms about gender-appropriate fields than will her counterpart in more elite systems. The association between structural differentiation and sex segregation by field of study warrants further study.[19]

The postwar feminization of higher education has been achieved largely through expansion of the tertiary system, as discussed above. All else being equal, this suggests a positive relationship between the size of the tertiary system and overall female enrollment rates (see Table 2, line 2b). As concerns distributions within the tertiary system, however, recent analysis of data for 12 countries suggests no clear effect of system size, net of structural diversification (Charles & Bradley, 2002). We were somewhat surprised by this result, as we had anticipated greater sex segregation by level and by field in larger tertiary systems.[20] Based on these results, our tentative conclusion was that expansion in and of itself is less consequential to women's tertiary status than is the particular structural form by which the expansion is achieved. Given the discrepancy between our initial expectation and the empirical evidence that is currently available, we have entered "0/−" in the second and third columns of line 2b (Table 2). This relationship also requires further study.

Curricular differentiation at the secondary level is another factor that may influence gender distributions within higher education (see line 2c). To our knowledge, this relationship has not yet been empirically examined in a comparative context. We posit a tendency for greater sex segregation across fields of study in countries characterized by differentiated, vocationally-oriented secondary systems (e.g. Germany) than in countries with comprehensive programs of secondary education (e.g. the United States; see Kerckhoff, 1996; Shavit & Müller, 1998 on cross-national variability in secondary systems). First, highly differentiated systems provide more opportunities for gender-differentiated choices and placements (UNESCO, 1995), and second, they generally require that these choices are made during adolescence, when pressure to conform to sex-role stereotypes is particularly intense (Entwisle & Greenberger, 1972; Gaskell, 1984).[21] Segregation at the secondary level often translates directly into segregation across tertiary fields of study, since secondary programs in such gender-typed fields as health care, education, industrial design, and information technology feed into corresponding tertiary programs (primarily in nonelite institutions and two-year colleges). The OECD has also suggested a segregative effect of secondary specialization, especially coupled with early choices:

> Postponement of choice may well be a necessary prerequisite, if not a sufficient one, to bring about greater equalization of the sexes in different educational programs and occupations (1986, p. 78).

Finally, we suggest that female access to tertiary education and to the elite university sector therein may be greater in educational systems characterized by greater state control (Table 2, line 2d).[22] Because legitimacy and popular opinion are crucial organizational resources in the public sector, domestic and international pressures for equal educational access are likely to be particularly salient in government-controlled institutions. Indeed, research on labor market inequality suggests that public-sector firms are more tightly bound by equality legislation than are their private-sector counterparts (Beggs, 1995; Kaufman, 1986). It seems unlikely that government control will directly affect the (less visible, and less manipulable) programmatic distributions of women within the university, except with respect to particular fields that rise to national attention.[23]

CONCLUSION

In recent decades, systems of higher education have undergone extensive organizational transformation as they have expanded and diversified to accommodate a larger and more heterogeneous student population. Given the scope and magnitude of the structural and ideological changes affecting higher education, it is surprising that there has not been more research on how these trends have influenced distributional flows within national educational systems – in particular, how they affect the relative distributions of men and women. Our descriptive data for 26 countries suggests that researchers and policy makers interested in making such an assessment must consider three distinct dimensions of female status in higher education: overall enrollment rates, segregation across tertiary levels, and segregation across fields of study. Building upon existing macro-culturalist accounts, as well as available empirical evidence, we have offered a conceptual framework for understanding both cross-national similarity and cross-national variability on these status dimensions.

As revealed in Table 1, industrial and industrializing countries are characterized by near gender-parity in overall tertiary enrollment rates, by female overrepresentation in non-university (i.e. two-year or vocational) programs, and by strong sex segregation across fields of study. We have argued that these similarities reflect the historical interaction of universalistic pressures for expansion and democratization of higher education with essentialist notions of male and female roles and predispositions. Cultural mandates for gender equality today exist alongside essentialist notions of gender difference because the latter have proven to be highly resilient in the face of modern universalistic pressures. Equality and difference are reconciled ideologically by virtue of a "separate-but-equal" model of female emancipation that treats sex segregation as the outcome of free choices by naturally different male and female individuals.

Sex segregation by field and by level have been exacerbated by global trends toward expansion and diversification of higher education. As programmatic "choice" has been emphasized in recent rounds of educational restructuring, and as options have proliferated within systems of higher education, opportunities have increased for gender-essentialist ideologies to influence men's and women's educational trajectories. Differences in the ways in which structural reforms have been implemented help account for variability among countries in patterns and processes of tertiary gender stratification.

Modern cultural and structural pressures affect each dimension of tertiary gender stratification in distinct ways, producing patterns of cross-national variability that are uneven and sometimes counterintuitive. As a result, increased female participation in higher education overall does not necessarily imply more gender-neutral distributions within the system, and strong representation of women in elite tertiary institutions does not coincide with gender integration of historically male-dominated engineering and physical science programs. Similar complexities have been revealed in studies of occupational sex segregation (e.g. Charles, 1992; Charles & Grusky, in press).

While emphasizing different causal mechanisms, modernization and neoinstitutionalist accounts of ascriptive inequalities both imply the gradual convergence of men's and women's public-sector roles. Consistent with these arguments, some clear signs of "degendering" can be found in most national systems of higher education – most notably, we find that female representation in tertiary education reaches or exceeds gender parity in most industrialized countries today.

Available evidence suggests two inadequacies of existing explanatory frameworks, however. First, these scholars' implicit treatment of "women's status" as a unidimensional quantity is difficult to reconcile with growing evidence that modernity (of whatever variety) is associated with erosion of some forms of gender stratification, but persistence – and even exacerbation – of others. Second, these "evolutionary" accounts provide no framework for understanding the variability and contextual dependence of equalizing pressures. If cross-national differences are considered at all, they are generally attributed to different levels of cultural or structural modernity. This is problematic, because national systems of higher education differ with respect to *patterns*, not just overall *levels*, of gender inequality. We have suggested a variety of macro-level factors that may underlie this qualitative variability.

In emphasizing the global ideological forces that support educational democratization and feminization, we draw heavily upon arguments made by neoinstitutionalist scholars (e.g. Meyer et al., 1977; Ramirez & Wotipka, 2001). While sympathetic to neoinstitutionalist accounts in this general sense, we have offered three qualifications. First, we have suggested that modern norms of equality have proven to be quite compatible with at least some cultural representations of gender difference. Second, we have suggested that effects of gender-egalitarian mandates are not uniform across the different dimensions of female status in higher education, but are targeted and sector-specific (see Table 2). Third, we have argued that the structural dynamics of tertiary expansion and restructuring contribute to increased gender stratification *within* modern tertiary systems. Our account is, we think, more easily reconciled with the existing empirical evidence – in particular with evidence of weak intercorrelations among the different dimensions of women's "status" in higher education.

NOTES

1. The argument that unfolds in this paper is intended to apply to countries with established systems of higher education and highly differentiated labor markets; therefore, we do not consider countries with predominantly agricultural economies.

2. Furthermore, there is considerable cross-national variation in the extent to which students change majors or do not complete degrees. Italy presents an extreme case with an approximate 60% university dropout rate (Windolf, 1997); see Jacobs (1989) on the "revolving door" of field selection in the United States.

3. Jacobs estimates the first-year earnings of social science graduates in the United States to be about 70% of those of their counterparts with engineering degrees (1995; see also NSF, 2000). Studies in the U.S. have suggested that a large part of the gender gap in income can be attributed to sex segregation by field of study (Fuller & Schoenberger, 1991; Wilson & Smith-Lovin, 1983).

4. Some scholars have documented an inverse association between prestige rankings of programs and female representation (Bourdieu & Passeron, 1977; Randour, Strasburg & Lipman-Blumen, 1982). Research on occupational prestige and gender composition (e.g. Bose & Rossi, 1983) suggests that this relationship may be reciprocal. See also Ayalon and Yogev (1996) and Bourdieu (1984) on the contextual dependence of curricular prestige hierarchies.

5. Although the absolute number of women graduating from these programs has increased since the 1970s, women's share of engineering and computer science graduates has grown much more slowly than hasfemale tertiary participation overall (Barber, 1995; Ramirez & Wotipka, 2001). For the United States, Jacobs (1995) reports a modest increase in female access to male-dominated programs prior to 1985, followed by a marked slowdown in gender integration (see also Roemer, 1983; Wilson & Boldizar, 1990 on earlier trends).

6. The moderate positive correlations shown in column 1 are not surprising, since women's overall share of tertiary graduates and their share of graduates within the various levels and programs are mathematically related (e.g. the overall share is equal to the weighted average of female shares across all levels).

7. See Article 10 of the 1979 Convention on the Elimination of All Forms of Discrimination Against Women which directs states to take action to eliminate discrimination against women in access to and participation in education at all levels (United Nations, 1996).

8. Although neoclassical economists often account for the sexual division of labor with reference to gender-differentiated "preferences," these scholars do sometimes acknowledge structural and cultural effects in the generation of preferences (e.g. Polachek, 1978, p. 505).

9. Switzerland adopted a more conservative approach to educational restructuring and did not reclassify teacher-training until the 1990s (Heidenheimer, 1997).

10. Many explanations for such cultural differences can be found in the sociological literature. Modernization theory implies that different levels or patterns of economic development will result in different levels of cultural "modernity" (Kerr et al., 1960); Lipset, Bendix, and Zetterberg have suggested that the absence of a feudal past has helped sustain ideological "equalitarianism" in the United States (1959); and Ruggie attributes the cultural transcendence of particularistic gender distinctions in Sweden to the turn-of-the-century development of comprehensive industrial unionism (as opposed to more divisive craft- or occupation-based forms) (1984).

11. Cultural norms are influenced by both available symbolic resources and socioeconomic conditions. Organizational structures, for example, both enact and reinforce gendered notions of "childhood," "motherhood," and "career" (Epstein, 1992; Leira, 1992). These understandings provide the context for women's and men's educational investments. See also Wuthnow (1989) and Lamont and Thévenot (2000) on the dynamic relationship between social structure and ideology.

12. Among the countries included in Table 1, data on this particular survey item are available for the following fourteen countries: Austria, Czech Republic, Germany, Ireland, Italy, Japan, New Zealand, Norway, Poland, Slovenia, Spain, Sweden, United Kingdom, and United States.

13. Consistent with the predictions of neoinstitutionalist theory, official government endorsements of gender egalitarian principles through national constitutions, laws, and organizational practices have proliferated in recent decades (Berkovitch, 1999; Ramirez, 2001). In previous research we found effects of "legal egalitarianism" on tertiary sex segregation that were similar to, but weaker than, those of direct measures of gender-egalitarian attitudes (Charles & Bradley, 2002).

14. The positive effect of gender-egalitarianism on overall female enrollment rates is also relatively weak, since aggregated female enrollment figures reflect women's participation in both elite and non-elite tertiary levels.

15. Neither structural nor cultural egalitarianism is likely to promote integration of female-labeled educational programs. Given the low pay and status of "women's" occupations, there is little incentive for men to seek access to such positions, even in the most egalitarian of contexts (Reskin & Roos, 1990; see Sumsion, 2000 for a discussion of men's decisions concerning teacher training programs in Australia).

16. See also Baker and Jones (1993), Hanson, Schaub and Baker (1996) on the relationship between market opportunities and educational choices and performance. Debates concerning whether gender segregation in higher education *causes* gender inequality in the labor market, or vice versa, present a conundrum that is unlikely to be empirically resolved. We suggest that more diffuse processes are at work that simultaneously affect expectations concerning women and men in both the educational and occupational spheres.

17. By attending to the organizational features of higher education systems, we are not implying that structure exists independently of its cultural meaning. As we mentioned previously, higher female enrollment rates have sometimes been achieved through efforts to expand female-labeled programs and institutional sectors, reinforcing extant gender stereotypes. Even so, it is useful at any given point in time to distinguish structural effects from the broader cultural pressures that may have influenced their development.

18. Countries vary strongly in their degrees of structural diversification. In 1997, for instance, 60% of Canadian but only 7% of Spanish tertiary degrees were awarded to level 5 graduates (Charles & Bradley, 2002, Appendix C).

19. We have indicated a stronger effect of this variable on sex segregation by level than by field based on past research, which suggests that the latter relationship is uneven and partially indirect (see Charles & Bradley, 2002, Table 5).

20. The rationale here was that participation in small, selective systems of higher education is restricted to an intellectual and cultural elite, while larger systems necessarily draw students from a broader cross-section of the population. Female students in larger systems should therefore be less inclined, on average, to transgress prevailing gender norms and more inclined, on average, to enroll in gender-appropriate institutions and fields than should their counterparts in smaller systems (see Hakim, 1996 for a similar argument on female heterogeneity in the labor market).

21. Past research suggests that early educational and occupational choices tend to be more gender-typed than those made later in life (Charles et al., 2001; Gerson, 1985; Jacobs, 1989; OECD, 1986). See Mortimer and Kruger (2000) on the effects of educational tracking on German and American students' career aspirations and identities.

22. The degree of educational centralization is also relevant here, since any equalizing effects of public-sector funding will be diluted by decentralization of day-to-day educational operations.

23. Women's underrepresentation in engineering and information technology fields has begun to draw the attention of national and international policy makers (European Parliament, 1999; The Council of Economic Advisers, 2000; National Science Foundation, 1996). Studies and pilot programs designed to promote female access to technical programs and occupations have recently proliferated (e.g. AAUW, 2000; Evaluation Associates, Ltd. 2000). Such efforts, if successful, could have substantial effects on women's participation in these particular fields in the future.

ACKNOWLEDGMENTS

Authorship is equal. This research was supported by grants from the National Science Foundation to Bradley and Charles, a grant to Bradley from Western Washington University's Bureau of Faculty Research, and a grant to Charles from The Spencer Foundation. We gratefully acknowledge the comments of John Meyer, Chiqui Ramirez, and the reviewers and editors of *RSE*. Colin Ong-Dean provided excellent research assistance. Direct correspondence to Karen Bradley (Karen.Bradley@wwu.edu) or Maria Charles (mcharles@ucsd.edu).

REFERENCES

Alwin, D. F., Braun, M., & Scott, J. (1992). The separation of work and the family: Attitudes toward women's labour-force participation in Germany, Great Britain, and the United States. *European Sociological Review*, *8*, 13–37.

American Association of University Women (2000). *Tech-savvy: Educating girls in the new computer age*. Washington, DC: AAUW.

Arum, R., & Hout, M. (1998). The early returns: The transition from school to work in the United States. In: Y. Shavit & W. Mueller (Eds), *From School to Work* (pp. 471–510). Oxford, England: Clarendon Press.

Ayalon, H., & Yogev, A. (1996). The alternative worldview of state religious high schools in Israel. *Comparative Education Review*, *40*, 7–27.

Baker, D. P., & Jones, D. P. (1993). Creating gender equality: Cross-national gender stratification and mathematical performance. *Sociology of Education*, *66*, 91–103.

Barber, L. A. (1995). U.S. Women in science and engineering, 1960–1990: Progress toward equity? *Journal of Higher Education*, *66*, 213–234.

Beasley, I. M. (1968). Education is the key for women. *Annals of the American Academy of Political and Social Science*, *375*, 154–162.

Becker, G. S. (1991, 1981). *A treatise on the family*. Cambridge, MA: Harvard University Press.

Beggs, J. J. (1995). The institutional environment: Implications for race and gender inequality in the U.S. labor market. *American Sociological Review*, *60*, 612–633.

Berkovitch, N. (1999). *From motherhood to citizenship*. Baltimore, MD: Johns Hopkins Press.

Berkovitch, N., & Bradley, K. (1999). The globalization of women's status: Consensus/dissensus in the world polity. *Sociological Perspectives*, *42*(3), 481–498.

Berryman, S. E. (1983). *Who will do science?* New York: Rockefeller Foundation.

Bose, C., & Rossi, P. (1983). Gender and jobs: Prestige standing of occupations as affected by gender. *American Sociological Review*, *48*, 316–330.

Bourdieu, P. (1984). *Homo academicus*. Stanford, CA: Stanford University Press.

Bourdieu, P., & Passeron, J. (1977). *Reproduction in education, society and culture*. Thousand Oaks, CA: Sage.

Bradley, K. (2000). The incorporation of women into higher education: Paradoxical outcomes? *Sociology of Education*, *73*, 1–18.

Bradley, K., & Ramirez, F. O. (1996). World polity and gender parity: Women's share of higher education, 1965–1985. *Research in Sociology of Education and Socialization*, *11*, 63–91.

Brinton, M., & Lee, S. (2001). Women's education and the labor market in Japan and South Korea. In: M. C. Brinton (Ed.), *Women's Working Lives in East Asia* (pp. 125–150). Stanford: Stanford Press.

Buchmann, M., & Charles, M. (1995). Organizational and institutional factors in the process of gender stratification: Comparing social arrangements in six European countries. *International Journal of Sociology*, *25*, 66–95.

Catsambis, S. (1994). The path to math: Gender and racial-ethnic differences in mathematics preparation from middle school to high school. *Sociology of Education*, *67*, 199–215.

Chabbott, C., & Ramirez, F. O. (2000). Development and education. In: M. T. Hallinan (Ed.), *Handbook of the Sociology of Education* (pp. 163–87). New York: Kluwer Academic/Plenum Publishers.

Charles, M. (1992). Cross-national variation in occupational sex segregation. *American Sociological Review*, *57*, 483–502.

Charles, M. (1998). Structure, culture and sex segregation in western Europe. *Research in Social Stratification and Mobility*, *16*, 89–116.

Charles, M. (2002). Schweizerische Besonderheiten im Vergleich mit anderen westlichen Ländern. In: M. Buchmann, I. Kriesi, A. Pfeifer & S. Sacchi (Eds), *Halb Drinnen – Halb Draussen: Analysen zur Arbeitsmarktintegration von Frauen in der Schweiz* (pp. 207–228). Zurich: Rüegger.

Charles, M. (2003). Deciphering sex segregation: Vertical and horizontal inequalities in ten countries. *Acta Sociologica*, *46*, 265–286.

Charles, M., & Bradley, K. (2002). Equal but separate? A cross-national study of sex segregation in higher education. *American Sociological Review*, *67*, 573–599.

Charles, M., Buchmann, M., Halebsky, S., Powers, J., & Smith, M. (2001). The context of women's market careers: A cross-national study. *Work and Occupations*, *28*, 371–396.

Charles, M., & Grusky, D. B. (in press). *Occupational ghettos: The worldwide segregation of women and men*. Palo Alto, CA: Stanford University Press.

Chaton, J. H. (1968). The UNESCO long–range program for the advancement of women. *Annals of the American Academy of Political and Social Science*, *375*, 145–153.

Clark, B. R. (1960). The cooling-out function in higher education. *American Journal of Sociology*, *65*, 569–575.

Clark, B. R. (1996). Diversification of higher education: Viability and change. In: V. L. Meek & L. Goedegebuure (Eds), *The Mockers and the Mocked: Comparative Perspectives on Differentiation, Convergence and Diversity in Higher Education* (pp. 16–25). Paris: IAU Press.

Correll, S. J. (2001). Gender and the career choice process: The role of biased self-assessments. *American Journal of Sociology*, *106*(6), 1691–1730.

Davies, S., & Guppy, N. (1997). Fields of study, college selectivity, and student inequalities in higher education. *Social Forces, 75*, 1417–1438.

Della Fave, L. R. (1980). The meek shall not inherit the earth: Self-evaluation and the legitimacy of social stratification. *American Sociological Review, 45*, 955–971.

Den Dulk, L. (2001). Work-family arrangements in organizations. In: T. Van der Lippe & L. Van Dijk (Eds), *Women's Employment in a Comparative Perspective* (pp. 59–84). New York: Aldine de Gruyter.

Donaldson, E., & Dixon, E. (1995). Retaining women students in science involves more than course selection. *The Canadian Journal of Higher Education, 25*, 29–50.

Elgqvist-Saltzman, I. (1988). Educational reforms: Women's life patterns: A Swedish case study. *Higher Education, 17*, 491–504.

Entwisle, D. R., & Greenberger, E. (1972). Adolescents' views of women's work role. *American Journal of Orthopsychiatry, 42*, 648–656.

Epstein, C. F. (1992). Tinkerbells and pinups: The construction and reconstruction of gender boundaries at work. In: M. Lamont & M. Fournier (Eds), *Cultivating Differences: Symbolic Boundaries and the Making of Inequality* (pp. 232–256). Chicago: University of Chicago.

Epstein, C. F. (1999). Similarity and difference: The sociology of gender distinctions. In: J. Saltzman Chafetz (Ed.), *Handbook of the Sociology of Gender* (pp. 45–61). New York: Kluwer.

Erwin, L., & Stewart, P. (1997). Gendered perspectives: A focus-group study of how undergraduate women negotiate their career aspirations. *Qualitative Studies in Education, 10*, 207–220.

European Commission (2000). *Science policies in the European Union: Promoting excellence through mainstreaming gender equality*. A Report from the ETAN Expert Working Group on Women and Science. Luxembourg: Office for Official Publications of the European Communities.

Finley, M. K. (1992). The educational contest for middle- and working-class women: The reproduction of inequality. In: J. Wrigley (Ed.), *Education and Gender Equality* (pp. 225–247). Washington, DC: Falmer Press.

Fiorentine, R. (1987). Men, women, and the premed persistence gap: A normative alternatives approach. *American Journal of Sociology, 92*(5), 1118–1139.

Fjelde, H. V. (1991). Public-private tendencies within higher education in Norway from a women's perspective. In: G. P. Kelly & S. Slaughter (Eds), *Women's Higher Education in Comparative Perspective* (pp. 117–130). Netherlands: Kluwer Academic Publishers.

Fujimura-Fanselow, K. (1988). Women's participation in higher education in Japan. *Comparative Education Review, 29*, 471–489.

Fuller, R., & Schoenberger, R. (1991). The salary gender gap: Do academic achievement, internship experience, and college major make a difference? *Social Science Quarterly, 72*, 715–726.

Gaskell, J. (1984). Gender and course choice: The orientation of male and female students. *Journal of Education, 166*, 89–102.

Gecas, V. (1991). The self-concept as a basis for a theory of motivation. In: J. A. Howard & P. L. Callero (Eds), *The Self-Society Dynamic: Cognition, Emotion, and Action* (pp. 171–187). New York: Cambridge University Press.

Gerson, K. (1985). *Hard choices: How women decide about work, career, and motherhood*. Berkeley: University of California Press.

Goode, W. J. (1963). *World revolutions and family patterns*. New York: Free Press.

Gornick, J. C., Meyers, M. K., & Ross, K. E. (1997). Supporting the employment of mothers: Policy variation across fourteen welfare states. *Journal of European Social Policy, 7*, 45–70.

Grubb, W. N. (1997). The returns to education in the sub-baccalaureate labor market, 1984–1990. *Economics of Education Review, 16*, 231–245.

Hakim, C. (1991). Grateful slaves and self-made women: Fact and fantasy in women's work orientations. *European Sociological Review, 7*, 101–121.
Hakim, C. (1996). *Key issues in women's work: Female heterogeneity and the polarisation of women's employment*. London: Athlone Press.
Hall, R., & Sandler, B. (1982). *The classroom climate: A chilly one for women*? Washington, DC: Project on the Status and Education of Women, Association of American Colleges.
Haller, M., & Hoellinger, F. (1992). Female employment and the change of gender roles: The conflictual relationship between participation and attitudes in international comparison. *International Sociology, 9*, 87–112.
Hanson, S. L. (1996). *Lost talent: Women in the sciences*. Philadelphia: Temple University Press.
Hanson, S. L., Schaub, M., & Baker, D. (1996). Gender stratification in the science pipeline: A comparative analysis of seven countries. *Gender and Society, 10*, 271–290.
Hatchell, H. (1998). Girls' entry into higher secondary sciences. *Gender and Education, 10*, 375–386.
Heidenheimer, A. (1997). *Disparate ladders*. New Brunswick, NJ: Transaction Publishers.
Inglehart, R. (1997). *Modernization and postmodernization: Cultural, economic, and political change in 43 Societies*. Princeton, NJ: Princeton University Press.
Inkeles, A., & Smith, D. H. (1974). *Becoming modern*. Cambridge, MA: Harvard University Press.
Jackson, R. M. (1998). *Destined for equality: The inevitable rise of women's status*. Cambridge, MA: Harvard University Press.
Jacobs, J. A. (1989). *Revolving doors*. Stanford, CA: Stanford University Press.
Jacobs, J. A. (1995). Gender and academic specialties: Trends among recipients of college degrees in the 1980s. *Sociology of Education, 68*, 81–98.
Jacobs, J. A. (1996). Gender inequality and higher education. *Annual Review of Sociology, 22*, 153–185.
Jones, J., & Castle, J. (1986). Women in U.K. universities, 1920–1980. *Studies in Higher Education, 11*, 289–297.
Karen, D. (2002). Changes in access to higher education in the United States: 1980–1992. *Sociology of Education, 75*, 191–210.
Kaufman, R. L. (1986). The impact of industrial and occupational structure on black-white employment allocation. *American Sociological Review, 51*, 310–323.
Kelly, G. P. (1991). Women and higher education. In: P. Altbach (Ed.), *International Higher Education* (pp. 290–323). Albany: SUNY Press.
Kerckhoff, A. C. (1996). Building conceptual and empirical bridges between studies of educational and labor force careers. In: A. C. Kerckhoff (Ed.), *Generating Social Stratification: Toward a New Research Agenda* (pp. 37–56). Boulder, CO: Westview Press.
Kerr, C., Dunlop, J. T., Harbison, F. H., & Myers C. A. (1960). *Industrialism and industrial man*. Cambridge, MA: Harvard University Press.
Kilkey, M. (2000). *Lone mothers between paid work and care: The policy regime in twenty countries*. Burlington, VT: Ashgate.
Lamont, M., & Thévenot, L. (2000). Introduction: Toward a renewed comparative cultural sociology. In: M. Lamont & L. Thévenot (Eds), *Rethinking Comparative Cultural Sociology: Repertoires of Evaluation in France and the United States* (pp. 1–22). New York: Cambridge University Press.
Leira, A. (1992). *Welfare states and working mothers: The Scandinavian experience*. New York: Cambridge University Press.
Lipset, S. M., Bendix, R., & Zetterberg, H. L. (1959). Social mobility in industrial society. In: S. M. Lipset, R. Bendix & H. L. Zetterberg (Eds), *Social Mobility in Industrial Society* (pp. 11–81). Berkeley: UC Press.

Meek, V. L., & Goedegebuure, L. (Eds) (1996). *The mockers and the mocked: Comparative perspectives on differentiation, convergence and diversity in higher education*. Paris: IAU Press.

Meyer, J. W., Ramirez, F. O., Rubinson, R., & Boli-Bennett, J. (1977). The world educational revolution 1950–1970. *Sociology of Education, 50*, 242–258.

Morgan, C. S. (1992). College students' perceptions of barriers to women in science and engineering. *Youth & Society, 24*, 228–236.

Mortimer, J. T., & Kruger, H. (2000). Pathways from school to work in Germany and the United States. In: M. T. Hallinan (Ed.), *Handbook of the Sociology of Education* (pp. 475–497). New York: Kluwer Academic/Plenum Publishers.

Murphy, J. L. (1995). *Gender issues in World Bank lending*. Washington, DC: World Bank.

National Research Council (1992). *Science and engineering programs: On target for women?* Washington, DC: National Academy Press.

National Science Foundation (2000). *Science and engineering indicators 2000*. Washington, DC: National Science Foundation.

Neave, G. (1985). Elite and mass higher education in Britain: A regressive model? *Comparative Education Review, 29*, 347–361.

OECD (Organisation for Economic Cooperation and Development) (1973). *Report of conference concerning the problem of post–secondary education structures*. Paris: OECD.

OECD (1986). *Girls and women in education*. Paris: OECD.

OECD (1997). *Education at a glance*. Paris: OECD.

Persell, C. H., James, C., Kang, T., & Snyder, K. (1999). Gender and education in comparative perspective. In: J. C. Saltzman (Ed.), *Handbook of the Sociology of Gender* (pp. 407–439). NY: Kluwer Academic/Plenum Publishers.

Pieterse, J. N. (1995). Globalization as hybridization. In: M. Featherstone et al. (Eds), *Global Modernities* (pp. 98–104). London: Sage.

Polachek, S. W. (1978). Sex differences in college major. *Industrial and Labor Relations Review, 31*, 498–508.

Ramirez, F. O. (1987). Global changes, world myths, and the demise of cultural gender: Implications for the United States. In: T. Boswell & A. Bergesen (Eds), *America's Changing Role in the World System* (pp. 257–273). New York: Praeger.

Ramirez, F. O. (2001, October). World society and the political incorporation of women. In: B. Heintz (Guest Ed.), *A Special Issue on Gender Studies of the Kölner Zeitschrift für Soziologie und Sozialpsychologie* (pp. 356–374).

Ramirez, F. O., & Cha, Y.-K. (1990). Citizenship and gender: Western educational development in comparative perspective. *Research in Sociology of Education and Socialization, 9*, 153–173.

Ramirez, F. O., & Wotipka, C. M. (2001). Slowly but surely? The global expansion of women's participation in science and engineering fields of study, 1972–1992. *Sociology of Education, 74*, 231–251.

Randour, M. L., Strasburg, G. L., & Lipman-Blumen, J. (1982). Women in higher education: Trends in enrollment and degrees earned. *Harvard Educational Review, 52*, 189–202.

Research Institute for Higher Education (1992). *Higher education and employment in Japan*. Hiroshima, Japan: Research Institute for Higher Education.

Reskin, B. F., & Roos, P. A. (1990). *Job queues, gender queues: Explaining women's inroads into male occupations*. Philadelphia: Temple University Press.

Roemer, R. E. (1983). Changing patterns of degree selection among women: 1970–1978. *Research in Higher Education, 18*, 435–454.

Rosser, S. V. (1995). Potential effects of increasing the number of women in the scientific and technological workforce. In: D. Bills (Ed.), *The New Modern Times: Factors Reshaping the World of Work* (pp. 235–249). Albany, NY: SUNY Press.

Ruggie, M. (1984). *The state and working women: A comparative study of Britain and Sweden*. Princeton, NJ: Princeton University Press.

Rumberger, R. W., & Thomas, S. L. (1993). The economic returns to college major, quality, and performance: A multilevel analysis of recent graduates. *Economics of Education Review, 12*, 1–19.

Schultz, T. W. (1961). Investment in human capital. *American Economic Review, 51*, 1–17.

Seymour, E., & Hewitt, N. M. (1997). *Talking about leaving: Why undergraduates leave the sciences*. Newbury Park: HarperCollins.

Shamai, S. (1996). Elementary school students' attitudes toward science and their course of studies in high school. *Adolescence, 31*, 677–689.

Shavit, Y., & Müller, W. (1998). *From school to work: A comparative study of educational qualifications and occupational destinations*. New York: Clarenden Press.

Shu, X., & Marini, M. M. (1998). Gender-related change in occupational aspirations. *Sociology of Education, 71*, 44–68.

Sirowy, L., & Benavot, A. (1986). Higher education in an era of equality: A cross-national study of institutional differentiation on the tertiary level. *Research in Sociology of Education and Socialization, 6*, 1–44.

Stolte-Heiskanen, V., Ananieva, N., Gaudart, D., with Furst-Dilic, R. (Eds) (1991). *Women in science token women or gender equality*? New York: St. Martin's Press.

Sumsion, J. (2000). Rewards, risks, and tensions: Perceptions of males enrolled in an early childhood teacher education program. *Asia-Pacific Journal of Teacher Education, 28*, 87–100.

Teichler, U. (1996). Diversity in higher education in Germany: The two–type structure. In: V. L. Meek & L. Goedegebuure (Eds), *The Mockers and the Mocked: Comparative Perspectives on Differentiation, Convergence and Diversity in Higher Education* (pp. 117–137). Paris: IAU Press.

Thomas, G., Meyer, J., Ramirez, F., & Boli, J. (1987). *Institutional structure*. Newbury Park, CA: Sage.

Trappe, H., & Rosenfeld, R. A. (2001). In: T. Van der Lippe & L. Van Dijk (Eds), *Women's Employment in a Comparative Perspective* (pp. 109–150). New York: Aldine de Gruyter.

UNESCO (United Nations Educational, Scientific, and Cultural Organisation) (1975). *UNESCO and the international decade for women*. Paris: UNESCO.

UNESCO (1995). *Secondary technical and vocational education: Female participation in the various fields of study 1980 and 1992. STE–17*. Paris: UNESCO.

UNESCO (1997, 1998). *Statistical yearbook*. Paris: UNESCO.

United Nations (1995). Beijing declaration and platform for action adopted by the 1995 fourth world conference on women. A/CONF.177/20.

United Nations (1996). *The United Nations and the advancement of women, 1945–1996*. NY: The United Nations.

Van Dijk, L. (2001). Macro changes in public childcare provision, parental leave, and women's employment: An international comparison. In: T. Van der Lippe & L. Van Dijk (Eds), *Women's Employment in a Comparative Perspective* (pp. 37–58). New York: Aldine de Gruyter.

Van Nught, F. (1996). Isomorphism in higher education? Towards a theory of differentiation and diversity in higher education systems. In: V. L. Meek & L. Goedegebuure (Eds), *The Mockers and the Mocked: Comparative Perspectives on Differentiation, Convergence and Diversity in Higher Education* (pp. 42–58). Paris: IAU Press.

Vincens, J. (1995). Graduates and the labour market in France. *European Journal of Education, 30*, 133–155.

Waite, L. J., & Berryman, S. E. (1985). *Women in non-traditional occupations: Choice and turnover*. Santa Monica, CA: Rand Corporation.

Williams, J. (2000). *Unbending gender: Why family and work conflict and what to do about it*. New York: Oxford University Press.

Wilson, K. L., & Boldizar, J. P. (1990). Gender segregation in higher education: Effects of aspirations, mathematics achievement, and income. *Sociology of Education*, *63*, 62–74.

Wilson, K., & Smith-Lovin, L. (1983). Scaling the prestige, authority and income potential of college curricula. *Social Science Research*, *12*, 159–186.

Windolf, P. (1997). *Expansion and cultural change. Higher education in Germany, the United States, and Japan, 1870–1990*. Boulder, CO: Westview Press.

Wuthnow, R. (1989). *Communities of discourse: Ideology and social structure in the reformation, the enlightenment, and European socialism*. Cambridge, MA: Harvard University Press.

COMMENTARY: INEQUALITY AND SCHOOLING AS AN INSTITUTION

Regina E. Werum and David P. Baker

INTRODUCTION

As guest editors, we welcomed the opportunity to help compile a volume that reflects current trends in cross-national analyses of educational stratification. Our interest in macro-comparative stratification research stems from a shared dissatisfaction with the extensive amount of research on schooling and social stratification exclusively on American education. Of course, studying what is close at hand is less complicated (and less fraught with data limitations), and investigations of a single nation or society often provide the basis for more or less universal generalizations.

But stratification research over the past 30 years has increasingly used explicit comparative studies to answer central questions, and we believe that a parallel emphasis on comparative study of educational stratification would increase the connection of sociology of education to major advances in contemporary stratification research (Baker, 1994; Ramirez & Meyer, 1981). Applying our best approaches to understanding educational stratification – which are developed chiefly on the American system – to a broader set of nations will yield a more robust sociology of education (Buchmann & Hannum, 2001).

The chapters in this volume offer new bridges to an expanded comparative study of educational stratification. Our commentary focuses on the first five chapters (see Hannum and Fuller's essay for commentary on the remaining chapters). At

Inequality Across Societies: Families, Schools and Persisting Stratification
Research in Sociology of Education, Volume 14, 275–284
(Formerly Research in Sociology of Education and Socialization)

ISSN: 1479-3539/doi:10.1016/S1479-3539(03)14012-8

first glance, these chapters seem to share little in common, because they differ in method and levels of analysis: Bradley and Charles examine gender stratification in higher education, relying on aggregate data from 26 largely industrialized countries; Wong uses individual-level data to examine educational transitions in five socialist countries; and McManus uses individual-level data in comparing educational credentials for women and men in two highly industrialized, capitalist countries. The other two chapters are single-nation case studies: Morgan and Morgan examine the effects of educational pathways on local employment patterns in pre-capitalist Nigeria; and Yair, Khatab and Benavot focus on the genesis of educational aspirations among Arab Israelis.

These differences notwithstanding, we find it striking that all five chapters share a substantive and theoretical focus on the interplay between institutional dynamics and specific stratification patterns. And it is precisely this simultaneous study of stratification and institutional changes in schooling that we find so promising as an emerging research strategy. Macro-comparative research (e.g. cross-national studies) on education has always tended to incorporate institutional perspectives, but institutionally-based analyses of questions relating to educational stratification have remained rare. Thus, the chapters at hand strengthen a growing and much needed trend in comparative international research. To highlight how they enhance our understanding of education as an institution that plays a significant role in social stratification, we first describe the potential advantages of linking institutional and stratification perspectives on education.

INSTITUTIONS AND THE PRODUCTION OF INEQUALITY

Using broad strokes, we can divide perspectives on the sociology of education into "institutionalist" and "structuralist" schools of thought (Baker, forthcoming). To some degree, the differences between institutional and structural perspectives can be traced back to each framework's respective roots in Weberian and Marxian thought (Bidwell, forthcoming). Although these perspectives also share some theoretical traditions, they have led to differing research questions and empirical approaches.

Most research on institutional aspects of schooling examines processes by which the institution expands. In other words, drawing on neo-institutionalism as the main theoretical tradition, these studies test theoretical arguments about how education develops as an institution. Taking a cue from the older functionalist idea of social institutions, neo-institutionalism expands arguments about the origins and consequences of institutions. Specific topics in this literature include: institutional formation as both emergence and deliberate action (e.g. Durkheim, 1911, 1961); institutionalization as value formation (Selznick, 1949) and as basis for the production of social power through formal organizations (Parsons, 1956); the politics of institutions and dynamics within an environment of overlapping institutional structure (e.g. Stinchcombe, 1965); and the collective cognitive process that forms socially constructed institutional sectors (Berger et al., 1973; Meyer, 1977).

Applying these topics to education has generated a research literature on the growth of mass schooling and its power as an institution to legitimate and regulate social mobility, credentials, and human capital formation (e.g. Boli, 1989; Fuller & Rubinson, 1992). This perspective on schooling helps us understand how macro forces – such as political, economic, and cultural factors – influence institutional growth (or in theory, decline) in terms of enrollments, organizational diversification, bureaucratization, and so forth (see Baker, 1999; Fuller & Rubinson, 1992; Meyer et al., 1977; Meyer, Ramirez & Soysal, 1992; Richardson, 1986; Rubinson & Ralph, 1984; Tyack, 1974). The related "world-polity" or "global culture" perspective stresses the role of international, non-governmental organizations in spreading a common institutional ideology about the role of mass schooling in society (e.g. Boli & Thomas, 1999; Frank et al., 2000; LeTendre et al., 2001; Meyer & Hannan, 1979; Shafer, 1999).

In contrast, studies in the structuralist tradition examine processes that produce *educational stratification*. In short, this perspective addresses the question: How does schooling contribute to an already stratified structure of modern society? Studies in this tradition examine the role of schools in the reproduction of social inequalities based on existing class, ethnic, racial, language, gender, and other factors. At times, structuralists even point to mass schooling in its institutionalized form as a key source of social stratification. Literature in this broad field ranges from research on educational sorting mechanisms, over-manifest and latent stratification processes in schools, to schooling's capacity to exert cultural dominance (e.g. Ayalon, 1994; DiMaggio, 1982; Grant, 1984; Hallinan, 2000; Lareau & Horvat, 1999).

Neither of these frameworks has generated a comprehensive theory of educational stratification. Structuralists in the field succeed at honing in on the processes that facilitate the reproduction of inequalities, but their focus often prevents them from specifying the institutional roots of the unequal patterns observed (see also Oswald, Baker & Stevenson, 1988; Powell, Werum & Steelman, 2003). At the same time, neo-institutionalists succeed in identifying long-term and comparative trends in the growth of schooling, but their arguments have some difficulty explaining continued conflict and tension in institutional expansion. Compare, for example, the lack of class conflict imagery in institutional accounts of educational expansion with historical and contemporary accounts of class conflict in school expansion (e.g. Katz, 1968; Reese, 1986; Wrigley, 1982).

Institutionalist analyses accept the now global mantra that education maximizes human capital formation (and presumably intergenerational mobility), prepares future generations for an increasingly industrialized world, and creates democratically minded citizens. In the process, stratification processes often remain implicit, although mass schooling includes stratification processes that are perceived as both legitimate (via meritocratic principles) and illegitimate (via social reproduction).

To summarize, the extent to which the movement towards universal schooling influences social stratification patterns remains unclear. This causes us to ask: Who benefits from these long-term trends? How do schools/institutions structure access to specific types of education? How can comparative historical and international studies help us pinpoint these dynamics? To work towards a more integrated theory of educational stratification, we need more analyses that examine how the institutionalizing process of schooling reduces or exacerbates existing stratification patterns, or how it creates new patterns. Comparative international studies of education like the five chapters in this volume help us examine these links between institutional dynamics and stratification.

Incidentally, some of our own work also provides examples of how comparative institutional approaches yield new ways to examine stratification. For example, Baker et al.'s work (2002a) illustrates this idea, focusing on the growth and consequence of shadow education worldwide as a function of greater institutionalization of formal schooling *and* as a new source of educational stratification and status reproduction. Similarly, Werum's research on the institutionalization of vocational education in the U.S. shows that federal efforts to expand such training were shaped by prevalent gender and racial ideologies (Werum, 1997) and produced disparate effects on access to training (Werum, 2001, 2002). But state-sponsored efforts to expand programs often missed their mark. Political mobilization and the expansion of academic high schools produced unintended long-term consequences, sometimes exacerbating inequalities, at other times ameliorating them (Werum, 1999a, b). Not surprisingly, our own work leads us to welcome the chapters discussed below, which combine institutional and structural approaches using a comparative lens.

ADVANCING INSTITUTIONAL AND STRUCTURAL PERSPECTIVES

The first five chapters of this volume illustrate a useful and thought-provoking nexus between institutional and structural frameworks. They highlight that, while stratification occurs regardless of institutional parameters, the specific stratification mechanisms differ depending on the actual institutional context. For instance, McManus' comparison of gender patterns in the U.S. and Germany demonstrates that formal credentials seem to have little influence on people's transitions in and out of self-employment. While educational attainment (human capital) generally matters, its effects are particularly weak on self-employment patterns among women in the U.S.

This contradicts the common perception that public policies aimed at educational expansion shape overall employment patterns. Instead, McManus finds that traditional pathways linked to family status shape self-employment patterns in both countries, but the specific ways in which families influence occupational trajectories differ by country. In both countries, men's self-employment typically follows an intergenerational pattern, while women tend to follow spouses into self-employment. But only in the U.S. does women's self-employment follow what she calls the "caretaker path," where women with small children choose self-employment, typically in low-paid caretaker roles as an alternative to part-time work.

Bradley and Charles'(B&C) study of gender stratification in higher education shows that whether or not we can "see" social inequalities may depend on which aspect of educational expansion we examine. When we focus on overall tertiary enrollment rates (i.e. the spread of mass higher education), women have made great strides throughout the industrialized world. But a closer look reveals that strong enrollment growth at the tertiary level has produced a new form of inequality, leading to pronounced gender segregation by type of higher education institution and curricular specialization. B&C conclude that *two* coexisting global ideologies help produce these countervailing patterns, an argument that challenges institutionalist/world polity theory as well as classic human capital and modernization theories. B&C suggest that international support for educational democratization helps increase women's enrollments, but a similarly global (read "institutional") ideology based on essentialist gender expectations limits women's access to certain educational credentials.

Further, B&C's analysis clearly plays into the analysis of gender-specific employment paths presented by McManus. Together, these chapters raise a number of future research questions. For example, if sex segregation within an educational system leads to different credentials and thus influences subsequent career trajectories, will that ameliorate or exacerbate the impact of the "caretaker path" McManus describes as typical for self-employed women in the U.S.? In addition, does reliance on part-time jobs and self-employment explain the higher poverty rate among American women compared with women in other industrialized countries (whose educational experiences reflect similar gender-segregated patterns)? And lastly, what are the long-term implications regarding the effects of continued institutionalization of higher education on gender or other forms of stratification?

On a related note, Werum (2002) demonstrates similar gender dynamics regarding the expansion of vocational training in the U.S. Rather than reducing social inequalities, curricular diversification and concomitant expansion produced new stratification mechanisms. The cross-national tertiary enrollment patterns and employment trends described by B&C and McManus, respectively, contain obvious and long-term implications for social stratification, including persistent gender segregation at work and related wage gaps, even among professionals.

Wong's chapter on educational transitions in five socialist nations takes on egalitarianism as a key element in the global ideology of education – an argument articulated in the neo-institutional ideas behind world polity theory, as well as specifically examined in B&C's chapter. Wong's study also shares crucial aspects of the human capital argument made by economists, as well as by McManus in this volume. Finding that the usually substantial effect of parents' educational background on their children's educational outcomes weakens when parental cultural capital is controlled, he interprets this as evidence that institutional global ideas about egalitarianism do not prevent class reproduction.

The fact that class reproduction remains alive and well, even in socialist countries, suggests that educational stratification persists, regardless of specific institutional arrangements. While this particular article neither invokes nor tests standard institutionalist ideas about educational expansion, Wong essentially critiques the notion of a world polity, as well as modernization theories that suggest that ideology alone can serve as the "great equalizer." For a contrasting interpretation of this conclusion, see the comparative analysis of family and school effects on achievement and the institutional ramifications of this empirical trend by Baker et al. (2002b).

Morgan and Morgan's (M&M) analysis of local employment patterns in Nigeria takes a comparative historical rather than cross-national approach. Its innovativeness lies in applying a framework originally designed with developed nations in mind to a pre-capitalist African country. The study focuses on how competing educational pathways, some of which constitute the institutional legacy of colonialism, have affected the earnings of two cohorts of men in Kano, Nigeria.

M&M conclude that the traditional apprenticeship system may continue to help workers maximize earnings or, in other words, returns to their human capital. They recommend expanding and formalizing vocational training, and ask whether this might be more useful than heavy emphasis on academic (westernized) or indigenous, religiously-based programs. In substantive terms, this chapter connects to Wong with its attention to cohort and long-term effects, and to McManus in sharing a focus on the impact of vocational credentials on employment patterns as the outcome of interest.

In contrast, the single-nation study by Yair, Kathab and Benavot (YK&B) focuses explicitly on intra-group differences, trying to explain the determinants of educational aspirations among Arab Israelis of different religious backgrounds: Christian, Muslim, and Druze. More grounded in a traditional structural approach to education stratification than the other four chapters, YK&B complement them by turning our attention to exogenous factors at the micro-level left largely unexplained by the more macro-theoretical approaches. They demonstrate that role models can play a key role in "heating up" the aspirations of these adolescents, a finding that resonates with an earlier study by Shavit and Pierce (1991).

Their main finding contradicts commonly held assumptions about minorities in other industrialized nations (i.e. having low aspirations or at least exemplifying an "attitude-achievement paradox;" see Mickelson, 1990). This raises an important question for institutional and stratification researchers alike. Is it possible that the formal segregation of Arab and Jewish schools not only facilitates institutional discrimination, but also unintentionally produces an intellectual and political elite among Arab Israelis? YK&B's answer is yes. "Arab Israelis understand that their unusually high aspirations are probably unattainable, yet such aspirations can serve as a catalyst for social change and . . . a potent, non-violent means for fighting prejudice and discrimination."

YK&B's chapter leads one to consider institutional parallels between the Israeli situation and the Jim Crow system that was in place in much of the U.S. until the mid-20th century. That system at once embodied the principles of segregation ("separate and unequal") but also played a key role in the production of Afro-American leaders for the ensuing civil rights movement. For example, almost exactly 100 years ago, W.E.B. Du Bois argued that "Negro institutions should be at the forefront of training leaders of the Talented Tenth, standing conspicuously among the best of their time" (Paschal, 1971, p. 33). Historically black colleges and universities have played that key role in higher education in the U.S. It remains to be seen whether, in the long run, formally segregated educational institutions in Israel will help produce an Arab-Israeli rights movement.

CONCLUSION

These five chapters show that comparative research on stratification can help us understand the institutional parameters that shape educational opportunities for different groups, nations, and time periods. Moreover, they point to a theoretical framework that draws on both institutional and structural perspectives to explain educational stratification. Far from suggesting that one can either superimpose one framework on the other or create a merely additive framework, the chapters in this section illustrate that questions about institutionalization and stratification are intertwined.

Let us assume that the institutionalization of formal education will continue. This process will occur in different sectors and at different levels, depending on the country, and it will occur in ways that were not easy to predict even two decades ago. Thus, future research should focus on both the intended and unintended consequences of this process. To reiterate, stratification research is enhanced through incorporation of institutional dynamics (Baker, forthcoming). Similarly, research on institutional dynamics is enhanced through understanding how long-term institutional patterns of schooling create social inequalities (Meyer, 1977).

Pursuing this integrative direction through comparative educational research will have positive substantive and methodological consequences for the sociology of education in general. For instance, it might lead to additional studies on how institutional parameters in developing nations shape ethnic/gender inequality in educational opportunities and outcomes. It might also spur large-scale international data collection efforts that go beyond examining classic, individual-level status attainment factors and involve collecting organizational and aggregate, longitudinal data. At the same time, this new research direction might produce more in-depth, qualitative, historical, and ethnographic case studies to maximize insights into the policy formation and implementation processes.

REFERENCES

Ayalon, H. (1994). Monopolizing knowledge? The ethnic composition and curriculum of Israeli high schools. *Sociology of Education*, *67*, 264–278.

Baker, D. P. (1994). In comparative isolation: Why comparative research has so little influence on American sociology of education. *Research in Sociology of Education and Socialization*, *10*, 53–70.

Baker, D. P. (forthcoming). Can we predict institutional change? Evidence from cross-national comparisons of educational phenomena. In: H. Meyer & B. Rowan (Eds), *New Institutionalism in Education*. Albany, NY: SUNY Albany Press.

Baker, D. P. (1999). Schooling all the masses: Reconsidering the origins of American schooling in the postbellum era. *Sociology of Education*, *72*(4), 197–215.

Baker, D. P., Akiba, M., Letendre, G., & Wiseman, A. (2002a). Worldwide shadow education: Outside-school learning, institutional quality of schooling, and cross-national mathematics achievement. *Education, Evaluation, and Policy Analysis*, *23*(1), 1–17.

Baker, D. P., Goesling, B., & LeTendre, G. (2002b). Socio-economic status, school quality, and national economic development: A cross-national analysis of the 'Heyneman-Loxley effect' on mathematics and science achievement. *Comparative Education Review*, *46*(3), 291–312.

Berger, P., Berger, B., & Kellner, H. (1973). *The homeless mind: Modernization and consciousness*. New York: Random House.

Bidwell, C. E. (forthcoming). Varieties of institutional theory: Traditions and prospects for educational research. In: H. Meyer & B. Rowan (Eds), *The New Institutionalism in Education*. Albany, NY: SUNY Albany Press.

Boli, J. (1989). *New citizens for a new society: The institutional origins of mass schooling in Sweden*. New York: Pergamon Press.

Boli, J., & Thomas, G. (Eds) (1999). *Constructing world culture: International non-governmental organizations since 1875*. Stanford, CA: Stanford University Press.

Buchmann, C., & Hannum, E. (2001). Education and stratification in developing countries: Review of theories and research. *Annual Review of Sociology*, *27*, 77–102.

DiMaggio, P. (1982). Cultural capital and school success: The impact of status culture participation on the grades of United States high school students. *American Sociological Review*, *47*, 189–201.

Durkheim, E. (1911–1961). *The evolution of educational thought*. London: Routlege and Kegan Paul.

Frank, D. J., Wong, S.-K., Meyer, J., & Ramirez, F. (2000). What counts as history: A cross-national and longitudinal study of university curricula. *Comparative Education Review*, *44*(1), 29–53.

Fuller, B., & Rubinson, R. (Eds) (1992). *The political construction of education: The state, school expansion, and economic change*. New York: Praeger.

Grant, L. (1984). Black females' 'place' in desegregated classrooms. *Sociology of Education*, *57*(2), 98–111.

Hallinan, M. (Ed.) (2000). *Handbook of the sociology of education*. New York: Kluwer.

Katz, M. (1968). *The irony of early school reform*. Boston: Beacon Press.

Lareau, A., & Horvat, E. (1999). Moments of social inclusion and exclusion: Race, class, and cultural capital in family-school relationships. *Sociology of Education*, *72*, 37–53.

LeTendre, G., Baker, D. P., Akiba, M., Goesling, B., & Wiseman, A. (2001). Teacher's work: Institutional isomorphism and cultural variation in the U.S., Germany, and Japan. *Education Researcher*, *30*(6), 3–15.

Meyer, J. (1977). The effects of education as an institution. *American Journal of Sociology*, *83*(1), 55–77.

Meyer, J., & Hannan, M. T. (Eds) (1979). *National development and the world system: Educational, economic, and political change, 1950–1970*. Chicago: University of Chicago Press.

Meyer, J., Ramirez, F., & Soysal, Y. N. (1992). World expansion of mass education, 1870–1980. *Sociology of Education*, *65*(2), 128–149.

Meyer, J., Rubinson, R., Ramirez, F., & Boli-Bennett, J. (1977). The world educational evolution, 1950–1970. *Sociology of Education*, *50*(4), 242–258.

Mickelson, R. (1990). The attitude-achievement paradox among black adolescents. *Sociology of Education*, *63*(1), 44–61.

Oswald, H., Baker, D. P., & Stevenson, D. L. (1988). School charter and parental management in West Germany. *Sociology of Education*, *61*, 255–265.

Parsons, T. (1956). Suggestions for a sociological approach to a theory of organizations I. *Administrative Science Quarterly*, *1*, 63–85.

Paschal, A. (Ed.) (1971). *A W.E.B. Du Bois Reader*. New York: MacMillan.

Powell, B., Werum, R., & Steelman, L. C. (2003, forthcoming). Macro causes, micro effects: Linking public policy, family structure, and educational outcomes. In: D. Conley (Ed.), *After the Bell: Educational Solutions Outside of School*. Routlege.

Ramirez, F., & Meyer, J. (1981). Comparative education: Synthesis and agenda. In: J. Short (Ed.), *The State of Sociology: Problems and Prospects* (pp. 215–238). Beverly Hills, CA: Sage.

Reese, W. J. (1986). *Power and the promise of school reform: Grassroots movements during the progressive era*. Boston: Routlege & Kegan Paul.

Richardson, J. G. (Ed.) (1986). *Handbook of theory and research for the sociology of education*. New York: Greenwood Press.

Rubinson, R., & Ralph, J. (1984). Technical change and the expansion of schooling in the United States, 1890–1980. *Sociology of Education, 57*, 134–152.

Selznick, P. (1949). *TVA and the grass roots*. Berkeley, CA: University of California Press.

Shafer, M. (1999). International non-governmental organizations and third world education in 1990: A cross-national study. *Sociology of Education, 72*, 69–88.

Shavit, Y., & Pierce, J. (1991). Sibship size and educational attainment in nuclear and extended families: Arabs and Jews in Israel. *American Sociological Review, 56*, 321–330.

Stinchcombe, A. (1965). Social structure and organizations. In: J. March (Ed.), *Handbook of Organizations*. Chicago: Rand-McNally.

Tyack, D. (1974). *The one best system*. Cambridge, MA: Harvard University Press.

Werum, R. (1997). Sectionalism and racial politics: Federal vocational policies and programs in the pre-desegregation south. *Social Science History, 21*(3), 399–453.

Werum, R. (1999a). Elite control in state and nation: Racial inequalities in vocational funding in North Carolina, Georgia, and Mississippi, 1918–1936. *Social Forces, 78*(1), 145–186.

Werum, R. (1999b). Tug-of-war: Political mobilization and access to schooling in the southern racial state. *Sociology of Education, 72*, 89–110.

Werum, R. (2001). Warehousing the unemployed? Federal job training programs in the depression-era south. *American Journal of Education, 109*(2), 228–265.

Werum, R. (2002). Matching youth and jobs? Gender dynamics in new deal job training programs. *Social Forces, 81*(2), 472–503.

Wrigley, J. (1982). *Class politics and public schools: Chicago, 1900–1950*. New Brunswick, NJ: Rutgers University Press.

ABOUT THE AUTHORS

David P. Baker is a Professor of Education and Sociology at the Pennsylvania State University, where he is also the associate director of the Social Science Research Institute. He publishes widely on the comparative analysis of education and stratification, and the global impact of education as an institution. Recent publications include "Student Victimization: National and School System Effects on School Violence in 37 Nations" (*American Journal of Education Research*, 2002) and "Socio-Economic Status, School Quality, and National Economic Development: A Cross-National Analysis of the 'Heyneman-Loxley Effect' on Mathematics and Science Achievement" (*Comparative Education Review*, 2002).

Aaron Benavot is a Senior Lecturer in Sociology at the Hebrew University of Jerusalem. Grounded in an institutional approach to education and development, his research has examined historical and cross-national patterns in official school curricula, the consequences of educational expansion on economic development and democratization, the economic impacts of curricular contents, and the origins and expansion of mass education. He is currently studying the diversification of educational knowledge in local Israeli schools and also the dynamics of transnational social science research projects in the European Union.

Karen Bradley is an Associate Professor of Sociology at Western Washington University. Her research examines women's participation in higher education cross-nationally. Recent publications include "Equal but Separate? A Cross-National Study of Sex Segregation in Higher Education" (with Maria Charles, American Sociological Review, 2002) and "The Incorporation of Women into Higher Education: Paradoxical Outcomes?" (Sociology of Education, 2000). She is currently collaborating with Maria Charles on a project sponsored by the Spencer Foundation and the American Educational Research Association that examines factors underlying women's underrepresentation in engineering and math/computer science programs in several countries.

Wendy Cadge is an Assistant Professor of Sociology at Bowdoin College. She received her Ph.D. in sociology from Princeton University. Her research focuses on the cultural aspects of globalization in the United States and Southeast Asia. Her first book, *Heartwood: the First Generation of Theravada Buddhism in America*, is forthcoming from the University of Chicago Press.

Maria Charles is an Associate Professor of Sociology at the University of California, San Diego. Her research explores how cultural ideologies and social structures affect the economic and social status of individuals and groups. Most recently, Charles is author of "Deciphering Sex Segregation: Vertical and Horizontal Inequalities in Ten Countries" (*Acta Sociologica* 46:265–286, 2003), and coauthor of *Occupational Ghettos: The Worldwide Segregation of Women and Men* (with David Grusky, Stanford University Press, in press) and "Equal but Separate: A Cross-National Study of Sex Segregation in Higher Education" (with Karen Bradley, *American Sociology Review* 67: 573–599, 2002).

Chang Y. Chung is a Statistical Programmer at the Office of Population Research, Princeton University. He received his Ph.D. in sociology from the University of South Carolina and M.S.E. in systems engineering from the University of Pennsylvania. He is involved in multiple research projects as statistical programmer, data manager, and co-author. A recent publication is "Employment and Earnings of Foreign-Born Scientists and Engineers in U.S. Labor Markets" (with Thomas Espenshade and Margaret Usdansky, *Population Research and Policy Review*, 2001).

Sara R. Curran is an Assistant Professor and Director of Undergraduate Studies in Sociology at Princeton University. She received her Ph.D. from the University of North Carolina, Chapel Hill. She has research interests in demography, migration, gender, economic development, environment, aging and Southeast Asia. She is currently writing a book, *Shifting Boundaries, Transforming Lives: Globalization, Gender, and Family in Thailand*. Recent publications include: *Ambio*. Special Issue: Population, Consumption, and Environment, (with Tundi Agardy, 2002) and "Engendering Migrant Networks: The Case of Mexican Migration," (with Estela Rivero Fuentes, *Demography*, 2003).

Bruce Fuller is a Professor of Education and Public Policy at the University of California, Berkeley. His work focuses on the dilemmas around the decentering of public aims and institutions within the worlds of child care, family welfare, and school reform. Prior to becoming a full-time teacher, he worked for a state legislature, a governor, and then as a heretical sociologist at the World Bank. His most recent books are *Inside Charter Schools: The Paradox of Radical Decentralization* (Harvard, 2000), and *Government Confronts Culture* (Taylor & Francis, 1999).

Emily Hannum is Assistant Professor of Sociology at the University of Pennsylvania. Her research focuses on education, poverty, and social inequality, particularly in China. Recent publications include "Ethnic Differences in Basic Education in Reform-Era Rural China" (*Demography*, 2002) and "Education and Stratification in Developing Countries: A Review of Theories and Empirical Research" (with Claudia Buchmann, *Annual Review of Sociology*, 2001). Currently, she is working on a project sponsored by the Spencer Foundation and National Institutes of Health that investigates factors in the family, school, and community that support rural children's education and healthy development in Northwest China.

Nabil Khattab completed his Ph.D. at the University of Jerusalem. He is currently a Marie Curie postdoctoral research fellow at the Cathie Marsh Centre for Census and Survey Research, University of Manchester. His main areas of interest are sociology of education, the ethnic and gender aspects of the labor market, and social inequality. His most recent publication is "Segregation, Ethnic Labor Market, and the Occupational Expectations of Palestinian Students in Israel" (*The British Journal of Sociology*, 2003). In his current project, he is looking at the labor market prospects for Pakistani-Bangladeshi women in the U.K. and Muslim women in Israel.

Patricia McManus is an Associate Professor of Sociology at Indiana University, Bloomington. Her research centers on gender and family inequality under advanced capitalism. She will spend 2003–2004 in Berlin at the Max Planck Institute's Center for the Study of Sociology and the Life Course, where she will study welfare state policy and married women's work careers in the United States, Germany, and Great Britain. Current projects also include a study of the impact of residential mobility on gender inequality within households (with Claudia Geist), and a cross-national comparison of the wage penalties for motherhood in the United States and Germany (with Markus Gangl).

Stephen L. Morgan is an Associate Professor of Sociology at Cornell University. His main areas of interest are social stratification, sociology of education, and methodology. Recent publications include "Modeling Preparatory Commitment and Non-Repeatable Decisions: Information Processing, Preference Formation and Educational Attainment" (*Rationality and Society*, 2002) and "Counterfactuals, Causal Effect Heterogeneity, and the Catholic School Effect on Learning" (*Sociology of Education*, 2001). His current projects include studies of black-white differences in educational achievement and changes in labor market inequality in the 1980s and 1990s.

William R. Morgan is a Professor of Sociology at Cleveland State University. He has been studying and developing education in northern Nigeria over a period of 25 years. In Cleveland, he recently completed data collection for a seven-year study of the impact of the treatment and recovery process for cocaine-addicted women on their children's development, sponsored by the National Institute on Drug Abuse. His new project is a pilot study of the peer recruitment method to deliver HIV/AIDS education to networks of high-risk adolescents and young women.

Hiroshi Ono is an Assistant Professor at the European Institute of Japanese Studies, Stockholm School of Economics. He is interested in social stratification and inequality, and the sociology and economics of education, family, and work. Currently he is working on two projects. The first is examining Internet inequality in five countries, and the second is comparing human resource practices between foreign-owned versus domestic firms in Japan. His recent publications include "College Quality and Earnings in the Japanese Labor Market" (forthcoming, *Industrial Relations*), and "Gender and the Internet" (with Madeline Zavodny, *Social Science Quarterly*, 2003).

Hyunjoon Park, a doctoral student in Sociology at the University of Wisconsin-Madison, is interested in social stratification, education, and health inequality with a particular focus on East Asian countries. His current project examines the process of the transition to adulthood among Japanese, Korean, and Taiwanese young people across several dimensions, including educational and occupational attainment, and family formation. Two forthcoming publications include "Intergenerational Social Mobility among Korean Men: In Comparative Perspective" (*Research in Social Stratification and Mobility*, 2003), and "Racial/Ethnic Differences in Voluntary and Involuntary Job Mobility among Young Men" (with Gary Sandefur, *Social Science Research*, 2003).

Susan E. Short is an Associate Professor of Sociology and Associate Director of the Population Studies and Training Center at Brown University. She specializes in family sociology, social demography, and social inequality. Recent coauthored publications include "Use of Maternity Services in Rural China" (*Population Studies*, forthcoming); "Maternal Work and Time Spent in Child Care in China: A Multimethod Approach" (*Population and Development Review*, 2002); "China's One-Child Policy and the Care of Children: An Analysis of Qualitative and Quantitative Data" (*Social Forces*, 2001); and "Birth Planning and Sterilization in China" (*Population Studies*, 2000). In on-going research, funded by the NICHD, she examines the consequences of China's one-child policy for child well-being.

Rongjun Sun is an Assistant Professor of Sociology at Cleveland State University. His research focuses on population aging, and family relations in both the United States and China. Recent publications include "Old Age Support in Urban China from both Parents' and Children's Perspectives" (*Research on Aging*, 2002) and "Community-Acquired Pneumonia in Older Veterans: Does the Pneumonia Prognosis Index Help?" (with Lona Mody and Suzanne Bradley, *Journal of the*

American Geriatrics Society, 2002). He is currently studying the mortality of the oldest-old in China.

Anchalee Varangrat is a Lecturer at the Institute for Population and Social Research, Mahidol University, Thailand. Her research focuses on family formation, population, and development. She is the author of *Population Projection for Thailand, 2000–2025* (Thailand Ministry of Public Health and Mahidol University, 2003). Currently, she is working on a project sponsored by the Wellcome Trust on factors affecting Thai marriage patterns.

Regina E. Werum is Associate Professor of Sociology at Emory University. Her research focuses on educational inequality from comparative historical and international perspectives. Recent publications include "Warehousing the Unemployed? Federal Job Training Programs in the Depression-Era South" (*American Journal of Education*, 2001), and a forthcoming chapter with B. Powell and L. Steelman titled, "Macro Causes, Micro Effects: Linking Public Policy, Family Structure, and Educational Outcomes" (in *After the Bell: Educational Solutions Outside of School*, edited by D. Conley). Currently, she is working on a project sponsored by the NAE/Spencer Foundation and NSF that investigates cross-cultural differences in how social capital affects academic outcomes.

Raymond Sin-Kwok Wong is a Professor of Sociology at the University of California, Santa Barbara. His research interests include inequality and stratification, sociology of education, quantitative methodology, urban poverty, and economic sociology, particularly Chinese entrepreneurship in East Asia. His recent publications include "Multidimensional Association Models: A Multilinear Approach" (*Sociological Methods & Research*, 2001), "Occupational Attainment in Eastern Europe Under Socialism" (*Research in Social Stratification and Mobility*, 2002), and "Chinese Business Firms and Business Entrepreneurs in Hong Kong" (*De-Essentializing Capitalism: Chinese Enterprise, Transnationalism, and Identity*, edited by Edmund Terence Gomez and Hsin-Huang Michael Hsiao, 2003).

Gad Yair is a Senior Lecturer at the Department of Sociology and Anthropology at the Hebrew University of Jerusalem. His research interests include the sociology of schools and schooling, organizational theory, the sociology of learning, sociological theory and its history, and the theory-methodology nexus. Recent relevant publications are "Educational Battlefields in America: The Tug-of-War over Students' Engagement With Instruction" (*Sociology of Education*, 2000) and "Decisive Moments and Key Experiences: Expanding Paradigmatic Boundaries in the Study of School Effects" in *The International Handbook on the Sociology of Education: An International Assessment of New Research and Theory*, 2003).

SUBJECT INDEX

www.ingramcontent.com/pod-product-compliance
Ingram Content Group UK Ltd.
Pitfield, Milton Keynes, MK11 3LW, UK
UKHW021032041026
15470UKWH00014B/1553

9 780762 310616